George Bartle

A Synopsis of English History

Salzwasser

George Bartle

A Synopsis of English History

1. Auflage | ISBN: 978-3-84605-012-5

Erscheinungsort: Frankfurt, Deutschland

Erscheinungsjahr: 2020

Salzwasser Verlag GmbH

Reprint of the original, first published in 1869.

SYNOPSIS

OF

ENGLISH HISTORY.

A SYNOPSIS

OF

ENGLISH HISTORY,

FROM THE

EARLIEST PERIOD TO THE PRESENT TIME,

ARRANGED ON A PLAN ENTIRELY NEW,

COMPRISING

A CONCISE YET FULL ACCOUNT OF THE WARS, LEADING EVENTS, AND PERSONS OF NOTE IN EACH REIGN ; TOGETHER WITH GENEALO-GICAL CHARTS, CHRONOLOGICAL TABLES, TERMS OF THE VARIOUS TREATIES, CONTEMPORARY SOVEREIGNS, BRITISH COLONIES, HISTORIC RHYMES, AND EXPLANATORY REMARKS.

EXPRESSLY DESIGNED

To assist Students preparing for the Oxford and Cambridge Local Examinations, and other Competitive Tests; and also for the use of Schools and Private Families.

BY THE REV. GEORGE BARTLE, D.D.,

Author of "The Scriptural Doctrine of Hades," "An Analysis and Exposition of the Church Catechism," "Dissertation on the Sacrifice of Christ," "Epitome of English Grammar," &c., &c., &c.

ENTERED AT STATIONERS' HALL.

THIRD EDITION.

LONDON:
LONGMANS, GREEN, READER, AND DYER.
1869.

PREFACE.

ALL who have been engaged in Education—particularly in that branch of it relating to English History—must have felt the need of a work of this description, at once clear, concise, and comprehensive—embracing, as it does, an amount of information not to be found in any similar work. This book has been compiled from the most authentic sources, and neither time nor pains have been spared to ensure accuracy.

Those who know anything about competitive examinations must be painfully conscious of the numerous failures in English History. In looking over the result of the Oxford Local Examination held in 1863, we find that the total number of candidates rejected was 175, of whom 102 failed in this important subject, and at the Local Examination held by the same University in June 1868, no fewer than 104 junior candidates failed in English History. To remedy this lamentable state of things is a leading object of the present work, which contains the substance of every notable event connected with the history of our country. It is planned and written in a style adapting it to the use not only of the advanced student, but also to pupils of the most slender capacity.

The value of this Synopsis has been fully ascertained, by its having been found to furnish appropriate answers to the University questions, and by its having enabled the Author's own pupils to pass the competitive examinations *without a single failure in the subject under consideration;* and although he designed the work expressly with a view to the Oxford and Cambridge Local Examinations, yet he *feels confident that it will be found of great assistance to teachers in testing* the progress or proficiency of their pupils to examiners, in propounding questions, or in ascertaining the correctness of the candidates' answers; and equally useful to schools, private families, general readers, and to all who wish to save time, trouble, and expense in acquiring an accurate knowledge of English History.

The work is divided, where practicable, into three sections, distinguished by the letters **A, B, C**; the first denoting wars; the second, Chief Events; the third, Celebrated Persons. Candidates for examination should bear in mind, that in giving the leading events of a reign, they must not omit to mention the Wars, which in this book are kept distinct for the sake of clearness.

The Author only wishes to add that, in dealing with those points in history concerning which there are different opinions, he has, after an impartial examination, followed that side of the question which appeared the best authenticated. There are, for instance, two dates given for Magna Charta, namely, June 15 and 19. A person knowing little of history, merely from having made himself acquainted with one writer on the subject, who uses the former date, would be inclined to consider the latter date an error in another author. The truth of the matter is, that the Charter was drawn up on the 15th, but not signed till the 19th. Hence, the latter date is the correct one. There are great discrepancies among historians, not only as to dates, but also in reference to persons. For instance, some historians consider Hans Holbein a Dutchman; others a German; while a third class say that he was a Swiss. The last opinion is the correct one, inasmuch as he was born at Basle.

Walton-on-the-Hill, 1869.

PREFACE TO THE SECOND EDITION.

The great and increasing demand for this work has called forth a Second Edition, which is offered to the public in a revised, corrected, and enlarged form, and to which are added a list of *British Colonies, and Historic Rhymes*.

PREFACE TO THE THIRD EDITION.

On the completion of my labour on bringing out the First Edition of the Synopsis of English History, I fancied that I had nothing further to do with it but sit down patiently for its sale, to remunerate me for the time and labour I had expended upon it; but the rapid and unexpected sale of the book, and the demand for a second edition, rendered it necessary that I should again set to work. I carefully revised it, and made many little improvements, correcting typographical and other errors that had crept in, unavoidably, in its progress. I then expected I should have some rest; but a Third Edition being called for, compelled me again to delve in the Historic field. I have, therefore, in the Third Edition, added considerably to the information the two previous editions contain, and have brought down the work to the present time.

It will be noticed that the writer of the "Historic Rhymes" has added some three hundred or more lines to his part of the work, which will render it still more acceptable to the learner of English History.

TABLE OF CONTENTS.

NORMAN LINE.

LINE OF PLANTAGENET.

HISTORIC RHYMES,

FOR ASSISTING THE PUPIL'S MEMORY.

By learning well these **Dates** and **Rhymes**,
You'll recollect each Monarch's times :
If they be on your minds impressed,
Then History will be read with zest.

ROMAN PERIOD.

In fifty-five and fifty-four,	B.C. 55
Ere Jesu's birth, came **Cæsar** o'er ;	54
At Hythe or Deal, on Cantuar's coast,	
First lands the mighty Roman host.	
'Twas then the Standard-bearer cried,	
While dashing through the surging tide,	
" Now, fellow soldiers, follow me,	
Or th' Eagle falls to th' enemy ! "	
The forty-third year of our Lord,	A.D 43
Brought **Claudius** fierce, with fire and sword.	
Caractacus, in fifty-one, .	51
Was by Ostorius overcome :	
With wife and daughters torn from home,	
As prisoner was he sent to Rome.	
From fifty-eight to sixty-four,	58
First Britons learnt Christ to adore.	64
'Twas in the year of sixty-one,	61
Th' **Icenian Queen** burnt London down.	
One seven and nine to mem'ry brings	179

SAXON PERIOD.

Began to rule, nine nought and one.	901
Comes **Athelstane** nine twenty five,	925
He made religion greatly thrive.	
Came **Edmund** "First" nine four and nought,	940
He with the Danes oft battles fought.	
In nine four six, King **Edred** reigned,	946
Who Abbot Dunstan made his friend.	
Came **Edwy** next, in nine five five,	955
Who with the Church did ever strive.	
Then **Edgar**, who made **Britain great**,	
Ascends the throne in nine five eight.	958
This seat by **Edward** next was filled,	
He, nine seven nine, was basely killed.	979
King **Ethelred, Unready** called,	
In nine seven nine was King installed.	979
Then **Edmund Ironside** was seen	
As England's Monarch, ten sixteen.	1016

DANISH PERIOD.

In that same year, **Canute** the **Dane**,	1016
Did England's throne and crown obtain ;	
Through him did **Harold** pow'r derive,	
Succeeding him, one nought three five.	1035
Then **Hard'canute, Queen Emma's** son,	
In ten four nought succession won.	1040

SAXON LINE RESTORED.

Next **Edward, the Confessor** named,	
In ten four two, dominion claimed.	1042
With **Harold** ten six six we see,	1066
The **close of Saxon Monarchy**.	

NORMAN PERIOD.

The **Conqueror, William**—**Harold** fought,	
The Normans, Hastings' victory wrought ;	
In ten six six his sway began,	1066
When Saxon England he o'erran.	

In ten seven seven the Conqueror   **1077**
Attacks his son at Gerberoi ;
And there he Robert's castle storms,
For rising 'gainst him up in arms.
In ten and eighty-seven, his son,   **1087**
Will Rufus, then to rule begun.
In ten nine six, the first Crusade,   **1096**
Through Europe great excitement made :
Each Christian Monarch pledged his word
To aid the cause by purse and sword,
To send forth men to Syria's strand,
To wrest from Moslems th' Holy Land.
In one, one hundred, **Henry** reigned,   **1100**
'Twas he the name of " **Beauclerc** " gained.
In one and one and nought and six,   **1106**
To pay off Robert's evil tricks,
Doth **Henry**, Normandy o'errun ;
When Tinchebrai's fierce fight was won,
In Cardiff Robert he confines,
And Normandy to England joins.
King **Stephen**, one one thirty-five,   **1135**
To win the crown, did frauds contrive ;
His reign was full of wrong and strife,
Embitt'ring all his way of life.
In one and one and thirty-eight,   **1138**
King Stephen's troops the Scots await
In Yorkshire, at North Allerton,
By him was **Standard Battle** won.
In '41 was Lincoln fought,   **1141**
Where Stephen was to ruin brought ;
For there was he a prisoner made,
And thence to Bristol Gaol conveyed.
At Winchester, 'leven fifty-three,   **1153**
By treaty Stephen did agree :
That he, with Henry ceasing strife,
Should reign in peace throughout his life ;
And, furthermore, did he ordain,
That at his death should Henry reign.

PLANTAGENET PERIOD.

With **Henry Second**, 'leven five four,	1154
First England's name began to soar.	
Then Becket rose to great renown ;	
A humble cit in London town,	
Warmed up by bright ambition's flame,	
He England's Primate soon became.	
To curb the Church's power vast,	
The laws of **Clarendon** were passed.	
Betwixt à Becket and the King,	
These brought on constant bickering.	
They on the clergy mainly bore,	
Their date was one one sixty-four.	1164
In one and one and seven and nought,	1170
A Becket's life to close was brought,	
For four of Henry's knights combine	
To slay him hard by Cantuar's shrine.	
In one and one and seventy-two,	1172
Did Ireland Henry's troops subdue.	
Then **Richard First** the "**Lion Heart,**"	
In **Holy War** took active part ;	
His reign of glory 'gan to shine,	
In one and one and eighty-nine.	1189
In one and one and ninety-one,	1191
He gained the fight at Ascalon ;	
'Twas there that Saladin he sought,	
And hand-to-hand in combat fought.	
The Moslem power that year he shook,	
When he their stronghold, **Acre**, took.	
Next Richard's brother, **John**, succeeds,	
And stains his reign by cruel deeds.	
In one one nine and nine, dates he ;	1199
His course was marked by tyranny.	
We, one and two and fifteen, find	1215
That John the Magna Charta signed :	
Which long as England shall endure,	
Will make of Freedom, men secure !	
In twelve sixteen, was pow'r conferred	1216
On gentle-minded **Henry Third** ;	

For six and fifty years he sway'd,
While traitors oft foul plots display'd.
In twelve one seven, by Lincoln's Wall,   1217
Invading Frenchmen thickly fall ;
And off the coast of Kent their fleet,
By brave De Burgh, sustain defeat.
In one and two and sixty-four,   1264
The Barons make 'gainst Henry war ;
Such strength at Lewes they displayed,
That Henry was a prisoner made.
At Evesham the Barons strive
With Edward's force, one two six five ;   1265
They beaten were, and Leicester slain,
When Henry was made free again.
In this same year the towns first sent   1265
Their members up to Parliament.
Next "**Edward First**" to him succeeds,
A Monarch famed for gallant deeds ;
His reign began twelve seventy-two,   1272
'Twas he that Wallace overthrew.
In twelve eight two his power prevails,   1282
At Llan-deil'vawr he conquered Wales.
To "**Edward Second**" sway is given
In one and three and nought and seven.   1307.
At Bannock-burn, one three one four,   1314
Led on by Bruce, did Scots once more
For independence nobly fight,
And Edward's army put to flight.
Thirteen two seven ceased Edward's reign,   1327
At Berkely Castle was he slain.
To **Edward Third** the crown was given,
In one and three and twenty-seven ;   1327
At Hal'don Hill, thirteen three three,   1333
King Edward gained a victory ;
There Regent Douglas was o'erthrown,
And Baliol won the Scottish crown.
'Twas said that forty thousand men
Were altogether slaughtered then.
Thirteen four six, at Neville's Cross,   1346
The Scots sustained a frightful loss,

King David was a prisoner ta'en,
While fifteen thousand men were slain.
In one and three and forty-seven, 1347
From Calais wall were Frenchmen driven;
For nigh a year they held the place,
Tho' famine haggered every face.
'Twas said when entered Edward's hosts,
The town seemed peopled but by ghosts.
In thirteen fifty-six, appears 1356
The famous battle of Poitiers;
Where, by the fate of war's mischance,
Was prisoner made the King of France.
In thirteen seventy-seven, we find 1377
A King of brave but fickle mind,
No trace of Edward's great renown
In Second Richard's conduct shone.
At Otterburn, one three eight eight, 1388
The English met disasters great,
They by the Scots were put to flight,
Their leaders falling in the fight.
It was the Battle at this place
That gave the theme of "Chevy Chase."

House of Lancaster.

Next Henry Fourth, thirteen nine nine, 1399
Found traitors 'gainst him oft combine.
'Tis now the Order of the Bath,
Through Henry its commencement hath.
Northumberland, who often strove
King Henry from his throne to move,
At Bramham Moor bow'd down to fate,
In one and four and nought and eight. 1408
Then Henry Fifth, fourteen one three, 1413
Assumed the English Monarchy.
When he his father's throne ascends,
He casts aside his worthless friends,
Who, in his wild and youthful days,
Had led him oft from virtue's ways.
'Twas he, when Prince, in wanton sport,

Struck Judge Gascoigne in open court.
On **Agincourt's** well-foughten field,
'Twas he compelled the French to yield ;
A fight more fatal scarce was seen,
The date was fourteen and fifteen. 1415
Next **Henry Sixth**, fourteen two two, 1422
Whom troubles oft seemed to pursue.
With blood and strife was filled his reign ;
He was by fierce assassins slain.
The **Wars of Roses** then began,
When Englishman fought Englishman :
St. Albans ope'd the dreadful work
Betwixt the King and Duke of York ;
The date is fourteen fifty-five 1455
When these two kinsmen fiercely strive.
At **Bloreheath**, fourteen fifty-nine, 1459
The Star of York appeared to shine.
In one and four and six and nought, 1460
Northampton Battle next was fought ;
At **Wakefield** fight, in that same year,
Yorkists met disasters drear.
At **Mort'mer's Cross**, fourteen six one, 1461
Were frightful deeds of slaughter done ;
They at **St. Albans** met again,
Where hosts of Yorkist men were slain.
'Twas in this reign that **Joan of Arc**
Threw light o'er France's fortunes dark.
Fourteen two nine, by her brave means 1429
Was raised the siege before Orleans.
Joan when a prisoner sad became,
Was burnt—to England's endless shame.

HOUSE OF YORK.

Next **Edward Fourth** assumed the crown,
In one and four and sixty-one. 1461
This year was **Towton's** battle fought,
Which to the King great victory brought,
Great nobles mingled with the dead,
While Henry and Queen Marg'ret fled.

At **Barnet**, fourteen seventy-one,　　　　　　1471
Was Margaret's cause nigh well undone ;
In that same year on **Tewkesbury's** field
Both Queen and Prince as prisoners yield.
By Edward's orders, in a butt
Of Malmsey wine was Clarence put.
Crook'd Richard HENRY SIXTH struck down,
And seized his nephew Edward's crown.
One four eight three, the hapless boy　　　　　1483
His ruffians in the Tow'r destroy.
Tho' Richard has been oft defamed,
And by historians greatly blamed,
His laws, tho' few, were just and sage,
And shewed a mind before his age.
On **Bosworth Field**, one four eight five,　　　　1485
'Gainst **Richmond** did he bravely strive,
No dangers could his spirit quell,
And there he as a soldier fell.

TUDOR LINE.

See **Henry** at the throne arrive
In one and four and eighty-five ;　　　　　　1485
He claimed the Crown, first, by descent ;
Next, by a conqueror's argument ;
The third, that marriage would foreclose
The wranglings of each rival Rose.
Now, scarcely had his reign begun
When **Simnel** came, the baker's son,
To lay a claim to regal state,
And **Warwick's** Earl to personate.
With friends to Furness first he went,
Then marched in force to Stoke-on-Trent,
Whereat, in fourteen eighty-seven,　　　　　1487
To flight he was by Henry driven.
Next **Perkin Warbeck** went to Cork,
And styled himself the Duke of York ;
In fourteen nine and nine was he　　　　　　1499
As *traitor hung on Tyburn* tree.

Fourteen nine two, in Henry's reign,   1492
Columbus won new worlds for Spain :
Next Cabot trod Newfoundland's shore,
Then Gamas' ships South Seas explore ;
Then, in fifteen and nought and nought,   1500
Cabral back news of Brazil brought.
With Henry Eight, fifteen nought nine,   1509
The light of Truth began to shine.
King Henry's troops to conquer France,
In fifteen thirteen, see advance :   1513
At Guinegate such a rout occurs
(Of French) 'twas called the " Fight of Spurs."
In that same year came " Flodden Field,"   1513
Where James the Fourth his life did yield.
At Solway Moss, fifteen four two,   1542
Did James the English troops subdue.
Six times was burly Henry wed,
And wretched lives his consorts led.
In fifteen forty-seven, his son,   1547
King Edward Sixth, to reign begun.
That year was famed for Pinkie's fight,
When Scotland's Chiefs were put to flight.
Next Mary, who was " Bloody " called,
Fifteen five three, was Queen installed.   1553
Then numbers died for conscience sake,
On scaffold, gibbet, and the stake.
In fifteen fifty-four, we find   1554
Jane Grey, the lovely, good, and kind,
Led forth to die on Tower Hill,
With Dudley, whom she loved so well.
'Twas in the year fifteen five eight,   1558
That Calais changed its captive state :
Re-taken by the Duke de Guise,
All English claims on it surcease ;
Its loss did grief so keen impart
To Mary, that upon her heart
She said they'd find it graven deep
When she in death would calmly sleep.
Succeeding next, at Mary's death,
We find the great Elizabeth.

Her reign commenced—noteworthy date—
In one and five and fifty-eight.   1558
At **Zutphen**, England's forces meet—
By th' Earl of Leicester led—defeat ;
'Twas there, amid stern battle's tide,
The brave **Sir Philip Sidney** died.
A plot was laid in that same year
By **Babington** of Derbyshire,
The Queen to slay, and place instead
The crown on **Mary Stuart's** head.
In that great age are some dark spots :
As when died Mary Queen of Scots ;
Upon the scaffold was she driven
In one and five and eighty-seven.   1587
Her hapless fate must ever stain
The glory of Eliza's reign !
The Armada vast her fleets destroyed,
Though Spain its utmost strength employed.
In fifteen eighty-eight it sailed,   1588
And in the English Channel failed.
'Twas in this time that Shakespeare wrote,
With many other men of note.

HOUSE OF STUART.

Next Scottish **James**, that learned fool,
Sixteen nought three, commenced to rule.   1603
In conference held at **Hampton Court**,
Were differences religious brought ;
'Mongst other things decided there,
Were changes in the Common Prayer.
Foul schemes were in this reign begot,
The "Main," the "Bye," and "Powder Plot."
This latter was designed so vast,
The Christian world all stood aghast ;
Its object demons might contrive,
Its date was one six nought and five.   1605
'Twas in the year sixteen eleven,   1611
Our Bible to the world was given.
In *one and six and one and eight*,   1618

Sir Walter Raleigh met his fate ;
This soldier, author, bard, and sage,
Stands first of all his time and age.
Succeeding to the crafty James,
Came **Charles the First**, who pity claims.
Sixteen two five, his reign began,
And through its course great trouble ran.
"Petition of Rights" doth take its date,
In one and six and twenty-eight ;　　　　1628
Was Freedom made by it secure
As long as England shall endure.
Then **Buckingham** was doom'd to feel
The deadly blow of **Felton's** steel.
Sixteen three seven, did Hampden stand　　　　1637
Against extortion in the land ;
He, Charles' orders disobeyed,
Nor odious tax Ship-money paid ;
By **Judges Twelve** was **Hampden** tried,
When 'gainst him all but two decide ;
The date of this great verdict given,
Was one and six and thirty-seven.　　　　1637
In one and six and forty-one,　　　　1641
The Irish to rebel began,
The Cath'lics could not hate restrain,
By them were hosts of English slain.
At Nottingham, sixteen four two,　　　　1642
Charles' friends around his standard drew ;
In that same year was Edge Hill fought,
To neither side it vantage brought.
It was on Chalgrove's fatal day,
That Hampden's spirit passed away.
At Athr'ton, Lansdown, Roundway Down,
Did victory Charles' army crown.
These all took place sixteen four three,　　　　1643
Besides the fight of Newbury.
"Nantwich," "Cropredy," "Marston Moor,"____
Were fought sixteen and forty-four ;　　　　1644
'Twas in the latter field of fame,
That Cromwell first in notice came.
At Naseby, sixteen forty-five,　　　　1645

Was Charles a vanquished fugitive ;
There, routed by the Parl'ment host,
Were baggage, arms, and treasures lost.
That year for treason Laud was tried,
And on the scaffold calmly died.
To England's shame it must be said,
See Charles before his Commons led,
With treason charged, arraigned by them,
In spite of law, him they condemn ;
And at Whitehall, sixteen four nine,   1649
Him to the headsman they consign.
The **Commonwealth** was next began,
And civil war the land o'erran.
Altho' profusely blood was shed,
A "crowning mercy," Cromwell said,
Was Worcester fight, sixteen five one ;   1651
Where Roundheads made the Roy'lists run.
The stout Van Tromp, sixteen five two,   1652
Off Goodwin's sand, Blake's ships o'erthrew.
In one and six and five and three,   1653
We Cromwell now in power see;
By Barebone Parliament installed,
Was he the "Lord Protector" called.
Died Cromwell, sixteen five and eight,   1658
'Mongst Englishmen most truly great.
At Cromwell's death his son succeeds,
But him the Commons supersedes,
In one and six and six and nought,   1660
To England back King **Charles** was brought.
The first of Charles' acts we see,
Is that known as "th' Indemnity."
Was th' act of Uniformity passed
To hold the clergy bound and fast ?
Its date was sixteen sixty-two,   1662
When numbers from the Church withdrew ;
Th' act Conventicle, in sixty-four,   1664
Let but five meet, God to adore.
Then raged in **London Plague** most dire ;
And next broke out the dreadful **Fire**;
The first dates *sixteen sixty-five*,   1665

When thousands stricken ceased to live :
The second ruin dire inflicts
On London, sixteen sixty-six.   **1666**
In one and six and seventy-three,   **1673**
The **Commons** to the " **Test** " agree ;
To check the Catholic's growing power,
Which over England seem'd to lower.
In one and six and seventy-nine,   **1679**
Is passed of laws that grand design,
The **Habeas Corpus**, which takes care
A prisoner shall have trial fair.
Sixteen eight three, by knaves begot,   **1683**
We find collapse the Rye House Plot.
In one and six and eighty-five,   **1685**
King Charles the Second ceased to live.
The **Second James** came to the throne,
Of Papist faith was he well known.
Sixteen eight five, at Sedgemoor fight,   **1685**
Was Monmouth's army put to flight.
In one and six and eighty nine,   **1689**
'Gainst James his subjects all combine ;
When driving Stuarts from the throne,
They **William** honor with the crown.
Sixteen eight nine, with France's aid,   **1689**
Was Derry placed in close blockade ;
By General Kirk the siege was raised,
Which has for bravery oft been praised.
So stoutly were the walls maintained,
That at the last no food remained,
Were horses eaten, dogs and cats,
Small birds and mice, and even rats.
Sixteen nine nought, was fought the **Boyne**,   **1690**
Where **James** and **Louis** once more join :
There **William** in each charge was found,
While **James** looked on from rising ground.
The **Irish** troops fought ill throughout,
While **Frenchmen** broke in perfect rout.
James fled to France, where at its court,
His friends gave aid to his support,
For twelve years there did he reside,

In one six seven and one he died.   **1671**
The mighty "**BANK**" in William's reign,
The London merchants entertain :
So highly was esteemed the plan,
The "Bank of Scotland" next began.
King William's horse his master threw,
And caused his death, one seven nought two.   **1702**
To him succeeds the **Good Queen Anne**,
Whose rule, one seven nought two began.   **1702**
Then men so shone on history's page,
They termed her reign th' **Augustan Age**.
'Twas in her time that Marlboro's star,
Arose in Continental war.
In seventeen nought and four, we find   **1704**
The **Duke of Marlboro's** troops, combined
With those led on by **Prince Eugene**,
A victory great at **Blenheim** gain.
At **Ramilies** and **Oudenarde**,
Still great success these chiefs reward ;
While from the fight of **Malplaquet**,
They palms of honor still display.
One seven nought four, Leake, Byng, and Rooke,   **1704**
From Spain strong **Gibraltar** took ;
Then **France** we find supporting Spain,
Strove hard to take it back again ;
But these allies at each attack
Where by the English driven back.
'Twas in this reign was **Scotland** joined
To England, and her rights defined.

·HOUSE OF HANOVER.

Upon Anne's death, one seven one four,   **1714**
George First from Hanover came o'er.
Rebellious Scotland then uprose,
And th' **Old Pretender** folly shows.
Next smash'd the **Mississippi** scheme,
Which brought on all distress extreme :
Then next the South Sea **Bubble** burst,
Which *one Sir John Blunt* started first ;

The date when this such ruin brought,
Was one and seven and two and nought.   1720
George "First" died seventeen twenty-seven,   1727
When rule to George his son was given.
But little talent he displayed,
And scant advancement England made.
At Dettingen, one seven four three,   1743
He gained o'er France a victory :
This fight was last on foreign land
Where th' English Monarch took command.
When next we fought at Fontenoy,
Our Dutch allies our fame destroy ;
For when they should have led the van,
They wheel'd about, and off they ran.
'Tis in the year of "Forty-five,"   1745
The Stuarts for their birthright strive.
At Preston Pans sprung high their hope,
When Charles defeated sleepy Cope :
But, next year, on Culloden's plain,
Their star sunk ne'er to rise again.
It was the Seven Years' War wherein
We find great Clive's career begin ;
To him doth England owe the sway
She holds o'er India to this day.
The pride of France received a check
On Minden's plain, and at Quebec,
'Twas there that Wolfe and Montcalm died,
The leaders brave on either side.
Hawke's Victory great in Quiberon Bay,
From England kept the French away.
The year one seven and six and nought,
King George the Third to power brought.   1760
Americans, seventeen seven five,   1775
Bad councils to rebellion drive ;
They British rule, "seven six," foreswear,   1776
And Independence they declare.
In one and seven and nine and eight,   1798
Rash men in Ireland agitate,
Mad schemes these traitors then devise,
And in rebellion wicked rise.

One seven nine eight saw victory smile   1798
On gallant **Nelson** at the **Nile**.
On **Alexandria's** sandy coast,
The French a desperate battle lost :
'Twas there when " See, they run ! " was cried,
That **Abercrombie** stricken died.
The date was eighteen nought and one.   1801
That same year, Nelson's glory shone
Off **Copenhagen**, when the fleet
Of Denmark met with dire defeat.
One eight nought five, at **Trafalgar**,   1805
Died Nelson, England's noblest Tar :
He fell upon the " Victory's " deck,
'Midst foes defeated, flames, and wreck.
The Peninsular war next came,
When rose resplendent Wellesley's name ;
O'er which bright laurels history strews,
From Vimeira down to dark Toulouse ;
With one bay more of purer green
For Waterloo,—eighteen fifteen.   1815
Next cometh he of little worth,
The Sybarite gross, King George the Fourth.
On him was regency conferred
When reason fled from George the Third.
His reign, one eight two nought began,   1820
And inglorious ten years ran.
The act that tarnished most his life,
Was conduct to his hapless wife.
In one and eight and twenty-four,   1824
We find commence the **Burmese War**;
Which brought within our **Indian sway**,
Rich provinces the cost to pay.
Next war with **Ashantees** we wage,
And oft with them in fight engage.
Then next to make the conflict cease
'Twixt **Turkey** and mis-governed **Greece**,
We—joined with Russia and with France—
A fleet to **Nav'rino's Bay** advance ;
And there this mighty force employ,
The *fleet of Turkey to destroy.*

To order keep, and hinder vice,
Then Peel enrolled the **New Police**.
'Twas in this reign that **Canning** died,
A statesman honest, true, and tried.
In one and eight and three and nought,   **1830**
Was George's reign to finish brought.
Then **William Fourth** the throne ascends,
Whose honest purpose won him friends.
As he from boyhood went to sea,
His manners were—though courteous—free ;
As bye-names from our habits spring,
Was William called "the Sailor King."
'Mongst measures wise that then were passed,
The Great Reform act may be classed ;
One eight and thirty-two its date,   **1832**
It brought wise changes in the state.
In one eight thirty-seven, is seen   **1837**
Th' accession of **our gracious Queen**.
In Canada, a few unwise,
'Gainst England in rebellion rise.
In one and eight four nought was seen   **1840**
The nuptials of our much loved Queen ;
The nation at this act rejoice,
And with true hearts approve her choice.
Round ALBERT's name will history throw
A radiance that must ever glow ;
For in his brief career was rife
The glories of a well spent life.
To every virtue close allied,
In eighteen sixty-one he died.   **1861**
In one and eight and four and nought,   **1840**
The **Syrian War** to close was brought.
In that same year, on various pleas,
We war declare against **Chinese**.
Next comes, in eighteen forty-three,   **1843**
The fight with Affghans, Meanee.
The noble **Sikhs** we next subdue,
And teach the **Kaffirs** lessons too.
In one and eight and fifty four,   **1854**
Breaks out the great Crimean war,

When fierce the waves of battle roll
One year before **Sebastopol**;
In fifty-five, this fortress fell,   1855
That Russia had defended well.
In **India**, one eight fifty-seven, 1857
The signal of alarm was given,
When at "**Meerut**" the fierce Sepoy
The British rule strove to destroy.
At **Delhi, Lucknow,** and **Cawnpore,**
The streets and dwellings ran with gore.
In one and eight and fifty-eight, 1858
The mutineers we subjugate,
By forces led by Havelock, Neill,
By Barnard, Outram, Lawrence, Steele,
And by Sir Colin Campbell brave,
Whose presence India helped to save.
The year one eight and sixty sees, 1860
War waged once more against **Chinese.**
For Missionaries' release delayed,
We th' **Abyssinian** land invade ;
In one and eight and sixty-eight, 1868
The interior we penetrate ;
"Magdala" there we storm and gain,
And find the King amongst the slain.
Stirred up by scheming selfish men,
See Ireland much disturbed again :
To arms some hare-brained "Fenians" rush,
Expecting th' English rule to crush ;
But everywhere did they disperse,
As they to "fighting" seemed averse.
If in eighteen six nine we search, 1869
We find a change i' th' Irish Church ;
Though 'gainst the measure some cried loud,
'Twas by both Houses disendowed.

O, may a watchful Providence
 O'er us be ever thrown,
To prosper brave old England,
 And guard VICTORIA's throne.

ENGLISH HISTORY.

BRITISH PERIOD.

The accounts given of Britain before the Roman Invasion are conflicting. While the inhabitants are represented by one writer as civilised, another speaks of them as a race of savages. An examination, however, of the works of different authors, who have written on the subject, with legitimate inferences from those works, will justify us in concluding that the Ancient Britons were more enlightened, and held a higher position among the nations of the earth, than we have been led to believe. It is probable that some writers have been induced to call the Ancient Britons savages, because Cæsar, in his commentaries, designates them " Barbarians." In so naming the people of this Island, the Roman General did not mean that they were actually savages, but **foreigners**. For it is well known to the classical scholar that both Greeks and Romans denominated all nations barbarians who could not speak Greek and Latin. Among the many proofs which could be easily adduced, it may suffice to furnish the reader with two taken from classical authors, and one from the Bible. Ovid actually applies the word to himself, in Pontus, Trist. v. 10, 37, thus:—"*Barbarus hic ego sum, quia non intelligor ulli.*" "In this place I am a Barbarian, because no one understands my language."

And in Euripides, Hecuba 328, we have these words addressed by Ulysses to the Queen of Troy:—

"But ye Barbarians neither regard your friends as friends, nor do ye hold up to admiration those who have nobly died."

1 Cor. xiv. 14, the Apostle thus speaks:—

"Therefore if I know not the meaning of the voice, I shall be unto him that speaketh a **Barbarian**, and he that speaketh shall be a **Barbarian** unto me."

It may hence be inferred that the error in supposing the Britons savages, because the Romans called them Barbarians, has arisen from ancient and modern writers using the expression in totally different senses.

THE ORIGINAL SETTLERS AND DIVISON OF THE COUNTRY.

According to some Welsh poetical records, called Triads, because written in verses of three lines each, Britain was first peopled by a colony of Celts, whom HUGH the Mighty conducted from Defrobani, or Summer Land, a country in Asia. At a very remote period the land was divided into three parts, and called Lloegr (England); Alban (Scotland); and Cymry (Wales); each being governed by a king. The whole territory was also named " Honey Island;" the "Waterguarded Island;" and afterwards Prydian or **Britain**, in honour of the distinguished chief who first established and organised the new settlers. This Prydian or Brito enacted laws, and gave the people a regular form of Government, which every subsequent colony was bound to observe and obey. Some have derived the word Britain from two Celtic words, signifying the painted people, but it most probably comes from **Baratanac**, signifying the **Land of Tin**, which would easily be changed into Britannia. This derivation of the word Britain agrees with the name given to the Island by the Greeks, who called it **Cassiterides**, denoting **Tin Islands**. At the time, however,. of the Roman Invasion, the inhabitants of Britain were divided into no fewer than forty-five tribes, of which the following are given as the chief:—

1. **The Bibroci**,—who dwelt in Surrey, Kent, Sussex, and part of Berkshire.

2. **The Segontiaci**,—Hampshire, and part of Berkshire.

3. **The Durotriges**,—Dorsetshire.

4. **The Carnabri,**
5. **The Cimbri,** } in Devonshire.

6. **The Hedui**,—Somersetshire, a portion of Gloucestershire, and Wiltshire.

7. **The Ancalites** inhabited the district near Henley-on-Thames.

8. **The Dobuni**,—Oxfordshire, part of Gloucestershire, and part of Worcestershire.

9. **The Cassii**, in Hertfordshire, Bedfordshire, Buckinghamshire, Middlesex, and Essex.

10. **The Iceni Magni**,—Huntingdonshire, Cambridgeshire, Norfolk, Suffolk, and part of Northamptonshire.

11. **The Coriceni,** including the **Jugantes,** in Lincolnshire, Derbyshire, Leicestershire, Nottingham, Rutlandshire, and part of Northamptonshire.

12. **The Carnabii,** in Warwickshire, Staffordshire, Shropshire, and Cheshire.

13. **The Brigantes,** in Durham, Yorkshire, Westmoreland, Cumberland, and Lancashire.

14. **The Voluntii,**
15. **The Sistunii,**
16. **The Parisi,**
17. **The Ottadini,**
18. **The Gadeni,**

> in the Countries North of the Tyne, extending into Scotland.

19. **The Silures,**
20. **The Dimetæ,**
21. **Ordovices,**

> in Wales, except the Isle of Anglesea, and a small tract near Bangor.

22. **The Cangiani,** in the Isle of Anglesea, and a small tract near Bangor.

RELIGION.

As the Ancient Britons were descendants of **Gomer,** the grandson of **Noah,** they could hardly be ignorant of the knowledge of the true God, which knowledge seems never to have been quite extinct, though in subsequent ages they added to it a gross system of idolatry called **Druidism,** so named from the Celtic **Dru,** or the Greek **Drus, an Oak,** because they performed their religious services most frequently in groves of Oak. Some derive the word from the Hebrew **Drussim,** meaning those who are devoted to study. PLINY informs us that the "Druids hold nothing more sacred than the **Mistletoe,** and the tree on which it is produced, provided it be the oak. They choose groves of oaks on their own account, nor do they perform any of their sacred rites without the leaves of those trees, so that one may suppose that they are for this reason called by a Greek Etymology, **Druids.** And whatever mistletoe grows upon the oak they think is sent from heaven, and is a sign of God Himself having chosen that tree. This, however, is very rarely found, but when discovered is treated with great ceremony. They call it by a name, which in their language signifies the curer of all ills, and having duly prepared their feasts and sacrifices under the tree, they bring to it two white bulls, whose horns are then for the first time tied. The Priest, dressed in a white robe, ascends the tree, and with a golden *pruning-hook cuts off the mistletoe,* which is received in a white sheet. Then they sacrifice the victims, praying that God would bless His own gift to those on whom He has bestowed it." Perhaps the best way of conveying an outline of what the Druids believed and taught, will be by giving a summary of their chief doctrines, which are said to be the following:—

1. The Mistletoe must be cut with a golden bill.
2. Everything derives its origin from heaven.
3. Great care is to be taken in the education of children.
4. The disobedient are to be shut out from the sacrifices.
5. Souls are immortal.
6. The soul after death goes into other bodies.
7. If the world is destroyed, it will be by fire or water.
8. Upon extraordinary emergencies a MAN must be sacrificed.
9. According as the body falls, or moves after it has fallen; according as the blood flows, or the wound opens, future events are foretold.
10. Prisoners of war are slain upon the altars, or burnt alive enclosed in wicker, in honour of the gods.
11. Children are brought up apart from their parents, until they are fourteen years of age.
12. There is another world; and they who kill themselves to accompany their friends thither, will live with them there.
13. Money lent in this world will be repaid in the next.
14. Letters given to dying persons, or thrown on the funeral piles of the dead, will be faithfully delivered in the other world.
15. The moon is a sovereign remedy for all things, as its name in Celtic implies.
16. Let the disobedient be excommunicated; let him be deprived of the benefit of the law; let him be avoided by all, and rendered incapable of any employment.

The **Druids** were divided into three classes, and exercised different functions:—

The **Bards,** who were poets and musicians.

The **Vates,** who were priests and physiologists.

The **Druids** proper, who were moral philosophers.

At the head of these was one invested with supreme authority, called the **Arch-Druid,** who was elected by a plurality of voices and retained his distinguished and wealthy office for life. These sacred characters were chosen from the best families, and on this account, together with their holy calling, were held in great estimation by the people.

LEARNING.

The British Druids were skilled in Moral and Natural Philosophy, Astronomy, Politics, Geometry, and Geography; while in the opinion of DIOGENES LAERTIUS, their knowledge was not inferior to that of the Chaldeans, or the Magi of Persia. In fact, the Druids of Britain were so celebrated for their learning that the distinguished families of Gaul sent their sons into England to finish their education under the guidance of these preceptors, who had stored their memories with such a fund of knowledge, that their disciples needed twenty years to acquire all they were taught. **Writing** was also well known to the Britons, and we are told by CÆSAR that they used **Greek letters.** If we may judge from **Stonehenge,** on Salisbury plain, and other vestiges of art found in various parts of the country, the Britons were not by any means destitute of mechanical skill.

Like the Pharisees among the Hebrews, the British Druids, on account of their position and superior knowledge, exercised absolute control over the minds of the people, and discharged the functions of teacher, prophet, priest, judge, and legislator. Speaking of the Druids, ST. CHRYSOSTOM says:—" They in truth reigned; for kings, though sitting on thrones of gold, and dwelling in magnificent palaces, and partaking of sumptuous banquets, were subservient to them."

And CÆSAR informs us that "They neither went to war, nor paid tribute with the rest of the people; they had an exemption from military service, and a dispensation in all matters." If any, either in public or private, refused to obey the Druids, they were immediately interdicted from the sacrifices and placed among the impious and the criminal, whom all avoided, lest by their society and conversation they should become contaminated.

GOVERNMENT.

Though the Britons at the time of the Roman Invasion were divided into forty-five independent tribes, over each of which was a prince or petty king; yet in times of danger, when threatened by a common enemy, they laid aside their wonted differences, and many of the small states united their forces under one superior leader whom they elected, and to whom they entrusted the entire management of the war, as in the case of **Caswallon** or **Cassivelaunus,** by whom CÆSAR was opposed.

In times of peace, however, it appears that not only the common people, but even their chiefs, were subject to the authority of the Druids. **Succession** to the throne was generally **hereditary.** Sometimes the father would divide his dominions among his children, or bequeath them to his widow, who, in case of necessity, led her troops to the field of battle.

ARMY.

The British forces consisted of **Infantry, Cavalry,** and **Charioteers.** Their war-chariots were of two sorts; each had two wheels, and was drawn by a pair of horses. To both ends of the axletree were fastened sharp scythes, which became very destructive when the vehicles were driven into the midst of the enemy, cutting and maiming any one who attempted to oppose them. The other sort of war-chariots contained the chiefs, who were conducted into the ranks of the enemy, hurling their darts in every direction, and inspiring their troops to deeds of extraordinary valour. The Britons showed great military tactics and considerable judgment in selecting their ground for an engagement. They even astonished the veteran soldiers of Rome, and made them hesitate on one occasion, like cowards, till the Standard-bearer of the **Tenth Legion** made a bold dash which so inspired the other men that they followed his example. As to their mode of fighting, CÆSAR thus speaks : " The Britons first drive about in all directions, throw their weapons, and break the ranks with the dread of their horses, and the noise of their wheels, and after working themselves in between the troops of the horse, leap from their chariots and engage on foot. In the meantime the Charioteers withdraw a short distance from the battle, and so place themselves with the chariots that, if their masters are overpowered by the number of the enemy, they may have a ready retreat for their own troops. And therefore, in battle they combine the speed of horse with the firmness of infantry ; and by daily practice and exercise acquire such expertness, that they are accustomed, even in a steep place, to stop their horses at full speed, manage and turn them in an instant, and run along the pole, and stand on the yoke, and thence betake themselves with the greatest celerity to their chariots again."

COMMERCE.

Britain was known to the **Phœnicians** and other nations in that part of the globe even more than a thousand years before the dawn of Christianity ; and at a subsequent period these Phœnician merchants carried on an extensive system of commerce with the natives, who, about the time of the Christian Era, exported iron, tin, gold, copper, dogs, skins, and even slaves; and received from foreign countries, salt, brass, and earthenware. Britain is mentioned, or alluded to, in the writings of several ancient authors, of whom the first is **Herodotus** (B.C. 484), a Grecian Historian, who speaks of it under the name of **Cassiterides,** or the **Tin Islands.** **Aristotle** (B.C. 340) mentions Albion as known to the Greeks. **Strabo** (A.D. 50), the Geographer, refers to the extensive commerce of Britain, specifying tin, lead, and skins, as the principal exports; while other authors, including **Ptolemy, Diodorus Siculus, Polybius, Pliny,** and **Tacitus** have furnished us with their united testimonies respecting Britain.

MANNERS, CUSTOMS, AND CHARACTER OF THE ANCIENT BRITONS.

The old Britons did not lead an artificial but a natural life, which resulted in longevity. Like other Celtic Nations, they had an inbred love of liberty, and a decided horror of anything approaching slavery. Some of the tribes were extremely quarrelsome, and kept up a continual warfare with each other. These unhappy differences made the task of the Romans much more easy than it would otherwise have been. **The Britons forgot that unity is power!** Tacitus, speaking of the Britons after their submission to the Romans, says: " They pay their taxes and obey the laws so long as no arbitrary or illegal demands are made upon them; but these they cannot bear without the greatest impatience, for they are merely reduced to the state of **subjects**, not of **slaves.**" CÆSAR tells us that the Southern inhabitants were more civilised than the rest, and that they had passed over from Gaul (the Ancient name of France) for the purpose of plundering and making war upon the natives. Historians ascribe the superior civilisation of the tribes on the coast to their intercourse with foreign nations.

Those on the coast grew large quantities of corn, and used marl for manure. The people in the interior of the country had large pasture grounds, which were well stocked with cattle, sheep, and hogs. Milk and flesh were the chief articles of food, but it is absurd to suppose they lived entirely upon this diet. They deemed it unlawful to eat the cock, the goose, and the hare, though they bred them for pleasure and amusement. They used either brass or gold coins; or, instead of money, iron rings of a specified weight. The houses of the Britons were numerous, simple in their architecture, and greatly resembled those of Gaul. The people, says CÆSAR, were multitudinous.

They made their own clothes. The men were dressed in trousers and waistcoats, which were covered with a large cloak. The women had a plaited tunic fastened round the waist by a belt, over which was thrown a mantle, similar to that worn by the men. Their ornaments were simple, comprising a ring on the second finger of each hand, and a heavy metallic chain suspended from the neck. Some of the least civilised inland inhabitants painted certain parts of their bodies with a blue dye extracted from a plant called **woad,** and occasionally **tattooed** themselves in order to present to their enemies, in *times of war,* a more formidable appearance.

REMARKS.

From what has been said concerning the Ancient Britons, it may be inferred, that they have not on all occasions been justly represented. Admitting, indeed, that even the more refined part of the nation had not reached the culminating point of civilisation, and that others were in a rude condition, it is surely unfair to conclude that the whole island contained only hordes of savages. We have scarcely any more reason for asserting that the Britons were savages, than for concluding that the English are heathens, because some of the inhabitants in the villages are only a few degrees removed from barbarism. It is impossible to read Cæsar's account of these ancient people without perceiving that he in some respects at least, secretly admired them, and he acknowledges that he learnt from the Britons what enabled him to make improvements in the Roman navy. We are also informed by SIR JOHN FORTESCUE, in his work on the Constitution of England, "De Laudibus legum Angliae," "that the realm of England was first inhabited by the Britons; then by the Romans; then again by the Britons; after whom the Saxons possessed it, and changed its name from Britain to England; then the Danes for some time had the dominion of it; then again the Saxons; last of all the Normans. Yet in the time of these different nations and kings, this kingdom has always been governed by the same customs by which it is governed at present. If these Ancient British customs had not been most excellent, reason, justice, and the love of their country, would have induced some of their kings to change or abolish them, especially the Romans, who ruled all the rest of the world by Roman laws." This author wrote in the reign of Henry VI., and if it is true that the Ancient Britons were in possession of the same laws as those who lived so many ages afterwards, it is most inconsistent to regard such a people as savages.

THE ROMAN PERIOD.

B.C. 55, A.D. 426.

FIRST INVASION.

Julius Cæsar, the celebrated Roman General, invades Britain. He embarks two legions, which amount to 12,000 men, sets sail from **Portus Itius,** between Calais and Boulogne, arrives the following day (August 26), and finds swarms of Britons already armed to prevent his landing. He sails about seven miles along the coast, and disembarks near the place where **Deal** now stands, though others believe that he landed at **Hythe.** His troops were *for some time afraid of* leaping from their vessels to fight with the natives, till the standard-bearer of the Tenth Legion jumped into the water, and exclaimed, " Follow me, fellow soldiers, unless you will betray the Roman Eagle to the enemy. For my part I am determined to do my duty to Cæsar and the Commonwealth." The soldiers instantly imitate his bold example, and a terrible struggle ensues, in which the Britons are overcome. The Britons again attack Cæsar's camp, though without success. After this the General finds that his stay in Britain is by no means safe, and therefore he returns to Gaul (now France) after obtaining promises of submission and hostages from a few of the tribes.

SECOND INVASION.

As the Britons did not send the hostages they promised, Cæsar undertakes a second invasion the following spring, and brings with him 800 vessels, containing five legions and 2,000 horse, altogether making 32,000 men. At this time, according to his own statement, Cæsar crossed the Thames, destroyed Verulamium (St. Alban's), the fortress of Caswallon or Cassivelaunus, chief of the Trinobantes, replaced him by Mandubratius, after which he returned to Gaul.

Three reasons are assigned for Cæsar's invasion of Britain:

1. Cæsar states that he wished to punish the Britons for assisting his Gallic enemies with whom he was waging war.

2. Some think he was induced to invade Britain on account of her pearls and rich tin mines.

3. Others are of opinion that Cæsar was prompted by ambition, and a desire to extend the Roman Empire.

REMARKS.

It is true that the veracity of Julius Cæsar has generally been thought worthy of credit; still, by a careful perusal of what he has written in his Commentaries respecting the invasion of our country, there can be no doubt that his account is exceedingly partial. Indirectly he praises himself, and extols his own achievements. He entered the country with two legions at first, and after being a very short time in the Island, he returned without accomplishing anything of importance. He makes a second attempt upon Britain with nearly three times the forces with which he attacked the Island the first time, which clearly shows that he had found the Britons formidable enemies. Dion Cassius states that Cæsar left Gaul with the intention of subduing Great Britain, and making it a Roman Province. If such were his intentions, and he gained all the advantages mentioned by him, is it not evident that he has suppressed many principal facts, simply because they made against him? He is even charged by Lucan with having turned his back upon the Britons. Dion Cassius informs us that in one of *the battles the Britons* completely routed the Roman Infantry, but were afterwards thrown into confusion by the Cavalry. Horace and Tibullus speak of Britain as unconquered in their time. Tacitus observed that Cæsar rather showed the Romans the way to Britain than put them in possession of it. And in addition to all this we ought not to pass over the very significant fact, that when Cæsar is addressing his own soldiers, he reminds them of the many successful battles they and he had fought in Gaul, but not one syllable falls from his lips in respect of Britain. If he had really gained any important and decisive victory over the Britons, why did he not mention the fact? His silence is against him, and proves that things were not exactly as he represents them in his Commentaries. Cæsar gives one side of the question, but we require both before we can draw genuine conclusions. All we can say is, that he achieved what no predecessor ever did, and prepared the way for the Romans to plant and establish their influence in Britain.

BRITAIN from 54 B.C. to A.D. 43.

When released from the second hostile visit of Julius Cæsar, the Britons do not appear to have been molested for 97 years. The next who resolved on subjugating Britain was the Emperor **Augustus**, but he was prevented on three different occasions from carrying out his intention. On two occasions the Britons warded off the invasion by sending embassies to the Emperor. On the third he was prevented through a revolt of the Panonians (Austrains) and other urgent affairs at home. His successor, Tiberius, did not molest Britain, alleging that the Roman empire was large enough. Tiberius was succeeded by Caligula, to whom **Adminius**, the banished son of Cymbeline, went and surrendered Britain.

The Emperor hastened with his army to Boulogne, went out a short distance on the sea, returned, and gave signal for battle. The soldiers asked where the enemy was; Caligula told them they had subdued the ocean, and ordered them to gather the shells on the shore as a proof of victory. The Emperor then marched back to Rome, in order to honour himself with a triumph.

A.D. 43.

Claudius, the fourth Roman Emperor, instigated by **Beric**, an expelled British chief, sent 50,000 men, under the command of Aulus Plautius, who met with a vigorous resistance from the British forces, headed by **Caractacus**, the son of Cymbeline. Many engagements ensued, in which the success of the Romans may be ascribed to their German Auxiliaries, who, in fighting with the Britons were more serviceable to Plautius than his own men. Plautius was now joined by Claudius with reinforcements. The Britons were driven beyond the Thames, and routed with the loss of Togidumnus. Claudius received the submission of the Britons at **Camolodunum** (Maldon, in Essex), after which he left his army under the command of PLAUTIUS and VESPASIAN, returned to Rome in triumph, and surnamed himself **Britannicus.** **Vespasian,** after thirty battles, subdued the Belgae and Vectis (the inhabitants of the Isle of Wight): PLAUTIUS reduced the country as far as the Thames.

A.D. 51.

CARACTACUS, after having bravely opposed the Romans for nine years, was defeated by **Ostorius Scapula,** the successor of PLAUTIUS, at **Caer-Caradoc,** in Shropshire; his wife and daughters were taken captive, and his brother surrendered, whilst CARACTACUS himself was betrayed to the Romans by his stepmother, CARTISMANDUA, Queen of the Brigantes, to whose residence he had fled for protection. CARACTACUS and the noble captives were sent by OSTORIUS SCAPULA in chains to Rome, and brought before the Emperor CLAUDIUS and his wife AGRIPPINA. The arms and ornaments of the British hero were carried first; then followed his wife, daughters, and brothers, all manifesting the greatest distress at their misfortunes. Last in the procession was **Caractacus,** who appeared in no way dejected by his altered condition, but on beholding the multitudes of people, and the splendour of Rome, while they were leading him through the city, could not refrain from exclaiming : " How is it possible that a people having such palaces at home, can envy me a humble abode in Britain ?" When presented to the Emperor he thus addressed him : " My present state is as humiliating to me as it is glorious to you ; with these chains you can confine my person, but heaven has given me a mind out of the reach of human power to enslave. I once had horses, men, arms, and riches ; was it strange I should be unwilling to part with them ? If your ambition aims at universal sway, it does not follow that all men should submit to the yoke. If to defend my life, my liberty, and my country, be a crime, punish me with death, and my misfortunes will end with it. If I am suffered to live, I shall remain to future ages a monument of your clemency." CLAUDIUS and the Empress were so deeply affected by this short address, that CARACTACUS and his whole family were immediately set at liberty.

A.D. 51—61.

Ostorius dies, and is succeeded by **Aulus Didius,** who did nothing worthy of record. Then came **Veranius,** who scarcely surpassed his predecessor DIDIUS. The next governor was **Suetonius Paulinus,** a very distinguished general. He slaughtered the Druids, by whose instigation it was thought the Britons so obstinately resisted the Romans. *They had fled to* **Mona** *(Isle of Anglesea),* whither Suetonius pursued them. The Druids presented such an extraordinary appearance, from the women running about, shouting and raving, that the Roman forces became alarmed, and were struck with superstitious fear. Their General, however, led them on, and sacrificed the priests and priestesses on the fiery altars which the Durids had prepared for their enemies. Whilst SUETONIUS was in the Isle of Anglesea, an **insurrection** broke out in Britain. **Prasatagus,** King of the **Iceni,** and Roman Ally, divided his dominions between the Emperor and his two daughters, trusting that by such liberality the property of his children would be more secure. **Catus,** however, the Roman Procurator, seized all the estate, caused the daughters of PRASATAGUS to be violated, and his widow, **Boadicea,** when she remonstrated with him for his conduct, to be scourged. **Boadicea** appealed to the people, who took up arms and joined her cause. She led her forces, 230,000 fighting men, to **Maldon,** where a temple was erected to CLAUDIUS, the conqueror of Britain, destroyed it and also the Ninth Legion, which had been brought by **Petilius** to aid the Romans. **London** and **Verulam** immediately suffered the same fate, whilst SUETONIUS was driven from the former place. They slew 70,000 Romans. A battle, however, was afterwards fought beween the forces of BOADICEA and those of SUETONIUS, in which 80,000 Britons were slain, and numbers made prisoners. To avoid falling into the hands of the Romans, BOADICEA poisoned herself. **Paenius Posthumius,** Prefect of the Second Legion, having refused to join the army of SUETONIUS against the Britons, and wishing in consequence to escape the accusation of cowardice, also committed suicide.

A.D. 75.

PETILIUS CERIALIS reduces the Brigantes.

A.D. 75.—78.

The Silures are subdued by JULIUS FRONTINUS.

A.D. 78.

The most noted of all the Roman Generals was **Cneius Julius Agricola,** who carried the Roman power in Britain to its **greatest height.** He punished the **Ordovices** for slaughtering a troop of Roman horse; and once more subdued the sacred Isle of Mona.

A.D. 80.

He subjugated the inhabitants from Manchester to the Tweed.

A.D. 81.

He extended his victorious arms from the Solway to the Friths *of the Clyde and the Forth.*

A.D. 82—83.

He subdues all along the north-east of Scotland.

A.D. 84.

In the following year, being his seventh campaign, he completely routed 30,000 **Caledonians**, under **Galgacus, on the Grampian Hills**, in which battle 10,000 of the natives were slain. On this occasion the shock to the Caledonians was so terrible, that they slew their own wives and daughters to save them from the insults to be expected from the cruel victors. **The Roman power was now at its highest point.** The famous commander, **Agricola**, introduced a code of laws, and had the natives instructed in the Roman language, many of them adopting the dress, manners, and customs of their conquerors. Thirty years after his time, peace seems to have prevailed in the Island, which was broken by the incursions of the Caledonians, or the inhabitants of Scotland. To put a stop to these incursions, **Hadrian**, the fourteenth Roman Emperor (A.D. 120) visits Britain, and raises a new rampart, **Hadrian's Wall**, from Solway Firth to the German Ocean. During the reign of **Antoninus, Lollius Urbicus**, Governor of Britain, drove the Caledonians beyond the Friths of Forth and Clyde, repairing the rampart and forts of AGRICOLA.

A.D. 183.

The Caledonians break through the ramparts, and several battles ensue between them and the Romans; a feeling of dissatisfaction manifests itself among the different legions in Britain.

A.D. 207.

The Emperor **Severus** entered the northern districts and punished the barbarians, though with the terrible loss of 30,000 of his men: a loss said to be occasioned by the heavy work the soldiers had to undergo in cutting down forests, and making roads. And not far from the rampart of **Hadrian** he re-built a stone wall, four yards high and nearly three yards thick, with eighty-one castles, about three hundred towers, and a deep ditch. This wall was seventy-four miles in length, and extended from **Newcastle to Carlisle.** It was first erected by AGRICOLA, A.D. 79.

A.D. 211.

Severus marched a second time against the northern tribes, but was taken ill, and expired at **Eboracum** (York). **Caracalla** (son of SEVERUS) and the Caledonians lived on better terms, because *he granted them the* ground between the Solway and Tyne,

and the Friths of Clyde and Forth. From this time, for the next seventy years, we have little information concerning Britain.

A.D. 288.

Britain is now ravaged by **Saxon** and **Scandinavian pirates.** **Diocletian** and **Maximian,** then joint emperors, appoint **Carausius** a Menapian, to command the fleet in the British Channel. The pirates are defeated by him, after which he is ordered to be put to death for his collusion with the enemy. He sets the Emperors at defiance, who are obliged to purchase peace by giving him the government of Britain, Boulogne, and the neighbouring parts of Gaul, as well as the title of Emperor. **Under Carausius, Britain** becomes a great naval power. He is, however, murdered at York, by **Allectus,** a Briton, by whom he was succeeded in 293.

A.D. 296.

Constantius Chlorus, the successor of Diocletian and MAXIMIAN, defeats and slays **Allectus,** who reigned about three years.

A.D. 306.

Constantius Chlorus, who had married **Helena,** daughter of a **British Prince,** dies at Eboracum, and is succeeded by his son **Constantine,** afterwards called the **Great,** who assumed the title of **Cæsar.** Having carried on a war for a short time north of the wall of Severus, he left Britain, and took with him a great number of youths to serve in his army. From 306 to 337, when Constantine died, the Island seems to have enjoyed peace. About this time the **capital** of the empire was removed from **Rome** to **Constantinople.** While this change is going on, the **Southern** coasts of the Island are ravaged by the Frank and Saxon pirates, and the **northern** parts by the Picts and Scots. The **Picts** were the original Britons who dwelt beyond the Roman frontier; the **Scots** were Irish, but both occupied the country which is now called Scotland. **Ireland** was formerly designated **Scotia.**

A.D. 368.

The Picts and Scots plundered **Augusta** (London) and carried away the people as slaves. When **Theodosius,** the father of the Emperor THEODOSIUS, was governor of Britain, he made them give up their booty and prisoners.

A.D. 382.

Maximus, General of the Roman army in Britain, assumed the title of Emperor, and marched forth to take possession of **Gaul,**

pain, and Italy. He took nearly all his troops with him, and
as followed by so many Britons that there were very few left to
efend the country. MAXIMUS was put to death, A.D. 388. Owing
his absence, the Picts and Scots again invaded Britain, but were
pulsed by **Chrysantus,** the Lieutenant of **Theodosius.**

A.D. 402—410.

Italy having been invaded by the famous **Alaric,** King of the
oths, the Emperor **Honorius** was obliged to withdraw the
oman legion, which was stationed along the wall of Severus, in
nsequence of which the Picts and Scots recommenced their in-
ursions. Through the renewed incursions of these Picts and Scots,
e soldiers in Britain revolted, and appointed an Emperor for
emselves. They first chose **Marcus,** and destroyed him four
onths afterwards. The next fixed upon as the successor of
ARCUS was **Gratian,** whom they dethroned and put to death.
fter GRATIAN, the soldiery elected **Constantine,** a common
ldier, who aimed at the whole empire of the West, and was
lled while fighting to obtain it. The Picts and Scots still con-
nued their terrible ravages. The Britons in vain implored the
mperor to send them aid. HONORIUS could afford them no assis-
nce, because he was now heavily oppressed by the **Goths** under
laric, who had taken and sacked the city of Rome, although a
w years previously (404) the Emperor had concluded a treaty
ith him. **Gaul,** too, being now occupied by the **Vandals, Suevi,**
d the **Alani,** HONORIUS, in order to save himself from further
nportunities, **renounced his sovereignty over Britain, and
eleased the inhabitants from their allegiance, A.D. 410.**

A.D. 410—426.

Aetius, in the reign of **Valentinian III.,** out of pity to the
d state of the Britons, sends into the Island a legion under
aximian, who quickly drove the northern enemies back to their
wn territories. This legion being recalled, the general informed
e Britons that they were not to expect any further aid from
ome, as the Emperor had other urgent matters requiring his
ttention. In their unfortunate condition MAXIMIAN offered the
ritons both counsel and assistance. He advised them not to
epend upon others for aid, but to accustom themselves to arms and
repair the wall of Severus as a barrier against the incursions of
eir enemies. The Britons and the Roman Legion, under the
perintendence of MAXIMIAN himself, repaired the wall, after
hich the general and his men bade a final farewell to our Island,
ever to return. This event *occurred* A.D. 426, at which time the
oman *domination in Britain* ended.

DIVISION OF BRITAIN.

BRITAIN UNDER THE ROMANS WAS DIVIDED INTO SIX PROVINCES.

I. **Britannia Prima,** which embraced the country south of the Thames and Bristol Channel.

II. **Britannia Secunda,** comprising Wales, Monmouthshire, Herefordshire, and parts of Worcestershire, Shropshire, and Gloucestershire.

III. **Flavia Caesariensis,** in which was included the country north of the Thames, east of the Severn, south of the Mersey and Humber.

IV. **Maxima Caesariensis,** which extended from the wall of Hadrian, on the Tyne, to the Dee and Wash.

V. **Valentia,** which lay between the walls of Hadrian and Antonine. It was erected by THEODOSIUS (A.D. 369), and called **Valentia,** in honour of the Emperor **Valens.**

VI. **Vespatiana,** which consisted of the tract of land north of Antonine's wall.

Number six was never conquered by the Romans.

ROMAN GOVERNMENT.

CONSTANTINE divided the whole Roman Empire into four **Prefectures,** namely, Italy, Gaul, Illyria, and the **East,** which comprised fourteen provinces. Britain being one of the provinces, was governed by a **Vicarius,** or deputy, who was responsible to the Prefect of Gaul. The Vicarius had five Magistrates under him, two **Consulares,** or men of Consular rank, and three with the title of **Presides,** or Presidents. All civil and criminal affairs were regulated by these magistrates, and a few inferior officers. **Military** matters were under three officers:—

I. The **Count of Britain,** who maintained peace in the inland parts and on the western coast.

II. The **Duke of Britain,** who was expected to defend the north against the Picts and Scots.

III. The **Count of the Saxon Coasts,** whose business was to protect the southern and eastern coasts from the incursions of the Saxon pirates.

The combined number of troops under these three officers amounted to 20,000 foot, and 2,000 horse.

For the management of private business there were:

1. A **Registrar;** 2. A **Treasurer;** 3. A **Procurator.**

ROMAN CIVITATES.

The Roman Civitates were classified and named according to their privileges.

MUNICIPIA.

To the Municipia belonged **Eboracum** (York), and **Verulamium** (St. Alban's), whose inhabitants enjoyed all the rights of Roman citizens. They were allowed to enact their own laws, and to elect their own magistrates.

COLONIAE.

These consisted of **veteran legionaries**, who held lands on condition of rendering **military service** when required. Under this head there were nine towns :—

   I. **Londinium,** also called Augusta, London.

  II. **Camelodunum**—Colchester or Maldon.

 III. **Thermae or Aquae Solis**—Bath.

 IV. **Glevum or Claudia**—Gloucester.

  V. **Isea Silurum**—Caerleon.

 VI. **Deva**—Chester.

 VII. **Lindum**—Lincoln.

VIII. **Rhutupiae**—Richborough.

 IX. **Camboricum**—Cambridge.

CIVITATES LATIO JURE DONATÆ.

These **Civitates** possessed the **Latian right,** and consisted of Roman colonists to whom lands were granted. There were ten of this class :—

   I. **Durnomagus**—Water Newton.

  II. **Durobriae**—Castor-on-Nene.

 III. **Cambodunum**—Slack, in Yorkshire.

 IV. **Catarractonum**—Catterick, in Yorkshire.

  V. **Coccium**—Ribchester.

 VI. **Luguvallium**—Carlisle.

 VII. **Pteroton**—Burgh Head, in Morayshire, Scotland.

VIII. **Victoria**—Dealgin Ross, in Perthshire.

 IX. **Corinium**—Cirencester.

  X. **Sorbiodunum**—*Old Sarum.*

STIPENDIARIAE CIVITATES.

The inhabitants of these towns, twelve in number, were subject to the **payment of tribute** :—

   I. **Venta Belgarum**—Winchester.

  II. **Venta Silurum**—Caer-Went, or Caer-Gwent, in Monmouthshire.

 III. **Venta Icenorum**—Caister, near Norwich.

 IV. **Segontium**—Caer-Seiont, near Caernarvon.

  V. **Muridinum**—Seaton, near Colyton, Devon.

 VI. **Ragae**—Leicester.

 VII. **Cantiopolis** or **Durovernum**—Canterbury.

VIII. **Durinum** or **Dunium**—Dorchester.

 IX. **Isca**—Exeter.

  X. **Bremenium**—Riechester, Nothumberland.

 XI. **Vindonum**—near Andover, Hants.

XII. **Durobrivae**—Rochester.

The Roman towns contained baths, temples, and other noble buildings, as Cirencester and Lincoln.

INTRODUCTION OF CHRISTIANITY.

In speaking of the introduction of **Christianity**, it is necessary to distinguish between the **British** and the **Anglo-Saxon** Church. The former existed in the **first century**; the latter began under **Augustine**, who was sent by Gregory, bishop of Rome, to convert the Saxons, A.D. 596. This remark seems to be required, because so many are under an impression that the Ancient Britons knew nothing of the Gospel before the arrival of Augustine. It is certain that the Gospel made the most rapid strides in a very short space of time, and its introduction into **Britain** at a very early period seems evident from the following testimonies :—

1. **St. Paul.**—Col. i., 6, 23.—We learn that "the Gospel had come into all the world and was preached to every creature under heaven." And in Rom. i., 8, the Apostle declares that "the faith of the Roman converts was spoken of throughout the whole world." This declaration decidedly implies that Christianity was very widely disseminated so early as A.D. 63.

2. **Tertullian,** an African Presbyter, wrote a book against the Jews, in which he asserts that "those parts of Britain into which the Roman arms had never penetrated were become subject to Christ." A.D. 160—245.

3. **Eusebius,** an ecclesiastical historian, who, in speaking of the Apostles, exclaims: "What madness were it in such poor illiterate men, understanding only their mother tongue, to go about to deceive the world by preaching the Gospel to the Romans, the Persians, and those called the **British Isles.**" A.D. 270—338.

4. **Chrysostom,** Bishop of Constantinople, says, "The **British Isles,** which lie beyond this sea—those, I mean, lying in the very ocean—have felt the power of the word." A.D. 354—407.

5. **Jerome.**—This Latin Father's testimony is to the following effect: "Equally from **Britain** as from Jerusalem, the gates of heaven lie open. The churches of Gaul and Britain, as well as those of Asia and the East, observe one rule of truth." JEROME died A.D. 420.

6. **Gildas,** the earliest English writer, informs us that "the cheering beams of the sun, the sun of righteousness, shone upon this frozen island, shivering with the icy cold of heathenism and idolatry, **a little before the defeat of Boadicea by the Roman legions.**" GILDAS flourished, A.D. 493—570. According to this author, Christianity reached Britain during the first century, because BOADICEA was defeated A.D. 61.

THROUGH WHAT CHANNEL CHRISTIANITY
WAS INTRODUCED.

1. **Claudius** (A.D. 53) published a decree, commanding all **Jews** "to depart from Rome," and it is hence inferred that Christianity might be introduced by some of them who must have been scattered among the Gentiles.

2. It has been conjectured that the Gospel reached this island from the East by means of the **Mediterranean commerce,** through Gaul, which contained multitudes of Christians in the second century.

3. **Pomponia Grecina,** the wife of AULUS PLAUTIUS, the first Roman governor in Britain, is thought to have been a Christian, because **Tacitus,** a Roman historian, says, "she was accused of having a strange and foreign superstition." Now, if Pomponia were a Christian, and accompanied her husband to Britain, she might have been instrumental in bringing the Gospel into this island, and diffusing it among the inhabitants.

4. Some of the family of **Caractacus** are said to have become Christians while at *Rome, among whom the Welsh Triads place Brân, his father. This account carries with it the appearance of*

truth, for, according to respectable authority, the detention of the British hostages at Rome, and St. Paul's imprisonment in that city, happened at the same time. On this account Brân has been celebrated as "one of the three blessed sovereigns; and his family as one of the three blessed lineages of Britain."

5. There are strong reasons for believing that the Gospel was preached in Britain by some of the Apostles, and especially by St. Paul, the great Apostle of the Gentiles. The following testimonies ought to carry weight with them :—

Jerome says, St. Paul preached the Gospel in the **Western parts**. **Theodoret**, Bishop of Cyprus, states that "the Apostles persuaded even the **Britons** to receive the laws of the Crucified Lord." The same author informs us that "St. Paul, after his release from imprisonment at Rome, went straightway to Spain, and thence, hastening away to **other nations**, carried the light of the Gospel to them also." **Clement**, a fellow labourer with St. Paul, states that the Apostle "was a preacher both in the East and in the West, that he taught the whole world righteousness, and travelled as far as the utmost bounds of the West." Now Britain is called by **Catullus** "the utmost Island of the West." And **Theodoret** describes the Britons as "inhabiting the utmost part of the West." When **Clement**, therefore, says that Paul went to the utmost bounds of the West, "we do not conjecture," says **Calmet**, "but are sure that he meant Britain, not only because Britain was so designated, but because Paul could not have gone to the utmost bounds of the West without going to Britain."

Not only was Christianity widely spread in the Island, but there were also **churches**, whose Bishops attended various general councils in different parts of the world. At the Council of **Arles**, in France, held A.D. 314, there were three **British Bishops**, namely, **Eborius**, of York; **Restitutus**, of London ; and **Adelfius**, of Lincoln. It is supposed that some English Bishops were present at the Council of Nice, A.D. 325. At the Council of **Arminium**, A.D. 359, there were 400 Bishops of the West, including those of Britain. Though the **Arian** heresy had found its way into England, the British Bishops at the Council of **Antioch**, A.D. 363, were declared to be orthodox.

The first British Bishop is supposed to have been **Aristobulus**, whom St. Paul salutes in his Epistle to the Romans. The **Diocletian** persecution began in the year A.D. 303, during which, many Christians were cruelly put to death, being torn limb from limb in the most savage manner. In this persecution perished St. Alban, the British Protomartyr. Constantine befriended *the Christians*, so that under him and his sons, they enjoyed *comparative tranquility* for upwards of fifty years.

ROMAN INFLUENCE IN BRITAIN.

Rome and Britain having been connected for nearly **five** centuries, it seems natural to ask what influence the former exercised over the latter. I shall therefore endeavour to lay before the student what I conceive to be the **advantages** and **disadvantages** which resulted from Roman dominion in Britain.

THE ADVANTAGES.

I. **Christianity.**—The Romans probably became the indirect means of introducing Christianity into Britain, and thereby preparing the way for a more ready diffusion of its saving truths, by familiarising the natives with their language. In fact, the extension of the Roman language among so many nations before the dawn of Christianity, may be regarded as a grand preparation for spreading the Gospel.

II. **Commerce.**—British Commerce increased under the Romans. The chief articles imported into Britain were :—brass wares, chains, bridles, drinking glasses, cups of amber, and trinkets. The exports from Britain to Rome consisted of corn, cheese, lime, chalk, oysters, baskets of wickerwork, earth, metals, ivory, pearls, horses, dogs, and slaves. The horses of the Britons were greatly admired by the Romans, who mounted their cavalry with them ; nor did they think little of the English dogs, especially the bull-dog and mastiff. British pearls were highly prized, insomuch that JULIUS CÆSAR, on his return dedicated a costly breast-plate, made of these pearls, to his favourite goddess, **Venus Genetrix.**

III. **Civilisation.**—The refined civilisation of the Romans produced its effects upon many of the Britons, especially in the case of the youth, who attended the same schools with the sons of the conquerors.

IV. **Agriculture.**—British soil was turned to the best account under Roman cultivation. Such quantities of corn were grown that the Romans annually sent 800 ship-loads into Germany for the use of their armies. For this reason Britain was called the "**Western Granary.**"

V. **Roads.**—Britain is indebted to the Romans for some excellent roads, which they either made or improved. These roads were paved with stones and called **strata**, from which is derived our word street. The most remarkable of these ways were :—

1. **Watling Street,** extending from the coast of Kent, by London, to Caernarvon.

2. The **Foss-way,** between Cornwall and Lincoln.

3. **Ikenild** or **Rikenild Street,** leading from Tynemouth, through York, Derby and Birmingham, to St. David's.

4. **Irmin** or *Hermin Street,* extening from St. David's to Southampton.

VI. **Architecture.**—The Britons were instructed in architecture by the Romans, whose towns and stations in the island were upwards of 300. Traces of Roman occupation are found in the names of those towns ending in **Chester, caster,** or **cester,** (from the Latin, **castra,** a camp); as Manchester, Lancaster, Cirencester. **Colne** and **Lincoln** are probably derived from the Latin **colonia.** Bath was a Roman watering-place, and had its temples, palaces, and theatres. Where Westminster Abbey now stands, there was a temple to Apollo; and another to Diana on the site occupied by St. Paul's.

VII. **Protection.**—The imperial arms were frequently employed in defending the Roman subjects against the united forces of the Picts, Scots, and those native Britons who relinquished their possessions and fled northward rather than become the slaves of their conquerors.

VIII. **Municipal Law.**—The effects of those municipal laws enjoyed by some of the Roman **Civitates** have come down to the present day, and may be said to form the basis of those privileges and regulations which are still in force in many of our own towns.

THE DISADVANTAGES.

I. The Britons were compelled to pay the most exorbitant taxes, which were levied on commerce, mines, houses, heads, and legacies. According to **Lipsius,** Rome received from Britain an annual tribute of **two millions sterling** !

II. Many of the Britons were deprived of their estates, which were given to Roman veterans, numbers of whom flocked into the Island.

III. Britain was stripped of the flower of her youth, who were trained for Soldiers, and despatched into remote parts of the empire, whence they seldom, if ever, returned.

IV. The Romans did not allow the Britons to use arms, except those whom they sent abroad.

Such was the treatment of the Romans towards those whom they subdued. In dealing with conquered nations, the Romans invariably adopted a policy which redounded to their own advantage. For, as RAPIN observes, "they sent away whole bodies, levied in a conquered country, into other remote regions. For instance, the **Britons** into **Pannonia,** the **Batavians** into **Illyria,** the **Germans** into **Britain,** to keep them at a distance from their own country. By thus draining the conquered nations of their main strength, they disabled them from revolting, and at the same time made use of them to acquire new conquests." There were twelve bodies of British soldiers in the Roman armies; and it is said that **Vespasian,** at the sacking of Jerusalem, had **20,000 British Soldiers.** These facts will account for the deplorable condition in which the Britons found themselves, after they were deprived of Roman protection. They had not been accustomed to arms, and therefore were not prepared at once to cope with their enemies. Those who could, and *ought to have defended* their native country, were scattered abroad for the purpose of fighting the Emperor's battles in distant parts of his dominions. It is, however, generally admitted that Roman influence produced happy effects upon Britain. The flourishing condition of our Island under these mighty conquerors is strikingly set forth by Eumenius, in his laudation on CONSTANTINE the great. "Oh, fortunate Britannia," says the orator, "thee hath nature deservedly enriched with the choicest blessings of heaven and earth. Thy harvests reward thy labours with so great an increase as to supply thy tables with bread and thy cellars with liquors. Innumerable are thy herds of cattle and flocks of sheep, which feed thee plentifully and clothe thee richly." Such may be considered the chief advantages and disadvantages which resulted from the connection of Rome with Britain.

THE LEADING EVENTS AND PRINCIPAL DATES
OF THE ROMAN PERIOD.

The Romans under Julius Cæsar invade Britain	B.C. 55
Britain invaded a second time by Cæsar, who defeats Cassivelaunus, a British Chief	54
Britain invaded by Claudius	A.D. 43
London founded by the Romans	49
Caractacus subdued and sent prisoner to Rome	51
Christianity probably introduced into Britain	58-64
The Britons under Boadicea slay 70,000 Romans and burn London	61
The Romans slay 80,000 Britons under Boadicea, who poisons herself	61
Julius Agricola appointed Governor of Britain	78
Battle of the Grampian Hills	84
Lucius, the first Christian King of Britain and in the world, reigns	179
Hadrain visits Britain and constructs a rampart	120
In the reign of Antonine the rampart of Agricola is repaired by Lollius Urbicus, and called Antonine's Wall	140
Severus builds a wall near Hadrian's rampart	210
Severus dies at York	211
Carausius, Commander of the Roman fleet, usurps the throne of Britain	286
He is slain by his minister, Allectus, who also usurped the British throne	293
Allectus is slain and *Britain recovered* by Constantinus	296

BRITAIN INDEPENDENT.

A.D. 426—449.

The history of Britain from the departure of the Romans to the arrival of the Saxons (a period of 23 years), is both scanty and indefinite, for want of accurate sources of information. The following is a summary of the chief events during this obscure period :—

1. The Picts and Scots hearing that the Roman legion had been withdrawn, commenced hostilities, and drove the Britons from the northern to the more southern parts of the Island.

II. About this time the heretical doctrines of **Pelagius**, a native of Britain, whose real name was **Morgan**, were spreading in the Island, through the zealous preaching of **Agricola**, one of his disciples. The chief doctrines taught by PELAGIUS were :—

1. That **Adam** was constitutionally mortal, or that he would have died, had he never sinned.

2. That man might be saved by his own merits, without the special grace of God.

3. That infants do not inherit original sin, and are as pure as ADAM was when he came from the hands of his Creator.

4. That the general resurrection of the dead is not the result of Christ's resurrection.

Germanus, Bishop of Auxerre, and **Lupas**, Bishop of Troyes, are sent into Britain to refute the doctrines of PELAGIUS. During the stay of these two Bishops in the island, GERMANUS, at the request of the Britons, led them against the Picts and Scots, who had advanced as far as Mold, in Flintshire. The Bishop having been a military commander during his youth, placed his men in an advantageous position. GERMANUS desired his followers to shout Hallelujah at the onset, which they did so vociferously, that the hills, echoing with the sound, terrified their enemies, causing them to flee in all directions. They were pursued by the Britons, who slew the greater part of them. This was called the **Hallelujah Victory**, from the cry uttered by the Britons at the onset, A.D. 429.

III. During the minority of **Eugenius II.**, King of Scotland, **Graham**, regent of that country, concluded a **Treaty** with the Britons, by which it was agreed:—

1. That the wall of Severus should be the boundary between the two nations.

2. That the Britons should pay the Scots a large sum of money.

IV. This treaty is broken by EUGENIUS, who demands from the Britons all the lands previously possessed by the Scots. The Britons hold a council to determine upon the best means of satisfying the King of Scotland. Their deliberations end in a rejection of the claims of EUGENIUS. A battle ensues, in which the Britons lose 14,000 men and all the lands north of the Humber.

V. The miseries of the wretched Britons are increased by **pestilence and famine**, which destroy the people by thousands. To escape these ravages many of the inhabitants fly to **Armorica**, and others join the Picts and Scots.

VI. After the departure of the two Bishops, Pelagianism revived. GERMANUS, therefore, accompanied by SEVERUS, Bishop of Troyes, undertook a second mission into Britain. Finding it impossible to convince the Pelagians by arguments, he procured their expulsion under the edict of **Valentinian III.**, A.D. 446. While in Britain, GERMANUS is said to have founded some excellent schools, from which emanated many pious and learned men.

VII. The sad affairs of the Britons compelled them to apply once more to Rome. They sent a letter to the famous ÆTIUS, Prefect of Gaul, in which they set forth their miseries in these pitiable words: "The barbarians drive us to the sea, and the sea forces us back to the barbarians; between which we have only the choice of two deaths; either to be swallowed by the waves, or to be butchered by the sword." ÆTIUS returned the Britons an answer to the effect that he could not help them, because at that time he was opposed by **Attila**, King of the **Huns**, who had entered Gaul with 80,000 soldiers, A.D. 446.

Harrassed by the continued attacks of the Picts and Scots, and influenced by the advice of **Vortigern**, a native prince, the Britons, call in the assistance of a people known by the general name of **Saxons**, who landed at **Ebbsfleet**, in Kent, under two brothers, **Hengist** and **Horsa**, A.D. 449. These people were divided into three principal tribes:—

1. The **Jutes**, *who occupied the* peninsula of Jutland.

2. The **Angles**, who inhabited the duchy of Schleswig, in Denmark, and where some traces of their name are still said to be found, near **Anglen.**

3. The **Saxons**, including the **Frisians**, whose country lay between the shores of the Baltic and Friesland.

HENGIST and HORSA were followed at different periods by many of their countrymen, who invaded Britain, and formed themselves into separate kingdoms, which are specified in their proper place. The following are the five invasions of the Saxons:—

1. Five thousand in seventeen vessels, arrived, 455.

2. Another tribe, under the leadership of **Ella** and his three sons, invaded our island, 477.

3. **Cerdic** and his son, **Cynric**, landed 495.

4. Another tribe of Saxon invaders made their appearance on our shores, 527.

5. A body of Angles, under **Uffa**, invaded Britain, 527.

ANGLO-SAXON PERIOD.

A.D. 449—827.

This period, which lasted about 377 years, was distinguished by a gradual extension of the Saxon power, and a great many battles, which are said to have been caused by the Britons refusing to furnish the Saxons with an additional supply of provisions; but it is more probable that the Saxons were ambitious of becoming masters of the country, and therefore put forth their unreasonable request as a pretext for an open rupture.

A   **WARS.**

1. **Battle of Stamford**, Lincolnshire, in which the united forces of the Britons and Saxons, under HENGIST, HORSA, and VORTIGERN, completely routed the Picts and Scots, A.D. 449.

2. **Battle of Aylesford**, Kent, in which the Saxons, under HENGIST and HORSA, probably defeated the Britons, who were commanded by VORTIMER. In this engagement HORSA was killed, and HENGIST slew CATIGERN, the youngest brother of VORTIMER, 455.

3. **Battle of Crayford**, Kent, in which HENGIST obtained a ecisive victory over VORTIMER, who lost 4,000 men and the reater part of his best officers, 457.

CIVIL WARS.

After **Vortimer's** defeat at Crayford, the Britons lose con- dence in him, and therefore solicit aid from **Androen**, King of rmorica, who sends **Ambrosius**, a Roman by descent, with 0,000 men, 458. Some of the Britons suspecting the intentions f AMBROSIUS, join VORTIMER. Britain is now troubled by two ctions, and civil wars rage for seven years, from 458 to 465, when he contending parties, for the safety of both, resolve on a division f the country. VORTIGERN and VORTIMER have the eastern, and MBROSIUS the western part of the Kingdom.. **Watling Street** ivided their territories.

THE WARS RENEWED BETWEEN THE BRITONS AND SAXONS.

1. **Battle of Wipped's-Fleet** (Ipswich) in which the Britons rere led by VORTIMER and AMBROSIUS against the united forces f the Saxons; but it is uncertain which party was victorious. In nis engagement HENGIST lost an officer named WIPPED, after rhom the field of battle is called Wipped's-fleet, 466.

2. **Battle of Chardford**, Hampshire, in which the Saxons, nder **Cerdic** and his son **Cynric**, defeated the Britons, headed by MBROSIUS, who was slain, with 5,000 of his men, 508.

3. **Battle of Mount Badon**, near Bath, in which ARTHUR ained a complete victory over the Saxons under CERDIC, 511.

4. **Battle of Camelford**, Cornwall, in which ARTHUR and is nephew slew each other, 542.

5. **Battle of Heathfield** (now called Hatfield), Yorkshire, in rhich PENDA, King of Mercia, and CADWALLO, King of Wales, ught against EDWIN, who ruled over Northumbria. The allied overeigns were victorious, 633.

6. **Battle of York.**—This encounter took place between OSRIC, ing of Deira, and CADWALLO, who was conqueror in the battle of leathfield. . The troops of OSRIC were defeated, and their leader lain. The men of Deira might have been assisted by the Berni- ians, had not jealousy alienated the two kingdoms, 634.

7. **Battle of Haledon** (formerly styled Heofen, or Heaven- eld.) The contending parties were OSWALD, brother to ANFRID, ing of *Bernicia* (*who had lately · been slain in Battle*), and

CADWALLO, the warlike monarch of Wales. It is said that the favour of heaven on this occasion was shown in a most marked manner to the soldiers of OSWALD, who gained a signal victory, 634.

B   **CHIEF EVENTS.**

The Saxon Heptarchy or Octarchy.

The different parts of England over which the confederate tribes of the Saxons spread themselves were as follows:—

I. **Cantia,** or **Kent,** founded by **Hengist,** and comprised the county of Kent, 457.

II. **Sussex,** founded by **Ella,** and contained Sussex and Surrey, 490.

III. **Wessex,** founded by **Cerdic,** and embraced Berks., Southampton, Wilts., Somerset, Dorset, Devon, and part of Cornwall, 519.

IV. **Essex,** founded by **Ercenwine,** and extended over Essex, Middlesex, and part of Herts., 527.

V. **Northumbria,** founded by **Ida,** and composed of Lancaster, Cumberland, York, Westmoreland, Durham, and Northumberland, 547. At first Northumbria was divided into two kingdoms, **Bernicia** and **Deira,** on which account some historians consider **Octarchy** a more correct term than **Heptarchy.**

VI. **East Anglia,** founded by **Uffa,** and consisted of Norfolk, Suffolk, Cambridge, and the Isle of Ely, 575.

VII. **Mercia,** founded by **Crida,** and comprised the counties of Chester, Hereford, Gloucester, Stafford, Worcester, Oxford, Salop, Warwick, Derby, Leicester, Bucks., Northampton, Notts., Lincoln, Bedford, Rutland, Huntingdon, and part of Herts., 586.

Though each of the preceding kingdoms was governed by a prince, yet one had to some extent power over the others, and was styled **Bretwalda,** which signifies the controller of Britain ; or, **Rex Gentis Anglorum,** King of the English nation. After the Saxons had established themselves over a greater part of the country, they began to wage war against each other, which led to the destruction of the different kingdoms of the Heptarchy ; causing them at last to fall under the power of **Egbert,** King of Wessex, 827.

The doctrine of Predestination was maintained by ST. AUGUSTINE in the fifth century, and taught by LUCIDUS, a Gallic priest, 470.

The custom of turning the face towards the East, while engaged in prayer, was instituted by Pope BONIFACE II., 532.

The Danes cruelly massacre the monks of Bangor, 580.

Prayers addressed to the Saints, and the Virgin MARY, were introduced by Pope GREGORY, 593.

The doctrine of **Purgatory** was received into the Romish Church, 593.

The **Anglo-Saxons** were converted to Christianity by ST. AUGUSTINE and forty other monks, whom Pope GREGORY the Great was induced to send into Britain, from having seen three English youths exposed for sale in the slave-market at Rome, 596.

London was made a bishopric, 650.

Britain was ravaged by a terrible disease, called the **yellow plague,** which began 664, and lasted twenty years.

The manufacture of glass, and the art of building with stone, were introduced into England by a monk named **Benedict**; the former in 663, and the latter in 670. Gothic architecture was also invented in the seventh century.

Ina, King of Wessex, issued a code of laws, about seventy-nine in number, 709.

Consecrated places were first used for the burial of the dead in 750; and churchyards, 758.

Offa, King of Mercia, murders ETHELBERT, King of the East Angles, and obtains absolution from the Pope by paying £243 6s. 8d. He also orders that every house of the annual value of thirty pence should pay the yearly tax of a Saxon penny for the maintenance of an English college at Rome. This tax at first received the name of **Romescot,** but was afterwards called **Peter's Pence,** because paid on the first of August, the day dedicated to that saint, 793.

Some writers assert that INA, King of the West Saxons (Wessex) first ordered the payment of Peter's Pence for the maintenance of the English college at Rome which he founded, and that what OFFA did was merely a confirmation of the same.

CELEBRATED PERSONS.

C

Vortimer, the son of VORTIGERN, opposed the Saxons under HENGIST and HORSA, and is said to have been poisoned by **Rowena,** his stepmother, 475.

Vortigern, a British king, first invited the Saxons to England; and was burnt to death in a Welsh castle, 485.

Hengist, a Jute, by whose energy the Picts and Scots were soon driven out of England. To him the **Heptarchy** owes its origin. His death took place 488.

St. Patrick, a native of Scotland, converted the Irish to Christianity, and founded many churches and schools of learning. Died 493.

Ambrosius, a British King, opposed the Saxons, and was slain by CERDIC, 508.

Dubricius, Archbishop of Caerleon, famous for his piety and learning; he also built many schools. Died, 522.

St. David, the son of a British Prince, and successor of DUBRICIUS, in a synod held at Vittoria, ratified the decisions of BREVI (Wales). From him MENEVIA received the name of St. David's. He died 529, aged 150 years.

Cerdic, a Saxon General, is noted for three reasons :—

1. His conquests.

2. His founding a kingdom which ultimately subdued all the rest.

3. From him are descended all the Kings of England, in the male line, down to EDWARD the confessor; and in the female line, to Queen VICTORIA. CERDIC arrived in Britain 495, and died 534.

Arthur, son of UTHER PENDRAGON, and a great warrior, defeated the Saxons in twelve battles. He instituted an order of chivalry, called **"The Knights of the Round Table,"** whom he made his principal officers. They were forty in number, and took their names from a large round marble table, at which they used to sit. Historians inform us that he led the life of a soldier for seventy-six years, and was at last mortally wounded by his nephew **Medrawd,** 542.

Gildas, the first British historian, was a native of Dumbarton, and Monk of Bangor Monastery. He wrote a treatise entitled " De Excidio Britanniæ," (On the Destruction of Britain). Died 570.

Cadoc, Abbot of Lancarvan, noted for spending all his income in the maintenance of 300 priests. Died 570.

St. Asaph wrote the life of his master, **Kentigan,** Abbot of Glasgow, presided over a Welsh Monastery, and gave his name to the city of St. Asaph. Died 590.

St. Columba, of noble Irish descent, entered Scotland, and preached the Gospel to the Northern Picts, 565. He resided in the Isle of Iona, which after him was called Columb-cylle and now Colchil. Died 598.

Augustine introduces Christianity among the Anglo-Saxons, and converts to the faith ETHELBERT, King of Kent, whose example has a powerful effect upon his subjects, causing vast numbers to embrace the doctrines of the Cross. He is consecrated at Arles, and appointed the first Archbishop of Canterbury. AUGUSTINE tries to bring the British Bishops under the dominion of himself and the Pope, but signally fails in his attempt. The doctrines of the Roman and British Christians were the same, but some difference prevailed between them as to **baptism,** and the **celebration** of **Easter.** The questions of AUGUSTINE, addressed by letter to Pope GREGORY, are not calculated to raise him in one's estimation. These enquiries related to the consecration of Bishops; the division of Church-offerings; Marriages; how he should demean himself towards the bishops of Gaul and Britain; and the appropriate age for the baptism of infants. Died 605.

Ethelbert, King of Kent, was converted to Christianity by ST. AUGUSTINE. His queen, **Bertha,** daughter of CARIBERT, King of the Franks, had previously embraced the truths of the Gospel. ETHELBERT died in the year 616.

Sebert, King of Essex, is said to have founded the University of Cambridge. Died 616.

Nennius, who is supposed to have lived in the beginning of the seventh century, wrote a "History of the Britons."

Caedmon, a monk of Whitby (Yorkshire), wrote poetry on the "Creation." Died 680.

Aldhelm, the most ancient British poet, and said to have been the first Englishman that wrote in Latin. Died 709.

Bede (the Venerable), author of an Ecclesiastical History, was so distinguished for his learning, that Pope SERGIUS desired an interview with him at Rome; but he declined the honour. Born at Wearmouth (Durham), 672, and died 735.

Offa was the most renowned King of Mercia. In order to protect the Anglo-Saxons from the Welsh, he constructed a dyke, called "**Offa's Dyke,**" extending from the mouth of the Dee, to that of the Wye, in Monmouthshire. Died 796.

Alcuin, an English divine, educated first under BEDE, and afterwards by EDWIN, Archbishop of York, was tutor to **Charlemagne,** from whom he received some rich Abbeys. He wrote poetry and theology, and was the most accomplished man of his time. Died at Tours in France, 804.

REMARKS.

I. The **Saxons,** so called from seax, a short sword (usually worn by them), were a **Germanic** race, noted for their courage, cruelty, and love of war. They are described as having a dignified mien, athletic frames, blue eyes, and flaxen hair. To their chiefs they paid implicit obedience, showed great regard for the female sex, and were passionately fond of liberty. Great cruelty was shown by them towards their enemies, whom, if taken in war, they usually sacrificed to their gods. Their mode of government *may be thus described:*—

1. They divided their dominions into twelve provinces.

2. At the head of each province they placed a chief, who was responsible to the general council of the nation.

3. While engaged in war, they elected a general to conduct their armies, and invested him with supreme power until the termination of the conflict, after which his authority ceased.

II. Before the arrival of AUGUSTINE, they were idolaters, having a god for each day of the week. From the Saxon deities are thus derived the names of our days:—Sun, Sunday; Moon, Monday; Tuisco, Tuesday; Woden, or Oden, Wednesday; Thor, Thursday; Frea, or Friga, Friday; Seater, Saturday. The chief deity of the SAXONS was Woden, the god of battles, to whom they sacrificed their prisoners of war. All the SAXON leaders professed to have descended from Woden. They believed in a future state, in which the valiant would have the enjoyment of drinking ale from the skulls of their enemies.

III. The SAXONS were induced to establish themselves in our island for the following reasons:—1. The barrenness of their own country; 2. The fertility of the soil of Britain; 3. Because they saw that the conquest of Britain would be an easy task.

IV. It is probable that many of the Britons, after they had been dispossessed by the SAXONS, were made the slaves of their conquerors. Others, however, escaping the slaughter, and not willing to submit to the invaders, fled into Holland, Wales, Cornwall, and Armorica (in France), which place they subsequently called after their own name, Brittany.

V. The success of ST. AUGUSTINE's mission may be attributed in a great measure to the influence of BERTHA (the queen of ETHELBERT), who was a Christian before her marriage. BERTHA's anxiety for the conversion of the King might possibly have induced her to open a correspondence with Pope GREGORY, and request his aid in accomplishing the object she had so much at heart. This will explain why AUGUSTINE landed in Kent, and sent a message to the sovereign of that kingdom.

VI. The causes tending to facilitate the SAXON conquest of Britain were:—

1. Internal dissensions among the BRITONS.

2. The enervation of character, and incapacity for war, produced by their long subjection to the ROMANS.

3. The want of a competent leader. In the same way, discord among the different kingdoms of the Heptarchy led to their ruin.

VII. During the SAXON conquests, the invaders made dreadful havoc, destroying the churches of the Christians in every direction, and sacrificing the ministers of religion to their merciless fury, so that *Christianity in some parts* of the kingdom was almost extinguished.

GENEALOGICAL TABLE,

Showing the descent of Henry II. from Cerdic.

Cerdic

Cynric

Ceawlin

Guthwine

Cutha

Ceolwald

Cenred

Ingild

Eoppa

Eafa

Ealhmund

Egbert

Ethelwulf

...ne ETHELBALD   ETHELBERT   ETHELRED   Alfred

Ethelwald

Edward the Elder   5 other childre...

ATHELSTANE   Edmund   EDRED

Edgar

EDWARD THE MARTYR   Ethelred

...l Ironside   Alfred   EDWARD THE CONFESSOR

Edward the Outlaw

...ar Atheling   Margaret   Christina

Matilda
M. Henry I., King of England

Matilda

Henry II.

LIST OF THE KINGS OF ENGLAND,

From the Accession of Egbert to the Norman Conquest.

		(Began to reign.) A.D.	(Reigned.) Years.
SAXONS.			
Egbert	...	827	9
Ethelwulf	...	836	22
Ethelbald	...	858	2
Ethelbert	...	860	6
Ethelred I.	...	866	5
Alfred	...	871	30
Edward the Elder	...	901	24
Athelstane	...	925	15
Edmund I.	...	940	6
Edred	...	946	9
Edwy	...	955	3
Edgar	...	958	17
Edward II., the Martyr	...	975	4
Ethelred II., the Unready	...	979	37
Edmund II., Ironside	...	1016	(6 mths.)
DANES.			
Canute, the Great	...	1016	19
Harold I., Harefoot	...	1035	5
Hardicanute	...	1040	2
SAXON LINE RESTORED.			
Edward III. the Confessor	...	1042	24
Harold II.	...	1066	(9 mths.)

Egbert was the Son of Ealhmund. A.D. 827—836.

A   **WARS.**

1. Battle of Camelford, in which EGBERT defeats the Bri
tons, and reduces Cornwall under his power, 809.

2. He subdues Venedotia, one of the three Principalitie
into which Wales was divided, 810—813.

3. Battle of Wilton (Wilts.), in which EGBERT gained
decisive victory over BEORNWULF, King of Mercia, 823.

4. EGBERT advances with his army, and receives submissio
from ANDRED, King of Northumbria, 827.

5. **Battle of Charmouth** (Dorset), in which Egbert was defeated by the Danes, 833.

6. **Battle of Hengston Hill** (Cornwall), in which Egbert defeated the combined forces of the Danes and Cornish Britons, 836.

B   **CHIEF EVENTS.**

Egbert (surnamed Bright Eye) formed all the Saxon kingdoms into one monarchy, 827.

Organs are said to have been first used in the Western Churches, 828.

The name **England** (from the *Angles*, and *lond*, the *Saxon* for country) was first given to Britain in 688; which name Egbert ratified in a Council held at **Winchester**, the capital of his dominions, 829.

Ethelwulf was the eldest son of Egbert. A.D. 836—858.

A   **WARS.**

1. Several battles were fought beween the English and Danes with varying success. The latter, however, were defeated at **Ockley** (Surrey), 851.

B   **CHIEF EVENTS.**

The first act of Ethelwulf was to divide his dominions by giving the kingdoms of Kent, Essex, and Sussex, to his son Athelstane. The inhabitants of London, Canterbury, and Rochester were slaughtered by the Danes, 838. Every Wednesday was set apart for public prayer against the Danes. The Picts were almost annihilated by the Scots, 840. Tithes were granted to the Church, 853. Ethelwulf's first wife was Osberga (daughter of Oslac, his cup-bearer), by whom he had five sons. Accompanied by his son **Alfred**, the King made a pilgrimage to Rome, and on returning home, married Judith (who was then only 12 years of age), daughter of Charles the Bald, King of France. Ethelbald attempted to usurp the throne of his father, and, in order to prevent a cival war, Ethelwulf allowed him to have the kingdom of Wessex. Ethelwulf's death took place at Stambridge (Essex), and he was buried at Steyning, in the county of Sussex. This King made a curious will, in which he expressed a wish that his sons should succeed each other to the throne.

Ethelbald was the second son of Ethelwulf. A.D. 858—860.

B **CHIEF EVENTS.**

ETHELBALD married JUDITH, his mother-in-law; but St. Swithin, Bishop of Winchester, procured a separation. Judith afterwards returned to her father's Court, and married Baldwin, Forester of France, from which union descended MATILDA, the wife of the conqueror. ETHELBALD died in 860, and was buried at Sherborne, but his remains were subsequently removed to Salisbury.

Ethelbert was the third son of Ethelwulf. A.D. 860—866.

B **CHIEF EVENTS.**

The Danes invaded England, and burnt Winchester, but ETHELBERT's forces repulsed them with great loss, 861. They made a descent upon the Isle of Thanet, and received large sums of money to abstain from ravaging the country, 862—863. Kent was afterwards laid waste by them. ETHELBERT died 866, and was buried at Sherborne.

Ethelred I. was the fourth son of Ethelwulf.
A.D. 866—871.

A **WARS.**

1. ETHELRED in one year fought with the DANES no fewer than nine pitched battles, in most of which they were defeated; but in the last, which took place at Merton (Surrey), he received a wound from which he died, and was buried at Wimborne (Dorset), 871.

B **CHIEF EVENTS.**

During this reign, England was not only afflicted with famine and pestilence, but was also molested by the DANES, who made themselves masters of Northumberland, subdued East Anglia, extorted money from the people of Mercia, and marched into Wessex. They also demolished the monasteries of Peterborough, Ely, and Coldingham (Scotland). ETHELRED was distinguished for piety and valour.

C **CELEBRATED PERSONS.**

Alfred, afterwards King, was the first Earl created in England. This title was conferred upon him by ETHELRED, whom he *greatly assisted against* the DANES.

Edmund, Prince of East Anglia, is taken prisoner by the Danes, who *insist* on his paying them tribute and renouncing Christianity. The Prince rejects these demands with horror, in consequence of which the Danes bind him naked to a tree, discharge arrows at him, and, last of all, sever his head from his body, 874. The place of his interment is called **Bury St. Edmunds**, where a splendid monastery was erected to his memory.

Bruen Bocard, exasperated at the ill-treatment of his wife by Osbert, the governor of Northumberland, went and prevailed upon Ivar, King of Denmark, to attempt the conquest of England.

Alfred the Great was the fifth and youngest son of Ethelwulf, and Grandson of Egbert. A.D. 871—901.

A   **WARS.**

Many battles were fought between the Saxons under Alfred and the Danes, of which we need mention only the following :—

1. **Battle of Wilton** (Wilts.), between Alfred and the Danes, who suffered so severely in the engagement, that they were obliged to conclude a **treaty** with the King, and withdraw their troops from Wessex, 871

2. **Battle of Ethandune**, near Westbury (Wilts.), in which Alfred completely routed the Danes, who were willing to have peace on any terms. Alfred ceded to them the kingdom of East Anglia, with portions of Essex and Mercia, on condition that they would embrace Christianity. The proposal was accepted by the Danish Prince Guthrum, who, with thirty of his nobles, received baptism. Alfred became sponsor for Guthrum, to whom he gave the name of Athelstane, 878.

3. A powerful fleet of Danish vessels, under the command of Hastings, their famous chief, landed near Kent, and laid waste the country, 893. They were, however, defeated by the King, who again restored his dominions to tranquility.

B   **CHIEF EVENTS.**

The Danes never became the real subjects of Alfred, but formed an independent State, which continued to the end of the Saxon Monarchy. A portion of the country situated to the north and east of *Watling Street* was called Danelagh, or the Danes' Community, because it remained under the dominion of the invaders.

The Danes renewed their ravages, and compelled ALFRED to flee to **Athelney** (or the Isle of Nobles), in Somersetshire, 878, where a costly gold enamelled jewel has since been found, bearing this inscription:—"**Aelfred mec heht Gewurcan**" (Alfred ordered me to be wrought.) At the accession of ALFRED, England was in a deplorable state, owing to the frequent incursions of the Danes, who had become masters of a great part of the Island.

ALFRED was the first to establish a regular militia, and to equip a fleet of ships. London and Shaftesbury were rebuilt, and the kingdom was fortified with castles, and walled towns. The division of England into **counties, hundreds,** and **tithings,** and the institution of **Trial by Jury,** are said to have originated in this reign, but the statement is not well authenticated. A code of laws was issued by ALFRED, comprising—

1. Judicial laws of the Old Testament.

2. Some of those enacted by INA, King of Wessex.

3. Certain statutes ordained by OFFA, King of Mercia.

4. Others framed by himself.

ALFRED's laws were marked by lenity, united to a rigorous administration of justice.

The King instituted three judicial assemblies—

1. **A Cabinet Council,** to which only royal favourities were admitted.

2. **A Council of Noblemen,** including Thanes, Viscounts, Earls, Judges, &c., which was identical with our Privy Council.

3. The **Witenagemot,** or Assembly of Wise Men, consisting of two Archbishops, the Bishops, Earls, Viscounts, and Sheriffs. They frequently met together, formed the Supreme Judicial Court, and on a political emergency, were always summoned by the King.

In his measurement of time ALFRED was very exact; and is said to have divided his days into three parts of eight hours each; one portion being chosen for acts of devotion and study; another for public affairs; and a third for sleep and refreshment. **Lanterns** were also invented by him.

His religious zeal induced him to re-people the various monasteries whose inmates had all previously been destroyed by the cruel ravages of the DANES. To effect this object, he was obliged to call in foreign monks.

Learning was extensively patronised by this King, as shown by the energy which he devoted to the foundation of four schools *or colleges at* Oxford, and the eagerness which he exhibited in sending for men of science to come and instruct his subjects. He himself was skilled in poetry, rhetoric, grammar, history, and logic; which rendered him one of the best scholars of his time.

He translated into the Anglo-Saxon tongue, "Bede's History," The Psalms, "Æsop's Fables," &c. This Prince justly earned the title of "Great," and "Founder of the English Monarchy."

The famous **Rollo**, of Norway, (ancestor of WILLIAM THE CONQUEROR) visited England, but shortly afterwards returned to France; and having taken Normandy, assumed the dukedom of his newly-acquired territory.

By his wife **Alswitha**, ALFRED had three sons and three daughters:—

1. **Edmund**, the eldest son, died before his father.

2. **Edward** succeeded to the throne.

3. **Ethelward**, who was educated at Oxford, and became a very learned man. He died at the age of 40, A.D. 922.

ALFRED expired at Farringdon (Berkshire), A.D. 901, and was buried at Winchester.

C   **CELEBRATED PERSONS.**

Grimbald, teacher of divinity at Oxford.

John Scotus Erigena, an Irishman, noted for his classical learning and astronomy. He lived in the ninth century.

Edward the Elder was the second son of Alfred. A.D. 901—925.

A   **WARS.**

1. ETHELWALD, the son of ETHELRED (ALFRED'S elder brother), claims the crown; a battle takes place near **Bury**, in which ETHELWALD is slain, 905.

2. The King gains a decisive victory over the ANGLIAN DANES and **Five Burghers**, viz: the DANES occupying the five towns of Nottingham, Derby, Leicester, Stamford, and Lincoln, 911.

3. EDWARD subdued the Welsh, and compelled their leader (REES-AP-MADOC) to continue the tribute imposed on him by ETHELFLEDA, daughter *of* ETHELRED (governor of Mercia), 921.

B   **CHIEF EVENTS.**

EDWARD ordered CONSTANTINE III., King of Scotland, to do homage, 922. This monarch was the first to assume the title of "**Rex Anglorum,**" King of the Angles. During this reign, EDWARD and his sister ETHELFLEDA built the castles of Stafford, Bridgnorth, Runcorn, Warwick, Bedford, Colchester, Stamford, Bamborough, and Nottingham. Clocks are said to have been used for the first time in Churches. In military virtues, EDWARD equalled his father, but in other respects was greatly inferior. He had three wives, and twelve children, as well as an illegitimate son, named **Athelstane,** who succeeded to the throne. The King died at Farringdon, 925, and was buried at Winchester.

C   **CELEBRATED PERSONS.**

Asser, Bishop of Sherborne, was a native of Wales. He wrote the life of ALFRED THE GREAT. Died, 909.

Ethelfleda, called the "wisest lady in all England," and "the Lady of Mercia," greatly assisted the King, her brother, in fighting against the Danes. She died, 920.

Guy, Earl of Warwick, is noted for many wonderful deeds, and especially for his killing in single combat the Danish giant Colbrand.

Athelstane was the illegitimate son of Edward the Elder.

A.D. 925—940.

A   **WARS.**

Battle of Brunanburgh (Northumbria), in which ATHELSTANE and TURKETUL completely defeated the united forces of the Welsh, Irish, and Northumbrian Danes, under ANLAFF, and CONSTANTINE, King of Scotland, 938.

B   **CHIEF EVENTS.**

As the nobility of England were unwilling to be governed by a **bastard,** they formed a conspiracy, at the head of which was ALFRED, for the purpose of dethroning ATHELSTANE, and appointing EDWIN to be King. ALFRED, however, declared on oath in the presence of POPE JOHN, that he had not been guilty of complicity in the rebellion. He, however, was immediately seized with *illness which* terminated fatally in three days.

The King suppressed an **insurrection**, headed by **Anlaff and Jodfrid**, the two sons of SITHRIC. CONSTANTINE, King of Scotland (who afforded refuge to PRINCE GODFRID), was obliged to sue for peace. ATHELSTANE entered Wales, and raised the yearly tribute of that country to 20 pounds weight of gold, 300 pounds of silver, and 5000 head of cattle. An impetus was given to commerce by granting the title of **Thane** to every merchant who made three voyages on his own account. The **basis of a political alliance between England** and **France was first laid in this reign.** From ATHELSTANE, the title of **"King of all Britain,"** received its origin.

A royal order was issued that the **Bible** should be translated into the **Anglo-Saxon language,** and a copy placed in every church. ATHELSTANE was zealous in the cause of religion, erecting many churches, and manifesting a charitable disposition to the poor. **St. Germain's Priory** (Cornwall) was built by the King.

The coronation of ATHELSTANE took place at Kingston-on-Thames, the ceremony being performed by ATHELM, Archbishop of Canterbury. ATHELSTANE died at Gloucester, in 940, aged 46, and was buried at Malmesbury (Wilts.)

This monarch's character is stained by the death of his brother EDWIN, who was accused of being concerned in ALFRED's conspiracy. ATHELSTANE was not destitute of good qualities. He brought to his exalted position, courage, wisdom, and great aptitude for government. He was chosen to be King, because he possessed greater administrative talent than his brothers, who were the lawful heirs to the crown.

C   **CELEBRATED PERSONS.**

Howel, King of Wales, was defeated by ATHELSTANE, and agreed to submit to his demands.

Constantine, King of Scotland, was slain at the battle of Brunanburgh, 938.

Turketul, cousin of ATHELSTANE, and grandson of ALFRED the Great, contributed much by his valour to gain the battle of Brunanburgh. In the reign of EDMUND, whose Chancellor he was, TURKETUL rebuilt and restored to its former grandeur the Abbey of Croyland (Lincolnshire), which had been demolished by the DANES. He afterwards became a monk, and was made Abbot of Croyland by EDRED, from whom he also obtained a very advantageous charter for his abbey.

Edmund I. (the Magnificent) was the second son of Edward the Elder. A.D. 940—946

A   **WARS.**

Battle of Chester, between EDMUND and the DANES under ANLAFF, which ended in the former ceding all the kingdom north of Watling Street, 942.

B   **CHIEF EVENTS.**

The King expelled the **Five Burghers,** because they were always ready in times of disquietude to admit foreign DANES into the kingdom. EDMUND subdued Cumberland, and presented it to MALCOLM, King of Scotland, on condition that the latter should do homage, and defend the north of England against the DANES, 945.

EDMUND was the first English King that made **robbery a capital offence.** He was killed at Pucklechurch, near Gloucester, by LEOLF, a man whom he had banished for his notorious crimes, 946. The remains of EDMUND were interred at Glastonbury. His valour and abilities caused him to be respected both at home and abroad.

By his wife ELGIVA, he had two sons, EDWY and EDGAR, neither of whom was old enough to ascend the throne. EDMUND's brother EDRED was therefore made King, as decided by an assembly of the **Witan.**

Edred was the youngest son of Edward the Elder. A.D. 946—955.

B   **CHIEF EVENTS.**

EDRED was obliged to put down several insurrections of the Northumbrian DANES, who were aided by ANLAFF and ERIC, as well as by MALCOLM, King of Scotland. After these events EDRED kept a strict watch over the DANES, and placed strong English garrisons in all their principal towns.

This King yielded, both in church and state matters, to the authority of **Dunstan,** abbot of Glastonbury, who excluded all the married clergy from their benefices, and attempted to enforce celibacy. Glastonbury Abbey was rebuilt in this reign. Christianity was introduced among the NORMANS in Ireland, 951.

EDRED's death was caused by a quinsy (955), and he was buried at Winchester. His children, ELFRID and BEDFRID, being *infants, he was* succeeded by his nephew EDWY, son of EDMUND.

Edwy the Fair, was the eldest son of Edmund I. A.D. 955—958.

B **CHIEF EVENTS.**

EDWY's unpopularity with the MONKS arose from the following causes :—

1. He opposed the growing power of DUNSTAN, who aimed at making the authority of the Church supreme in State matters.

2. He resisted DUNSTAN in his efforts to enforce celibacy among the clergy.

3. DUNSTAN and the MONKS asserted that EDWY had violated the canon law by his marriage with the beautiful ELGIVA, who was a near relative of the King.

On the day of his coronation, EDWY was outraged by DUNSTAN, who, having dragged him out of the Queen's apartment, thrust him back into the presence of the guests, from whom he had previously withdrawn. To punish the offender for this insult, EDWY accused DUNSTAN of malversation and banished him the kingdom. He also adopted severe measures with the MONKS, who were expelled from their monasteries, and replaced by the secular clergy. Instigated by DUNSTAN and his fraternity, the DANES of Northumbria, Mercia, and East Anglia, revolt and proclaim EDGAR King. Wessex alone remained under the sovereignty of EDWY; the rest of the kingdom having been ceded to PRINCE EDGAR, his brother. Elgiva was persecuted by ODO, Archbishop of Canterbury, who burned her face with a red-hot iron, in order to destroy her beauty, and banished her to Ireland. Having obliterated the scars, she returned to England in hopes of seeing the King, but was again taken by ODO's spies, and put to death in the most barbarous manner. These wretches having cut the sinews of her legs, she expired shortly after in the most excruciating agony, at Gloucester. The King died, 958; but whether his death was caused by violence or not, is uncertain. EDWY is represented by some historians as being very handsome, and possessing many good qualities; whilst other writers describe him as a vicious and profligate monarch.

C **CELEBRATED PERSONS.**

St. Dunstan, nephew of ATHELM, Archbishop, of Canterbury, by whom he was persuaded to enter into Holy Orders. After having adopted the clerical profession, he became very studious and austere. He was made Abbot of Glastonbury by King Edmund, banished by Edwy for insulting that Monarch on the day of his coronation, *and recalled by Edgar,* who made him Archbishop of

Canterbury. DUNSTAN is regarded by many as the first that sought to introduce celibacy among the clergy. He was born at Glastonbury, A.D. 925, and died A.D. 988.

Edgar the Pacific, was the son of Edmund I. A.D. 958—975.

B .   **CHIEF EVENTS.**

EDGAR's partiality to the monks was shown by his recalling DUNSTAN, whom he appointed to the See of Worcester, 958. In the following year DUNSTAN was made Bishop of London ; and soon afterwards became Archbishop of Canterbury. Several monasteries were now founded by EDGAR, who also erected Corfe Castle in Dorsetshire, and Cranborne Priory in the same County. By an order issued in 969, none of the clergy could marry, under pain of deprivation.

This reign was never troubled by any foreign enemy, neither did civil wars disturb the kingdom. EDGAR protected his dominions from the Scots, by placing a powerful army in the north. Another body of troops in the west kept the Welsh in subjection ; whilst a fleet of 360 ships prevented any outbreak on the part of the Danes. The King was held in such high estimation, that not only the sovereigns of Wales, but also the Kings of Scotland and Ireland, paid him submission. Under Edgar, the Saxon power in England reached its greatest height, and he soon became the most absolute monarch of that period. Foreigners were at this time encouraged to settle in England.

To rid the country of wolves, he adopted the following expedient :—

1. A yearly tribute of 300 wolves' heads was demanded from the Welsh, instead of the gold, silver, and cattle, exacted from them by ATHELSTANE.

2. Proclamation of a general pardon was made throughout England to all criminals, who, within a specified time, brought a certain number of wolves' tongues in proportion to their offences. In three years, 900 wolves were thus destroyed, and the whole race nearly extirpated.

EDGAR travelled over a part of his kingdom every year, in order to see that justice was administered impartially among all classes. He also heard the complaints made against the judges and magistrates, who frequently abused their authority. A law was enacted, imposing a fine of twenty shillings upon any judge who, in ignorance, gave sentence not according to justice. If he knowingly passed an erroneous decision, he was never afterwards permitted to exercise his functions.

In this reign weights and measures were regulated.

This monarch was ostentatious, arrogant, and licentious. He caused ETHELWOLD to be murdered, in order to obtain possession of his wife (ELFRIDA). A nun was forced from her seclusion by the King, who, for this crime, was ordered by DUNSTAN seven years' penance, on the following conditions :—

1. That the King should lay aside his crown.

2. That he should found a nunnery.

3. That he should observe a strict fast twice every week.

4. That he should be very liberal in the distribution of alms.

5. That he should frame good laws for the government of his kingdom.

6. That he should expel the married clergy from their benefices and replace them by monks.

Though EDGAR ascended the throne in 958, he was not crowned till 971, which event took place at Bath. He then proceeded to Chester, where his barge was rowed up the Dee to the priory of St. John by eight tributary Kings. This last mentioned circumstance is a proof of his ostentatious character.

EDGAR died at the age of 33, and was buried at Glastonbury Abbey. By his wife, ETHELFLEDA the fair, he had a son named EDWARD, who afterwards became King; ETHELRED was the offspring of his second wife, ELFRIDA.

C.   CELEBRATED PERSONS.

Elsin, appointed Archbishop of Canterbury, but died while going to Rome for his pall.

Odo, Archbishop of Canterbury, the son of an East Anglian Dane, was by birth a Pagan, but embraced Christianity, on account of which he was expelled from his father's house. Having entered the service of an English nobleman, his master had him baptised and educated. He entered into orders in the reign of EDWARD THE ELDER, and was made, by ATHELSTANE, Bishop of Sherborne. When EDWARD wished to elect ODO Archbishop of Canterbury, the latter raised several objections, but at the urgent request of the King, he afterwards accepted the appointment. ODO was a vigorous champion of *the monks*. *Died, 959.*

Edward the Martyr was the son of Edgar.   A.D. 975—979.

B   CHIEF EVENTS.

On the death of EDGAR there were two candidates for the throne.   A powerful faction was headed by ELFRIDA, who wished her son ETHELRED to be made King, while the monks and DUNSTAN preferred EDWARD, who, they asserted, had been nominated by EDGAR.   DUNSTAN'S influence, however, secured the crown for EDWARD.

When hunting near Corfe Castle, the King called to see his stepmother, who gave him a glass of wine, and instigated one of her domestics to stab him while he was drinking it.   Finding himself wounded, he galloped off, but soon fainted from the loss of blood. He fell from his horse, and was dragged in the stirrups for a considerable distance along the road, till he died, 979.

At the **Council of Calne** (Wiltshire), it was decreed that the Monks should hold their benefices, 978.   Many synods were held, in which it is pretended that the crafty DUNSTAN wrought miracles.

Ethelred II., the Unready, was the younger son of Edgar, by his second wife Elfrida.   A.D. 979—1016.

B   CHIEF EVENTS.

This reign was a very miserable one, owing to the terrible ravages of the Danes.   In order to remove them from his dominions, the King adopted the following measures, each of which failed:—

1. He paid them large sums of money, which were obtained from his subjects by the imposition of a tax called **Danegelt,** or Dane-money.

2. By marrying EMMA, the beautiful sister of RICHARD II., Duke of Normandy, A.D. 1001.

3. By a general massacre of the Danes, on the festival of St Brice, November 13, 1002.

Gunhilda, sister of SWEYN, King of Denmark, who had embraced Christianity, was put to death by ETHELRED'S orders, and in her dying agonies she declared that England would soon suffer for that barbarity. The Danish Prince hearing of the cruelty towards his countrymen, and especially to his sister, took signal vengeance.   He continually invaded the country, till in 1013 ETHELRED and his Queen were obliged to fly to Normandy.   SWEYN was *proclaimed* King first at Bath, and afterwards in London, but died bout three weeks afterwards at Gainsborough in Lincolnshire. s the coronation of SWEYN is not mentioned by historians, we may irly conclude that it never took place. SWEYN left England to is son CANUTE, but the Saxons recalled ETHELRED, and gave him ll their support, so that CANUTE was compelled to leave England; ut on taking his departure he ordered the hands, noses, and ears of is Saxon hostages to be cut off. CANUTE still continued to trouble ngland till the death of ETHELRED, 1016.

CELEBRATED PERSONS.

Aelfric, said to have been the Bishop of Wilton about the ear 990, and the Archbishop of Canterbury four years after, was elebrated as a writer, being the author of homilies, a Latin grammar, Saxon translation of the historical books of the Bible, and other rorks.

Edmund Ironside was the eldest son of Ethelred II.
A.D. 1016.

A   **WARS.**

Several indecisive battles were fought between the Danes nder CANUTE, and the English headed by EDMUND; till at length he latter agreed to a partition of the kingdom. CANUTE held the orthern provinces; all the country south of the Thames, the rhole of East Anglia, London, and part of Essex, being assigned to DMUND. Both parties agreed to pay the tax called Danegelt, r the support of the Danish fleet.

B   **CHIEF EVENTS.**

About a month after the partition of the kingdom, EDMUND ras assassinated at Oxford by his two chamberlains, who were istigated by the traitorous EDRIC, Duke of Mercia, Nov. 30, 1016. Ie was buried at Glastonbury.

Canute was the son of Sweyn, King of Denmark. A.D.
1016—1035.

A   **WARS.**

1. CANUTE, with the aid of EARL GODWIN and the English, efeated the Vandals, 1019.
2. OLAUS, the Monarch of Norway, was put to flight, and ANUTE crowned king *of that country,* 1027.

3. He marched against the Swedes, but the expedition was not altogether successful, 1035.

4. MALCOLM, King of Scotland, and his nephew, DUNCAN, King of Cumberland, were both reduced to a state of vassalage, for refusing to do homage to the English sovereign. These two rulers withheld their obedience on the ground that CANUTE was a usurper.

B   **CHIEF EVENTS.**

Canute was converted to Christianity on coming to the English throne. In order to atone for the many acts of violence committed in his younger days, he built several churches; one of these buildings was erected over the tomb of KING EDMUND, and gave the name of ST. EDMUND'S BURY to the town in which the church stood. The King married EMMA, widow of ETHELRED II., and stipulated that any children he might have by that union should succeed to the English throne, 1017. He created his General, GODWIN, EARL OF KENT, 1022. CANUTE insisted on the payment of Peter's pence. Musical notes were invented, 1024. At one time the English were heavily taxed by the King, who wished to reward his Danish followers. He restored the Saxon customs, and protected both the laws and property of his subjects; nor was he at all partial in the administration of justice. In 1030, CANUTE made a pilgrimage to Rome. While on the beach at Southampton, his courtiers began as usual to flatter him, and even asserted that the waves were in subjection to his royal authority. In order to put a stop to their flattery, the King requested his followers to place a chair near the water, in which he seated himself, and then commanded the billows to stop, and not to wet the feet of their sovereign. The waves quickly rolled over his feet, upon which he administered a sharp rebuke to his courtiers, by informing them that "there was only one Being, the Supreme God, to whom the waves and wind are in subjection." It is said that CANUTE never wore a crown afterwards. In this reign, the first regular standing army, since the departure of the Romans, was formed, which they called "Hus-Carls," or "Household Troops." The King enacted a law, by which he imposed a very heavy fine upon any who shed the blood of one of his subjects; he himself being the first to break it, by killing a soldier while in a violent passion, paid a fine nine times greater than that which he had previously fixed by law. CANUTE died at Shaftesbury, and was buried at Winchester.

C   **CELEBRATED PERSONS.**

Elnothus, and Edsine, Archbishops of Canterbury.

Edric, the traitor, who expired on the gallows, by order of the King.

Harold I. was the son of Canute, by his first wife. A.D. 1035—1040.

B   **CHIEF EVENTS.**

On the death of CANUTE, HAROLD and HARDICANUTE aspired to the throne. According to CANUTE's marriage contract with EMMA, the latter ought to have succeeded. By an assembly at Oxford, it was agreed to divide the kingdom; HARDICANUTE was to rule over the country south of the Thames, while HAROLD had all the provinces north of that river, with London for his capital. As HARDICANUTE was in the north of Europe at the time of his father's death, EMMA and Earl GODWIN governed his portion of the kingdom till he returned. EDWARD and ALFRED, EMMA's sons by ETHELRED, endeavoured to enforce their claims, but without success. The former landed at Southampton with forty ships, but was opposed by his mother, and obliged to return to Normandy. At the head of 600 followers, ALFRED shortly after landed in Kent, whence he marched to Guildford, where nearly all his men were murdered; he himself was taken to Ely, where his eyes were put out, and his death took place soon afterwards. From his agility HAROLD was called Harefoot. He died at Oxford, and was buried at Winchester.

C   **CELEBRATED PERSONS.**

Leofric, Earl of Mercia, who espoused HAROLD's cause.

Ethelnoth, Archbishop of Canterbury, who refused to crown HAROLD I.

Hardicanute was the son of Canute, by Emma, the widow of Ethelred. A.D. 1040—1042.

B   **CHIEF EVENTS.**

To avenge the death of ALFRED, HARDICANUTE ordered HAROLD's corpse to be taken out of the grave, and cast into the Thames. He oppressed the people with the tax called Danegelt, and sent his soldiers to destroy the town of Worcester, because the inhabitants had killed two of the tax collectors. The King had his mother and PRINCE EDWARD brought from Flanders to reside at his Court.

At the marriage-feast of TOWEL the Proud, a Dane of note, HARDICANUTE fell to the ground while raising the cup to his lips, and died a few days after at Lambeth. With the death of this monarch, the Danes were banished from the kingdom, in commemoration of which the festival called Hocktides was established, a Saxon word denoting " the period of triumphing and scorning."

Edward III., the Confessor, was the second son of Ethelred. A.D. 1042—1066.

A **WARS.**

1. **Magnus**, King of Norway and Denmark, made an attempt upon England, but was alarmed at the fleet which EDWARD assembled at Sandwich, and declared that he would let EDWARD enjoy his crown in peace, 1044.

2. By the King's orders, **Siward**, Duke of Northumberland, led an army into Scotland, against **Macbeth**, the murderer of DUNCAN, whom he slew, and restored MALCOLM to the throne, 1054.

B **CHIEF EVENTS.**

EDWARD abolished **Danegelt.** He stripped his mother, EMMA, of her large treasures, and even compelled her to spend the remainder of her life in a convent at Winchester. As a proof of EDWARD'S reconciliation with EARL GODWIN, and in order to gain that nobleman's influence, he married his daughter, EDITHA. EDWARD founded Westminster Abbey, and there built his own tomb. The King, who had received his education in Normandy, nearly involved the country in a civil war, on account of the jealousy caused by his predilection for the natives of that country. Among the distinguished guests at EDWARD'S court was WILLIAM, afterwards the Conqueror, to whom it is said he promised the kingdom. He confined his own Queen in Wherwell nunnery. EDWARD banished GODWIN for refusing to punish the people of Dover, because they had a conflict with the King's brother-in-law, EUSTACE, Count of Boulogne, 1051. EDWARD selected a code of laws out of those enacted by the Saxons, Mercians, and Danes, upon which it is said that our **Common Law** is based. By his order the Saxon laws were translated into Latin. He was the first monarch that touched for the King's evil, it being supposed in those superstitious times that the touch of a King would effect a cure. EDWARD died 1066, and was canonised with the surname of the "Confessor," by POPE ALEXANDER III.

C **CELEBRATED PERSONS.**

Godwin, Earl of Kent, one of the most influential noblemen *of his time*, was the son of Ulnoth, a distinguished lord and Thane of Sussex. In the war between the Danes and Vandals, GODWIN was appointed by CANUTE leader of the English troops, by whose aid he gained a decisive victory over the latter. As a reward for this victory, CANUTE made him Earl of Kent. ALFRED, one of the sons of ETHELRED II., is said to have been murdered by GODWIN, who declared upon oath that he was innocent of the charge. On the death of CANUTE, he united himself to HARDICANUTE against HAROLD, and subsequently joined the latter. Shortly after the death of HARDICANUTE, he took part with EDWARD, to whom he gave his daughter in marriage. Having raised an unsuccessful rebellion against the King, he was obliged to make his escape to Flanders. He, however, returned to England with strong forces, which induced EDWARD to enter into negotiations for peace. GODWIN was afterwards restored to his estates. He died suddenly, 1053.

The tract of land called the **Goodwin** or **Godwin Sands,** upon which many ships have been wrecked, lying off the coast of Kent, derived its name from GODWIN, to whom it formerly belonged. This piece of land was afterwards given to the Monastery of St. Augustine at Canterbury; but owing to the neglect of the Abbot in not repairing the wall which defended it against the sea, the whole became submerged in the year 1100.

Siward, Duke of Northumberland, who vanquished Macbeth, and died, 1055.

Robert, Archbishop of Canterbury.

Guido Aretino, an Italian Monk, invented musical notes.

Harold II. was the son of Earl Godwin. A.D. 1066.

A **WARS.**

1. **Battle of Stanford Bridge,** afterwards called **Battle Bridge,** near York; in which HAROLD defeated his brother, TOSTI, and HAROLD HARDRADA, both of whom were slain, 1066.

2. **Battle of Hastings,** in which HAROLD was defeated by WILLIAM, Duke of Normandy, October 14, 1066.

B **CHIEF EVENTS.**

The death of HAROLD ended the Saxon Monarchy, which had lasted 600 years.

C **CELEBRATED PERSONS.**

Edgar Atheling, grandson of EDMUND IRONSIDE, was the lawful heir to the throne.

Tosti, the King's brother, was slain in the battle of Stamford.

Morcar, Earl of Northumberland, and Edwin, Earl of Mercia, brothers-in-law to the King.

Stigand, Archbishop of Canterbury.

REMARKS.

Kingston-on-Thames was the customary place for the Coronation of Saxon Monarchs, on which account it was called Kingston, or the town of the King.

The seven Saxon Bretwaldas were: CEAWLIN of Wessex, ELLA of Sussex, ETHELBERT of Kent, EDWIN of Northumbria, OSWY of Northumbria, REDWALD of East Anglia.

England, Ireland, and Scotland were much harassed by Danish invasions. The first series of these irruptions began in 788, and ended with their defeat by ETHELWULF, 853. Another succession of Danish inroads began 867, and terminated with their conquest of England, 1017. The third series dates from 1020, when they settle in Scotland, and ends 1074, when they again invade England, but are bribed by WILLIAM THE CONQUEROR to leave the kingdom. On the death of EDWARD the Confessor (so called because of his superstitious piety) there were three candidates for the throne: EDGAR ATHELING, who was the rightful heir; HAROLD II., son of EARL GODWIN, who prevailed upon the nobles and prelates to make him their king; WILLIAM, Duke of Normandy, who assigned the five following reasons for his claiming the English crown:

1. His relationship to EDWARD the Confessor.

2. The wish expressed by EDWARD on his deathbed, that WILLIAM should succeed him.

3. HAROLD's perjury.

4. PRINCE ALFRED's murder.

5. The expulsion of a Norman Archbishop from the See of Canterbury.

WILLIAM had little trouble in collecting an army for the invasion of England, when it was known on the continent that it had the sanction of POPE ALEXANDER II., who wished the tax of Peter's pence to be re-established.

There were three classes among the Saxons:

1. The Thanes, or Nobles.

2. The Ceorls, who were of low birth.

3. The Slaves, who consisted of criminal Saxons, or conquered *Britons.*

Saxon delinquents were generally punished by a pecuniary fine. When a man committed murder he was obliged to exonerate himself by paying—

1. The wer to the relatives, which was considered the value of the person's life.

2. The wite to the King for breaking the laws.

The estimation of a person's life was as follows :—

1. The life of a King's Thane was valued at 1200 shillings.

2. The life of a lower Thane at 600 shillings.

3. The life of a Ceorl was valued at 200 shillings.

For the administration of justice they had the following courts :—

1. The Hall-mote, in which the lord of a tithing could punish thieves or others with a fine. This court took the name of Hall-mote, on account of its being held in the Lord's Hall.

2. The Folk-mote, or The Hundred-court, assembled every month, and was composed of the landlords of the hundred; the Alderman and Bishop of the diocese, being its Presidents. Contracts for the sale of land were made in this court, and such criminals tried as could not be dealt with in the Hall-mote.

3. The Shire-mote, or The County-court, which was higher than the two preceding. It met twice every year, in the early part of May and October, to settle ecclesiastical matters and the rights of the crown. The presidents of the County-court at first, were the Earlderman or Earl, and the Bishop, assisted by the Sheriff, whose business was to execute its decrees, and who ultimately became the Sole President.

4. The Witena-gemot, the parliament, a great council of the nation, was held at Christmas, Easter, and Whitsuntide. Accompanied by his Nobles and Officers, the King presided over this council. Much of the business transacted in the Witena-gemot or Witan comprised :

1. The enacting of laws.

2. The making of grants.

3. The imposition of taxes.

4. The trial of state offenders.

5. The nomination of a successor to the throne.

To ascertain the innocence or guilt of accused persons, they resorted to—

1. Compurgation.

2. Ordeal.

By the first method the criminal was acquitted if a number of persons would depose, upon oath, their belief in the accused individual's innocence.

Ordeals were *either by fire or water.*

If the accused person could grasp a piece of red-hot iron without injury, he was declared innocent; if he could not he was pronounced guilty.

In the ordeal of water, if the offender was able to place his arm in boiling water without injury, or plunge into a river and float without any swimming action, he was regarded as innocent.

The Saxons practised their ordeals under a belief that GOD would work a miracle on behalf of a guiltless man. They had the law of **Frankpledge**, by which neighbours were bound for each other's good conduct.

Gavelkind.—By this law, which is said to have originated with the Saxons, the property of any person dying **intestate** was equally divided among the surviving male children.

Expenses for mending the roads, keeping the royal castles, and fitting out military expeditions for the defence of the country, were defrayed by imposing a land-tax, which was called "**Trinoda Necessitas.**" **Danegelt** was the **first direct land tax** known in England.

During the Saxon period water-mills were introduced; till then corn was ground by handmills.

CANUTE the Great was the most powerful monarch of his time in Europe; being King of England, Denmark, Norway, and part of Sweden.

The law of **Primogeniture** did not prevail among the Anglo-Saxons; a father divided his property among his children, and often bequeathed the largest share to his youngest son. The Anglo-Saxons were an agricultural people, and were very fond of eating and drinking.

Division of the Soil.—Land belonging to the general commonality, was called **Folkland**, that is, the *land* of the *folk* or people. It could be let out for a term, but at the expiration of that term, it reverted to the State.

Bocland.—Land parcelled out to private individuals, was called *Bocland*, that is, land held by *boc*, charter, or deed. This species of tenure is the origin of our **modern freeholds.**

We may remark that the priests of this period were not ashamed of working in gold, silver, iron, lead, and jewels. DUNSTAN, who acquired so great a celebrity, was the best blacksmith, brazier, and goldsmith in his day. The Anglo-Saxon ladies were remarkable for their spinning, embroidery, weaving, and dyeing.

GENEALOGY OF VICTORIA FROM WILLIAM THE CONQUEROR.

WILLIAM 1

Robert.   Richard.   WILLIAM II.   Henry I.   6 daughters, of whom Adela, the fourth, m. Stephen.

William.

Matilda, m. 1. Henry V. of Germany. 2. Geoffrey of Anjou.   STEPHEN.

Henry II.

William.   Henry.   RICHARD I.   Geoffrey   John.   3 daughters.

Arthur.   Eleanor.

Henry III.   Richard, Earl of Cornwall.   3 daughters.

Edward I.   Edmund, Earl of Lancaster.   2 daughters.

John.   Henry.   Alfonso.   Edward II.   Thomas, Earl of Norfolk.   Edmund, Earl of Kent.   2 daughters.

Edward III.   John of Eltham.   2 daughters.

/ENTS AND PRINCIPAL DATES
IE SAXON PERIOD.

A LIST OF THE KINGS AND QUEENS OF ENGLAND.

NORMAN LINE.

	Born.	Began to Reign.	To whom Married.	Reigned years.		Age at d'th.
William I., the Conqueror	1027	1066	Matilda of Flanders	21	...	60
William II., Rufus	1057	1087	Unmarried	18	...	42
Henry I., Beauclerc	1070	1100	Matilda of Scotland	35	...	67
			Adelais of Louvain			
Stephen Blois	1105	1135	Matilda of Boulogne	19	...	49

LINE OF PLANTAGENET.

	Born.	Began to Reign.	To whom Married.	Reigned years.		Age at d'th.
Henry II., Plantagenet	1133	1154	Eleanor of Guienne	35	...	57
Richard I., Cœur de Lion	1157	1189	Berengaria of Navarre	10	...	42
John Sansterre or Lackland	1167	1199	Earl Montague's Daughter	17	...	49
			Isabella of Angouleme			
			Avisa of Gloucester			
Henry III., Winchester	1207	1216	Eleanor of Provence	56	...	65
Edward I., Longshanks	1239	1272	Eleanor of Castile	35	...	68
			Mary of France			
Edward II., Caernarvon	1284	1307	Isabella of France	20	...	48
Edward III., Windsor	1312	1327	Philippa of Hainault	50	...	65
Richard II., Bordeaux	1867	1377	Ann of Bohemia	22	...	33
			Isabella of France			

HOUSE OF LANCASTER.

	Born.	Began to Reign.	To whom Married.	Reigned years.		Age at d'th.
Henry IV., Bolingbroke	1866	1399	Mary Bohun	14	...	46
			Joanna of Navarre			
Henry V., Monmouth	1388	1413	Catherine of France	9	...	34
Henry VI.	1421	1422	Margaret of Anjou	39	...	50

HOUSE OF YORK.

	Born.	Began to Reign.	To whom Married.	Reigned years.		Age at d'th.
Edward IV., Earl of March	1441	1461	Elizabeth Woodville	22	...	42
Edward V.	1470	1483	Unmarried	2m.	...	13
Richard III., Crook-back	1450	1483	Ann Neville	2	...	35

TUDOR LINE.

THE HOUSES OF YORK AND LANCASTER UNITED.

	Born.	Began to Reign.	To whom Married.	Reigned years.		Age at d'th.
Henry VII., Tudor	1456	1485	Elizabeth of York	24	...	52
Henry VIII., (Defender of the Faith)	1491	1509	Catherine of Arragon	38	...	55
			Anne Boleyn			
			Jane Seymour			
			Ann of Cleves			
			Catherine Howard			
			Catherine Parr			
Edward VI.	1537	1547	Unmarried	6	...	16
Lady Jane Grey	1537	1553	Lord Guilford of Dudley	10d.	...	16
Mary, the bloody	1516	1553	Philip, King of Spain	5	...	42
Elizabeth, the maiden	1533	1558	Unmarried	45	...	70

LINE OF STUART.

	Born.	Began to Reign.	To whom Married.	Reign-ed years.	Age at d'th.
James I., Solomon	1566	1603	Ann of Denmark	22	59
Charles I., the Martyr	1600	1625	Henrietta of France	24	48
Commonwealth began		1649		lasted 11	
Charles II., Merry Monarch	1630	1660	Catherine of Portugal	24	55
James II.	1633	1685	Anne Hyde	4	68
			Maria d'Este of Modena		
William III., Orange	1650	1689	Mary, Daughter of James II.	13	52
Anne, the Good	1665	1702	George of Denmark	12	49

LINE OF HANOVER OR BRUNSWICK.

	Born.	Began to Reign.	To whom Married.	Reign-ed years.	Age at d'th.
George I., Guelph	1660	1714	Sophia of Zell	12	67
George II.	1683	1727	Wilhelmina of Anspach	33	77
George III.	1738	1760	Charlotte of Mecklenburgh	60	82
George IV.	1762	1820	Caroline of Brunswick	10	68
William IV., Clarence	1765	1830	Adelaide of Saxe-Meiningen	7	71
Victoria	1819	1837	Albert of Saxe-Gotha	—	—

THE NORMAN LINE.

William I. was the illegitimate son of Duke Robert, of Normandy. A.D. 1066—1087.

A   WARS.

1. **Battle of Hastings,** between HAROLD II. and WILLIAM, for the crown of England. WILLIAM was victorious, 1066.

2. WILLIAM enters Scotland, and compels MALCOLM to do homage for having invaded England, 1072.

3. The king attacked the **Castle of Gerberoi,** to punish his son ROBERT, who had taken up arms against him, 1077.

4. WILLIAM commenced war with PHILIP I., King of France, because the latter had uttered a few rude words about him, 1087.

B   CHIEF EVENTS.

WILLIAM was crowned at Westminster Abbey on Christmas-day, 1066. Soon after this event, the odious tax, Danegelt, was imposed by royal authority, 1067.

The King appointed his half-brother, Odo, Bishop of Bayeux, and William Fitz-Osborne, to govern the country during his absence on the continent. Their injustice towards the English caused an insurrection, which William, after his return, succeeded in putting down, 1067.

The sons of Sweyn, King of Denmark, and Edgar Atheling, with other Saxons, slew the Norman garrison at York, but they were defeated by William, who in revenge, laid waste the country between the Humber and the Tyne, 1069.

Stigand, Archbishop of Canterbury, was deposed by the King, who placed in the See Lanfranc, an Italian. The French language instead of the English now began to be used in courts of law, 1070.

The King, aided by three legates sent by Pope Alexander II., deprived the Saxon prelates of their benefices, and put foreigners in their places, 1071

William permitted the payment of **Peter's pence**, but declined doing homage to the Pope, 1076.

During this reign the insurrections were numerous, especially in the North and West of England, all of which the King quelled.

The **Feudal System** was developed, **Domesday-Book** compiled, **Curfew Bell** established, the **Cinque Ports** fortified, Westminster National School founded, and the Tower of London erected for state prisoners; the Courts of **Chancery** and **Exchequer** were established; the Lord Chief Justice and Justices of the Peace were appointed.

The **New Forest** (Hampshire) was made; the Forest and Game Laws, Surnames, and the punishment of beheading were introduced; William built Battle Abbey, to commemorate his victory at Hastings. The Channel Islands, **Jersey, Guernsey, Alderney,** and **Sark,** being part of William's Duchy of Normandy, were added to England.

William's death resulted from a bruise which he received while burning the town of **Nantes.** His horse's feet coming in contact with some hot embers, the animal plunged with great violence, causing the King to hurt himself against the pommel of his saddle. He died shortly afterwards, at the Abbey of St. Gervais, Sept. 9, 1087, and was buried at St. Stephen's, Caen.

C   CELEBRATED PERSONS.

Stigand, a Saxon prelate, much esteemed by Edward the Confessor, became in 1052 Archbishop of Canterbury. William refused to be crowned by Stigand, who was at that time suspended *by the Pope, on* the ground of his being an intruder into the See of

Canterbury—ROBERT, the former primate, never having been canonically deprived. Notwithstanding the sentence of suspension, STIGAND continued to exercise archiepiscopal functions till 1070, when he was stripped of his honours and committed to prison, where, it is said, he died.

Lanfranc, Prior of the Abbey of Bec (Normandy), came to England with WILLIAM, by whom he was appointed to succeed STIGAND as Archbishop of Canterbury. Canterbury Cathedral was re-built by LANFRANC, who also founded several churches and hospitals. He was a learned man and the author of several religious works. Born at Pavia (Italy), 1005; died 1089.

Aldred, Archbishop of York, by whom HAROLD II. and WILLIAM I. were crowned. He is said to have been the first English Bishop that visited Jerusalem. Died 1069.

Ingulph, Abbot of Croyland (Lincolnshire), and Secretary to the King, wrote the "History of Croyland Abbey." (1030—1109).

Waltheof, a Saxon Nobleman, to whom WILLIAM'S niece, JUDITH, was married. Having joined two Norman Earls in a conspiracy against the King, he was betrayed by his own wife, and executed, 1075.

Hereward, "England's Darling," through whom the Saxons maintained their independence for a long time in the Island of Ely.

Edwin, Earl of Mercia, rebelled against WILLIAM, but was betrayed by his followers, and slain by the Normans while in the act of making his escape to Scotland, 1071.

Edgar Atheling, being the grandson of Edmund Ironside, was the lawful heir to the English throne. He submitted to the Conqueror, from whom he received a pension, and is said to have lived at Rouen (France). This Prince was created Earl of Oxford by HAROLD II., which was confirmed by WILLIAM.

Malcolm Canmore, King of Scotland, married MARGARET, sister of EDGAR ATHELING. He invaded England, and was slain near Alnwick Castle, 1093.

William II. was the third son of William I.

A.D. 1087—1100.

A   **WARS.**

1. Desirous of placing ROBERT, Duke of Normandy, on the throne, ODO, Bishop of Bayeux, WILLIAM, Bishop of Durham,

ROGER, Earl of Shrewsbury, assisted by other barons, formed a conspiracy against the King, but he suppressed it and confiscated the estates of most of the conspirators, 1087.

2. In 1090 WILLIAM invaded the dominions of his brother in Normandy, but through the influence of the nobles on both sides, hostilities terminated in the **Treaty of Caen**, by which it was agreed that, if either of the two brothers died without heirs, the survivor should govern both countries, 1091.

3. HENRY, being annoyed at his brothers, ROBERT and WILLIAM, for ignoring him in the treaty of Caen, withdrew to the fortress of **Mount St. Michael**, and made incursions upon Normandy. Here he was besieged by his brothers, and through want of water soon compelled to surrender, 1091.

4. ROBERT and WILLIAM having returned to England, undertook an expedition against Scotland, and obliged MALCOLM CANMORE to do homage to WILLIAM, and cede Cumberland to England, 1091.

5. MALCOLM CANMORE, King of Scotland, invaded England, but being attacked by ROBERT MOWBRAY near Alnwick, Northumberland, both he and his son were slain, 1093. On hearing of the deaths of her husband and son, MARGARET, sister of EDGAR ATHELING, was taken ill, and in three days expired.

6. The **First Crusade** was undertaken by various European princes to rescue **Palestine**, or the **Holy Land**, from the Mahometans. The cause of this war was the bad treatment which Christian pilgrims, going to the tomb of our Saviour at Jerusalem, received from the Mahometans, 1096.

7. MAGNUS, King of Norway, having reduced the Isle of Man and the Orkneys, made an attack upon Anglesea, but he was repulsed by the Earl of Shrewsbury, 1098. It is worthy of remark, that the Scandinavians from this time made no further attempt upon England.

B   CHIEF EVENTS.

On arriving in England, WILLIAM RUFUS, aided by EADO, High Treasurer, proceeded in the following manner :—

1. He seized the fortresses of Dover, Pevensey, and Hastings.

2. He secured the royal treasures at Winchester, which amounted to £60,000, besides the plate and jewels.

3. His next step was to deliver his father's letter to LANFRANC, which authorised that prelate to crown him instead of ROBERT, *who had a prior claim* to the English throne. WILLIAM was crowned,

ig 30 years of age, at Westminster, by Archbishop LANFRANC, . 26, 1087, just 17 days after his father's death.

After the death of LANFRANC, in 1089, WILLIAM appropriated revenues of the see of Canterbury till 1091, when a severe ill- brought him to his senses, in consequence of which he pre- ed upon ANSELM, abbot of Bec, to accept the Archbishopric.

A great part of London was burnt down, 1092.

To improve his revenues, WILLIAM ordered all the lands to be veyed, and Domesday Book to be corrected. He induced the glish to aid him against his brother ROBERT and the Norman ons by fair promises, which he never fulfilled; but instead reof, extorted heavy fines from his subjects. After appointing SELM to the see of Canterbury, he deprived him of its tempor- ies, while his continued disputes with that prelate caused the ar to leave the kingdom, 1093.

ROBERT MOWBRAY, Earl of Northumberland, having rendered LLIAM signal service, and feeling that he had not been sufficiently arded for what he had done, raised a rebellion against him, and k refuge in Bamborough Castle, Northumberland. MOWBRAY ag captured, was confined in Windsor Castle, where he remained risoner for 30 years, 1095.

For furthering the Crusade, which was first projected by rer the Hermit, POPE URBAN II. summoned a council of all tions, at Clermont, in Auvergne, 1095, and in the following r ROBERT, in order to raise money for joining in this holy War, rtgaged to WILLIAM, for five years, the Duchy of Normandy for 000 marks.

The Duke of GUIENNE and POITIERS also mortgaged his rtes to WILLIAM, and joined the Crusade, 1099. Jerusalem was en by the Crusaders in 1099, and GODFREY of Bouillon elected first King.

The sea overflowed the coast of Kent, sweeping away numbers people and cattle, while the tract of land thus covered with ter received the name of Goodwin Sands, because it formerly onged to GODWIN, Earl of Kent, 1100.

RUFUS built Westminster Hall, a bridge over the Thames, and all round the tower.

WILLIAM's death was caused by the shot of an arrow, which is said to have received while hunting in the New Forest, gust 2, 1100; and his remains were buried at Winchester.

C   **CELEBRATED PERSONS.**

Godfrey of Bouillon, a French knight and one of the leaders in the Crusades. · After Jerusalem had been taken from the Turks he was made its first King. (1060—1100).

Ralph Flambard, the King's chief minister, by whom he was greatly assisted in extorting money from his subjects. As a reward for his nefarious services, WILLIAM, shortly before his death, made him Bishop of Durham, 1099.

Odo, Bishop of Bayeux, maternal brother of WILLIAM THE CONQUEROR, and uncle to the King, was imprisoned by the former in Normandy for aspiring to the Popedom, 1082. On being liberated, he entered into a conspiracy against RUFUS for placing ROBERT, Duke of Normandy, on the English throne; but being unsuccessful he was banished the kingdom, 1087.

Anselm, created Archbishop of Canterbury by WILLIAM, whose oppressions he resisted. Having thereby fallen into disgrace he thought it prudent to leave the kingdom, but was restored to the Archbishopric on the accession of HENRY in 1100. ANSELM was born at Aosta, in Piedmont, 1033, and died at Canterbury, 1109.

Walter Tyrrel, a French knight, said by some historians to have accidentally shot the King while hunting in the New Forest.

Peter the Hermit, a French monk, was born at Amiens, in Picardy. Having made a pilgrimage to the Holy Land, he saw with great indignation the cruel manner in which the Christians were treated by the Turks, or Mahometans. On his return to Europe, PETER communicated the state of the Christians in Palestine to Pope URBAN II., by whom he was authorised to preach the **First Crusade** throughout Christendom. He was engaged in the siege of Jerusalem, 1099, on which occasion he displayed great valour, and after its capture was made Vicar-General. Died 1115.

Henry I. was the youngest son of William I.

A.D. 1100—1135.

A   **WARS.**

1. HENRY's elder brother ROBERT having a prior claim to the throne, invaded England; but an agreement was eventually made that ROBERT should receive 3,000 marks a year and give up his *pretensions to the* English crown, 1101.

2. Through ROBERT's bad government, HENRY invaded Nor-
dy, and at Tinchebrai finally defeated his brother, 1106.
BERT was taken prisoner, brought to England, and confined in
diff Castle, Glamorganshire, where he remained twenty-eight
s, and died, 1135. Shortly after ROBERT's defeat, the Duchy
Normandy was united to England.

3. ROBERT's son WILLIAM, assisted by LOUIS VI. of France,
DWIN, Earl of Flanders, and FULK, of Anjou, made an unsuc-
ful attempt to regain Normandy, 1116.

4. **Battle of Brenville,** in which HENRY defeated LOUIS,
9.

CHIEF EVENTS.

On the death of RUFUS, HENRY seized the royal treasures at
nchester, and was crowned at Westminster by MAURICE, Bishop
London, August 5, 1100. To win the affections of his people, he
nted a **charter,** in which he promised :—

1. To govern by the laws of EDWARD the Confessor.

2. To remove some of the burdens of the feudal system.

3. To return to the Church its immunities, and to refrain from
ing the benefices as they became vacant.

In order to strengthen himself on the throne, HENRY married
TILDA, also called **"the good Queen Maud,"** daughter of
LCOLM, King of Scotland, and niece of EDGAR ATHELING, the
of the Saxon princes. During this reign Woodstock Park was
out. Rents now began to be paid in **money** instead of in kind.

HENRY abolished the Curfew, and altered several of the laws
cted by his father. His son WILLIAM, heir apparent to the
glish throne, was drowned, at the age of eighteen, on returning
n Normandy, where he had been taken to receive the homage
the Barons, and with him perished 140 noblemen, and some
ies of distinction. The fatal calamity was caused through the
xication of the captian and crew, who ran the vessel upon a
k. The only one who escaped was a butcher of Rouen, named
ROLD, Nov. 25, 1120. The King left his crown to his only
timate child, MATILDA. The order of **Knights Templars**
established, 1118. HENRY was married to ADELAIS, daughter
GEOFFREY, Duke of Louvain, 1121. Weights, measures, and
age were regulated; while the yard measure is said to have
n taken from the length of HENRY's arm.

A colony of **Flemings,** who fixed their abode at Worsted,
r Norwich, were the first to introduce the manufacture of
llen stuff.

Stealing was first made a capital offence. The Thames was dry for three days, 1114.

Pope CALIXTUS II. convoked the **First Lateran Council** 1123.

The first arched bridge, called **Bow Bridge** on account of its shape, was built over the Lea, near Stratford, 1130.

During this reign the different states of the kingdom were summoned by HENRY to meet at Winchester; and this meeting is represented by some historians as the **First Parliament.**

HENRY died from eating too many lampreys (a kind of eel), at the Castle of Lyon, Normandy. His remains were conveyed to England, and buried in the abbey of Reading (Berks.), of which he was the founder, Dec. 1, 1135.

C CELEBRATED PERSONS.

Anselm, Archbishop of Canterbury, mentioned in the preceding reign, was restored to his office by HENRY.

Simeon of Durham, a learned monk, who taught Mathematics at Oxford, and wrote a history of England from 616 to 1130. He was also the author of a history of Durham Cathedral, called "Historia Ecclesiae Dunhelmensis." (1061—1131).

Oderieus Vitalis, a monk of St. Eurold's, Normandy, author of an Ecclesiastical history, in thirteen books, in which are found many particulars relating to our history. (1075—1132).

William of Malmesbury, a learned monk of the Monastery of Malmesbury (Wilts.), whose father was of Norman and his mother of English extraction. He was the author of "The History of the Kings of England," "The History of the Prelates of England," and other works; and he is considered one of the most veracious and impartial of the early writers. (1095—1150).

Eadmer, an English historian, wrote the lives of Archbishop ANSELM, ST. DUNSTAN, &c. His chief work, however, is the "Historia Novorum," or "History of his own times." Died 1124.

Fitz-Stephen, captain of the vessel in which Prince WILLIAM perished.

William, son of ROBERT COURTHOSE, was mortally wounded at Alost, in Flanders, 1127.

tephen, **Earl of Blois**, was the youngest son of Adela, daughter of the Conqueror. A.D. 1135—1154.

A ## WARS.

1. **Battle of the Standard**, so called from a high crucifix hich the English carried, was fought at **Northallerton**, Yorkire. In this encounter, STEPHEN's forces, led by THURSTAN, rchbishop of York, defeated DAVID I., King of Scotland, who had vaded Northumberland in support of his niece MATILDA. On is occasion more than 12,000 Scots were slain, Aug. 22, 1138.

2. MATILDA, aided by ROBERT, Earl of Gloucester, her natural other, invaded England, 1139. This occasioned a civil war, ıring which the people were plundered by the nobles, the lands ft uncultivated, and all parties were in consequence oppressed by severe famine.

3. **Battle of Lincoln**, between the forces of MATILDA, and ose of STEPHEN, in which the latter was defeated, made prisoner, ıd conveyed to Bristol Castle, in which he was detained about ne months. Feb. 2, 1141.

4. MATILDA held **Oxford**, where she was besieged by the ing, and compelled through want of provisions to leave the Castle, ec. 20, 1142. As there was snow on the ground, MATILDA and ree knights dressed themselves in white, and thus, unobserved by rEPHEN's sentinels, effected their escape at midnight, and fled to ʃallingford. Oxford capitulated the next day.

5. War with HENRY, son of MATILDA, which resulted in the **reaty of Winchester**, by which it was stipulated that STEPHEN ıould reign for life, and be succeeded by HENRY, Nov. 7. 1153.

B ## CHIEF EVENTS.

STEPHEN was crowned at Westminster Abbey by CORBOIL, rchbishop of Canterbury, Dec. 26, 1135; and his title to the rone was confirmed by the Pope. That he might secure the own which he had gained as a usurper, STEPHEN granted a harter, containing the following privileges:—

1. The Barons obtained permission to fortify old castles, build w ones, and also to hunt in their own forests.

2. The Clergy were allowed to fill up their vacant benefices.

3. The people were to enjoy the laws of EDWARD the Confessor, 35.

STEPHEN abolished the tax Danegelt. After he was made prisoner, the people became disgusted with MATILDA'S conduct, deposed her, and placed him on the throne. During the civil wars, Nottingham, Winchester, and Worcester were burnt. A great part of London, from Aldgate to St. Paul's Church, was destroyed by fire, 1136.

STEPHEN converted the Tower into a royal residence, and in this reign sugar was imported.

Pope INNOCENT II. summoned the **Second Lateran Council,** 1139.

Under the auspices of LOUIS VII. of France, and CONRAD of Germany, the **Second Crusade** was preached by ST. BERNARD, 1147.

Queen MATILDA founded St. Catherine's Hospital, 1148.

The Cathedral of Rochester, the City of York, including the Cathedral and thirty-nine churches, and the City of Bath, were burnt down, 1137.

England suffered from a **severe famine,** 1150—1151.

STEPHEN died of **Colic,** at Canterbury, where he had gone to have an interview with the Earl of FLANDERS, Oct. 25, 1154; and was buried by the side of his wife MAUD, and son EUSTACE, in the Abbey of Faversham, Kent, which he had founded.

C   **CELEBRATED PERSONS.**

Matilda, or Maud, daughter of HENRY I., was the rightful heir to the English throne. On the death of her first husband, HENRY IV. of Germany, she married GEOFFREY PLANTAGENET, Earl of Anjou, by whom she had a son, afterwards HENRY II. of England. In accordance with the wishes of the late King, MATILDA claimed the crown; but was opposed by STEPHEN, and being defeated, she ultimately fled to the Continent.

Robert, Earl of Gloucester, was the natural brother of MATILDA, and her chief supporter against STEPHEN for the crown of England. Died 1146.

Thurstan, Archbishop of York, by whom the English forces were led at the battle of the Standard, 1138.

Henry of Huntingdon, Canon of Lincoln and Archdeacon of Huntingdon, wrote a History of England to the year 1154, and also a Latin work, called "Contempt of the World," (1100—1168).

Vacarius, said to have been the first Professor of Canon Law in the University of Oxford.

REMARKS.

According to modern notions as to the right of succession, all the orman Kings of England were usurpers.

WILLIAM'S success in the conquest of England, may, in a great easure, be ascribed to the want of a competent man to lead the Anglo-xons, after the death of HAROLD and his two brothers at the Battle Hastings. During the reign of the Conqueror, a change was made the law, by which the Ecclesiastical and Civil jurisdictions were se-rated. All the proceedings in the King's Court were conducted in the orman language, because WILLIAM'S Justiciaries were comparatively norant of English.

Trial by Jury.—Some historians inform us that this mode of deter-ining the innocence or guilt of an offender, originated in the time of LFRED the Great, and was abolished in the reign of WILLIAM the Con-ueror, who substituted in its place **Trial by Single Combat.** This state-ent is rejected by others, who strenuously deny the existence of Trial y Jury during the Anglo-Saxon period. The confusion on this subject ridently arises from the want of a proper distinction between the *ncient* and *modern* mode of Trial by Jury. In the former, the Jury-en determined the merits of the case from their own personal know-dge, and, therefore, were virtually witnesses; but in the latter, the erdict is arrived at, not by personal knowledge, but through the testi-ony of others, which is brought forward during the process of the ial. The absence, therefore, of all previous personal knowledge of ie merits of the case would have disqualified a man from becoming a uryman among the Anglo-Saxons; while the same absence of that nowledge would rather be a recommendation for his serving on a odern jury. The exact time when the functions of witnesses and urymen were separated and established, has not been ascertained. The rst instance of the practice is found in the twenty-third year of the ign of EDWARD III.

Livery of Seisin consisted in—

1. Delivering up the possession of lands and tenements.

2. Release from wardship. A person was put in corporal posses-on of a freehold by being furnished with the ring, latch, or key of the oor ; or if land, a turf or twig was delivered to him.

Congé d' élire.—This is the King's licence empowering a Dean and hapter to elect a Bishop.

The Forest Laws were so stringent, that any one who killed a deer ad his eyes plucked out or one of his hands cut off.

Purveyance.—This was the royal prerogative or right by which the ing had authority to buy provisions and necessaries at an apprised alue, in preference to his subjects and without the owner's consent. ; also empowered him to seize horses, carriages, &c. Purveyance was troduced into England at the time of the Conquest.

Curfew, or Cover-fire bell, was tolled every night about eight o'clock, when the English were obliged to extinguish all lights.

Domesday Book was compiled by order of WILLIAM the Conqueror. It consists of two volumes, and contains an account of all the lands of England, except Cumberland, Westmoreland, Northumberland, and Durham. The value of each man's property, and the number of inhabitants upon it, are specified. To carry out the feudal system properly, the King required this knowledge.

The Anglo-Norman Kings reduced most of the population of England to a slavish condition, which was called **Villenage**.

While England was under the government of the Saxons, the *Ceorls* or *Freemen* held a middle rank between the Thanes and the *Serfs*, but the Normans reduced the Ceorls to a level with the Serfs, both of whom subsequently became the Norman **Villeins**. According, however, to Domesday Book, some of the Ceorls were allowed to enjoy their freedom and retain their land. In this monument of antiquity we find the following classes of persons specified :—

1. **Norman Barons.**

2. **Saxon Thanes.**

3. **Socmanni**, or **Socmen**, who were small land-owners.

4. **Villeins**, who were divided into two classes :—

> 1. *Villeins regardant*, who occupied land, but could be sold with it.
>
> 2. *Villeins in gross*, who were slaves, and the property of their masters.

Feudalism.—The germ of this system we find among the Saxons, but its development in England is justly ascribed to the Conqueror. The letting out of lands on condition of **Military Service** constitutes the essence of the feudal system. The term is derived from *feud* or *feod*, meaning a piece of land.

In this system all lands were owned by the King, who divided them among his Norman Barons. The Barons subdivided their lands among the *Saxon* Thanes, whom the Normans called *Franklins*. The Thanes or Franklins sublet these lands to their vassals, but with a clear understanding that in every case the inferior should serve his superior in time of war. If, for instance, the King waged war, he would demand military service from the Barons, who held their lands immediately from him as their superior lord. The Barons in like manner required military service from the Franklins, who held lands under them. The Franklins in the same way demanded military service from their vassals. So the King summoned the Barons ; the Barons, the Franklins ; and the Franklins, their vassals. As WILLIAM I. divided England into about 60,000 parts among his Norman Barons, on condition that each Baron, who received a part, should furnish him in time of war with a horse-soldier properly equipped, he would have from that source alone *60,000 horse-soldiers* ready for active service.

In the feudal system the superior was called the *liege* lord ; the tenant, a *liege* man ; the land, a *liege* fee.

The word *liege* is derived from the Latin *ligare*, to *bind*, because the vassal was bound to serve his lord, while the lord was under obligation to protect his vassal.

Those who held lands immediately from the King were called **Tenants-in-Capite**, or Tenants-in-Chief. The lands which were not obliged to render service to a superior lord, but which might be taxed for the public defence, were designated **Allodial**, to distinguish them from the feudal lands.

The ceremonies connected with feudalism were :—

1. **Homage**, in performing which, the vassal, on bended knees and bareheaded, promised service to his lord.

2. The **Oath** of **Fealty**, by which the promise was confirmed upon oath.

3. **Investiture**, which consisted in the lord's putting his vassal in possession of the land.

The **Revenue** of the Anglo-Norman Kings was derived from the following sources :—

1. The rents of the **crown-lands**, which were generally paid in kind, and were used chiefly for the support of the King's household.

2. **Tallages**, which were heavy taxes levied at the King's pleasure upon the inhabitants within the royal demesne.

3. **Danegelt**, which was levied for some time without any just cause.

4. **Escuage or Scutage.**—Those Tenants-in-Capite who failed to furnish the King with a soldier for every knight's fee were obliged to pay him a certain sum of money instead, and this was called Escuage or Scutage.

5. **Reliefs.**—This was a fine paid by an heir to his lord on succeeding to his *fief* or *land*. It was the same as the Saxon **heriot**.

6. **Primer Seisin**, or one year's profits of the land, was an extra relief claimed by the King on the death of a Tenant-in-Capite, provided the heir was of age.

7. **Alienation.**—When a tenant transferred his *fief* or *land* to another, a fine upon the Alienation was paid.

8. **Escheat** (probably from the Latin *cadere*, to fall, to happen), was any *fief* or *land* which fell to the superior lord in consequence of the tenant having no heir to succeed him.

9. **Forfeiture.**—This resulted from the tenant's failing in duty to his lord or the state.

10. **Aids.**—These Aids were taxes demanded from the tenants by their lord under special circumstances. The three principal were:—

1. To *ransom the lord* when a prisoner.

2. To marry his eldest daughter.

3. To make his eldest son a knight. [1]

11. **Wardships**, by which the tenant's person during his minority was under the care of the lord, who received the profits of his estate.

12. **Marriage.**—While the female ward was under age, the lord could provide her with a husband; but on her refusal to accept him, she was obliged to forfeit a sum equal to that which he might have procured by the marriage.

WILLIAM I. suffered much from dissensions among his own children, whose disobedience, it is said, was encouraged by the Queen. The Conqueror had promised his continental dominions to his son ROBERT, provided his invasion of England succeeded. Failing, however, to keep his word, ROBERT became discontented, and, therefore, took up arms against his father. During the Conqueror's last illness, he confessed that he had no right to the English throne except what he had gained by the sword.

HILDEBRAND, the Pope, insisted that WILLIAM should do homage for the crown of England; this the King rejected, asserting that none of his predecessors ever rendered homage to the Pope. He also prohibited the English bishops from attending a council which had been summoned by that Pontiff. At Salisbury, WILLIAM I. received the fealty not only of the Tenants-in-Capite, but also of their tenants, which was a departure from the custom of the continent, 1085.

The Normans or Norsemen were Scandinavians, who became very formidable enemies to France in the ninth and tenth centuries. In the year 912, CHARLES the simple could only satisfy them by ceding a portion of his territory, which after them was called **Normandy**. At the time these Normans settled in France, their chief was the great Norwegian Sea King, **Rollo**, from whom descended WILLIAM the Conqueror. CHARLES the Simple gave his daughter in marriage to ROLLO, who, embracing Christianity, was baptised under the name of ROBERT, and became the first Duke of Normandy. The mother of WILLIAM I. was HARLOTTA, a tanner's daughter.

The most remarkable event in the reign of WILLIAM II. was the commencement of the Crusades or Holy Wars. There were altogether eight Crusades, which extended over a period of nearly 200 years, from 1095 to 1291, during which it is supposed that more than 3,000,000 Europeans perished in the East. These wars were termed *Crusades*, because those who were engaged in them wore a red cross on the right shoulder of their coats. Their motto was, "It is God's Will." The leading men in the Crusades were, **Robert**, Duke of Normandy; **Godfrey** of Bouillon; **Robert**, Earl of Flanders; **Baldwin**, Earl of Hainault; **Hugh** of Vermandois; **Raymond** of Toulouse; **Stephen** of Chartres; **Bohemond** of Tarentum, and his nephew **Tancred**.

The Knights Templars were a religious military order, first instituted *at Jerusalem* for protecting pilgrims travelling to the Holy Land. *They were denominated Templars* from an apartment of the palace of ᴸᴰᴡɪɴ II., in Jerusalem, near the Temple. This order, through ɘ alleged viciousness of its members, was suppressed by the Council of ɘnne, 1312.

Origin of the Stuart Family.—MALCOLM, King of Scotland, had a̶ ɴeral called WALTER, whom he appointed **Steward** or Master of his ʊsehold, as a reward for his signal services. From this individual ʀang the family of the STUARTS, who long wielded the sceptre both ɘr England and Scotland.

The Saxon Chronicle or Annals was a compilation from existing ɔuments which were preserved in the monasteries. These Annals ʀe an account of the wars between the Anglo-Saxons and Britons, ɹ indeed form the principal basis of our history to the time of the ɴquest. The work commences from the birth of our Saviour and ʀminates with the death of STEPHEN in the year 1154. The Chro-ɹle gives internal evidence of being composed at different periods.

The Cinque Ports were Dover, Hastings, Romney, Hythe, and ɴdwich.

A Mark.—The value of this coin was thirteen shillings and fourpence.

Investiture was the right of putting in possession of any benefice, ɩce, or manor. This right, in the reign of HENRY I. and STEPHEN, ɘ claimed by the **King** and **Pope**, which led to great contention. ɹe term **Investiture** is derived from the custom of *investing* the Bishop ɘ Abbot, who had been elected, with a ring and a crosier or pastoral ɘff, as marks of his authority.

WILLIAM I. demolished many houses in order to make the New ʀest in which to hunt, but it is remarkable that in the very Forest in ɘstion, three members of the royal family were killed, namely, ᴄHARD, his eldest son, who was gored by a stag ; WILLIAM RUFUS, ɘ third son, who was shot; and the son of Duke ROBERT of Nor-ɪndy, who expired in the same place.

HENRY I. punished offenders with such severity that he was called ɘ **Lion of Justice.** On one occasion, Forty-four robbers were executed ; ɘ another time, forty-six debasers of coin had, by his orders, their ɣht hands cut off.

In the reign of STEPHEN 126 new castles were built, so that in ɪgland there were no fewer than 1100 of these fortified structures.

During the Norman period a change was made in warfare, the ʈtle-axe being superseded by the use of the large bow and arrows.

At this period the chief towns were London (which in the reign ɘ HENRY II. became the capital of England), Bristol, Exeter, Glou-ɘter, Winchester, Lynn, Chester, Dunwich, Lincoln, York, Norwich, ɹ the Cinque or five ports already mentioned.

Among the many Cathedrals which arose during the Norman ʀiod we may mention those of Durham, Oxford, Peterborough, Win-ɘester, Norwich, *and Chichester.*

The Anglo-Normans had two meals a day, dinner at nine in the morning, and supper at five in the afternoon.

From them we obtained new terms for flesh meat. What the Saxons called oxen and sheep, the Normans, after the slaughtering of the animals, designated beef and mutton.

The chief study at this time was **Astrology**, whose professors were dignified with the name of Mathematicians.

The advantages England derived from the Conquest :—

1. **Architecture** was much improved; the Norman style being chiefly adopted in any buildings of note.

2. The more refined taste and polished manners of the Normans were introduced.

3. The Danish invasions received their death-blow.

4. Robbery and other crimes were considerably checked by means of a better police force.

5. The feeble Saxon Government was succeeded by one of a more powerful character, which in subsequent ages placed England at the head of European nations.

6. **Commerce** made rapid strides; the chief articles exported were tin, lead, wool, and hides.

It must, however, be remembered that these beneficial results were attained at the cost of much injustice and suffering on the part of the English. The period of the Danish invasions excepted, the state of England was the most wretched during the reign of STEPHEN.

The Norman period lasted from 1066 to 1154, a period of eighty-eight years.

THE LEADING EVENTS AND PRINCIPAL DATES
OF THE NORMAN PERIOD.

Invasion of the Normans, and Battle of Hastings ...	A.D. 1066
The Curfew Law was instituted	1068
The North of England reduced to a desert by the King, in consequence of an insurrection	1069
The marriage of Priests forbidden by Pope Gregory VII. ...	1074
The Tower of London built	1080
Domesday Book, after six years' labour, finished	1080
Cumberland was reduced to an English County	1091
The First Crusade was proposed in a council at Clermont	1095
The First Crusaders depart...	1096
William Rufus shot in the New Forest	1100

LINE OF PLANTAGENET.

Henry II. was the eldest son of Geoffrey Plantagenet,
Count of Anjou, and of Matilda, daughter of
Henry I. A.D. 1154—1189.

A   **WARS.**

1. MALCOLM IV. of Scotland was compelled by HENRY to
relinquish Cumberland, Northumberland, and Westmoreland, 1157.

2. Battle of Coleshill, Flintshire. The Welsh having made
incursions into England, HENRY resolved on chastising them, and
therefore led an army into their country, but it was routed, while
HENRY himself narrowly escaped death, 1157.

3. In right of his wife, HENRY claimed Toulouse, and besieged the city, but he was unsuccessful. On this occasion his
vassals were freed from military service by paying a certain sum of
money, called Escuage or Scutage, 1159.

4. HENRY again invaded Wales, and defeated the enemy on the
banks of the river Cieroc, Denbighshire, but he was afterwards
guilty of a shocking piece of cruelty, by ordering his male hostages
to have their eyes plucked out, and the female hostages to lose
their noses and ears, *1165.*

5. HENRY conquered Ireland and annexed it to the English crown, 1172.

6. Three of the King's sons claimed a portion of his dominions, namely: HENRY demanded Normandy; RICHARD, Aquitaine; and GEOFFREY, Brittany; and because he would not accede to their wishes, they rebelled against him. He was therefore obliged to have recourse to arms against these disobedient sons, who were aided by their own mother and the Kings of France and Scotland, 1173.

7. WILLIAM I. of Scotland, having invaded Northumberland, was taken prisoner at **Alnwick**, by the Chief Justiciary, RALPH DE GRANVILLE, July 12, 1174, and liberated the following year, but not until he had agreed to hold Scotland as a **fief** of the English crown, 1175.

8. In 1188 HENRY was involved in a war with his son RICHARD and PHILIP AUGUSTUS, King of France. The alleged ground of these hostilities was, that HENRY detained from RICHARD the Princess ALICE, PHILIP's sister, to whom he had been betrothed, and that he wished her to be married to Prince JOHN instead of RICHARD. HENRY was obliged to conclude a peace the following year on very humiliating terms, 1189.

B   CHIEF EVENTS.

HENRY was crowned at Westminster by THEOBALD, Archbishop of Canterbury, Dec. 19, 1154.

The first acts of HENRY after coming to the throne were:—

1. To dismiss from the kingdom all STEPHEN's mercenary soldiers.

2. To demolish the castles of the Barons, which were about eleven hundred in number.

3. To redress the grievances of the people.

4. To improve the coinage, which had become debased, and to check robbery and violence.

After the death of THEOBALD, HENRY raised THOMAS A BECKET, a London citizen, to be Archbishop of Canterbury, 1162.

In order to restrain the growing power of the Church, which had reached its climax in the shameful conduct of a clergyman in Worcestershire, who had not only violated a gentleman's daughter, but also murdered her father, the King summoned a council of the nobility and clergy, at Clarendon (Wilts.), Jan. 25, 1164, and passed some laws (sixteen in number) called the **Constitutions of** *Clarendon, the* most important of which were:

1. That clergymen accused of any crime should be tried by civil judges.

2. That no person should leave the realm without the King's permission.

3. That the revenue of vacant Sees should belong to the King.

4. That Bishops should be considered as Barons, and be subject to the burdens of that rank.

5. That no tenant-in-capite should be excommunicated, or his lands put under an interdict.

6. That appeals should be carried to the King, and no further, without his consent.

These constitutions caused the **quarrel** between the King and BECKET, who disapproved of them, and denied that they were binding.

The King was so highly displeased with BECKET's insolence, and his opposition to the laws enacted at Clarendon, that in the **Council of Northampton**, the Archbishop, by HENRY's direction, was charged with owing the crown 44,000 marks, which he ought to have paid during his **Chancellorship**, Oct. 12, 1164.

BECKET escaped to France (1164), where he remained about six years. LOUIS VII. afforded him some protection, which led to a three years' war between England and France. The hostilities ended with the **Peace of Montmirail**, 1169.

BECKET arrived in England, Dec. 1, 1170, and excommunicated the Archbishop of York and the Bishops of London and Salisbury, for having crowned Prince HENRY, whose coronation took place, June 15, 1170.

These three prelates proceeded to Normandy, where HENRY was, and laid their case before him. The King became highly exasperated, and exclaimed, "Is there no one who will rid me of this turbulent priest?" This speech induced four of HENRY's knights—HUGH DE MORVILLE, RICHARD BRITO, WILLIAM DE TRACY, and REGINALD FITZ-URSE—to hasten to Canterbury for the purpose of compelling BECKET to stop his violent measures. As he would not promise to revoke the excommunication of the Bishops, they assassinated him before the altar of St. Benedict, in Canterbury Cathedral, Dec. 29, 1170.

HENRY's queen was imprisoned for poisoning FAIR ROSAMOND, a mistress of the King, 1173.

Danegelt was not collected after the year 1174.

HENRY walked barefoot three miles, and did penance at the tomb of BECKET, *where he received lashes from the monks,* 1174.

In this reign a new mode of trial was adopted, called **"Trial by Grand Assize,"** upon which is based our modern Trial by Jury.

The **Common Law** of England is supposed by some writers to date from this reign.

For the proper administration of justice England was divided into six circuits; three judges (called **"Justices in Eyre"**) being appointed to each, 1176.

The building of London Bridge with stone was commenced, 1176.

Prince JOHN was appointed Lord of Ireland in 1177, but being unfit for the office he was recalled.

The **Third Lateran Council** was convoked by Pope ALEXANDER III. in 1179.

Charters were granted to several towns, and glass windows were first used in private houses, 1180.

Part of Lincoln was destroyed by an earthquake, 1185.

Jerusalem was taken by SALADIN, 1187.

HENRY FITZALWIN was made the first Lord Mayor of London, 1188.

HENRY died of grief, caused by the undutiful conduct of his sons, at Chinon (France), July 6, 1189; and was buried at Fontevraud.

C   CELEBRATED PERSONS.

Nicholas Breakspeare is remarkable as being the only Englishman that ever became Pope. He was called ADRIAN IV. On his elevation to the Papal See HENRY congratulated him, and afterwards received from ADRIAN a bull or edict, authorising him to conquer Ireland. ADRIAN was choked by a fly, in Sept., 1159.

Theobald, Archbishop of Canterbury. Died 1161.

Thomas a Becket, a man of great natural abilities, was a London citizen, whom HENRY made Lord High Chancellor, and Archbishop of Canterbury. After he was made Primate, BECKET became an altered man. In order to give indications of sanctity, he frequently scourged himself, put on sackcloth, lived upon the meanest food, such as dry bread and water, and washed the feet of *thirteen* beggars every day. He was murdered by four knights in *Canterbury* Cathedral, and two years after his death he was canonised by Pope ALEXANDER III. For three centuries his shrine was visited by vast multitudes of pilgrims. (1117—1170).

Dermot, King of Leinster, having carried off the wife of RODERIC, Prince of Leitrim, was driven from his country by the latter, 1167. DERMOT sought aid from HENRY, and obtained it on condition of becoming his vassal and doing homage for his kingdom. By the assistance, therefore, of the King's general, RICHARD DE CLARE, Earl of Pembroke, surnamed Strongbow, DERMOT regained his sovereignty. Died 1170.

Ralph de Granville, the Chief Justiciary, captured WILLIAM the Lion of Scotland at Alnwick. Having accompanied RICHARD I. on the Third Crusade, he was killed at the siege of Acre, 1190.

Strongbow, Earl of Pembroke, was sent by HENRY to assist DERMOT, King of Leinster, to regain his dominions, from which he had been expelled by O'RUARC or RODERIC, Prince of Leitrim. In 1169 he married DERMOT'S daughter EVA, and on the death of her father in 1170, STRONGBOW assumed the sovereignty of Leinster. Being attacked by RODERIC at the head of 30,000 men, this able general with a few followers routed the large Irish forces. HENRY marched into Ireland in 1171, received submission from most of the native princes, and in 1172 he appointed STRONGBOW governor of his newly acquired kingdom.

John of Salisbury, an eminent Latin scholar and author of a miscellany entitled "Frivolities of Courtiers and Footprints of Philosophers." (1116—1182).

Fitz-Stephen, a monk of Canterbury, wrote the life of THOMAS A BECKET, in which he also gives a curious description of London.

Robert Wace, HENRY's Chaplain, author of a History of the Normans. (1090—1176).

Joseph of Exeter, author of an Epic on the subject of the Trojan War, and said to be "a miracle in classical composition."

Walter Mapes, Archdeacon of Oxford, noted for his drinking song in rhyming Latin.

St. Gilbert, of Sempringham, a divine.

Richard of St. Victor, a divine.

Richard I. was the eldest surviving son of Henry II.
A.D. 1189—1199.

A   **WARS.**

1. **Battle of Ascalon,** in which RICHARD defeated 300,000 Saracens, under their brave leader, SALADIN, 1191.

2. **Acre,** which had been besieged for nearly two years by the Christians, and with a loss of 200,000 men, was taken by RICHARD, 1191.

3. **Battle of Gisors,** in which PHILIP OF FRANCE was defeated by RICHARD, who wished to punish the French monarch for having entered into a league to dethrone him, 1198.

4. **War with Vidomar,** lord of Limoges, a vassal of RICHARD. These hostilities were caused by VIDOMAR'S refusing to give up the whole of a treasure, which had been discovered by his servants when digging on the land held under RICHARD, who was mortally wounded by an arrow, while besieging his vassal in the castle of Chalus, 1199.

B   **CHIEF EVENTS.**

RICHARD was crowned at Westminster, Sept. 3, 1189.

The **Jews,** having incurred popular dislike for charging an exorbitant rate of interest on loans of money, were cruelly massacred in London, York, Norwich, Stamford, and other towns in England, 1189—1190.

In order to raise funds for the prosecution of the Holy Wars, RICHARD converted all that he could into money. He sold all his personal estates and the crown lands. He afterwards renounced his authority over Scotland for 10,000 marks. For the recovery of Jerusalem, RICHARD engaged in the **Third Crusade** with PHILIP OF FRANCE, and marched to Palestine, 1190. The united armies of both Kings amounted to 100,000 men. After various successes, the King, on coming in sight of Jerusalem, found his army so wasted by disease that he was glad to conclude with SALADIN a truce of three years, by which it was agreed :—

1. That Christians should not be molested when they made a pilgrimage to Jerusalem.

2. That they should hold the seaport towns of Palestine. 1192.

On his returning to England, the King was taken prisoner by LEOPOLD, Duke of Austria, who was maliciously disposed towards

RICHARD for having disgraced him by a kick, in the Holy Land, because the Duke refused to work as a common soldier. LEOPOLD delivered RICHARD into the hands of HENRY VI., Emperor of Germany, who detained him in the castle of Deirnstein. As soon as the place of RICHARD's detention was known, the English paid a ransom of £300,000 for the liberation of their King, who landed at Sandwich amid universal joy, March 13, 1194, and in the same year was crowned again at Winchester by HUBERT, Archbishop of Canterbury.

WILLIAM FITZ-OSBERT, surnamed Longbeard, considering the poor more heavily taxed than the rich, took up their cause, and raised an insurrection in London against the Government. The tumult was suppressed by Archbishop HUBERT, and Longbeard slain, 1196.

The Fourth and Fifth Crusades began and almost terminated during this reign. The former commenced in 1195 and ended 1197; the latter began in 1198 and terminated 1204.

The French motto, "*Dieu et Mon Droit*" (God and my right) was chosen for the Royal Arms.

Coats of Arms were invented and used by the Crusaders for the purpose of distinguishing one chief from another. RICHARD chose *Lions passant* as his device, which still continues to be used on the Royal Arms of England.

RICHARD was shot by one BERTRAND DE GOURDON, while besieging the Castle of Chalus (Normandy), expired eleven days afterwards, April 6, 1199, and was buried at Fontevraud.

C   CELEBRATED PERSONS.

Baldwin, Archbishop of Canterbury, built Lambeth Palace, near London. He died in the Holy Land. (1121—1191).

William Longchamp, Bishop of Ely, guardian of the kingdom during RICHARD's absence, was expelled from his office by PRINCE JOHN, and withdrew to France, 1191.

Eleanor of Guienne, became the wife of LOUIS VII. King of France, from whom she was separated, and afterwards married HENRY II. of England. She encouraged her sons in rebellion against their father, for which she was imprisoned sixteen years. On RICHARD's accession to the throne he released her. (1125—1204).

Layamon, a priest and historian. Died 1200.

Saladin, a Sultan of Egypt, by whom the Christian army at Jerusalem was conquered, 1187. He was, however, defeated by

RICHARD in 1191. SALADIN was a wise man and a very generous foe.

Blondel, a French minstrel, who had so great affection for RICHARD that he undertook to travel through Europe in pursuit of him. After wandering about for a year and a half, he found the King confined in a Castle in the Tyrol. BLONDEL returned to England, and informed the Barons that he had discovered their King, who was immediately ransomed.

Robin Hood, a notorious outlaw, the leader of a gang of robbers. His abode was chiefly in Sherwood Forest, Nottinghamshire. The poor and oppressed had a firm friend in ROBIN HOOD. Feeling unwell, he called at Berkeley Nunnery, and requested to be bled. On recognising that the patient was ROBIN HOOD, the operator bled him to death.

Little John, ROBIN HOOD's Lieutenant; though called "little," was in fact a giant.

William Fitz-Osbert, was executed for raising an insurrection in London, 1196.

Henry Fitz-Alwin, mentioned in the preceding reign, was the first Lord Mayor of London.

Bertrand de Gourdon, who shot RICHARD while the latter was besieging the Castle of Chalus.

William of Newburgh, author of a History of England from the Conquest to his own time. (1128—1198).

John was brother of the late King, and youngest son of Henry II. A.D. 1199—1216.

A   WARS.

1. As Queen ELEANOR supported the interests of her son JOHN, who had refused to give up certain continental possessions to his nephew ARTHUR, the youthful Duke of Brittany, the latter beseiged her in the Castle of Mirabeau (France), but JOHN raised the siege, and captured ARTHUR and his sister ELEANOR, August 1, 1202.

2. JOHN had several wars with PHILIP II. of France, who espoused the cause of young ARTHUR, the lawful heir to the crown, 1203—1214.

3. The King invaded Ireland, and reduced to obedience all those who resisted his authority, 1210.

4. John marched into Wales as far as Snowdon, and received submission from Llewellyn, the Welsh Chief, 1211.

5. Battle of Bouvines (France), in which the allied English, German, and Flemish forces were defeated by Philip, July 27, 1214.

6. War between John and his Barons, who invited to aid them Philip's son Louis, and to him they promised the crown of England, 1216.

B	CHIEF EVENTS.

John was crowned at Westminster, May 27, 1199.

Richard was induced by Constance, Arthur's mother, to appoint John as his successor. In this appointment England, Normandy, and Aquitaine agreed; but the interest of Arthur, the son of Geoffrey, John's deceased elder brother, was espoused by the people of Anjou, Touraine, and Maine.

Philip also favoured the cause of Arthur, and invaded Normandy, which resulted in a peace. During this reign the English lost nearly all their continental territories; even Normandy fell to the crown of France.

William the lion, King of Scotland, did homage to John at Lincoln, Nov. 22, 1200.

Shortly after his accession, John granted three charters to the citizens of London, by one of which they had power given them to choose their own sheriffs. John enacted a law in which he declared his authority over the British seas, and ordered all foreign vessels, under pain of confiscation, to lower their top-sails in respect to his flag, 1201.

John murdered his nephew Arthur at Rouen, and cast his body into the Seine, 1203. He imprisoned Arthur's sister Eleanor, known as the "Damsel of Brittany," in Bristol Castle.

The Inquisition, an infamous tribunal for examining and punishing all who did not adhere to the Romish Church, was established by Pope Innocent III. in 1204.

Pope Innocent III. appointed Stephen Langton to be Archbishop of Canterbury, but John refused to have him, in consequence of which the Pontiff laid England under an Interdict, excommunicated John, absolved the people from their allegiance to the King, and authorised Philip of France to dethrone him. Terrified at this, John yielded to the Pope, resigned his kingdom, and swore that he *would hold it* as the Pope's vassal, 1207—1213.

JOHN granted the London citizens power to choose a Mayor every year, 1208.

London bridge was finished, 1209.

A Crusade, under SIMON DE MONTFORT, against the Albigenses, a people in the South of France, who refused to be under the authority of the Romish Church, was commenced, 1210.

Magna Charta.—This important charter is justly considered the foundation of English liberty. The Barons compelled JOHN to sign it on a meadow called **Runnymede**, near Windsor, June 19, 1215.

Some of the most important privileges of this great charter were:—

1. That the Church of England should be free to enjoy her whole rights and liberties inviolable.

2. That there should be but one weight and measure throughout the realm; and that foreign merchants should have freedom of commerce.

3. That no **Scutage** or **Aid** (except in a few specified cases) should be imposed without the consent of the **Great Council**, consisting of the Archbishops, Bishops, Abbots, Earls, and Greater Barons assembled by writ, and the Lesser Barons by a general summons of the Sheriff.

4. That no freeman should be imprisoned, disseised of his lands, outlawed, or exiled, but by the lawful judgment of his Peers or the law of the land.

5. That the court of Common Pleas should be stationary at Westminster.

6. That the Judges of Assize should go on their circuits once a year, and administer justice fairly.

7. That justice should neither be sold, denied, nor delayed to any man.

8. That all men should pass from and return to the kingdom at their pleasure.

9. That the Crown should not seize the lands of a Baron for debt, while he had sufficient personal property to discharge it.

10. That all cities and boroughs should preserve their ancient liberties.

11. That the estate of every freeman should be regulated by his will; and if he died intestate, by the law of the land.

12. That no freeman should be fined to his utter ruin, nor a peasant be deprived of his instruments of husbandry.

Though JOHN granted this charter, which was solemnly ratified on *thirty-eight* different occasions by subsequent Kings, yet he

ually procured from the Pope a bull annulling it, and introduced
eign soldiers to fight against the Barons, who immediately offered
) kingdom to Louis, son of Philip II., King of France, an offer
iich was readily accepted.

The Jews had a great enemy in John, who ordered one of
em to pay 10,000 marks, and on his refusal, the King directed
it a tooth should be extracted every day, till the sum was paid.
ter losing seven teeth, the Jew yielded to the demand.

Sterling money was first coined by John, who introduced
iglish law into Ireland, and granted to the Cinque Ports certain
vileges, of which they have never been deprived.

The Fourth Lateran Council was convoked by Pope
nNOCENT III., in 1215.

The use of Chimneys; the Publishing of Banns; and Mar-
ges in Churches date from this reign; and also the Hanseatic
ague, for protecting commerce, was formed by some leading
rman towns.

While the King was marching into Lincolnshire, he had the
sfortune to lose all his carriages, baggage, and treasure, by the
erflowing of the Wash.   This loss so preyed upon his mind that
died shortly after at Swinehead Abbey (Newark), Oct. 18, 1216,
l was buried at Worcester.

CELEBRATED PERSONS.

Prince Arthur, son of Geoffrey, John's elder brother, was
e legitimate heir to the throne.   John captured him at the siege
Mirabeau in 1202, and is said to have murdered him in the castle
Rouen, 1203.

Gilbert Anglicus, astronomer and physician.

John de Courcy, Earl of Ulster, a man of prodigious strength.
e and his descendants were allowed by John to wear their hats
the royal presence.

Peter of Blois, Archdeacon of London, author of sermons,
d one hundred and thirty-four letters, containing descriptions of
e manners and characters of the times.   (1120—1200).

Gervais of Canterbury, the author of Chronicles of the
ngs of England, and a History of the Archbishops of Canterbury.
l33—1205).

Stephen Langton, born in Lincolnshire, became in 1213
rchbishop of Canterbury.   He divided the Bible into chapters
d verses, and was mainly instrumental in securing Magna Charta.

He boldly maintained the rights of Englishmen, resisted the encroachments of the Pope, and refused to excommunicate the Barons
after they had obtained the great charter. (1151—1228).

Roger de Howden, Prior of Howden (Yorkshire), wrote a
continuation of BEDE's Ecclesiastical History. (1129—1202.)

Giraldus Cambrensis, a distinguished Welshman, wrote a
Description of Wales, and a Topographical History of Ireland
(1146—1220).

Robert Fitz-Walter, General of the Army of the Barons.

Pandulph, the Pope's Legate, into whose hands JOHN resigned the Crown.

William Mareschal, Earl of Pembroke, was a leading man
in compelling the king to sign Magna Charta. On the death of
JOHN he became guardian to the young King, and was also appointed Regent. Died 1219.

Maimonides, of Cordova, a learned Hebrew, who was very
proficient in medicine, mathematics and philosophy. Died 1208.

Henry III. was the eldest son of John. A.D. 1216—1272.

A   **WARS.**

1. **Battle of Lincoln.**—The army of LOUIS being defeated at
Lincoln by the Earl of PEMBROKE, and his fleet almost destroyed
by HUBERT DE BURGH, off the coast of Kent, he quitted England
May 19, 1217. This battle was also called the **Fair of Lincoln**
because the victory was so easily obtained.

2. **Battle of Taillebourg** (France).—In order to recover the
possessions which England had lost, HENRY invaded France, but
was defeated at Taillebourg by LOUIS IX., 1242.

3. **Battle of Lewes.**—The Barons being displeased with the
arbitrary power of the King, and his partiality to foreigners, flew to
arms, with SIMON DE MONTFORT, Earl of Leicester, for their leader,
and defeated HENRY at the battle of Lewes, making him prisoner,
May 14, 1264.

4. **Battle of Evesham.**—EDWARD having escaped from prison
collected an army and defeated the Barons at Evesham, SIMON DE

rrfort being numbered amongst the dead, Aug. 4, 1265. ftr this encounter the King was released.

CHIEF EVENTS.

Henry being only nine years of age at his father's death, the ve and wise Earl of Pembroke was appointed Protector of the lm and guardian of the King. After his coronation, the King homage to the Pope, who assumed the title of feudal lord England. The crown having been lost with John's treasures, a clet of gold was used in its stead at the King's coronation, which k place Oct. 20, 1216.

The King solemnly confirmed the Great Charter in 1225, and subsequent occasions renewed the confirmation.

The Sixth Crusade began in 1227 and ended in 1229; the venth Crusade commenced in 1249 and terminated in 1250.

The Welsh were subdued and obliged to observe English law, 51.

In order to draw up some rules for the reform of Government, ouncil was held at Oxford, which the Royalists called the Mad rliament, because of its opposition to the king, 1258. The re- lutions passed by the Mad Parliament were called the Provisions Oxford, of which the following were the principal :—

1. That sheriffs should be chosen by vote every year.

2. That the freeholders of every county should be represented four knights.

3. That an annual account of the public money should be ren- red.

4. That Parliament should meet three times a year; February, ne, and October.

The King granted a charter to the people of Newcastle, by hich they had permission to dig in search of coal. Henry being liged to submit to the provisions of Oxford, referred the dispute Louis IX., whose award the Barons rejected, which caused renewal of the civil war, 1264.

Towns were first summoned to Parliament by Simon de Montfort, 1265.

By the Award of Kenilworth, passed in 1266, pardon was fered to all who had committed offences against the King, pro- ded they would at once return to their allegiance. The family f De Montfort was excepted.

Henry being defeated and made prisoner at Lewes (Sussex), is son Edward surrendered the following day. A treaty, called the **Mise of Lewes**, for the King's liberation, was concluded, but they did not carry it out.

On one occasion the Queen was grossly insulted by the Londoners. The Jews, too, were again persecuted.

Coal was first used for domestic purposes; the Flemish introduced linen cloth; magnifying glasses, gunpowder, and the mariner's compass were invented; gold coin first used; architecture was much improved, tiles being laid on roofs of buildings instead of thatch; the study of geography was introduced—and five colleges founded, one at Cambridge and four at Oxford; the Moors taught the art of distilling.

Prince EDWARD, with his wife ELEANOR, set out for the last Crusade, 1270.

HENRY died at Bury St. Edmund's, Nov. 16, 1272, and was buried at Westminster.

C   CELEBRATED PERSONS.

Earl of Pembroke, noted for his wise Regency, which lasted only three years.

Simon de Montfort, Earl of Leicester, and son of SIMON DE MONTFORT who headed the Crusade against the Albigenses, was the King's brother-in-law. He is noted for opposing HENRY's unconstitutional measures, and also for founding the House of Commons. He was slain, Aug. 4, 1265.

Hubert de Burgh, a great statesman, and Governor of Dover Castle, succeeded PEMBROKE in the Regency, 1219.

Robert of Gloucester, a monk of Gloucester Abbey, by whom the chronicles of GEOFFREY of Monmouth were turned into rhymes. He is said to have been the first that wrote verses in English. (1230—1285).

Matthew Paris, a monk of St. Alban's, in Herefordshire. His work, entitled Historia Major, is a History from the Creation to his own times. (1180—1259).

Robert Greathead or Grosstête, Bishop of Lincoln for twenty-three years, received his education at the Universities of Oxford and Paris. He was a patron of ROGER BACON, and distinguished for his learning, piety, and his opposition to the shameful exactions of the Romish Church. (1175—1258).

Peter des Roches, Bishop of Winchester, who had charge of the young King's person: he retired from England in 1224, because he had failed to obtain chief power, and returned in 1231. It was through him that HENRY imprisoned HUBERT for a time in the *Tower.*

Roger Bacon, a Franciscan friar, called the "Father of Philosophy," and the "Wonderful Doctor," was born A.D., 1214, and educated at Oxford. He afterwards studied at Paris, and became very proficient in Greek and Oriental literature. He devoted much time to the study of mathematics, natural philosophy, and chemistry, spending twenty years and a large amount of money in making experiments. He effected some extraordinary discoveries. He is said to have written eighty treatises on different subjects, and to have invented telescopes, microscopes, maps, &c. His superior learning and abilities roused the jealousy of the monks, who reported that he corresponded with evil spirits. He was therefore forbidden to lecture in the University, and committed to prison, where he remained ten years, and died, 1292.

Thomas Aquinas, an Italian monk, called the Angelic Doctor, author of seventeen folio volumes of Divinity. (1224—1274).

Edward I. was the eldest son of Henry III.
A.D. 1272—1307.

A ### WAR WITH WALES.

1. LLEWELLYN, the Welsh Prince, having refused to do homage to EDWARD for his fief of Wales, the latter entered the principality and compelled the former to yield, and also to surrender a portion of North Wales, 1277.

2. **Battle of Llandeilovawr,** in which the Welsh were defeated by EDMUND MORTIMER, LLEWELLYN himself being slain by ADAM FRANKTON, an English knight. **This victory completed the conquest of Wales, Dec. 11, 1282**

WAR WITH SCOTLAND.

1. **Battle of Dunbar.**—JOHN BALIOL having renounced his allegiance to EDWARD, the latter invaded his territories, and by the aid of the Earl of WARRENNE, defeated the Scottish army at Dunbar. BALIOL surrendered, and was committed to the Tower, April 27, 1296.

2. **Battle of Cambuskenneth** (Stirling), in which the English were vanquished by SIR WILLIAM WALLACE, the Scottish Chief, Sept. 10, 1297.

3. **Battle of Falkirk,** in which EDWARD routed WILLIAM WALLACE, the Scottish leader, July 22, 1298.

4. **Battle of Roslin,** in which the English were defeated by COMYN, the nephew of BALIOL, Feb. 24, 1303.

5. **Battle of Methven,** near Perth.—ROBERT BRUCE, son of one of the candidates for the crown of Scotland, having murdered COMYN, assumed the title of King, but his forces were overcome at Methven by the Earl of PEMBROKE, while he managed to escape, July 19, 1306.

6. **Battle of Loudon Hill,** in which BRUCE defeated the English under the Earl of PEMBROKE, May 10, 1307.

B   **CHIEF EVENTS.**

During EDWARD'S absence in Palestine, where he greatly distinguished himself in the last Crusade, his father died, but he was shortly after proclaimed King of England, Lord of Ireland, and Duke of Aquitaine, Nov. 20, 1272.

As EDWARD did not return to England for nearly two years after hearing of his father's death, the kingdom was in the meantime under the Regency of WALTER GIFFORD, Archbishop of York, and the Earls of CORNWALL and GLOUCESTER.

EDWARD landed at Dover, August 11, 1274, and was crowned with his Queen ELEANOR at Westminster, by ROBERT, Archbishop of Canterbury, August 19, 1274, on which occasion 500 horses were let loose and given to any who could catch them.

EDWARD took away from Scone, near Perth, the great stone upon which the Kings of Scotland sat when they were crowned, and sent it to Westminster; this stone was framed, and has been used as the Coronation Chair of England ever since. He built **Caernarvon Castle,** and made his eldest son the **First Prince of Wales.**

EDWARD did homage to the French King for his continental possessions, 1272—1274.

While in Palestine, EDWARD was stabbed by an assassin, which must have proved fatal had not his wife, QUEEN ELEANOR, at the risk of her own life, sucked the poison from the wound; and on his way to England he was challenged by the Earl of CHALONS to a Tournament, which, owing to the suspected foul play on the part of the Burgundians, ended in a real fight, called the **Little Battle of Chalons,** in which the English were victorious, 1273.

Coroners were appointed by EDWARD'S first Parliament, *1275.*

The Statute called **Peine forte et dure**, for the punishing of such as refused to plead, is supposed to have been enacted, 1275.

The first Attorney General, WILLIAM DE GISILHAM, was appointed, 1278.

In London 280 Jews were hanged for clipping the coin, a common practice in those days, 1278.

On the death of ALEXANDER III., of Scotland (1286), the heir to that throne was his grand-daughter, MARGARET, known as the "**Maid of Norway**," of which country, ERIC, her father, was King. On her voyage from Norway to Scotland, MARGARET died (1290), in consequence of which thirteen candidates aspired to the crown, the principal of whom were:—

1. **John Baliol**, who contended that he had a right to the crown, because he was the grandson of **Margaret**, the eldest daughter of DAVID, Earl of Huntingdon, and brother of WILLIAM, King of Scotland.

2. **Robert Bruce**, son of **Isabel**, the second daughter, whose claim rested on his being one degree nearer to the common stock.

3. **Hastings**, grandson of **Ada**, the third daughter, who asked for only a third part of the kingdom.

EDWARD being requested by the Parliament of Scotland to decide which of the three candidates ought to succeed to the throne, first insisted upon their acknowledging him as feudal lord, and then delivered his judgment in favour of BALIOL, 1292. BALIOL soon after revolted, which led to war with Scotland.

The Sicilian Vespers.—This was a terrible massacre of the French in Sicily, 8,000 of whom were slain *in one night*, 1282. The cause of this outrage arose from a French soldier having insulted a Sicilian bride while she was marching in procession to a church at Palermo.

The Statute of Mortmain, which prohibited the granting of lands to the Church without the King's licence, was passed, 1279.

The Statute of Acton Burnall, for enabling merchants and others to recover their debts more speedily, was enacted 1283. Acton Burnall or Burnell is a village in Shropshire, where the act was passed, hence its name.

Wales was formerly incorporated with England by a statute passed at Rhuddlan, called the **Statute of Wales**, 1284.

De Donis.—The statute known by this name provided that the Barons should be allowed to entail their personal property, 1285.

Many judges having been convicted of corruption in the administration of justice, were fined and deposed, 1289.

Instigated by his mother ELEANOR, EDWARD banished upwards of 16,000 Jews from the kingdom, 1290. This persecuted race was not permitted to return till the time of the Commonwealth.

The statute entitled **Quia Emptores** was passed in 1290, and allowed freemen to sell their lands, provided the purchaser would hold them of the Chief Lord, in order that the latter might receive his usual fees arising from marriages, wardships, &c.

A private quarrel between some English and Norman sailors involved France and England in a war, in consequence of which EDWARD lost Guienne, 1294.

On the clergy refusing to submit to the heavy taxation of the King, he outlawed them, and confiscated their property, which they only recovered by paying a large sum of money, 1297.

Owing to the King's frequent imposition of illegal taxes upon his subjects, and in order to put a check upon such arbitrary proceedings for the future, two distinguished patriots, HUMPHREY BOHUN, Earl of Hereford, and ROGER BIGOD, Earl of Norfolk, seconded by the people, compelled the King to sign a **Confirmation** of the **Charters**, with an additional clause called the statute "**De Tallagio non Concedendo,**" by which it was enacted—

1. That no tax should be imposed upon the people without the consent of the Lords and Commons.

2. That the crown should neither seize wool, hides, nor any other merchandise.

3. That neither tolls nor customs should be levied, except those provided by the charters, 1297.

On EDWARD I. was conferred the title of "The British Justinian," for making so many improvements in the English law. He was also designated "The Hammer of Scotland."

France and England concluded a peace, after which PHILIP restored Guienne to EDWARD, 1303.

To a monk of Pisa is attributed the invention of spectacles in this reign. FLAVIO GIOIA, of Amalfi, improved the mariner's compass. Windmills were introduced, paper brought from the East, and the amusements of tilting, quintain, and riding at the ring became popular. Striking clocks were also invented, and halfpence and farthings coined. A settlement was made in London by some Lombard merchants and money lenders, who fixed their abode in what is now called after them Lombard Street. Coal was used by some London brewers, and other tradesmen ; at last it was prohibit-*ed as a public* nuisance.

While advancing towards the north with a firm resolve to punish the Scots, Edward died at Burgh-on-Sands, Cumberland, July 7, 1307, and was buried at Westminster.

C. CELEBRATED PERSONS.

John Britton, Bishop of Hereford, was skilled in the common law. A book written by him under the title of "De Juribus Anglicanis," was deemed very valuable. Died 1275.

David, brother of LLEWELLYN, was made prisoner, taken to Shrewsbury, and after being tried was found guilty of high treason. He was hanged, his body taken down before life was extinct, and his bowels cut out and burnt in his presence. The cruel wretches then severed the head from the body, sending the former to be placed on the Tower of London; the latter, when quartered, they severally despatched to York, Winchester, Northampton, and Bristol, as a warning to traitors, 1283.

Margaret, called the **Maid of Norway,** daughter of **Eric,** King of Norway, was on the death of ALEXANDER III., the lawful heir to the crown of Scotland; but she died on her way to Scotland, 1290.

Cressingham, treasurer of Scotland, headed the English forces in the battle of Cambuskenneth, but he and 500 of his followers were left dead on the field. CRESSINGHAM was so hated by the Scotch that they flayed his dead body, and converted the skin into horse-trappings, 1297.

Sir William Wallace, the Scottish Champion, was treacherously betrayed to EDWARD by his professed friend, Sir JOHN MONTEITH. He was ultimately put to death in London as a common felon. (1276—1305).

John de Fordun, one of the earliest of the *Scotch* Chroniclers, wrote the History of Scotland, to the year 1153, but it was brought down to 1437 by WALTER BOWER. (1221—1308).

John Duns, or John Scotus, a Franciscan monk, author of ten folio volumes, and for his great learning was designated the **Subtle Doctor.** His "Commentaries" on the Bible and Aristotle are considered his best works. He became Professor of Divinity at Oxford, then at Paris, and finally at Cologne, where he died. He strongly opposed the teachings of AQUINAS, whose followers called the adherents of DUNS SCOTUS *Dunses,* meaning stupid persons. From this is derived our word *Dunce.* (1218—1309).

John Baliol, the successful claimant to the crown of Scotland. *Being defeated at the battle of Dunbar, he surrendered his* crown into the hands of EDWARD, who committed him and his son prisoners to the tower. By the intercession of the people they were released. BALIOL withdrew into Normandy, where he died in obscurity, 1314.

Aymer de Valence, Earl of Pembroke, one of EDWARD's leaders, who defeated BRUCE at Methven, in Perthshire; and was made Governor of Scotland by EDWARD II.

Robert Winchelsea, Archbishop of Canterbury, was so charitable, that 4,000 people were relieved by him twice every week.

Edward II. was the first Prince of Wales and the eldest surviving son of Edward I.   A.D. 1307—1327.

A   WARS.

1. **Battle of Bannockburn,** in which EDWARD's army was completely routed by the Scotch under ROBERT BRUCE, June 24, 1314.   By this victory Scotland secured her independence.

2. The Irish under EDWARD BRUCE, brother to the Scottish King, endeavoured to regain their independence, but were defeated near **Dundalk,** and BRUCE was slain by the Archbishop of DUBLIN, General of the English forces, 1318.

3. **The White Battle,** in which the Scotch, under the Earl of MURRAY, vanquished the English, headed by WILLIAM DE MELTON, Archbishop of York.   This engagement was called the White Battle, because some English priests were slain with their surplices on, 1319.

4. The King gained a decisive victory over his Barons at Boroughbridge, Yorkshire, in which LANCASTER, their leader, was taken prisoner and executed at Pontefract, March 16, 1322.

B   CHIEF EVENTS.

EDWARD was crowned at Westminster, Feb. 24, 1308, and in the same year he did homage to PHILIP IV., King of France, at Guienne.

Earthenware was invented and came into general use, 1309.

The palace of the Bishop of CHICHESTER was converted into a court of law, called Lincoln's Inn, 1810.

For the regulation of Government and his household, the King permitted the Parliament to choose seven Bishops, eight Earls, and six Barons, who were styled **Ordainers**, 1310. They demanded—

1. The banishment of GAVESTON.

2. The abolition of the new taxes on wool, cloth, and wine.

3. That the consent of the Baronage, in Parliament, should be necessary in order to enable the King to leave the realm, or wage war.

4. That the final choice of the officers of the crown should rest with Parliament.

5. That a **Parliament** should be held once or twice every year.

These laws were enacted 1311.

In this reign the House of Commons began to annex **Petitions** to their bills. The interest of money at one time was at the rate of 45 per cent. Bills of Exchange were first used in England.

GAVESTON, the son of a Gascon Knight, and a special favourite of the King, was put to death by the Barons at Blacklow Hill, near Warwick, on account of his haughty conduct towards them, June 19, 1312.

The Order of the **Knights Templars** was suppressed by POPE CLEMENT V., on account of their alleged wickedness, 1312, and their property given to the Knights of St. John, called the Knights of Malta.

The long wars between England and Scotland ended, and a truce for thirteen years was concluded at **Berwick**, 1323.

England and Venice entered into the **First Commercial Treaty**, 1325.

A religious sect, called **Lollards**, arose. They rejected the Romish rites of mass, penance, and extreme unction. The name was afterwards applied to the followers of WICKLIFFE by way of reproach.

During a portion of this reign England was grievously oppressed by the following destructive enemies :—

1. A most severe famine.

2. Unseasonable weather, which destroyed the harvests.

3. A murrain among the cattle; in consequence of which an enormous price was charged for provisions.

In this reign paper was produced from rags. Land lay fallow every third year. The people dined at eleven in the morning, and ate so much and had so many dishes served up, that they were forbidden by law to have more than two courses.

Headed by Tell, the Swiss threw off their allegiance to the House of Hapsburg, and were victorious at the **Battle of Morgarten,** 1315. They were also successful against their enemies at **Sempach,** 1386.

In 1305, the Papal Seat was transferred to Avignon, where it continued till the year 1375.

EDWARD was made a prisoner by his subjects, compelled to sign his own abdication, and murdered at Berkeley Castle, Gloucestershire, 1327. His body was interred in Gloucester Cathedral.

C   **CELEBRATED PERSONS.**

Piers Gaveston, a native of Gascony, a great favourite of the King, who created him Earl of Cornwall, and gave him his niece in marriage. The Barons becoming jealous of his growing power, compelled EDWARD to banish him in 1308. GAVESTON was recalled from Ireland, over which country he had been Governor during his absence from England, 1309. Being attacked a second time he withdrew to Flanders, but returning shortly afterwards, he was seized and executed at **Blacklow Hill,** near Warwick, June, 19, 1312.

Maltravers and **Gournay,** who murdered the King, by thrusting a red-hot iron into his intestines, 1327.

Robert Bruce, grandson of BALIOL's competitor, claimed the crown of Scotland, and enabled that country to achieve its independence. He routed EDWARD's army at the battle of Bannockburn, leaving 30,000 of the English dead upon the field, 1314. His coronation took place at Scone. Died 1329.

Baston, a Carmelite friar, whom EDWARD took to celebrate his victory at Bannockburn, instead of which the Scotch compelled him to eulogise EDWARD's defeat.

John Deydias, a tanner's son, of Exeter, tried to deprive the King of his crown, by asserting that he was EDWARD, and had been changed during infancy.

Earl of Lancaster, the first Prime Minister, and the **Earl of Warwick,** both noted for their opposition to EDWARD's favourites, GAVESTON and SPENSER.

Hugh Spenser and his father became great favourites of the King. The son was the King's chamberlain, and amassed much wealth. The barons becoming jealous of the SPENSERS, demanded their dismissal, and on EDWARD's refusal to comply a civil war was the result, 1327. The royal party were defeated, and the SPENSERS *hanged—the father* at Bristol, and the son at Hereford.

Isabella, EDWARD's Queen, formed an improper intimacy with ROGER MORTIMER, a powerful Baron of the Welsh Marches, who became her adviser and confidant in all her undertakings. Having contracted a dislike to her husband she joined his enemies; and while in France settling some differences about Gascony, between EDWARD and her brother, CHARLES IV., she upon her own authority, affianced the PRINCE OF WALES to PHILIPPA, daughter of the Count of HOLLAND and HAINAULT. Aided by this Prince, the Queen raised 3,000 men, set sail from Dort, and landed at Orwell, in Suffolk, Sept. 24, 1326, where she was joined by the Earls of KENT and NORFOLK, the King's brothers. She summoned a Parliament at Westminster, Jan. 7, 1327, which voted the King's deposition, and his son EDWARD was proclaimed in his stead. EDWARD was removed to Berkeley Castle, and by order of ISABELLA and MORTIMER, was murdered in the most cruel manner. The wicked career of the Queen and her paramour was checked in the following reign; for MORTIMER being seized in Nottingham Castle, was afterwards hanged on a gibbet at Tyburn, 1330; while ISABELLA was confined during the remainder of her life to her castle at Risings, Norfolk.

Roger Mortimer, a Welsh Baron, paramour of Queen ISABELLA, wife of EDWARD, was executed at Tyburn, 1330.

Edward III. was the eldest son of Edward II.
A.D. 1327—1377.

A   WARS.

1. A Scottish army under BRUCE invaded England, but it resulted in a peace, by which EDWARD was induced to recognise the complete independence of Scotland, and to restore the regalia, 1328.

2. EDWARD, in support of EDWARD BALIOL (son of JOHN BALIOL), a claimant of the crown of Scotland, invaded that country, and gained a decisive victory over the Regent DOUGLAS at Halidon Hill. In this conflict, 30,000 of the Scots and 15,000 of the English were killed; while BALIOL was made King, July 19, 1333.

3. On the death of PHILIP IV. of France, in 1328, EDWARD, in right of his mother ISABELLA, daughter of that monarch, claimed the crown of France. In 1337 he assumed the title of King of France, and quartered the French Lilies with the Arms of Eng-

land. His next step was to make friends with a noted brewer of Ghent, named JACOB VON ARTAVELDT, who had great influence in Flanders, the quarter fixed upon for commencing the attack. The English on this occasion, under EDWARD's command, gained their **first great Naval Victory** over the French off Sluys, capturing 230 sail of the enemy, June 24, 1340.

4. **Battle of Auberoche** (Perigord), in which the French were defeated by HENRY, Earl of Derby, Oct. 23, 1345.

5. **Battle of Cressy,** in which PHILIP of France was signally defeated by EDWARD and the BLACK PRINCE, then only 15 years old. The English army, consisting of 30,000 men, was commanded by the PRINCE OF WALES, the Earls of NORTHAMPTON and ARUNDEL, and Lord Ross, the King himself heading the body of reserve. The French forces were 120,000 men, under the command of ANTHONY DORIA, CHARLES GRIMALDI, and the Count of Alençon, brother to the King, who had charge of the third division. The loss of the English was very small, but that of the French was tremendous, being 1200 knights, 1400 gentlemen, 4000 men-at-arms, 30,000 of inferior rank, a large number of the French nobility, the King of MAJORCA, the Dukes of LORAINE and BOURBON, the Count of Alençon, and JOHN, the blind King of Bohemia, whose standard, on which were embroidered in gold three ostrich feathers, with this motto, *Ich Dien* (I serve), was seized and given to the Prince of WALES, who, in memory of that day, bore three ostrich feathers in his coronet, with the same motto, Aug. 26, 1346.

6. **Battle of Neville's Cross,** near Durham.—Instigated by PHILIP of France, DAVID II. of Scotland invaded England while EDWARD was prosecuting the French war. In the absence of her husband, Queen PHILIPPA raised an army, which was commanded by Lord PERCY, who defeated the Scots at Neville's Cross, 15,000 of whom were slain, and their King taken prisoner, Oct. 17, 1346. DAVID was released in 1357, on payment of 100,000 marks.

7. **Calais,** after a siege of 11 months, was surrendered to EDWARD, by JOHN DE VIENNE, the governor, Aug. 4, 1347; and remainded in the hands of the English 210 years, being retaken by the Duke of GUISE in the last year of the reign of MARY, Jan. 7, 1558. On this occasion it was, that six heroic citizens of Calais presented themselves before EDWARD for execution on condition that he would spare the garrison, all of whom he had resolved to put to death. EUSTACE DE ST. PIERRE, JAMES WISANT, PETER WISANT, JOHN DARCE, and two others, therefore, appeared, bareheaded, and barefooted, with ropes about their necks, before the English monarch, and laid at his feet the keys of *their city.* EDWARD ordered them to be led to execution, but was *induced to pardon* them through the supplication of his generous

ueen, who not only saved the lives of the unfortunate men, but
ve them an entertainment in her tent, provided them with clothes,
d on dismissing them, presented each with six pieces of gold.
DWARD ordered the inhabitants to quit Calais, which he peopled
ith English, and made it a market for tin, lead, wool, and leather.

8. **Battle of Poitiers.**—War being renewed with France, the
LACK PRINCE gained a great victory over JOHN, King of that
untry, at Maupertuis, near Poitiers, making him and his son
HILIP prisoners, Sept. 19, 1356. There were now two royal
isoners in England, DAVID of Scotland and JOHN of France.

9. The BLACK PRINCE espoused the cause of PETER THE
RUEL, of Castile, against his brother HENRY, who had driven him
om his throne, and was victorious at the **Battle of Najara,**
pain, April 3, 1367. The result of this encounter replaced PETER
the throne of Castile, but involved France and England in
rther hostilities, which arose from the BLACK PRINCE being
mpelled to tax his French subjects heavily to defray the ex-
nses he incurred in the Spanish war. PETER was afterwards
urdered by his brother HENRY.

10. The people of **Limoges** revolted from the BLACK PRINCE,
t he re-captured the town and ordered all the inhabitants to be
t to death, 1370.

11. The English fleet, under the Earl of PEMBROKE, was
arly destroyed off La Rochelle, by HENRY, King of Castile,
72.

B   **CHIEF EVENTS.**

EDWARD, in the 15th year of his age, was crowned at West-
inster by the Archbishop of CANTERBURY, Jan. 29, 1327; a
gency, with LANCASTER at its head, being appointed by Parlia-
ent to manage the affairs of the kingdom, which in reality were
der the control of the Queen and MORTIMER.

EDWARD married PHILIPPA of Hainault, Jan. 24, 1328.

In the year 1340, **Gunpowder** was improved and brought
to general use, by SCHWARTZ, a German monk; THOMAS
LANKET, of Bristol, set up looms for weaving woollen cloths,
hich are called after his name; copper money was first used in
eland and Scotland.

A Treaty of Peace between England and France was con-
uded for two years, 1342.

Cannon was first used by EDWARD in the battle of Creasy,
46; and in 1348 Stephen's Chapel, now the House of Commons,
as built.

The **Statute of Labourers** was passed, compelling peasan
to work for low wages, or be punished in the **Stocks,** then erecte
in every parish, 1349; and in the same year the **Order of th
Garter** was instituted by EDWARD.

A terrible pestilence, called the **Black Plague,** or the Blac
Death, wasted the inhabitants of England, destroying in Londc
alone upwards of 50,000 persons, 1349. There was also a **Secon
Plague,** in 1361, and another in 1369.

The **Second Statute of Labourers** was enacted for regt
lating artificers' and labourers' wages, 1351.

The **Statute of Treason** was enacted, and the Parliame
which passed it was called the "**Blessed Parliament,**" 135
This statute defines high treason, and limits it to seven offences,
which the following are the chief:—

1. Devising the King's death, or waging war against hi
within his realm.

2. Giving aid to the King's foreign enemies in his kingdom.

3. Violating either the Queen or the wife of the heir apparen

4. Slaying the Chancellor or Judges while engaged in tl
discharge of their judicial functions.

The **Statute of Provisors,** forbidding the presentation
benefices by the POPE, and securing the rights of all patrons
livings, upon which the Pontiff had encroached, was passed, 1353

EDWARD, by way of retaliation, entered Scotland in Januar
1356, and with fire and sword devastated the country as far
Edinburgh. This inroad the Scots called **Burnt Candlemas.**

A formidable insurrection of the peasants against the nobh
broke out in France, 1358.

The **Treaty of Bretigny,** called the **Great Peace,** betwee
England and France, was signed May 8, 1360. The followir
terms were agreed upon by this treaty :—

1. That King JOHN should be liberated and pay as his ransoi
three million crowns of gold, equal to £1,500,000 of our preset
money.

2. That EDWARD should renounce all claim to the crown (
France, as well as the possessions of his ancestors; and have instea
Calais, Guisnes, Montreuil, Ponthieu, Poitou, Guienne, Perigon
Agenois, Limousin, Quercy, Angoumois, Bigorre, and Rovergne.

After JOHN's liberation he went over to Paris for the purpo
of carrying out the stipulations of the treaty, but finding it im
possible to raise the money demanded for his ransom, he we
so honourable that he returned to England, and received for h
residence the Savoy Palace in the Strand, where he died, 1364.

The Black Prince married Joanna the fair, daughter of Edmund, Earl of Kent, who was beheaded in the early part of this reign through the intrigues of Isabella and Mortimer, 1361.

A statute was passed directing that all pleadings in law courts were to be conducted in English, instead of in French, 1362.

Owing to the state of his health, the Black Prince was compelled to give up the command of the army in France and return home, in consequence of which England had lost by 1374 all her French possessions except Calais, Bordeaux, Bayonne, and a few places on the Dordogne.

A statute was enacted for abolishing **Peter's Pence,** 1365.

The Parliament, called the **Good,** assembled in 1376, and passed an ordinance of banishment and confiscation against Alice Perrers, the King's mistress, with whom the people had become disgusted, but it was repealed in 1377.

Until this time the Lords and Commons in Parliament occupied the same chamber, but ever since they have sat in separate halls. The **Speaker** of the House of Commons was appointed in 1376, Peter de la Mare being the **First** to occupy that position.

The growing power of the House of Commons may be inferred from their establishing the following rights :—

1. The illegality of raising money without their consent.

2. No alteration to be made in the laws without the concurrence of both Houses of Parliament.

3. The right of the Commons to investigate public abuses, and to impeach public ministers.

Edward introduced the title of **Duke,** and created the Black Prince Duke of Cornwall and Earl of Chester, which dignities have been inherited by the Prince of Wales ever since. The **Heralds'** College and **Doctors'** Commons were erected, and the **Admiralty Court** established.

Windsor Castle was rebuilt by William of Wykeham, and made into a royal palace. Gold coin, chimneys, and glazed windows came into more general use. Justices of the Peace were appointed *by statute.*

Edward died at Shene (now Richmond) June 21, 1377, and was buried at Westminster Abbey.

C   **CELEBRATED PERSONS.**

Wallingford, Astronomer, and Abbot of St. Albans, died 1366.

John Gower, was contemporary with CHAUCER, who called him the "Moral Gower." His chief works are " Vox Clamantia," and " Confessio Amantis," the latter being a poem of 30,000 verses about love. He is said to have become a Professor of law in the Inner Temple. (1320—1402).

The Black Prince, eldest son of EDWARD III., was so called from the colour of his armour. The victories of Cressy and Poitiers were gained by this Prince, who was distinguished for his modesty, bravery, generosity, and military talents. Towards the end of his life, however, he perpetrated a piece of cruelty which must ever remain a blot upon his character. Having recaptured the town of Limoges, which had revolted from him, he ordered all the inhabitants to be slain, while he himself was carried on a litter to see the carnage. The bad state of his health obliged EDWARD to return to England, where, after a lingering illness, he died, and was buried in Canterbury Cathedral. (1330—1376).

Ralph Higden, a monk of Chester, author of a History of the World, from Adam to the year 1357.

Henry Knighton, to whom we are indebted for a History of England from the year 950 to the Deposition of RICHARD II.

Geoffrey Chaucer, called "The Father of English Poetry," was born in London. He was the noted author of the " Canterbury Tales." (1328—1400).

Sir Robert Knolles was born in Chester, and rose from a common soldier to be a general. Rochester bridge (Kent) was built by him. (1317—1407).

Thomas Bradwardin, called the Profound Doctor, became Archbishop of Canterbury, and was distinguished as a divine, philosopher, and mathematician. (1290—1349).

William Occam, designated the Invincible Doctor, was a disciple of DUNS SCOTUS. Having written against the Pope, JOHN XXII., he was in consequence excommunicated. (1280 —1347.)

Matthew of Westminster, a monk, author of a History of England from the creation to the present reign, called " Flowers of History."

William of Wykeham, a famous architect, who built Windsor Castle, founded Winchester School, and New College, Oxford. He was the son of a poor family in Hampshire, and became Bishop of Winchester, and Lord Chancellor of England. (1324—1404).

John Froissart, who wrote a History of the French Wars. (1337—1401).

John Barbour, a Scotch divine, who became Archdeacon of Aberdeen, and Chaplain to King David Bruce. He wrote a Metrical Chronicle of Robert Bruce. (1320—1395).

John Wickliffe, a celebrated English divine, called the "Morning Star of the Reformation," was educated at Merton College, Oxford, where he took the degree of Doctor in Divinity. He preached and wrote against the corruptions of the Romish Church, which induced Pope Gregory I. to issue a bull, ordering Wickliffe to be imprisoned and brought to trial. In accordance with this injunction Wickliffe, accompanied by John of Gaunt and Lord Henry Percy, appeared at St. Paul's, before Courteney, Bishop of London, to answer for his conduct, 1378, but owing to some altercation between Lancaster and the Bishop, a tumult ensued and put a stop to the proceedings. The Great Reformer was again summoned (1378) before a Synod held in the Archbishop's palace at Lambeth; but on this occasion he owed his safety to the King's mother (Richard II.), who sent a message by Sir Lewis Clifford, forbidding the Bishops to condemn him. Wickliffe's doctrines were similar to those which were restored at the Reformation. He formed a society of pious men to preach throughout England, 1379. He translated the Bible into English; wrote a tract on "The Schism of the Popes," and composed a treatise called "The Last Age of the Church," &c.

Wickliffe died from an attack of palsy, at Lutterworth, in Leicestershire, Dec. 31, 1384. Forty years afterwards, his bones were taken up and burnt by order of the Council of Constance, and his ashes cast into the river Swift.

Sir John Mandeville, born at St. Albans, traveller and historian. His Itinerary, which gives an account of his travels in Asia, China, and Palestine, is one of the earliest works written in English prose. (1301—1372).

Sir Walter Manny, a native of Belgium and page to Queen Philippa, founder of the Priory of Chartreux (now Charterhouse School) and Sir John Chandos, both distinguished warriors.

The Captel de Buch, captain to the Black Prince, was so distressed at his master's death, that he died the following year, 1377.

Blind Harry, one of the earliest English poets, author of a History of William Wallace in verse.

Dante and Petrarch, Italian poets, flourished in this reign.

Richard II. was the son of the Black Prince, and grandson of Edward III. A.D. 1377—1399.

A   WARS.

1. The truce between England and France having expired before the death of EDWARD III., CHARLES renewed hostilities, and invaded the English Channel with his French and Spanish forces, who burnt Plymouth, Hastings, Portsmouth, and other places, 1377.

2. A Scotch pirate named MERCER, having carried off some vessels from the port of Scarborough, JOHN PHILPOT, a London citizen, equipped a small squadron at his own expense and went in pursuit of the enemy, whom, after a severe battle, he took prisoner and captured sixteen Spanish ships, 1378.

3. The war with France continuing, and being further aggravated by the Papal Schism, England favouring URBAN VI., and France, CLEMENT VII., both of whom aspired to the Popedom, a large force, under SPENCER, Bishop of Norwich, was sent to Ghent to assist the burghers against the Count of Flanders and his supporter, the King of France. The Bishop routed 30,000 French and Flemings, captured Gravelines, Dunkirk, and several other places; but on learning that the King of France, with a mighty army, was marching to oppose him, he disbanded his forces, and was obliged to negotiate for a safe return to England, 1383.

4. The allied forces of France and Scotland, entered Northumberland and took three castles; but RICHARD marched against them with 60,000 men, and burnt Edinburgh, Melrose, Dunfermline, Perth, and Dundee. Jealousies, however, between the King and LANCASTER caused a sudden disbanding of the army, after which RICHARD returned to England without accomplishing anything of importance, 1385.

5. As the Duke of LANCASTER had married CONSTANTIA, a daughter of DON PEDRO the Cruel, he marched into Spain at the head of 20,000 men to enforce his claim to the throne of Castile, which ended in the Duke's concluding a marriage between his daughter, by CONSTANTIA, and HENRY, Prince of Austurias, the heir of Castile, 1386. The descendants of this union, which took place in 1388, ruled over Spain for many generations.

6. In order to assist the King in regaining his power, of which he had been deprived by the Duke of GLOUCESTER, DE VERE, Duke of Ireland, levied an army in Wales, but was defeated by the Earl of DERBY, eldest son of the Duke of LANCASTER, at **Badcot Bridge,** in Oxfordshire, 1387.

7. Battle of Otterburn, near Newcastle, between the English under the Earl of NORTHUMBERLAND and his two sons, and the Scots under Sir WILLIAM DOUGLAS, whom Sir HENRY PERCY slew. The advantage was with the Scotch, and the English leaders were made prisoners, Aug. 10, 1388. The ballad of "Chevy Chase" is founded upon this battle.

CHIEF EVENTS.

RICHARD being only eleven years old at his coronation, which took place at Westminster, July 16, 1377, a council of regency was appointed to govern the kingdom during his minority.

War expenses obliged Government to impose upon every individual a tax, which varied according to his *status;* a duke being assessed at £6 13s. 4d.; a labourer fourpence for himself and wife, 1379.

The Bible was translated into English by WICKLIFFE, 1380.

Insurrection of the Peasantry, headed by WAT TYLER, a blacksmith, and two priests, named JACK STRAW and JOHN BALL. Money being required for prosecuting the war with France and Scotland, it was enacted that every person above fifteen years of age should pay a tax of one shilling. TYLER refused to pay the tax for his daughter because she was under the specified age, and struck the collector dead for his insolence. The bystanders applauded TYLER's conduct, and appointed him their leader. About 100,000 of the insurgents assembled at Blackheath, June 12, 1381, and after committing some terrible outrages, they were put down by the King, who met them in Smithfield; while TYLER, on account of his disrespectful behaviour to RICHARD, was struck with a dagger by SIR WILLIAM WALWORTH, Lord Mayor of London, and killed by STANDISH, one of the King's knights. The Dagger was afterwards added to the city arms, where it has been ever since retained. The insurgents made the following demands :—

1. A general pardon for their past offences, and the abolition of slavery.

2. The reduction of rent on land to 4d. per acre.

3. Free liberty to buy and sell in all fairs and markets.

Charters granting their requests were issued, but shortly after revoked; while 1500 of the offenders, including BALL and STRAW, were hanged.

RICHARD married ANN of Bohemia, sister of the Emperor VENCESLAUS, Jan. 14, 1382.

RICHARD was compelled by Parliament to remove from office his favourites, DE VERE, Duke of Ireland, and DE LA POLE, Earl of Suffolk, the latter being impeached; and to entrust the Government to a council of regency, at the head of which was one of his uncles, the Duke of GLOUCESTER, 1386.

The Parliament designated both "Merciless" and "Wonderful" assembled, in which five of the King's councillors were convicted of high treason, 1388 :—

The Archbishop of York; ROBERT DE VERE, Duke of Ireland; MICHAEL DE LE POLE, Earl of Suffolk, all condemned to exile, and their estates confiscated.

Sir ROBERT TRESILIAN, the Chief Justice, was hanged, and Sir NICHOLAS BRAMBER, the late Lord Mayor of London, beheaded. DE VERE and DE LA POLE escaped from the country.

RICHARD recovered his authority and took the government into his own hands, 1389.

The First Navigation Act, ordering goods to be imported and exported in English vessels only, was passed, 1390.

In order to check the power of the Pope in England, and to prevent any evasion of the Statute of Provisors, another Act was passed (1393), called the **Statute of Praemunire,** which enjoined, that "whoever procures at Rome any translations, processes, excommunications, bulls, instruments, or other things, which touch the King, against him, his crown, and realm, and all persons aiding and assisting therein, shall be put out of the King's protection, their lands and goods forfeited to the King's use, and they shall be attached by their bodies to answer to the King."

A **Truce** of 25 years was concluded between England and France, 1396.

As the Duke of GLOUCESTER resumed his plots, RICHARD ordered him to be arrested and conveyed to Calais, where it is believed he was murdered, 1397.

The Duke of NORFOLK having intimated to the Duke of HEREFORD, that RICHARD intended to oppress the Duke of LANCASTER and the two Dukes of ALBEMARLE and EXETER, the words were repeated to the King by HEREFORD. A quarrel therefore arose between NORFOLK and HEREFORD, who agreed to settle the matter by single combat at Coventry. Just as the two Dukes were entering the lists, RICHARD, who wanted to rid himself of both these formidable rivals, interposed, and banished NORFOLK for life and HEREFORD for ten years. These arbitrary proceedings showed that the King's power had become absolute, 1398.

In this reign the Court of Chancery became a Court of Equity. Peers were first Created by Patent. Cards were invented to amuse CHARLES VI. of France, who had become *insane.* The LORD HIGH ADMIRAL and the CHAMPION are said to late from the present reign; the business of the latter being to throw down the gauntlet at the King's coronation as a challenge to any who denied his title to the throne. This custom is still continued. Westminster Hall was rebuilt.

While RICHARD was quelling a rebellion in Ireland, HEREFORD, now Duke of Lancaster by his father's death, landed at Ravenspur, in Yorkshire (July 4, 1399), where he was joined by the Earls of NORTHUMBERLAND and WESTMORELAND, and soon found himself at the head of 60,000 men. RICHARD hastened from Ireland, but on his return he was made prisoner, and deposed by Parliament on the alleged ground of tyranny and incapacity, Sept. 30, 1399; while the vacant throne was claimed by HENRY, Duke of Lancaster.

RICHARD was imprisoned in Pontefract Castle, Yorkshire, where he was murdered and his body shown to the Londoners for identification in 1400. His remains were interred at King's Langley, Herts, but removed by HENRY V. to the royal sepulchre at Westminster.

C   CELEBRATED PERSONS.

Fitz-Allen, Archbishop of Canterbury, was impeached and banished the kingdom.

Wat Tyler, or Wat the Tyler, leader of an insurrection in Essex, was killed, 1381.

Michael de la Pole, a favourite of the King, was created Chancellor in 1383, and Earl of Suffolk in 1386. Being accused of treason, he escaped to France, where he died, 1388.

Robert de Vere, Earl of Oxford, and a favourite of the King. RICHARD created him Duke of Ireland, and he was the first Englishman that bore the title of **Marquis**, which he received on his being made Marquis of Dublin. In 1388 he fled into the Low Countries, where he died a few years afterwards.

Duke of York, was appointed Regent during RICHARD'S absence in Ireland, but joined LANCASTER against the King, 1399.

John of Gaunt, or Ghent (so called from the place of his birth, in Belgium), Duke of Lancaster, fourth son of EDWARD III., was the friend and protector of WICKLIFFE. Died 1399.

Henry Bolinbroke, Duke of Hereford, was the eldest son of JOHN OF GAUNT, Duke of Lancaster. In 1398 RICHARD banished him for ten years, and on the death of HENRY's father, in 1399, confiscated his estates and made his exile perpetual. HEREFORD, who by his father's death had become Duke of Lancaster, invaded England (1399) to recover his estates, effected the deposition of his cousin RICHARD II., and was crowned HENRY IV.

REMARKS.

None of the Anglo-Norman kings had such extensive dominions as HENRY II., who, on his accession to the throne, was in possession of England and a third of France.

The slavish condition of the English people was such that, before the time of HENRY II., parents were debarred from bequeathing property to their children.

At the time that Ireland came under the English crown, it was divided into five parts—Leinster, Meath, Munster, Ulster, and Connaught; each of which was governed by a king.

When RICHARD was on his death-bed, he sent for GOURDON, and asked him what reason he had for taking away his life, to which the archer answered, "You killed with your own hands my father and my two brothers, and you intended to have hanged me. I am now in your power. You may revenge yourself by giving me over to the most severe torments, but I shall endure all this with pleasure, since I have rid the world of a tyrant." Instead of punishing the man, RICHARD ordered that he should have a sum of money given him, and be set at liberty. Marcadée, however, one of the English generals, disobeyed his dying master's injunction, seized GOURDON, had him flayed alive, and then hanged.

The **Laws of Oleron** were a famous code of laws, relating to maritime affairs, the framing of which has by some writers been ascribed to RICHARD I. of England, when he was in the Island of Oleron, in France, 1194. These regulations were considered so wise and just that they have been made the basis of naval constitutions by all the European nations.

During the reign of RICHARD, who spent little time in England, and who could scarcely speak a word of Saxon, the wages of a labourer were 2d. a day. An ox was sold for 3s. and a sheep for 4d.

When King JOHN consented to hold the kingdom as the Pope's vassal, he had to take the following oath :—

"I, JOHN, by the grace of God, King of England, and Lord of Ireland, in order to expiate my sins, from my own free will and the advice of my Barons, give to the Church of Rome, to Pope INNOCENT and his successors, the kingdom of England, and all other prerogatives of my crown. I will hereafter hold them as the Pope's vassal. I will be faithful to God, to the Church of Rome, to the Pope my master, and his successors legitimately elected. I promise to pay him 1000 marks yearly; to wit, 700 for the kingdom of England, and 300 for the kingdom of Ireland."

About the year 1170 the **Waldenses** rose from one PETER WALDO, a native of Lyons, who founded a society for preaching the Gospel among the poor. His followers were called "The poor men of Lyons."

The object of the **Lateran Councils** was to issue decrees, for the due regulation of the doctrines, discipline, and practice of the Romish *Church*. The **Fourth** Council declared the doctrine of **Transubstantiation** o be an article of faith, and obliged all persons to partake of the .ord's Supper at least once a year, on pain of excommunication, 1215.

Archbishop HUBERT held a national synod at Winchester, and .assed some canons, of which we note the following:—

1. Clergymen were forbidden to read the prayers during divine ervice, either too slowly or too quickly.

2. The Eucharist was not to be used more than once a day with-ut urgent necessity.

3. **Clandestine Marriages** were forbidden, and married persons not o go beyond the seas, unless they published their mutual consent.

The **Saladin Tax** was imposed upon ecclesiastical revenues by the 'ope, who wished to raise a crusade.

Another council was held in London by the Pope's legate, when he number of sacraments was stated to be seven, 1237.

Some blood, represented as a portion of that shed by our Saviour n the cross, was carried with great pomp and solemnity to Westmin-ter Abbey, 1250.

The Commons for the first time were admitted into the English 'arliament, 1265.

In 1268 a council was held in which certain constitutions, brought rom Rome, were published ; one authorises laymen to administer aptism in cases of necessity ; another ordains the marriage of people n public ; the third is levelled against pluralists.

Most of the councils held in the reign of HENRY III. were for the urpose of exacting money from the clergy for the benefit of the 'ope.

By the canon law, which chiefly emanated from the Popes, and as introduced into England in the reign of STEPHEN, it was decreed hat children born before marriage were legitimate. This was contrary o the laws of the realm.

The **Amalgamation** of the **Saxon** and **Norman races** was completed in he reign of JOHN. English literature dates from the thirteenth cen-ury, the **Ormulum** being the oldest specimen of the English language xtant.

The most prominent effects of the Crusades were :—

1. Extension in **Commerce**, and improvements in Agriculture, Navi-ation, Ship-building, and Literature.

2. Society became more civilised by intercourse with foreign ations.

3. A better feeling towards each other was engendered in the minds f all those who were engaged in the Crusades.

4. They were the means of exalting the middle classes at the ex-ense of the nobles, who, in order to raise money for going to the East, isposed of their estates to the former on disadvantageous terms.

The followers of WICKLIFFE were called **Lollards,** either from WALTER LOLLARD, a German who flourished about the year 1315 ; or from the word *Lolium,* signifying *tares ;* because they were considered by their enemies as **tares** in the field of God's church. Those who embraced the doctrines of the great Reformer were also *nicknamed* **Gospellers.**

The Tax, called **Annates** or **First-fruits,** by which the Popes claimed the first year's income from every clergyman on his appointment to a living, was abolished by the statute of provisors.

In the reign of EDWARD I. the title of **Baron** was exclusively confined to those whom the King summoned to Parliament.

EDWARD I. demanded one-half of the revenues of the Church in his dominions. He was opposed by the clergy, who at last were obliged to yield, 1292.

The **Statute of Mortmain** was so called, because the members of ecclesiastical bodies were considered dead in the eye of the law, consequently any property held by them was said to be *"in mortua manu,"* that is, in dead hands.

The soldiers of EDWARD III. wore plate armour instead of chain-mail, which was found to be very heavy for purposes of warfare.

The first recorded instance of Parliamentary impeachment was in the reign of EDWARD III. (1376), when Lords LATIMER and NEVILLE, as well as four merchants, were impeached for asking the King to remove the market from Calais, and for charging him a high interest for a loan of money.

The second instance was that of M. DE LA POLE, who was impeached in the following reign.

In the reign of RICHARD II. one-third of the land belonged to the Church.

The term **Subsidy** was first given to the Parliamentary grant in the reign of RICHARD II.

ANNE of Bohemia, first consort of RICHARD II., was the daughter of the Emperor CHARLES VI., and granddaughter of JOHN, King of Bohemia, who was slain at the Battle of Cressy. She was called "The Good Queen Anne," because she pleaded in behalf of the remaining rebels of WAT TYLER's insurrection.

Side-saddles, horned head-dresses, and the modern metal pin were introduced by her.

In 1344, EDWARD III. struck golden florins, which were valued at 6s., but being rated too high they were recalled, and the gold noble of 6s. 8d. coined. The motto, *"Dieu et mon droit,"* was on the coinage of this monarch, and it is said to have been originally adopted in reference to the claim to the French crown.

Elegant literature during this period was neglected ; Aristotelian logic and metaphysics being the leading subjects to which the students *directed* their attention.

atin language was principally employed by the learned during
genet period.

tecture was much improved by foreign workmen, who were
to a society called **Free Masons**, and were employed by the

e reign of EDWARD III., the wages of a labourer for hay-making
ny a day ; a reaper of corn received three pence ; a master
carpenter, fourpence.

t was sold for 3s. 4d. per quarter ; a fat ox cost 16s., a sheep
, hog 3s. 4d., ale 1d. per gallon, a pair of shoes 4d., and
1s. 4d. per yard. Threepence in the fourteenth century
equal to five shillings at the present time.

hief manufactures of England were those of leather and wool ;
s being tin, cheese, butter, honey, tallow, skins, worsted stuffs,
rs.

name Plantagenet is derived from *Planta Genista*, the Latin
room, which was worn as an emblem of humility by the first
NJOU when going on a pilgrimage to the Holy Land. From
mstance his successors took their crest and surname.

Plantagenets proper reigned from HENRY II. (1154), to
II. (1399), a period of 245 years.

LEADING EVENTS AND PRINCIPAL DATES

OF THE PLANTAGENET PERIOD.

., first King of the Plantagenet line, ascended the
le ...　...　...　...　...　...　...　...　A.D. **1154**
k of Venice, supposed to have been the first in
pe, was established ...　...　...　...　...　...　**1157**
introduced by Henry II. ...　...　...　...　...　**1159**
Exchange are said to have been invented by the
|　...　...　...　...　...　...　...　...　...　.**1160**
avers were established at Nottingham　...　...　**1161**
stitutions of Clarendon passed ...　...　...　...　**1164**
vas murdered ...　...　...　...　...　...　...　**1170**
conquered, and annexed to England　...　...　...　**1172**
. does penance at Becket's shrine　...　...　...　**1174**
better administration of justice, England was
led into circuits　...　...　...　...　...　...　**1176**
indows used for the first time in England ...　...　**1177**

The importance of the Magnet in Navigation is said to
have been mentioned in some verses of a Troubadour
Poet, at the court of the German Emperor ... A.D. 1181
Linen manufactured in England 1189
The Jews were massacred 1189
Cyprus conquered by Richard I. 1191
The Teutonic Order of Knights was founded in Palestine 1192
Richard was made prisoner by the Emperor, Henry VI,
of Germany 1192
Richard returned to England 1194
John's accession to the throne 1199
William, King of Scotland, did homage to the King of
England; the word "Parliament" began to be used in
England... 1200
The Inquisition was established by Pope Innocent III. ... 1204
The Pope placed England under an Interdict 1208
The first bridge in London was finished... 1209
The Albigenses, from Albi, a town in Languedoc, were first
persecuted 1209
John was deposed by the Pope 1212
John did homage to the Pope for England 1213
Battle of Bouvines, in which John's allies, Otho and
Ferrand, were defeated by Philip of France 1214
Magna Charta was granted 1215
Henry III. accedes to the throne 1216
Battle of Lincoln 1217
The sciences of Geography and Astronomy began to receive
special attention 1220
The re-building of Westminster Abbey was commenced ... 1221
Begging Friars made their first appearance in England ... 1221
Henry III. confirmed Magna Charta 1225
Cider was first made in England 1231
The first commercial company in England was established 1232
English houses were first covered with tiles 1246
University College, Oxford, was founded 1249
The first gold coin was struck by Henry III. 1257
The Parliament of Oxford, called the "Mad Parliament,"
was held 1258
Battle of Lewes was fought 1264
The House of Commons was founded by Simon de Mont-
fort, Earl of Leicester 1265
Battle of Evesham, in which Leicester was slain 1265
Edward I. accedes to the throne 1272

<table>
<tr><td>Richard II. accedes to the throne ...   .</td><td>A.D. 1377</td></tr>
<tr><td>The Bible was translated into English by Wickliffe...   ...</td><td>1380</td></tr>
<tr><td>Wat Tyler's rebellion ... ...</td><td>1381</td></tr>
<tr><td>The city of London was divided into wards ... ...</td><td>1386</td></tr>
<tr><td>Battle of Otterburn ... ...</td><td>1388</td></tr>
<tr><td>The Duke of Gloucester was murdered ... ...</td><td>1397</td></tr>
<tr><td>England invaded by Henry, Duke of Lancaster, who de-
throned Richard II.   ... ...</td><td>1399</td></tr>
</table>

HOUSE OF LANCASTER.

Henry IV. was the eldest son of John of Gaunt, fourth son of Edward III. A.D. 1399—1413.

A   **WARS.**

1. OWEN GLENDOWER having been deprived of certain lands by his neighbour, Lord GREY of Ruthyn, and finding that Parliament would not redress his wrongs, raised some Welsh forces, and defeated Lord GREY, making him prisoner, 1400.

2. **Battle of Knighton**, Radnorshire, in which GLENDOWER vanquished the English under Sir EDWARD MORTIMER, who was taken prisoner, June 12, 1402.

3. The Scots under HEPBURNE having entered England, were defeated at **Nesbit Moor** (Northumberland), by the Earl of NORTHUMBERLAND, who slew their leader, and seized all their booty, June 22, 1402.

4. The Scots again invaded England, but were vanquished at **Homildon Hill**, Northumberland, by the PERCIES, who captured their leader, Earl DOUGLAS, and several other of the Scotch nobility, Sept. 14, 1402.

5. **Battle of Shrewsbury.**—The Earl NORTHUMBERLAND, his brother, the Earl of WORCESTER, and his son, HOTSPUR, being exasperated with HENRY, because he had, contrary to the custom of that age, forbidden them to release Earl DOUGLAS and others whom they had taken in war, headed a rebellion against him for placing the Earl of MARCH on the throne, and were joined by SCROPE, Archbishop of York, GLENDOWER, and Earl DOUGLAS, *who was liberated* on condition that he would aid them with some

Scottish Knights. While marching to Wales in order to join his forces with those of GLENDOWER, HOTSPUR was intercepted by the royal troops under the command of the King, and a most obstinate and bloody battle was fought at Hateley Field, three miles from Shrewsbury, which ended in the defeat and death of HOTSPUR. The number on each side was about 14,000 men, nearly half of whom were killed or wounded. WORCESTER and DOUGLAS were taken prisoners. The former was beheaded, and the latter treated as a prisoner of war, July 21, 1403.

6. Battle of Grosmont, Monmouthshire, in which the Welsh under GLENDOWER were defeated by the English under PRINCE HENRY, March 11, 1405.

7. The Earl of NORTHUMBERLAND, who had already been pardoned by the King, entered into a new conspiracy with THOMAS MOWBRAY, Earl of Nottingham, and RICHARD SCROPE, Archbishop of York, for placing the Earl of March on the throne; but the Archbishop and MOWBRAY were taken by a stratagem of RALPH NEVILLE, Earl of Westmoreland, and executed; while NORTHUMBERLAND fled into Scotland, 1405.

8. Prince HENRY gained another victory over GLENDOWER at Mynydd pwl Melyn in Brecknockshire, and took his son prisoner, May 14, 1405.

9. The Earl of Northumberland having made another attempt to overthrow HENRY, was defeated and slain at Bramham Moor, near Tadcaster, by Sir THOMAS ROKEBY, Sheriff of Yorkshire, Feb. 18, 1408.

10. As France considered the truce with England nullified by the deposition of RICHARD II., she became very troublesome during the disturbances in Wales, ravaged the south coast of the country, and burnt Plymouth.

B   CHIEF EVENTS.

The usurpation of the crown by HENRY IV. caused the wars between the houses of York and Lancaster, which are usually called "The Wars of the Roses." The lawful heir to the throne of England at this time was the Earl of March, the great grandson of LIONEL, Duke of Clarence, who was the third son of EDWARD III., while John of Gaunt, or Ghent, the father of HENRY IV., was the fourth son of that monarch.

On the day of his coronation, which took place in Westminster Abbey, Oct. 13, 1399, HENRY issued a proclamation, declaring that he became King:—

1. By *right of conquest*, which was absurd.

2. By RICHARD's resignation and nomination of him as his successor, which was false.

3. By virtue of his being the next **male-heir** to the late King, which was not true.

Parliament not only adjudged the crown to HENRY IV., but also passed an act securing the succession to the House of Lancaster :—

1. On HENRY's eldest son, whom his father had already created Earl of Chester, Duke of Cornwall, and Prince of Wales.

2. Upon the heirs of the Prince of Wales.

3. On the Prince's three brothers and their children.

At the King's coronation, **Knights** of the **Bath** were created; which was a military order consisting of 46 esquires. They were designated **Knights** of the **Bath**, because they had to bathe themselves before the honour was conferred, to signify the purity and loyalty of their minds, 1399.

Shortly after the King's accession, the Earls of KENT and HUNTINGDON, half brothers to Richard II., headed a conspiracy for restoring the deposed sovereign; but the Earl of RUTLAND, one of the confederates, revealed the plot, and the conspirators were executed, 1400.

Wishing to ingratiate himself with the Romish Church, HENRY induced Parliament to pass the **Statute Heretico Comburendo**, by which it was enacted, that all persons guilty of heresy, who refused to abjure, or who relapsed after abjuration, should be publicly burnt, 1401; and in the same year Justices of Assize were empowered by Parliament to fine sheriffs £100 who made false returns.

A statute was enacted, making it felony to cut out any person's tongue, or to put out his eyes, 1403.

The Lack-learning Parliament assembled (1404), in which the Commons suggested that the King ought to seize the revenues of the clergy, because they possessed one-third of the lands of the kingdom, and because they rendered him no personal service.

The Commons did not succeed. This Parliament was so called, because the sheriffs were ordered by the King to return none but "illiterate persons."

While JAMES, son of ROBERT III. of Scotland, was on a journey to France, he was unjustly seized by HENRY in 1405, and detained as a prisoner in England till 1424, when £40,000 were paid for his ransom.

The Isle of Man was granted to Sir JOHN STANLEY, 1406.

.   England was ravaged by a terrible pestilence, which destroyed in London alone 30,000 persons, 1407.

.   The circulation of foreign money was forbidden by law in 1410.

This reign is remarkable for the increasing power of the House of Commons, and also for the great number of noblemen who were executed for high treason.

HENRY's anxiety to keep that crown which he had usurped shortened his days.   He died in the flower of his age, at Westminster, March 20, 1413, and was buried at Canterbury.

C   **CELEBRATED PERSONS.**

Rev. Sir William Sawtre, of St. Oswyth's in London, and formerly rector of Lynn, in Norfolk, was burnt as a heretic for denying Transubstantiation and other Popish dogmas, 1401. SAWTRE was the first that suffered by *fire* for his religious opinions.

Henry Percy, surnamed Hotspur on account of his valour and irritable temper, was the son of the Earl of NORTHUMBERLAND. He defeated Earl DOUGLAS at the battle of Homildon Hill, but afterwards united with him and OWEN GLENDOWER against the King, and was slain at the battle of Shrewsbury, 1403.

Richard Scrope, Archbishop of York, conspired against the King, but was taken and executed, 1405.   This is the first instance in English history of an Archbishop suffering capital punishment.

Earl of Northumberland, father of Hotspur, assisted HENRY in obtaining the crown, but afterwards tried to dethrone him. The King seems to have made an enemy of the Earl by forbidding him to receive any ransom for DOUGLAS, and other distinguished persons whom he had made prisoners at the battle of Homildon Hill.   NORTHUMBERLAND was slain by Sir THOMAS ROKEBY, at Bramham Moor, Yorkshire, 1408.

Sir William Gascoigne, a noted judge, was born in Yorkshire, and became distinguished for his impartial administration of justice.   He imprisoned the Prince of Wales (afterwards Henry V.) for striking him in open court, which is the first instance recorded in English history of a judge doing right in opposition to power.   GASCOIGNE was struck for condemning one of the Prince's dissolute companions.   (1350—1413).

Owen Glendower, a descendant of LLEWELLYN, the last Prince of Wales.   On applying for redress for the loss of some lands, he was told by one of the Peers that they " cared not for barefooted rascals."   Instigated by his wrongs, therefore, he took

ιp arms and gained several advantages over HENRY's f
Being afterwards defeated, he disbanded his army.   Died, 14

Edmund Mortimer, uncle to the Earl of March, the l
heir to the throne, was taken prisoner by OWEN GLENDOWI
1402.   The Earl of NORTHUMBERLAND and his son HOT
wished to ransom him, but were forbidden by HENRY.   MORT
married a daughter of GLENDOWER, and joined the King's ene

Archibald Douglas united with HOTSPUR against HI
but was taken prisoner at Shrewsbury.   After his release he
to France and was slain at Verneuil, 1424.

Sir Richard Whittington, a rich London tradesman
erected at his own cost Bartholomew and Christ's Hospital
who is often spoken of as " *Whittington and his Cat.*"   This
from his having realised the greater portion of his wealth l
first vessel, a ship which was called the " Cat."   Died 1430.

John Van Eyck, a Dutchman, invented oil-painting.
—1441).

═══════════════

Henry V. was the eldest son of Henry IV.
A.D. 1413—1422.

A   **WARS.**

1. France being in a deplorable condition in conseq'
the imbecility of CHARLES VI., and the Burgundian
leanist or Armagnac factions struggling against each
supreme power, HENRY was induced to take advantage of
fused state of that country.   He therefore demanded in
crown of France, as the heir of ISABELLA, daughter of P
This claim, which was invalid, being rejected, he comme
and having landed at the mouth of the Seine with 30
invested Harfleur, Aug. 17, 1415, and the town capitul
22, 1415, by which time war and disease had destroyed
of his army.

2. Battle of Agincourt or Azincourt, in wh
gained a decisive victory over the French, of whom 1(
ding D'ALBERT, Constable of France, the Dukes of BA
and ALENÇON, were killed, and 14,000 taken pris
whom were the Dukes of ORLEANS and BOURBON, v
of the English did not exceed 1600, with whom mus
the Duke of YORK and the Earl of OXFORD, Oct. 25.

3. HENRY again invaded France and took **Caen**, Sept. 4, 1417; he also captured **Rouen**, which had been besieged by the English nearly six months, Jan. 19, 1419, and concluded a **Treaty at Troyes**, called "**The Perpetual Peace**," by which it was agreed:—

That HENRY should marry CATHERINE, daughter of CHARLES VI., govern the kingdom of France in that monarch's name, and at his death succeed to the crown: that both kingdoms should be for ever under one sovereign, but each to have its own laws and privileges, May 21, 1420.

4. The Dauphin persisted in hostilities, and the French and Scotch under JOHN STEWART, Earl of Buchan, defeated and slew HENRY's brother, the Duke of CLARENCE, at Beaugé, in Anjou, March 22, 1421.

5. The King raised more troops, took **Meaux** after a siege of seven months, and subdued nearly all France north of the Loire, May 1422.

B　　　　　　　　**CHIEF EVENTS.**

HENRY V., when Prince of Wales, was called "Mad-cap," on account of his dissipation, but after his coronation, which took place April 9, 1413, he greatly changed for the better, dismissed his former bad companions, and received into his friendship Chief Justice GASCOIGNE, the judge whom he struck in court. He also liberated the Earl of MARCH, restored their forfeited estates to the family of NORTHUMBERLAND, ordered the body of RICHARD II. to be removed from King's Langley to Westminster Abbey, and founded three religious houses near Sheen, where RICHARD's soul was to be prayed for night and day.

It having been reported that the Lollards, headed by Sir JOHN OLDCASTLE, intended to seize the King, and that 25,000 were to assemble in St. Giles's Fields, Jan. 7, 1414, HENRY, accompanied by his guards, marched to the place at the appointed time and found only 80 persons, many of whom were executed.

A conspiracy, for placing the Earl of MARCH on the throne, was formed by Lord SCROPE, Sir THOMAS GREY, and the Earl of CAMBRIDGE, all of whom were condemned and executed, July 1415.

The revenue of the English crown amounted to £35,700. Calais is said to have cost England upwards of £19,000 a year.

Parliament granted tonnage, poundage, and also duties on leather and wool, to the King for life, 1415.

HENRY pledged his crown jewels for £20,000, because he required the money for his French wars; and is said to have been the first English King that established a proper navy, which was now separated from the Merchant Service. A ship called the **Great Harry** was built for him at Bayonne.

The assassination of the Duke of BURGUNDY, which took place in the presence of the DAUPHIN, contributed very much to HENRY's success in France, 1419.

Coining was declared to be treason by a statute passed in 1417.

In this reign there was a sanguinary persecution of the Lollards, commenced by Archbishop ARUNDEL; the streets of London were lighted by lanterns, one being placed at every door; moated castles began to fall into disuse; the fraternity of St. Giles without Cripplegate was founded by HENRY, who first instituted *Garter King at Arms*, and appointed a new Herald, by the title of *Agincourt King at Arms*. Guildhall was finished, and within its walls the King and Queen were entertained by Sir RICHARD WHITTINGTON (mentioned in the last reign), who was thrice Lord Mayor of London.

The King died from a fistula, at the Bois de Vincennes (France), August 31, 1422. His remains were brought to England and buried at Westminster Abbey, near the shrine of EDWARD the Confessor.

C   **CELEBRATED PERSONS.**

Thomas Arundel, Archbishop of Canterbury, was a noted persecutor of the Lollards. (1353—1413).

David Gam, a brave Welsh officer, was sent to ascertain the number of the enemy on the eve of the battle of Agincourt, and on his return informed the King that there were enough to be killed, enough to be taken prisoners, and enough to run away. He was knighted by HENRY for his bravery while dying on the field of Agincourt, 1415.

Thomas Walsingham, a Benedictine Monk of St. Alban's, is said to have been one of the best of our Latin chroniclers. He wrote a History of England from 1273 to the year 1422.

Sir Thomas Grey, united with others in a conspiracy to dethrone HENRY in favour of the Earl of MARCH, but was seized and executed, 1415.

John Huss, a celebrated Reformer, born about 1370, at Hussinetz, in Bohemia. During his rectorship of the University of Prague, he became acquainted with the writings of WICKLIFFE, from the study of which he was convinced of the errors of Popery. A Reformation in the University through his means was therefore *effected, to stop which* two decrees were issued by the Archbishop.

He was supported in spreading his doctrines by Winceslaus, King of Bohemia, till 1414, when he was summoned before the Council of Constance. Though the Emperor Sigismund promised Huss that he should not be hurt while going and returning from the Council, yet the members of that assembly decreed, " That no faith is to be kept with heretics," and Huss on refusing to retract his opinions was degraded and burnt alive, 1415.

Jerome of Prague, so called from the place of his birth, was a disciple of John Huss, with whom he was summoned to appear before the Council of Constance. Finding that Huss was imprisoned, he went to Uberlingen, where he applied for a safe-conduct, which he failed to obtain. On returning home he was arrested, sent in chains to Constance, cruelly tortured and consigned to the flames, which he endured with great fortitude, 1416.

Thomas, Earl of Salisbury, a renowned warrior, who displayed such courage during the French wars, that he was called the **Mirror of all martial men.** He was killed at the siege of Orleans, Oct., 1428.

Sir John Oldcastle, usually called, in right of his wife, Lord Cobham, was a distinguished soldier of the day. Having embraced the doctrines of Wickliffe, he was condemned as a heretic by Archbishop Arundel, and roasted alive in St. Giles's Fields. He was the *first nobleman* that suffered martyrdom for his religious opinions. (1360—1417).

John Sanspeur, Duke of Burgundy, entered into an alliance with the English against the Dauphin, in 1417; and in 1419, the Dauphin and Duke, who had apparently become reconciled, had an interview at Montereau, for concerting measures against the English, when Tannegui du Chastel, a leading adviser of the Dauphin, slew Burgundy in his presence, Sept. 10. Henry was benefited by this treacherous deed, for the young Duke and the Queen sought his protection, and the Treaty of Troyes followed soon afterwards.

Thomas Occleve, poet, flourished about the year 1420.

Henry VI. was the only son of Henry V.

A.D. 1422—1461.

A.   **WAR WITH FRANCE.**

1. On the death of Charles VI., and by virtue of the treaty of Troyes, Henry VI. was proclaimed King of France, but was

opposed by Charles VII., who seized the crown of France. This caused a bloody struggle between the two countries. The first contest took place at Crevant-on-Yonne, where the Earl of Salisbury defeated the allied forces of the French and the Scotch, July 31, 1423.

2. **Battle of Verneuil,** in which the English, under the Duke of Bedford, gained a complete victory over the French and Scotch who were commanded by the Count de Narbonne, and the Earls of Douglas and Buchan, Aug. 17, 1424.

3. **Battle of Herrings,** was fought at Rouvrai, while the English were besieging Orleans. As the season of Lent had begun, the Regent sent from Paris to the English camp at Orleans a convoy of salt fish or herrings, under the direction of a celebrated general named Fastolf. By order of Charles, the Earl of Clermont, at the head of 3000 men, attacked this convoy, but he was routed with great slaughter, no fewer than 120 principal officers being slain, Feb. 12, 1429. This engagement was called the "Battle of Herrings," on account of the fish which the English were taking to their friends at Orleans.

4. At **Patay** the French defeated the English, who lost upwards of 2000 men, Lord Talbot being taken prisoner, June 18, 1429.

5. Charles sent his troops into **Normandy** and conquered it, 1449.

6. Charles succeeded in making himself master of all the English possessions in France, except Bordeaux and Calais, 1451, the year in which the English were expelled from that country.

7. Bordeaux having revolted, the English under Talbot, Earl of Shrewsbury, were sent to quell the insurgents, but were defeated by the French at the **Battle of Chatillon,** and Talbot slain, July 20, 1453.

WARS OF THE ROSES.

These were civil wars between the Houses of York and Lancaster for the crown of England. The contest commenced in the reign of Henry VI., extended over a period of thirty years, and ended with the death of Richard III. They were called the "Wars of the Roses," because the Lancastrians wore as a badge of distinction a red rose; and the Yorkists a white one. Twelve battles were fought between the contending parties, six of which took place during this reign.

1. **Battle of St. Albans** (Herts.), between the King and the Duke of York, in which the Earls of Northumberland and Stafford, Lord Clifford, and the Duke of Somerset, were

slain; while the King was wounded and made prisoner, May 23, 1455. The Duke of YORK was now elected for the second time Lord-Protector.

2. **Battle of Bloreheath** (Staffordshire), in which the Lancastrians were defeated, and Lord AUDLEY slain by the Yorkists under the Earl of SALISBURY, Sept. 23, 1459.

3. **Battle of Northampton,** in which the royal army, under the Duke of BUCKINGHAM, was defeated by the Earl of WARWICK. BUCKINGHAM and the Earl of SALISBURY were slain, and the King was again made prisoner, while MARGARET and her son escaped to Scotland, July 19, 1460.

4. **Battle of Wakefield,** between MARGARET, the Queen of HENRY VI., and the Duke of YORK, in which the latter, with 3,000 Yorkists, perished on the field of battle; while his son, the Earl of RUTLAND, was murdered by Lord CLIFFORD, Dec. 31, 1460.

5. **Battle of Mortimer's Cross** (Herefordshire). EDWARD, Earl of March, now Duke of York, hearing of the death of his father and younger brother, at the head of 23,000 men, advanced and defeated the combined forces of the Welsh and Irish under the Earls of PEMBROKE and OXFORD, and Sir OWEN TUDOR, the husband of the widow of HENRY V., Feb. 2, 1461. Four thousand of the Lancastrians perished in this battle, while Sir OWEN TUDOR and others were beheaded the next day.

6. **Second Battle of St. Albans,** in which Queen MARGARET defeated the Yorkists, under the command of the Duke of NORFOLK and the Earl of WARWICK, and secured the person of the King, Feb. 17, 1461. In this conflict 2000 Yorkists perished.

B　　　　　　**CHIEF EVENTS.**

HENRY being only nine months old when he came to the throne, the Government of England was entrusted to the Duke of GLOUCESTER, and that of France to the Duke of BEDFORD. The imbecile CHARLES VI. died six weeks after his son-in-law, HENRY V. of England, 1422, and this induced the DAUPHIN to seize the crown of France under the title of CHARLES VII. After the English had besieged Orleans for some time, and were on the point of taking it, the siege was raised by JOAN OF ARC (May 8), and two months later CHARLES was crowned at Rheims, July 17, 1429.

A statute was passed, enacting that the right of voting for Knights of the Shire should be limited to freeholders, whose estates realized at least 40s. a year, 1430.

HENRY was crowned at Westminster, May 24, 1431; and in the same year Pope MARTIN V. convened the Council of Basle, its leading object being the reunion of the Eastern and Western Churches.

The Treaty of Arras was concluded between the French and the Duke of BURGUNDY, when the latter withdrew from the English Alliance, because he was displeased with BEDFORD for marrying JACQUETTA of Luxemburg without his consent, 1435. CHARLES regained Paris, 1436.

In 1444 a two years' **truce** with France was concluded at **Tours** by the Earl of SUFFOLK, who also negotiated a marriage between HENRY and MARGARET of Anjou, which took place in 1445. By the terms of this treaty England was to cede to her father Réné, Maine and Anjou.

The **Statute of Labourers,** compelling servants to give notice before leaving their situations, was enacted, 1444.

There was a remarkable insurrection headed by one **Jack Cade,** an Irishman, who assumed the name of MORTIMER, the rightful heir to the throne. He defeated the King's forces and slew their leader, Sir HUMPHREY STAFFORD, at **Seven Oaks** (Kent), but being forsaken by his followers, he was captured by IDEN, the sheriff of that county, and slain, 1450.

In 1453 HENRY became insane, and in 1454 YORK was appointed Protector, but the King, on his recovery, resumed the reins of Government, and released YORK's rival, SOMERSET, from the Tower. In 1455 the King became ill again, and YORK was made Protector a second time, but in 1456 HENRY recovered, and with the consent of Parliament resumed his authority.

An insincere reconciliation took place in London between the Yorkists and Queen MARGARET, March 25, 1458.

The **Inventions and Discoveries** of this reign were:—**Printing,** invented by JOHN GEINSFLEISH, of Haarlam, in the Netherlands, 1430, but the art was improved by LAURENTIUS COSTER, by cutting letters upon *separate wooden blocks*, 1431.

FAUST printed the Psalms from wooden blocks, 1442.

GUTTENBURG cut types from metal in 1444.

The roller printing press was invented in 1450; and the types cast by SCHOEFFER came into use, 1452.

HALLEY's Comet was first observed in 1456; and the manufacture of glass in England began in 1457.

The Senegal river was discovered by the Portuguese, 1440, the Azores by GONZALLO VELLO, a Portuguese, 1448, and Cape Verde Islands by ANTONIO DE NOLI, a Genoese, 1449. Engraving on copper was invented by a goldsmith of Florence, 1458; and **Etching** by ALBERT DURER, a German. **Electricity** was also *discovered* by OTTO DE GUERICK of Germany.

The **Public Institutions** founded in the present reign were:—

All Souls' College, Oxford, was founded by Archbishop **Chicheley** (1437); Queen's College, Cambridge, by Queen **Margaret** (1448); Eton College (1440); and King's College, Cambridge, by the King (1441); Glasgow University was established (1454); and Magdalen College, Oxford, was also founded by **William Wayneflete**, Bishop of Winchester (1458).

In this reign the title **Viscount** was adopted, Lord **John Beaumont** being the first English Viscount; the **National Debt** is said by some historians to have commenced; the first **Lord Mayor's Show** took place; freedom of speech was granted to both Houses of Parliament; foreigners were allowed to be tried by juries consisting of one-half of their own countrymen; and the winter of 1434 was so severe, that the Thames was frozen from London to Gravesend.

Ten years after **Henry** had been deposed, he was found dead in the Tower, May 22, 1471. He was interred at Chertsey (Surrey).

C   CELEBRATED PERSONS.

Joan of Arc (known as "**La Pucelle**," or the "**Maid of Orleans**"), the daughter of a small French farmer, was born at Domremy, in Lorraine, 1410. While employed as a servant at an inn, she fancied St. Michael, the tutelary angel of France, had authorised her to rescue her country from its enemies. The French gained some important advantages by the assistance of **Joan**, who raised the **Siege of Orleans** in 1429, then invested by the English, and saw the King crowned at Rheims by the title of **Charles VII.**, both of which events she had foretold should be accomplished. **Joan** was captured at the siege of Compiègne, and delivered up to the English, who ordered her to be tried by **Cauchon**, Bishop of Beauvais. She was unjustly condemned as a heretic and witch, and burnt in the market place of Rouen, May 30, 1431.

Eleanor Cobham, Duchess of Gloucester, was ordered to do public penance on an alleged charge of treason, 1431.

John, Duke of Bedford, third son of **Henry IV.**, was born in 1389. During the reign of **Henry V.**, he greatly distinguished himself in the French wars, and on the death of that monarch was appointed Regent of France. Died at Rouen, Sept. 1435.

Henry Chicheley, Archbishop of Canterbury, attended **Henry V.** during that monarch's wars with France. He founded All Souls' College, Oxford, and beautified Lambeth Palace.

Cardinal Beaufort, Bishop of Winchester, younger son of **John of Gaunt**, was tutor to **Henry V.** and VI. (1370—1447).

Humphrey, Duke of Gloucester, brother of BEDFORD and of HENRY V., was a great patron of learning. He was called the "Good Duke HUMPHREY." He was arrested for treason at Bury St. Edmunds, and is thought by some to have been murdered, by order of MARGARET, 1447.

Sir Humphrey Stafford, leader of the Royal army against JACK CADE, by whom he was slain, 1450.

William de la Pole, Duke of Suffolk, was impeached of high treason, and banished for five years, but was seized and beheaded, off Dover, while on his way to France, 1450.

Jack, or John Cade, leader of an insurrection, was slain, 1450.

John Talbot, Earl of Shrewsbury, so distinguished for the valour he displayed in the wars with France, that he was called the **English Achilles.** He was sent by HENRY V. as commander-in-chief to Ireland, where he put down a rebellion. He afterwards went to France and served under the Duke of BEDFORD. He was engaged at the siege of Orleans, and taken prisoner at the Battle of Patay, 1429. On recovering his liberty he was appointed Lord-Lieutenant of Ireland, in which office he continued for some time. He returned to France in order to command the English army, and was slain at the siege of Chatillon. (1373—1453).

Duke of Somerset, the King's minister, was slain at the Battle of St. Albans, while fighting for his sovereign, May 22, 1455.

Sir John Fastolf, born at Yarmouth in 1377, was a distinguished general. He defeated the French at the "Battle of Herrings." Died 1459.

Humphrey, Duke of Buckingham, was engaged in the French wars during the reigns of HENRY V. and VI. He was slain by the Yorkists at the Battle of Northampton, July 10, 1460.

Owen Tudor, a Welshman, married CATHERINE, widow of HENRY V. From this union sprang the Earl of RICHMOND, who was crowned under the title of HENRY VII. OWEN TUDOR was slain at Mortimer's Cross, 1461.

John Lydgate, a monk of Bury St. Edmunds, poet and imitator of CHAUCER. Chief Works, "Siege of Troy," and "Fall of Princes." (1375—1461).

John Capgrave, a divine and historian. (1393—1464).

Thomas a Kempis, a distinguished German monk, author of a book on "The Example of Christ." He died 1471.

Thomas Littleton, an eminent judge, author of a famous *work on "Tenures."* He became steward of the court to HENRY

VI., and was appointed by EDWARD IV. one of the judges of the Court of Common Pleas. Died 1481.

Sir John Fortesque, an able judge and author, was appointed in 1442 Chief Justice of the King's Bench. He subsequently went to Flanders, where he wrote his admirable book entitled "De Laudibus Legum Angliae." He returned to England with Queen MARGARET, and was made prisoner at the Battle of Tewkesbury, 1471; but being pardoned by EDWARD IV., he retired to his seat in Gloucestershire. (1395—1485).

THE LEADING EVENTS AND PRINCIPAL DATES OF THE LANCASTER PERIOD.

	A.D.
Henry IV. crowned	1399
Owen Glendower and other nobles revolt	1400
An Act passed for burning heretics	1401
William Sawtre burnt for Lollardism	1401
Battle of Nesbit Moor	1402
Battle of Homildon Hill	1402
Battle of Shrewsbury, and death of Hotspur	1403
Scrope, Archbishop, of York, executed	1405
A plague destroyed 30,000 persons in London	1407
The doctrines of Wickliffe condemned by the Council of London	1408
The University of St. Andrews founded	1411
Death of Henry IV., and accession of his son Henry V.	1413
Battle of Agincourt, or Azincourt	1415
London lighted for the first time with lanterns	1415
Siege of Rouen	1419
Sir Richard Whittington Lord Mayor of London for the third time	1419
Treaty of Troyes	1420
Death of Henry V., and accession of Henry VI.	1422
Prince James of Scotland released	1423
Battle of Crevant	1423
Battle of Verneuil	1424
Siege of Orleans raised by Joan of Arc	1429
Coronation of Henry VI. at Paris, and execution of Joan of Arc	1431
Printing from wooden Blocks commenced by Coster	1431
The Council of Florence declared Purgatory to be an article of faith	1439
The Portuguese began the African Slave Trade	1443

Metal Types cut by John Guttenburg ... ... A.D.
The King married Margaret of Anjou ... ...
Queen's College, Cambridge, founded by Margaret ... ...
Jack Cade's Rebellion ... ...
The English had lost all their possessions in France, except
    Calais ... ...
Expulsion of the English from France ... ...
Insurrection of the Duke of York ... ...
University of Glasgow founded ... ...
Wars of the Roses begin; first Battle of St. Albans ... ...
Mahomet II. took Constantinople, and overthrew the Greek
    Empire ... ...
Pawnbroking introduced ... ...
Battle of Bloreheath ... ...
Battle of Northampton ... ...
Battle of Wakefield ... ...
Battle of Mortimer's Cross ... ...
Second Battle of St. Albans ... ...
Out of these six engagements, the Yorkists were victorious
    in the first three, and in the fifth, which was fought at
    Mortimer's Cross.

HOUSE OF YORK.

Edward IV. was the eldest son of Richard, Duke of Y
and lineal descendant of Lionel, the third son
Edward III.   A.D. 1461—1483.

A   **WARS.**

1. Battle of Towton (Yorkshire), in which EDWARD ga
a decisive victory over the forces of Queen MARGARET; 28
Lancastrians being slain, among whom were the Earls of W
MORELAND and NORTHUMBERLAND, March 29, 1461.   HENRY
MARGARET fled into Scotland.

2. Battle of Hedgley-Moor (Northumberland), in w
Margaret's forces, consisting of English, Scotch, and French, u
Lord HUNGERFORD, were routed by the Yorkists under 1
MONTAGUE, brother to the Earl of WARWICK, April 25, 1461.

3. **Battle of Hexham,** in which MONTAGUE gained another ctory over Queen MARGARET. The Duke of SOMERSET and ords HUNGERFORD and ROOS were afterwards beheaded, May 15, 164.

4. **Battle of Barnet.**—This conflict took place on Easter nday, when the forces of MARGARET were defeated by EDWARD V., and all the Lancastrian leaders, as well as WARWICK and his other MONTAGUE, fell on the bloody field, April 14, 1471.

5. **Battle of Tewkesbury,** in which the Lancastrian army as completely routed, 3000 of whom fell on the field. The Earl Devonshire and Lord WENLOCK perished; Queen MARGARET id her son EDWARD were taken prisoners, May 4, 1471.

B **CHIEF EVENTS.**

EDWARD was 20 years old at his coronation, which took place une 29, 1461; and in the same year Parliament recognized his tle to the throne by hereditary descent through the family of IONEL, the third son of EDWARD III.

The King's marriage with ELIZABETH GREY, daughter of Sir ICHARD WOODVILLE, and widow of Sir JOHN GREY, greatly dis- leased his brothers and the Earl of WARWICK, and laid the undation of jealousy between the Nevilles and Woodvilles, 1464.

A Truce for 15 years was concluded with Scotland, the con- itions being—

1. That Prince ALEXANDER of Scotland, who had been cap- ured by the English, should be released.

2. That the Scots should in no way assist the Lancastrians, 464.

An Insurrection broke out at **Edgecote,** near Banbury, in hich the Royal forces, under the Earl of PEMBROKE and Sir ICHARD HUBERT, were defeated by the insurgents under Sir OHN CONGERS, who took up arms at the supposed instigation of VARWICK and the Duke of CLARENCE, July 26, 1469. The Earl f PEMBROKE and his brothers were taken prisoners and beheaded, revenge for the death of Sir HENRY NEVILLE, whom the oyalists had murdered in cold blood.

An Insurrection in favour of the Lancastrians broke out in incolnshire; but the rebels, under Sir ROBERT WELLES, were efeated by the King at **Erpingham,** near Stamford, March 12, 470. The confession of some of the offenders showed that the bject of the rebellion was to place CLARENCE on the throne. VARWICK and CLARENCE being proclaimed traitors, escaped to the ourt of LOUIS XI. of France, where a reconciliation between

WARWICK and MARGARET of Anjou took place, and the **Treaty** **Amboise** followed in 1470, by which it was agreed—

1. That HENRY should be restored to the throne.

2. That Prince EDWARD should marry WARWICK'S seco daughter.

WARWICK and CLARENCE returned from France, invad England, and compelled EDWARD to flee the kingdom, 147 HENRY was now proclaimed King. EDWARD, however, during l brief exile, obtained from his brother-in-law, the Duke of Bu GUNDY, some forces, with which he landed at the mouth of t Humber. Being afterwards joined by his brother CLARENCE completely routed the Lancastrians in two battles, and made Que MARGARET prisoner; while her son Prince EDWARD was murder by the Dukes of CLARENCE and GLOUCESTER, 1471.

The supplies voted by parliament not being sufficient for tl expenses of EDWARD, who was preparing to invade France, l obtained, without the consent of Parliament, large sums of mon from his subjects, which were called **"Benevolences,"** or fr gifts, 1474.

Treaty of Pecquigny.—To regain the English possessic lost in France during the preceding reign, EDWARD invaded tl country; but the expedition ended in the Treaty of Pecquigr Aug. 29, 1475, by which it was agreed—

1. That LOUIS should pay EDWARD 75,000 crowns witl fifteen days.

2. That EDWARD should receive the sum of 50,000 crowns year.

3. That the Dauphin of France should marry ELIZABETH England.

4. That 50,000 crowns should be paid to EDWARD for tl ransom of MARGARET.

Printing was introduced into England by CAXTON, who s up his first Printing Press at Westminster, 1471; and the fir book printed in England was called "The Game and Playe (Chesse," 1474. The export of plate or coin without royal pe: mission was made felony, 1478. In this reign **Posts** were estal lished. Horsemen were placed at twenty miles apart betwee Scotland and London, by which means despatches were conveye at the rate of 100 miles a day.

To PETER HALE, a German mechanic, we owe the **Inventio:** of **Watches.** Violins were invented by an Italian.

England was ravaged by a **Plague,** which made terrible havo *among the* inhabitants, 1479.

St. George's Chapel, Windsor was built, and St. Catherine's Hall, Cambridge, founded by ROBERT WOODLARK.

Those who followed the House of Lancaster in this reign were reduced to the most abject poverty, many (among whom was the Duke of EXETER) went barefoot in the streets begging their bread.

EDWARD manifested great cruelty in putting to death 1400 persons of high rank. He died April 9, 1483, and was buried in Westminster Abbey.

CELEBRATED PERSONS.

C

Sir Henry Neville, one of the leaders of the Yorkshire insurgents, was captured and put to death, 1469.

Richard Neville, Earl of Warwick, cousin to the King, was born in 1420. He was called the **King-maker,** because he deposed and reinstated HENRY VI. and EDWARD IV. He is said to have maintained on his estates 30,000 persons. Slain at the Battle of Barnet, 1471.

George Neville, Duke of Bedford, was stripped of his title by Parliament on the alleged ground of his poverty, 1478.

Duke of Clarence, brother to the King, was convicted of treason, and found dead in the Tower; though some writers assert that he was drowned in a butt of Malmsey wine, 1478.

Margaret, daughter of RENÉ, titular King of Sicily, and Queen of HENRY VI., remarkable for her courage and perseverance. Her life was made wretched by the incapacity of her husband. Died, 1482.

William Caxton, a native of Kent, noted for introducing into England the art of Printing, which he acquired during his residence in the Low Countries. He set up a press in the Almonry at Westminster in 1471, and issued in 1474 the first book printed in England. (1410—1491).

Elizabeth Woodville, widow of Sir JOHN GREY, was so admired by EDWARD that he married her. One of their children, the Princess ELIZABETH, married HENRY VII., by which the Houses of York and Lancaster were united.

Margaret Beaufort, Countess of Richmond and Derby, was a descendant of JOHN OF GAUNT, and mother of HENRY VII. She had three husbands, the first being EDMUND TUDOR, Earl of Richmond; the second, Sir HENRY STAFFORD; and the third was THOMAS, Lord STANLEY, who became Earl of DERBY. Christ and St. John's Colleges, Cambridge, are said to have been founded by her. Died 1509.

Edward V. was the eldest son of Edward IV. A.D. 1483.

B   **CHIEF EVENTS.**

EDWARD being only thirteen years of age at his father's death, his uncle RICHARD, Duke of Gloucester, was appointed Protector of the realm during the King's minority. In order to surmount every obstacle calculated to interfere with his nefarious plans, RICHARD put to death Earl RIVERS, Lord HASTINGS, and Sir JOHN GREY. Lord HASTINGS and JANE SHORE had been accused of plotting against the Protector's life by sorcery. JANE SHORE was the wife of a rich goldsmith in London, but she had been seduced from her husband by EDWARD IV. She was obliged to do penance for the charge, and at last (having been reduced to extreme poverty) is said to have died some years afterwards in a ditch near London, ever since called **Shoreditch.**

GLOUCESTER, wishful to obtain the crown for himself, commenced his cruel proceedings by lodging in the Tower EDWARD and his brother RICHARD, whom he ordered to be put to death. The two Princes were smothered with bolsters while fast asleep in bed, by Sir JAMES TYRREL, DIGHTON, FOREST, and SLATER. Their bodies were buried under a staircase, and remained undisturbed for more than 200 years. While the Tower was undergoing repairs (1674) the bones of the youths were discovered, and placed by order of CHARLES II. in Westminster Abbey, where a monument, designed by Sir CHRISTOPHER WREN, was erected to their memory. EDWARD reigned only two months, and was never crowned.

C   **CELEBRATED PERSONS.**

Anthony Woodville (Earl Rivers), and Sir JOHN GREY, put to death by RICHARD on account of their close relationship to the King, 1483.

Dr. Ralph Shaw, brother to the Lord Mayor of London, *preached a sermon at St. Paul's Cross, in which he unjustly attempted to convince his audience that* EDWARD IV. had been previously married to lady BUTLER, in consequence of which, EDWARD V. being his son by ELIZABETH WOODVILLE, was illegitimate, and therefore not the rightful heir to the crown, June 22, 1483.

Lord Hastings, a warm friend of EDWARD V., was beheaded by order of the Protector, June, 13, 1483.

Sir Richard Brackenbury, Lieutenant of the Tower, was ordered by the Protector to murder the young Princes, but he refused to imbrue his hands in innocent blood. He was therefore commanded to give up the keys and custody of the Tower for one night to Sir JAMES TYRREL, who with others carried out the Protector's instructions, 1483.

Richard III. was the youngest son of Richard, Duke of York, and brother of Edward IV.   A.D. 1483—1485.

A   **WARS.**

Battle of Bosworth Field (Leicestershire), in which RICHARD III. was defeated and slain by the Earl of RICHMOND (afterwards HENRY VII.) Aug. 22, 1485. This contest lasted about two hours, during which a thousand of RICHARD's men were slain, among whom were the Duke of NORFOLK, Lords BRACKENBURY, RADCLIFF, and FERRERS. After the battle, the crown of RICHARD was found in a hawthorn bush, and placed upon RICHMOND's head by Lord STANLEY, who afforded material aid in gaining the victory, not only by the 7000 men he brought, but also in warding off a blow levelled at RICHMOND by the King. This battle put an end to the Wars of the Roses, and established **a new dynasty** on the throne of England.

B   **CHIEF EVENTS.**

RICHARD, with his consort ANNE, daughter of the famous Earl of WARWICK, the king-maker, was crowned at Westminster, July 6, 1483; and in order to establish himself more firmly among the inhabitants of the north, with whom he was a favourite, repeated his coronation at York. Like most usurpers, RICHARD began his reign by dispensing favours; but these acts of kindness did not prevent plots which were formed against him.

A plan for placing HENRY TUDOR, Earl of Richmond, (
throne, was formed by MORTON, Bishop of Ely, who won o
his side the Duke of BUCKINGHAM, RICHARD's former adh
MORTON suggested that the crown should be offered to H
on condition of his marrying the Princess ELIZABETH of
eldest daughter of EDWARD IV. This plan met with approva
was immediately communicated to HENRY, with a request tl
would at once return to England. The day fixed for a g
insurrection in his favour was October the 18th, 1483. BUC
HAM collected his forces in Wales, and marched to the S
then rendered impassable by an extraordinary overflowing,
was called "The Great Flood," and "Buckingham's Fl
The latter name was probably given because it proved fatal
project. As the inundation continued for several days, the I
forces became short of provisions, and therefore deserted
Thus situated, he fled to the house of one BANNISTER, wh
formerly been a servant in his family. A reward of £1,000
offered for the apprehension of BUCKINGHAM, he was given
the Sheriff of Shropshire, through the treacherous conduct of
NISTER. The Duke was therefore condemned and execut
Salisbury, 1483.

RICHARD's Parliament met in January, 1484, and passe
following laws, which were the first drawn up in English; 1
or Norman-French being employed for that purpose up t
period :—

1. An Act, called Titulus Regius, was passed, by wh
was declared that RICHARD had a right to the throne bo
descent and choice of the people.

2. Benevolences were annulled, and the seizure o
person's goods before conviction forbidden.

3. Statutes for regulating commerce were enacted.

4. Another statute, usually designated Cutting off the Ei
was passed, by which the Alienation of Estates in Entail
made legal.

In the first year of this reign British Consuls were appo
by the King, who lessened the number of each nobleman's reta
or armed followers, and thereby prevented numerous quarrels.

On the death of his son, RICHARD declared his nephew.
DE LA POLE, Earl of Lincoln, heir to the throne, 1484.

The Sweating Sickness made its first appearance in Eng
1484.

The Earl of RICHMOND *set sail from Harfleur, in Norm*
with 3,000 men, and landed at Milford Haven (Wales) Aug

1485. Being now joined by 6,000 more, among whom were Sir WALTER HUNGERFORD, and Sir THOMAS BOURCHIER, HENRY marched to the field of battle, 1485.

RICHARD was killed at the battle of Bosworth Field, August 22, 1485, and buried at Grey Friars Church, Leicester.

C   CELEBRATED PERSONS.

Henry Stafford, Duke of Buckingham, not considering himself sufficiently rewarded for the aid he rendered RICHARD in obtaining the crown, joined a conspiracy to dethrone him. He was beheaded in the market place at Salisbury, 1483.

Henry Tudor, Earl of Richmond, afterwards HENRY VII.

Lord Stanley placed the crown on RICHMOND's head while on the field of battle.

Ratcliffe, Catesby, and **Lovel,** three wicked agents of the King.

Sir William Collingburn, executed for writing the following distich on the King and his nefarious agents :—

> "The Rat, the Cat, and Lovel our Dog,
> Rule all England under a Hog."

RICHARD's crest is said to have been a hog.

Ralph Bannister received the manor of Ealding in Kent, as a reward for his ingratitude to the Duke of BUCKINGHAM.

REMARKS.

The **House of York** and the **Plantagenet Line of Kings** ended with the death of RICHARD. The most marked features of the reigns of the Plantagenets were :—

1. A gradual decay of Feudalism and formation of a middle class of citizens.

2. Growth of the English constitution and consolidation of civil authority.

3. The manufacture of paper and the introduction of printing.

4. Rise of Lollardism, which tended to shake the Papal system in England.

5. Destruction of most of the nobility through the Wars of the Roses.

6. A constant struggle for liberty, and for restraining the power of the crown.

7. Great improvements in Arts, Commerce, and Literature.

8. Change in Architecture, by which the decorated style pas
into the perpendicular or florid style.

9. Translation of the Bible and spirit of free enquiry, which l
their influence in preparing the way for the Reformation.

10. The Amalgamation of the Norman and Saxon lines.

11. Change in the mode of warfare, effected both by the use of g
powder and the introduction of fire-arms.

12. Religious intolerance, followed by persecution.

During the Wars of the Roses, 100,000 Englishmen were kill
and many villages, churches, and castles were laid in ruins. 60 villa
and their churches within 12 miles of Warwick were demolished a
abandoned. It appears, from a statute passed in 1495 for regulat
wages, that the poor had to work very hard to procure the necessa
of life. From the middle of March to the same time in Septeml
labourers and artificers were ordered to begin work before 5 in
morning, and not to discontinue their labours till between 7 an
o'clock in the evening. They were allowed 2 hours each day
meals.

All clergymen, possessing a University degree, were formerly entit
Sir.

In the 15th century 40 new Universities were founded in Euro
Church livings were frequently bestowed on the ignorant ; while n
of literary attainments had to beg their bread.

Music appears to have been much cultivated.

This period has been spoken of as one of a most voracious charac
from the enormous quantities of food consumed.

The higher classes took four meals a day : breakfast, dinner, sup
and livery. The livery consisted of mulled wine and cakes, which t
took in their bed chambers.

The Lancaster and York Dynasties extended over 86 years.

THE LEADING EVENTS AND PRINCIPAL DAT

OF THE YORK PERIOD.

The Crown assumed by Edward IV.; Battle of Towton	A.D. 1
Henry VI. imprisoned in the Tower	1
Warwick's conspiracy against Edward IV.	1
Battle of Banbury	1
Battle of Stamford	1
Battles of Barnet and Tewkesbury ; death of Henry VI. in the tower	1
Printing introduced into England by William Caxton	1
St. Catherine's Hall, Cambridge, founded	1

LINE OF TUDOR.

Henry VII. was the son of Edmund Tudor and Margaret, daughter of John Beaufort, Duke of Somerset, son of John Beaufort, Earl of Somerset, who was an illegitimate son of Catherine Swynford and John of Gaunt, Duke of Lancaster, fourth son of Edward III.

Hence Henry VII. sprang from an illegitimate stock.
Edmund Tudor was the son of Owen Tudor, a Welsh gentleman, who married the widow of Henry V.

A.D. 1485—1509.

A   **WARS.**

1. An Insurrection under Lord LOVEL and HUMPHREY and THOMAS STAFFORD was easily suppressed by HENRY'S uncle, the Duke of Bedford. LOVEL escaped to the Duchess of BURGUNDY; HUMPHREY STAFFORD was executed; and THOMAS, the younger, was pardoned, 1486.

2. RICHARD SIMON, a priest of Oxford, instigated by the Duchess of BURGUNDY, sister of EDWARD IV., instructed one LAMBERT SIMNEL, the son of a baker (or joiner) at Oxford, to personate the Earl of WARWICK, son of the late Duke of CLARENCE.

SIMON and his pupil SIMNEL, a youth of fifteen years of age, landed in Dublin, where they were well received by THOMAS FITZGERALD, Earl of Kildare, the Lord Deputy of Ireland, and the young adventurer was proclaimed King, by the appellation of EDWARD VI. Being joined by JOHN DE LA POLE (son of the Duke of SUFFOLK, and ELIZABETH, eldest sister of EDWARD IV.), Lord LOVEL, and 2,000 Germans under MARTIN SCHWARTZ, they landed in Lancashire and advanced as far as Stoke, in Nottinghamshire, where the rebels, amounting to 8,000, were defeated by HENRY. The Earl of LINCOLN and FITZGERALD were slain; Lord LOVEL escaped, but was never heard of again; SIMON and SIMNEL were taken prisoners, the former being committed to close custody, while the latter was made a scullion, and afterwards a falconer, in the royal household, June 16, 1487.

3. HENRY being displeased with CHARLES VIII. for annexing **Brittany** to his crown, invaded France with 26,000 men; but in a few days the monarchs concluded a **Peace at Estaples**, by which it was agreed, that CHARLES should remove WARBECK from his dominions, and pay HENRY £149,000. Nov. 3, 1492.

4. In 1492 the English crown was claimed by a young man named **Perkin Warbeck**, son of a Jewish merchant living at Tournay, who appeared at **Cork**, and asserted that he was RICHARD, Duke of York (son of EDWARD IV.), said to have been murdered in the Tower. After appearing in Ireland he was invited to Paris by CHARLES VIII., who provided him with magnificent lodgings, settled on him a handsome pension, and gave him a guard for his person. When peace was concluded between the English and French monarchs at Estaples, WARBECK went to Flanders, where he was recognised by the Duchess of BURGUNDY as " her dear nephew," and the "*White Rose of England*," (1493.) In 1496 WARBECK proceeded to Scotland, where he was kindly received by JAMES IV., who gave him in marriage one of his kinswomen, Lady CATHERINE GORDON, daughter of the Earl of HUNTLY. To further the imposter's pretensions JAMES invaded England, but finding that the English would not join him, and not being satisfied with having all the trouble for nothing, plundered Northumberland, and returned home laden with spoils. Peace having been made with England, WARBECK next appeared in Ireland, and after remaining a short time in that country, he landed in Cornwall, 1497, where he found many followers. They besieged Exeter, and assembled at **Taunton** to the number of 7,000 men; but hearing the Royal forces were approaching, WARBECK deserted his followers, and fled to the **Sanctuary of Beaulieu** in Hampshire. He was made prisoner, and kindly treated by the King, till a secret correspondence between him and the Earl of WARWICK (*about eighteen* months after) for their escape was discovered.

The King accordingly ordered him to be tried and executed for high treason. WARBECK was hanged at Tyburn, and the Earl of WARWICK was beheaded a few days afterwards on Tower Hill, Nov. 1499.

5. **An Insurrection in Cornwall,** was caused by the levying of a tax voted by Parliament for prosecuting the war with Scotland. The insurgents were defeated by the King at **Blackheath,** near London, 1497. Two thousand of the rebels were slain, and their leaders, Lord AUDLEY, MICHAEL JOSEPH, and THOMAS FLAMMOCK were executed.

B   **CHIEF EVENTS.**

HENRY, knowing that he had no just right to the throne, began this reign by committing to the Tower EDWARD PLANTAGENET, the Earl of WARWICK, son of the Duke of CLARENCE, who was brother to EDWARD IV.; and he attempted to support his defective claim to the crown on the following grounds:—

1. By his descent from JOHN OF GAUNT, upon which the greatest stress was laid.

2. By right of conquest, as he was victorious at Bosworth Field.

3. By his projected marriage with ELIZABETH, daughter of EDWARD IV., by virtue of which it was expected that the rival Houses of York and Lancaster would be united. In consideration of the third claim, Parliament passed an act settling the crown upon HENRY and his heirs, 1485.

HENRY's coronation was postponed for a short time in consequence of the **Sweating Sickness** which broke out again in London, carrying off numbers of the inhabitants, among whom were the Lord Mayor and six Aldermen, 1485. The prominent symptoms of this disease were profuse perspirations, on account of which it was called the "Sweating Sickness." Unless checked, the malady proved fatal in 24 hours. The mode adopted for curing this terrible disease is said to have consisted in keeping the patient moderately warm, and administering to him cordials.

HENRY was crowned at Westminster by THOMAS BOURCHIER, Archbishop of Canterbury, Oct. 30, 1485; and as a reward for past services he created his uncle, JASPER TUDOR, Earl of Pembroke, Duke of Bedford, and Lord Stanley, Earl of Derby.

The Houses of York and Lancaster were united by HENRY's marriage with ELIZABETH of York, Jan. 18, 1486. The ends which the King kept constantly in view were:—

1. To retain his crown and humanise the people.

2. To ~~extend trade and commerce~~.

3. To gratify his avarice by hoarding up money.

4. To limit the power of the nobles and clergy.

For the accomplishment of the last two objects in particular, he caused certain laws to be enacted, and re-established a court called **The Star Chamber**, over which he himself presided, 1486. This court, which tried all cases without juries, and from which there was no appeal, had power to impose heavy fines for the following offences :—

1. Illegal combinations, or offences by maintenance, liveries, and retainers.

2. The taking of money by juries, riots, unlawful assemblies, and false returns of sheriffs.

The Statute of Fines, by which the nobility were permitted to dispose of their estates without paying the customary fines, was passed, 1489.

It was also enacted that disabled beggars should be maintained by the hundred to which they belonged.

The Statute of Drogheda was enacted in 1495. This statute is known by the name of "Poynings' Law," because it was passed by the Irish Parliament held by Sir EDWARD POYNINGS, the deputy. Its leading feature was that no bill could be brought into the Irish Parliament unless it had already met with the approbation of the English Council.

Parliament enacted a law, that no person should be impeached or attainted for assisting the King in possession of the throne, Oct. 13, 1495

The Magnus Intercursus, or great commercial treaty between the English and Flemings, was concluded, Feb. 24, 1496, by which the commerce between England and Flanders was not only settled to the satisfaction of both countries, but it was also stipulated—

1. That HENRY and Duke PHILIP should neither aid nor give refuge to each other's rebellious subjects.

2. That any vessel suffering shipwreck on the coasts of either Princes should not be confiscated, provided there was left alive a man, woman, or child ; a cat, dog, or cock.

JAMES IV. of Scotland having removed WARBECK from his dominions, concluded a Truce for seven years with England, Sept. 30, 1497.

In London alone 30,000 persons were destroyed by a **Plague,** 1500.

Prince ARTHUR, HENRY's eldest son, married CATHERINE of Arragon, daughter of FERDINAND and ISABELLA, Nov. 1501; but as ARTHUR died the following year, the King, in order to retain her dowry of 200,000 crowns, obtained a dispensation from Pope JULIUS II., by which his second son, afterwards HENRY VIII., was allowed to marry the widow.

In 1502, HENRY contracted his daughter MARGARET to JAMES IV. of Scotland, and the marriage was celebrated Aug. 8, 1503. From this union sprang the royal Houses of STUART and BRUNS-WICK. HENRY's Queen died in 1503.

While going from Flanders to Spain, PHILIP the Fair was compelled, through a violent storm, to shelter in Weymouth Harbour. Taking advantage of PHILIP's unfortunate situation, HENRY compelled him to make a new Treaty of Commerce, which being less favourable to the Flemings than the former treaty, they called Intercursus Malus, or the bad treaty. The King also compelled him to give up EDMUND DE LA POLE, Duke of Suffolk, the surviving grandson of GEORGE, Duke of Clarence. He promised PHILIP that SUFFOLK's life should be spared, but left a dying injunction with his son to put him to death. HENRY VIII., therefore, had him executed in 1513, and thus cut off the last male of the line of the Plantagenets, 1506.

The **Sweating Sickness** broke out again in 1507.

The **League of Cambray** was formed against Venice, which had now become formidable to all Italy, and was entered into by Pope JULIUS II., MAXIMILIAN I. of Germany, LOUIS XII. of France, and FERDINAND of Spain, Dec. 10, 1508. By this league, which takes its name from the place in France where it was signed, Venice was compelled to cede to Spain her possessions in the Kingdom of Naples.

The principal **Discoveries** of the present reign were :—

America was discovered by COLUMBUS in 1492 ; Newfoundland, by SEBASTIAN CABOT, in 1497 ; the Cape of Good Hope was doubled, and a new passage opened to the East Indies by VASCO DE GAMA in 1497 ; and Brazil was discovered by a Portuguese named PETRO ALVAREZ CABRAL, 1500.

The **Public Institutions** founded in this reign were :—

Jesus College, Cambridge, was founded by JOHN ALCOCK, Bishop of Ely, 1496 ; Christ's College, Cambridge, by MARGARET, Countess of Richmond, the King's mother, 1505 ; and Brazen Nose College, Oxford, by WILLIAM SMITH, Bishop of Lincoln, 1509.

Through the aid of two lawyers, named DUDLEY and EMPSON, the King extorted large sums of money from his subjects, and at his death left £2,000,000, which would be equal in value to £16,000,000 at the present time. In order that HENRY might give up all the English provinces in France, LOUIS XII. gave him £400,000.

During this reign the TUDOR style of architecture was introduced, shilling pieces issued, the brother of COLUMBUS brought maps and sea-charts to England, HENRY VII.'s chapel at Westminster was built, the King instituted at his own coronation a *body-guard*, consisting of fifty yeomen, who, from attending the *buffet* or royal sideboard, were called *buffetiers*, afterwards corrupted into *beef-eaters*.

Till this reign the country was much infested with gangs of robbers, called **Robertsmen.** During this and the two following reigns, Villenage was converted into **Free Tenantry.**

HENRY died of Consumption, April 21, 1509, and was buried in his own chapel at Westminster.

C   CELEBRATED PERSONS.

Christopher Columbus, a great navigator, was born at Genoa, 1445. In the year 1492 he discovered America. Died in the greatest poverty at Valladolid (Spain), 1506.

Americus Vesputius, a native of Florence, who coasted along South America, and unjustly called the whole continent after his own name; for the real discoverer was COLUMBUS. He was born at Florence, 1451, and died at Seville, 1512.

Ariosto, an Italian poet, born at Reggio, in Lombardy, 1474. His most celebrated work is entitled " Orlando Furioso." Died at Ferrara, 1553.

Sebastian Cabot, a Venetian, residing at Bristol, was sent by HENRY VII. on a voyage, and discovered the coast of North America, from Labrador to Florida. (1477—1557.)

Joan Boughton, burnt for heresy, is said to have been the *first* English female martyr, 1494.

Lord Audley, leader of the Cornish insurgents, defeated by the King at Blackheath, and taken prisoner. He was afterwards led (in a paper coat painted with his own arms reversed) from Newgate to Towerhill, and there beheaded, June 28, 1497.

Sir Edward Poynings, became Lord-Deputy of Ireland in 1494. He quelled PERKIN WARBECK'S insurrection, and in 1495 passed the Statute of Drogheda, commonly called Poyning's Law.

Lambert Simnel, born 1471, was instructed by one Simon, a priest, to personate the Earl of WARWICK.

Perkin Warbeck, assumed the person and character of RICHARD, Duke of York, son of EDWARD IV. He was acknowlodged by MARGARET of Burgundy as her dear nephew and the White Rose of England. He was taken prisoner and ultimately hanged, 1499.

Bartholomew Diaz, a Portuguese navigator, discovered the "Cape of Storms," called by the Spaniards the Cape of Good Hope.

Vasco de Gama, a famous Portuguese navigator, doubled the Cape of Good Hope and discovered the route to the East Indies by sea. JOHN III. appointed him Viceroy of Portuguese India, being the first who held that title. Died at Cochin, 1525.

John Morton, was made Bishop of Ely and Chancellor of England by EDWARD IV. In 1486 he became Archbishop of Canterbury, and in 1493 was created Cardinal by Pope ALEXANDER VI. He assisted HENRY VII. in exacting Benevolences, which had been condemned as illegal by RICHARD III. He told the rich that they could well afford to contribute, and those who were economical, he concluded, must have money, and therefore ought to give. This mode of reasoning was called Morton's Fork.

Sir Reginald Bray, an eminent statesman and celebrated architect, who superintended the erection of HENRY's chapel in Westminster. Died 1501, and was buried at Windsor.

Henry VIII. was the second son of Henry VII. and Elizabeth of the House of York. A.D. 1509—1547.

A   WARS.

1. HENRY and his father-in-law, FERDINAND of Spain, entered into a league (1511) for the conquest of Guienne, and with this object in view an army under the Marquis of DORSET was sent (1512) to Biscay, to assist the Spanish forces in making war against France. FERDINAND, however, merely used the English to check the French while he completed the conquest of Navarre, after which he refused to invade France, and the English Army, without having achieved anything of importance, returned home in disgust, 1512.

2. The French were defeated off Brest by Sir EDWARD HOWARD, but the largest ship in the English navy, called the *Regent*, was burnt, Aug. 12, 1512. To supply the loss of the *Regent*, a more magnificent vessel was ordered to be built, which the King called *Henri Grace Dieu*.

3. Sir EDWARD HOWARD was killed in a naval engagement with the French near Brest, April 25, 1513.

4. **Battle of Spurs.**—HENRY, aided chiefly by the Emperor MAXIMILIAN, invaded France, and during the **Siege of Terouenne** (which town as well as **Tournay** was captured by the King), some French forces advancing to relieve the place, were routed by the English at **Guinegate**, Aug. 16, 1513. From the way in which the French spurred their horses in galloping from the English, the encounter was called the "Battle of Spurs."

5. **Battle of Flodden Field** (near the Cheviot Hills).—JAMES IV. of Scotland sided with France and invaded England, but was defeated and slain with most of the Scotch nobility by the Earl of SURREY, at Flodden Field, Sept. 9, 1513.

6. **Battle of Pavia** (Italy), between the French and Imperialists, in which the former were defeated, and their King, FRANCIS I., made prisoner, Feb. 24, 1525.

7. Influenced by the Catholic party, JAMES V. of Scotland encouraged his subjects to make depredations on the English border, and this led to renewal of war between the two countries. The Earl of HUNTLY and Lord HOME defeated and made prisoner Sir ROBERT BOWES at **Halydon Rigg**, Aug. 24, 1542.

8. JAMES'S army was defeated by the English at **Solway Moss**, on the borders of Scotland, Nov. 25, 1542. In consequence of this defeat the Scottish Monarch died of grief (Dec. 14, 1542), and was succeeded by his infant daughter, the unfortunate MARY, Queen of Scots, who was only a week old.

9. HENRY invaded France and took **Boulogne**, but owing to his ally the Emperor CHARLES making a separate **Peace** with FRANCIS at Crépy, he was obliged to return to England, 1544.

10. FRANCIS, desirous of regaining Boulogne, made large preparations for war with England. An indecisive engagement took place between the English and French off the **Isle of Wight**, after which the latter returned to France under their Admiral ANNEBAUT, 1545.

11. HENRY sent some forces to Calais, but after a few skirmishes the two monarchs concluded a **peace**, by which it was agreed that HENRY should hold Boulogne for eight years, or till FRANCIS had paid the debt he owed to HENRY, June 7, 1546.

B   **CHIEF EVENTS.**

The Houses of York and Lancaster were **re-united** in the person of HENRY, who, at the age of eighteen, came to the throne *with an* undisputed title, and was crowned with his Queen at *Westminster,* June 24, 1509.

The King pleased his subjects by imprisoning the two noto-
us lawyers, EMPSON and DUDLEY, who after being confined
me time were executed on a frivolous charge of High Treason,
g. 18, 1510.

HENRY had six wives, whose names were as follow :—

1. **Catherine of Arragon,** widow of his brother ARTHUR,
l mother of **Mary** of England, was divorced from the King in
38, who said his conscience would not let him live any longer
th his brother's wife. The chief reason for divorcing CATHERINE
s HENRY's desire to marry ANNE BOLEYN, with whom he
l fallen in love. CATHERINE died, January 8, 1536.

2. **Anne Boleyn** (daughter of Sir THOMAS BOLEYN), maid
honour to Queen CATHERINE, and mother of **Elizabeth** of
gland, was beheaded by the King's orders on an alleged charge
infidelity to him, May, 1536.

3. **Jane Seymour** (daughter of Sir JOHN SEYMOUR and
ther of **Edward VI.**), whom HENRY married the day after
ne BOLEYN's death. JANE died a few days after she had
en birth to her son, October, 1537.

4. **Anne of Cleves** (daughter of the Duke of CLEVES), whom
NRY divorced on account of her ugliness (January, 1540).
e King was engaged to this lady without having seen her, and
en beheaded THOMAS CROMWELL for suggesting the marriage.

5. **Catherine Howard,** niece of the Duke of NORFOLK, was
eaded for alleged improper conduct before marriage, 1542.

6. **Catherine Parr** (widow of Lord LATIMER), who outlived
King, though he went so far as to give orders for her death,
ause she favoured the Reformed Religion, and ventured to
tradict him in his theological opinions.

Flattered by the prospect of being styled the *Most Christian
g,* which title LOUIS XII. had forfeited, HENRY was induced
Pope JULIUS II. to join the **Holy League,** which had been
ned (1510) by that Pontiff, MAXIMILIAN, and FERDINAND, for
bing the power of France, and for the defence of the Church,
1.

The Fifth and final Lateran Council, which was the
eteenth General Council, began in 1512, under Pope JULIUS II.,
was continued by LEO X. till 1517; one of its objects being
suppression of the **Pragmatic Sanction of France** against
Council of Pisa. This Pragmatic Sanction was published
1438 by CHARLES VII., and declared Papal Bulls to be of no
hority in France without the King's consent, and it also forbade
payment *of Annates to the Pope,* as well as any appeals to him.

Peace was concluded with Scotland, and also with France, the conditions with the latter country being :—

1. That Louis XII. should marry Henry's sister, the Princess Mary.

2. That Tournay should remain in the hands of the English.

3. That Henry should receive a million crowns, 1514. Mary's marriage with Louis took place in Oct., and she was crowned Queen of France, Nov. 5, 1514. Louis died in 1515.

Martin Luther began to preach against the Romish indulgences, which led to the **Reformation in Germany**, 1517.

"The Field of the Cloth of Gold."—There was an interview between Henry and Francis I. of France, at Ardres (a small town near Calais), where the nobility of England and France displayed such magnificence, that the place of meeting was called by the above name, 1520. Henry wrote a book against Martin Luther, in which he defended the Seven Sacraments of the Romish Church, and for which Pope Leo X. conferred on him the title of **"Defender of the Faith,"** which title our sovereigns have continued to use, 1521.

To carry on the war with France, Henry illegally raised a sum of money under the name of a loan or "benevolence," 1525.

Tyndale translated the **New Testament**, which was printed at Antwerp, 1526.

The **Concord of Madrid** was effected between Charles V. Emperor of Germany, and Francis I. of France, by which the latter obtained his liberty after consenting to surrender Burgundy, Flanders, and Artois, and to give up his claims on Italy, 1526.

As Rome had been sacked by the Imperialists under Bourbon, and Pope Clement taken prisoner, a new **Treaty** was concluded between England and France, by which it was agreed :—

1. That the Pope should be released, and the Imperialists expelled from Italy.

2. That Henry should renounce all claim to the crown of France, in consideration of which Francis and his successors were to pay to Henry and his successors an Annuity of 50,000 crowns, 1527.

Peace was restored to Europe by the **Treaty of Cambray**, which was concluded between Francis I. of France, and Charles V. of Germany, the conditions being :—

1. That Charles should relinquish his design on Burgundy.

2. That Francis should ransom his two sons for 2,000,000 *crowns*, and also give up Flanders and Artois, 1529.

The **League of Smalcald,** in Franconia, was entered into between the Elector of Brandenburg and the other Princes of Germany, for defending Protestantism, 1529.

Parliament passed a statute by which the King was released from his debts, 1529.

The English Reformation commenced in 1532, the immediate causes of which were :—

1. The intolerable abuses of the Papal Church; for many religious houses of the Roman Catholics being investigated, were found to be dens of vice rather than the abodes of virtue, which led to their destruction; still it is only fair to add that some of the larger monasteries were well conducted.

2. A more enlightened knowledge of the Bible, which had been translated into English, and placed in every parish church, so that all had an opportunity of reading God's Word, and judging for themselves.

3. The Pope's refusal to divorce HENRY from his Queen CATHERINE OF ARRAGON, which brought matters to a climax.

An act was passed, forbidding any appeal from the ecclesiastical courts to Rome, 1533.

CRANMER, Archbishop of Canterbury, held a court at Dunstable, and declared that the King's marriage with CATHERINE was null and void, 1533; while the Pope afterwards pronounced the said union valid. This completely severed the King from the Church of Rome. HENRY shook off the Papal supremacy, and was declared by Parliament the **"Supreme Head of the Church of England,"** 1534.

In 1535 TYNDALE and COVERDALE's Bible was published, and the religious order of **Jesus** or **Jesuits** founded by **Ignatius Loyola,** a Spaniard.

Wales was incorporated with **England** and became subject to English law, 1536.

The suppression of 376 smaller **Monasteries,** and changes in religion, produced an **Insurrection** in Lincolnshire, which was headed by MELTON, under the assumed name of Captain COBLER, and Dr. MACKAREL, the Abbot of Barlings; but the rebels dispersed on promise of a pardon, Oct. 1536.

Another **Insurrection,** caused by religious changes, broke out in Yorkshire, which the insurgents called the **Pilgrimage of Grace.** Its object was the suppression of heresy, restoration of the Church, and the expulsion of wicked counsellors from court. ROBERT ASKE, a barrister, led the rebels, who were also joined by Lords LUMLEY, LATIMER, SCROPE, DARCY, and the Archbishop of YORK, but when they were met at Doncaster by the

Duke of NORFOLK, with 5,000 men, the insurgents agreed to
armistice, on condition of being pardoned, and having their gr
ances discussed, Dec. 1536. In the following year the pe
again took up arms, but the presence of NORFOLK soon caused t
to disperse, and martial law being now proclaimed in the
affected parts of the country, Lords HASSEY and DARCY,
ROBERT ASKE, with many others, were executed.

A second edition of TYNDALE and COVERDALE's Bible
published under the name of "MATTHEW's;" and a law enac
called the Statute of Uses, declaring it illegal to leave land
churches and chapels for a period exceeding 20 years, 1537.

The notable events during the year 1539 were :—

1. Suppression of the larger monasteries, the revenues
which fell into the hands of the King.

2. Parliament was so subservient to the will of HENRY t
it yielded to his demand in passing a bill, which made the Ki
proclamations equal to laws.

3. The Statute of Six Articles, called the Bloody Stat
or the Whip with Six Strings, for abolishing diversity of opini
in certain Articles concerning the Christian religion, was pas
by which—1, Transubstantiation ; 2, Communion in one kir
3, The Celibacy of the Clergy ; 4, Private Masses ; 5, Vows
Chastity ; 6, and Auricular Confession ; were declared agree
to the law of God. Those who denied the First Article, wer
be burnt ; those who denied the others, were for the first offe
to lose their property, and for the second to suffer death as felo
In consequence of this statute, SHAXTON, Bishop of Salisb
and LATIMER, Bishop of Worcester, at once resigned their se
but were committed to prison.

4. Cranmer's Bible was ordered to be kept and read in
Churches.

CROMWELL, who had been created Earl of Essex, was execu
for high treason, 1540.

HENRY was declared King instead of Lord of Ireland in 15
and in the same year the aged Countess of SALISBURY, mothe
Cardinal POLE, and daughter of GEORGE, Duke of Clarence, a
two years' imprisonment, was beheaded on Tower Hill.

The King concluded a Treaty with Scotland, and stipula
that Prince EDWARD should marry the infant Princess, 1543.

In the present reign are said to have originated Bankrup
Laws, the first statute of Bankrupts being passed, 1544.

The Council of Trent (Austria), the decrees of which
considered binding by Roman Catholics, was in reality held

...rming the Reformed doctrines maintained by LUTHER, ...ius, and CALVIN, 1545.

The Earl of SURREY and his father, the Duke of NORFOLK, ...e committed to the Tower for high treason in 1546, and in the ...wing year, the former was put to death; the execution of the ...er, who had prepared to meet his end, being prevented by the ...den demise of the King, 1547.

The Inventions and Discoveries of this reign were:—

The South Sea or Pacific Ocean was discovered by VASCO ...NEZ DE BALBOA in 1513; Mexico, by J. DE GRIJALVA, who ...e it the name of New Spain, 1518; and in the same year the ... of Cochineal as a dyeing material made in Mexico, was dis-...ered by the Spaniards; the Straits of Magellan were discovered ...FERDINAND MAGELLAN, 1520; Peru by PIZARRO and ALMAGRO, ...4; Bermuda Isles in 1527; Japan by the Portuguese, 1542; ...d California, 1543. JURGEN, a German, invented spinning ...eels, which were greatly improved by JOHN HARGRAVE and ...RICHARD ARKWRIGHT in the reign of GEORGE III. Muskets ...d cotton thread were invented; and leaden pipes for the convey-...e of water.

The Public Institutions founded in this reign were, the ...llege of Physicians, founded by Dr. LINACRE, 1518; Trinity ...llege, Cambridge, and Christ Church, Oxford. Six bishoprics ...re also founded, namely, those of Bristol, Oxford, Chester, ...oucester, Peterborough, and Westminster, the last of which was ...corporated with the diocese of London in 1550.

HENRY converted an old hospital for leprous women into St. ...mes's Palace.

During this reign, currants, pippins, apricots, cherries, salads, ...rots, and turnips, were planted in England; hops were also ...roduced from the Netherlands.

The Reformers in this reign were first called Protestants, ...ince they protested at the Diet of Spires against the decree ...hat all reform in religion is unlawful."

JAMES V. of Scotland, instituted the Knights of the Thistle; ...eek professorships at both the universities were established; ...first Lord High Admiral appointed in 1512; and in the same ...ar was founded the Trinity House for the encouragement of ...vigation; the office of Secretary of State was instituted, 1530; ...s cannon first cast in England, 1535; and in 1543 mortars and ...nnons were cast in iron. HENRY'S fifth wife, CATHERINE ...WARD, introduced pins from France, and money allowed by ...bands to their wives for buying these articles, was called pin-money. The address, "Your most gracious Majesty," was first applied to HENRY. The King died of an ulcer in his leg, Jan. 28, 1547, and was buried at Windsor.

C   CELEBRATED PERSONS.

Sir Richard Empson, a distinguished lawyer, was the son of a sieve-maker. He became an instrument in the hands of HENRY VII. for extorting money from the people, and therefore rendered himself hateful to the nation. He was executed with his colleague DUDLEY, 1510.

Edmund Dudley, a noted lawyer and statesman, was the companion of EMPSON in extorting money for the benefit of HENRY VII. In the Parliament of 1504, he became Speaker of the House of Commons, and on the death of the King he and EMPSON were committed to the Tower, and in 1510 beheaded. During his confinement, DUDLEY wrote a piece called "the Tree of the Commonwealth."

Dr. John Colet was born in London, 1466. He founded St. Paul's School, of which the grammarian LILY became the first master. He was made Dean of St. Paul's, and by his preaching and labours furthered the Reformation. Died 1519.

Leonardo Da Vinci, a most distinguished Italian painter, sculptor, engineer, and architect. He studied under VERROCHIO, whom he very soon excelled, as well as all the painters of his time. His most noted work was a picture of "The Lord's Supper," at Milan. He constructed the aqueduct by which Milan is supplied with water, wrote a "Treatise on Painting," and was the first to lay down BACON'S great principle—that experiment and observation must be the guide to just theory. It is said that DA VINCI died in the arms of Francis I. of France. (1452—1519).

Sanzio Raffaelle was born at Urbino (Italy), and became the most eminent painter of modern times. His works are numerous, some of which are now in Hampton Court. The University of Oxford, too, has a fine collection of his drawings. (1483—1520).

Edward, Duke of Buckingham, and High Constable of England, was executed for high treason, 1521.

Lily, a celebrated English grammarian, author of a "Latin Grammar" and other grammatical pieces. He was born at Odiham (Hampshire), 1468, and died in London of the plague, 1523.

T. Linacre, a physician, and founder of the College of Physicians in London. (1460—1524).

Albert Durer, a famous German painter and artist, was the *son of a goldsmith* in Nuremberg, and is said to have been the first

ut printed woodcuts in two colours. He wrote a book on the
les of painting, and other works, and was held in such estimation
ut the Emperors MAXIMILIAN I. and CHARLES V. appointed him
ur artist. (1471—1528).

Thomas **Wolsey**, born at Ipswich, 1471, was educated at
ford, where he graduated at the age of 14, and was called the
y Bachelor. He became tutor to the three sons of GREY,
rquis of Dorset, and was appointed by that nobleman to the
ctory of Lymington in Hampshire. Being introduced at court
Sir JOHN NEFANT, treasurer of Calais, his great abilities and
t soon enabled him to gain the esteem of HENRY VII., who made
a Dean of Lincoln. On the accession of HENRY VIII., he was
ated the King's Almoner, and subsequently became Archbishop
York, Cardinal, and Chancellor. In 1518, he was appointed
al Legate, and also invested with power to suspend the laws and
ms of the Church. This rapid preferment inflamed his ambition,
induced him to aspire to the Popedom, to obtain which he made
or three attempts. Cardinals CAMPEGGIO and WOLSEY reed a commission from Pope CLEMENT VII., authorising them
quire into the validity of HENRY's marriage with CATHERINE,
se relationship to the Emperor prevented the Pontiff from giving
ment in favour of a divorce. In 1529 the **Legatine Court**
opened by the two Cardinals for trying the validity of the
iage, but without coming to any decision, the court was ad-
ed, and the cause by order of the Pope transferred to Rome.
SEY's conduct on this occasion showed that he was not will-
) facilitate the divorce, for which the King resolved that he
l be punished. He was, therefore, deprived of his offices, and
iced to imprisonment and forfeiture of goods for having
ed the **Statute of Praemunire**, Oct. 1529. In the fol-
g year he obtained a pardon, and retired to his See at York,
as soon after arrested on the false charge of treason. While
ling from York to London in order to undergo his trial, he
aken ill, and stopped at Leicester Abbey, where he died, Nov.
30. On his death-bed he said, "Had I served my God as
illy as I have the King, He would not have forsaken me in
d age." WOLSEY founded Christ Church College, Oxford,
iilt Hampton Court Palace.

Ulric **Zwingli** or **Zuingli**, the Swiss Reformer. He was a
of the Canton of Glarus in Switzerland, but seeing the cor-
ns of the Romish Church he began to declaim against them.
orks consist of commentaries upon the Scripture, contro-
l treatises, and a book on the Eucharist, in which the
ran doctrine of that sacrament is denied. He carried his
beyond those of the great German Reformer, and founded a
a of a *Presbyterian character*. (1484—1531).

William Dunbar, a Scottish poet, the author of several effusions, the chief of which are "The Thistle and the Rose," and "The Friars of Berwick." He was born in 1465, and died about 1530, or, according to others, in 1535.

Sir Thomas More, Chancellor of England after WOLSEY, was beheaded for refusing to acknowledge HENRY as head of the Church, 1535.

William Tyndale, a famous English divine, was educated at Oxford. He embraced the doctrines of the Reformers, and translated the New Testament into English. The Romish clergy being highly displeased with the work, began to persecute TYNDALE, who was condemned as a heretic and burnt near Antwerp, 1536.

Erasmus, an eminent scholar, was born at Rotterdam. Having been invited to England by HENRY VIII., he was appointed Professor of Divinity and Greek Lecturer at Cambridge. His chief works are "Praise of Folly," "Colloquies," "Ecclesiastes," and the Greek Testament. He approved of the principles of the Reformation, but had not sufficient courage to express himself openly; hence he incurred the displeasure of both parties. LUTHER called him a hypocrite, and said "he could point out error, but could not teach truth." The monks used to say "ERASMUS laid the egg, which LUTHER hatched." (1467—1536).

Thomas Cromwell, Secretary of State, was beheaded for suggesting the marriage between HENRY and ANNE OF CLEVES, 1540.

Sir Thomas Wyatt, a poet and diplomatist. He was the author of some elegant songs, and translated the Psalms of David into English verse. (1503—1542).

Nicholas Copernicus, a celebrated astronomer and physician, was born at Thorn in Prussia. In his great work entitled "De Revolutionibus Orbium Caelestium," he established the true system of the universe, which makes the Sun the "*Centrum Mundi*" round which the earth and other planets revolve. (1473—1543).

Martin Luther, the celebrated German Reformer, was the son of HANS LUTHER, a miner. In 1501 he entered the University of Erfurt, where he studied philosophy and civil law. While walking in the fields with a fellow-student, the latter was struck dead by lightning, which sad event produced such an impression upon LUTHER, that he resolved on retiring from the world, and entering a monastery of the order of St. Augustine, in which he spent a studious life. He was ultimately created Doctor in Divinity, and appointed Professor of Theology in the University of *Wittenberg.* In order to raise money, POPE LEO X. published plenary indulgences, granting pardon of sins to all who purchased them. The sale of these pardons in Germany gave great offence to LUTHER, who published a "**Thesis on Indulgences,**" in which he exposed and condemned the monstrous traffic. TETZEL, the papal agent, opposed the Reformer's thesis, but without much effect. He was cited to appear (1521) before the **Diet of Worms,** to retract his opinions. LUTHER obeyed the summons, and presented himself before the grand assembly, which was presided over by the Emperor CHARLES V., but he would not retract his errors, and as he had a safe-conduct, he was allowed to depart. He translated the New Testament into German, and published a reply to HENRY VIII., who had written against him in defence of the "Seven Sacraments." LUTHER's birth took place at Eisleben (Saxony) in 1483, and his death occurred in 1546.

Henry Howard, Earl of Surrey, a most accomplished English nobleman, and also a poet. He wrote some excellent poems, and translated part of the "Aeneid." HENRY becoming jealous of the Earl, charged him with treason, and had him executed. (1516—1547).

Martin Bucer, a Reformer, who was invited to England by CRANMER, and made Professor of Divinity at Cambridge. He was a voluminous writer, and assisted in revising EDWARD VI.'s second Prayer Book. He died in 1551, and in the reign of MARY his body was exhumed and burnt.

John Leland, a linguist and famous antiquary, died 1552.

Hans Holbein, a famous Swiss portrait-painter, was much patronised by HENRY. Among his earlier productions, "The Dance of Death" has been much celebrated. (1497—1554).

Gustavus Vasa, delivered Sweden from the Danish yoke, and was elected its Sovereign. (1490—1559).

Philip Melancthon, a great Reformer and friend of LUTHER. He was a most amiable man, and Professor of Greek in the University of Wittenberg. He drew up that system of Protestant opinions called the **Confession of Augsburg,** or the **Augsburg Confession of Faith,** which continues to be the creed of the Lutheran Church in Germany. (1497—1560).

Laelius Socinus, a native of Tuscany, who founded the sect of religionists called Unitarians, or Socinians. (1525—1562).

John Calvin, a celebrated Reformer, and founder of the religious sect called **Calvinists,** was born at Noyon (Picardy), 1509, and educated at Paris, under CORDERIUS. He published at **Basle** (1535) his "Institution of the Christian Religion," which he dedicated to FRANCIS I. By this work he acquired great celebrity. He was a very industrious man, as may be inferred from his yearly lectures and sermons, the former amounting to 186, the latter, 286. His works were published in nine vols. folio. CALVIN died, 1564.

Miles Coverdale, a Reformer, who assisted TYNDALE in translating the Bible. He was appointed to the See of Exeter in 1551, and died in London, 1568.

Edward VI. was the son of Henry VIII. and Jane Seymour. A.D. 1547—1553.

A   **WARS.**

1. **Battle of Pinkie** (near Edinburgh), in which the Duke of SOMERSET, the King's maternal uncle, defeated the Scotch with great slaughter, Sept. 10, 1547. This encounter was occasioned by an unwillingness on the part of the Scotch to carry out the treaty made in the last reign, by which it was agreed that EDWARD should marry MARY, the young Queen of Scotland. The day on which this victory was obtained the Scots called "Black Saturday." SOMERSET might have accomplished his object in enforcing a fulfilment of the treaty had he not been obliged to return to England through cabals formed against his authority by his brother, Lord SEYMOUR, and others.

B   **CHIEF EVENTS.**

In the will of HENRY VIII., made a short time before his death, he gave the following injunctions:—

1. That his crown should descend to EDWARD, then to the Lady MARY, and afterwards to the Lady ELIZABETH.

2. That EDWARD should not be considered of age till he had completed his eighteenth year.

3. That in the meantime young EDWARD and the kingdom were to be entrusted to sixteen executors and twelve councillors.

EDWARD, then in his tenth year, was crowned, Feb. 28, 1547; and contrary to the instructions left by the late King, Lord HERTFORD, EDWARD's eldest uncle, was created Duke of Somerset and Protector of the kingdom.

In the Parliament of 1547, were repealed—

1. The Statute of Six Articles, and Laws against the Lollards.

2. All the laws which extended the crime of treason beyond the limits prescribed by the Statute of EDWARD III.

No fewer than 2374 chantries, colleges, and chapels were abolished, and their revenues handed over to the Crown, 1547.

An Act was passed by which the King's supremacy was confirmed, and another by which priests were permitted to marry, 1548.

A law was made by which slaves, who ran away from their masters, were ordered to be branded on their breasts or foreheads with hot irons, and fed on bread and water.

After the death of SOMERSET, JOHN DUDLEY, Duke of Northumberland, was appointed Protector, and he induced EDWARD to nominate Lady JANE GREY as his successor to the Crown.

In this reign the English Reformation was almost completed.

An Act for the **Uniformity** of Divine Worship, and one confirming the **New Liturgy,** were passed, 1549. **The Prayer Book** was translated into English, and received the addition of forty-two articles of religion, which were drawn up by CRANMER.

England made peace with France, including Scotland, by which it was agreed:—

1. That Boulogne should be restored to France in six weeks.

2. That the King of France should pay the King of England 400,000 crowns of gold; viz., 200,000 at the taking possession of Boulogne, and 200,000 by the 15th of August. These stipulations were made on April 25, 1550.

The See of Westminster was incorporated with that of London in 1550, and RIDLEY appointed Bishop.

A treaty for the marriage of EDWARD with ELIZABETH of France (daughter of HENRY II.) was also concluded, July 19, 1551.

The **Book of Homilies,** or Sermons, was compiled by Archbishop CRANMER, and RIDLEY, Bishop of London; and the **Book of Psalms** translated and rendered into metre by STERNHOLD and HOPKINS.

Many Grammar Schools, still called King EDWARD's Schools, and St. Thomas's Hospital, were founded by EDWARD, who also confirmed his father's grant of Christ's and St. Bartholomew's Hospitals, and gave his palace at Bridewell to the citizens of London for a Workhouse.

The Sweating Sickness appeared again for the last time in England.

Knitting and leaden bullets were invented in this reign, and the new coins issued were—crown, half-crown, sixpenny, and threepenny pieces.

Religious changes and the enclosing of land caused **Insurrections** in many counties, the most formidable taking place in Cornwall, *Devon,* and *Norfolk.* The one in Norfolk was headed by Ket, a tanner, who addressed his followers under an oak, since known by the name of **The Tree of Reformation.** After the rebels had taken the city of Norwich and killed Lord SHEFFIELD, they were attacked by the Earl of WARWICK, who put them to flight. About 2,000 were killed, and **Ket** was hanged at Norwich Castle, 1549. In consequence of these risings, Lords-Lieutenant of Counties were appointed in this reign.

In this reign the eldest sons of Peers were allowed to sit in the Lower House, LORD FRANCIS RUSSELL being the first to enjoy that privilege; the Commons began to keep a journal of their proceedings; twelve persons assembling for riotous purposes not separating on proclamation, was declared high treason; a company was formed for discovering a north-east passage to India; and in 1553 an expedition of three ships left England under the command of Sir HUGH WILLOUGHBY. Two of the vessels were lost off Nova Zembla, while the third, under Captain CHALLONER, wintered at Archangel, and opened trade with Russia.

The young King died of consumption at Greenwich, in the sixteenth year of his age, July 6, 1553, and was buried at Westminster.

C   CELEBRATED PERSONS.

Admiral Lord Seymour, who married CATHERINE PARR, widow of HENRY VIII., was executed for plotting against his brother, the Duke of SOMERSET, 1549.

Joan Bocher, or **Joan of Kent,** burnt for denying that Christ was truly incarnate of the Virgin, 1550. CRANMER prevailed upon the young King to sign the warrant for the execution of this poor creature.

George Van Parre, a Dutch surgeon, was burnt for Arianism, 1552.

Lord Hertford, created Duke of Somerset and Protector, a friend of the Reformation, was executed for plotting the death of the Duke of NORTHUMBERLAND, 1552.

John Dudley, Duke of Northumberland, was the son of the notorious lawyer DUDLEY, mentioned in the two preceding reigns. After being created Viscount LISLE, Earl of WARWICK, and appointed Lord High Admiral, he became Duke of NORTHUMBERLAND. He induced EDWARD VI. to set aside the claims of his sisters MARY and ELIZABETH, and to nominate Lady JANE GREY, who was married to the Duke's son, Lord GUILDFORD DUDLEY. In the reign of MARY he was executed as a traitor, 1553.

John Heywood, the first writer of English Comedy, wrote "Gammer Gurton's Needle." (1500—1565).

Mary was the daughter of Henry VIII. and Catherine of Arragon. A.D. 1553—1558.

A   **WARS.**

Battle of St. Quentin.—The Queen was prevailed upon by PHILIP to declare war against France. The Spanish, therefore, under the command of PHILIBERT, Duke of Savoy, assisted by the English under the Earl of PEMBROKE, defeated the French at St. Quentin, Aug. 10, 1557. This encounter was also called the Battle of St. Lawrence, because fought on the day dedicated to that saint.

B   **CHIEF EVENTS.**

On the death of EDWARD VI., there were two competitors for the crown :—

1. The beautiful and accomplished Lady JANE GREY, who was, against her will, proclaimed Queen by her ambitious father-in-law, the Duke of NORTHUMBERLAND. She reigned only ten days, and then resigned the crown with the utmost satisfaction.

2. MARY, who was proclaimed Queen, and acknowledged as the lawful heir, July 19, 1553.

MARY began her reign by releasing GARDINER, BONNER, TONSTALL, DAY, and HEATH, who had been confined during the late reign for their religious opinions; by beheading NORTHUM-BERLAND, Sir THOMAS PALMER, and Sir JOHN GATES, for advocating the cause of Lady JANE GREY. She was crowned by GARDINER, Bishop of Winchester, Oct. 1, 1553. She repealed all the laws enacted in favour of Protestantism, and re-established Popery.

Insurrections.—In order to prevent the Queen's marriage with PHILIP. II. of Spain, and also to further the cause of Lady JANE GREY, an insurrection in Kent was headed by Sir THOMAS WYATT; another in Devonshire by Sir PETER CAREW; and a third in the Midland Counties, by the Duke of SUFFOLK; but they proved fatal to the Lady JANE, her husband, Lord GUILD-FORD DUDLEY, and WYATT; all of whom were in consequence beheaded, 1554. The Princess ELIZABETH was suspected of being concerned in these insurrections, for which she was imprisoned. The Queen's marriage with PHILIP took place July, 1554.

All the Clergy, who refused to be separated from their wives, were compelled to resign their livings, 1554.

The Marian Persecution began in 1555, and gained for the Queen the title of "The Bloody Mary;" for, during the short reign of that misguided and bigoted Queen, no fewer than 284 persons, of all ages and sexes, were put to death, making an average of 71 each year. Even infants were cast into the flames.

The **First Commercial Treaty** with Russia was formed, 1557.

Calais, which had been in the possession of the English ever since the time of EDWARD III., a period of 210 years, was taken by the Duke of GUISE, Jan. 7, 1558. This loss to the English nation so distressed Queen MARY, that she said the name of Calais would, after death, be found engraven upon her heart.

Nottingham was visited by a severe hailstorm, 1558.

In this reign the use of starch was discovered and hemp grown; glass beakers and bottles were invented.

The first general law relating to highways was enacted, declaring that they must be repaired by a parish duty over all England.

Trinity and St. John's Colleges, Oxford, were founded, the former by Sir THOMAS POPE, the latter by Sir THOMAS WHITE.

MARY died of fever, Nov. 17, 1558, and was buried at Westminster.

C   **CELEBRATED PERSONS.**

Sir Thomas Wyatt, executed for heading the insurrection in Kent, 1554.

Lady Jane Grey, the daughter of HENRY GREY, Earl of Dorset, and FRANCES, daughter of MARY, sister of HENRY VIII., was proclaimed Queen, and reigned only ten days. She was remarkable for her talents and accomplishments. FULLER says, "She had the innocency of childhood, the beauty of youth, the solidity of middle, and the gravity of old age. She had the birth of a princess, the learning of a clerk, yet the death of a martyr, for her parent's offences." She adhered to the Protestant religion, and after being confined in the Tower, was beheaded with her husband, Lord GUILDFORD DUDLEY, fourth son of the Duke of NORTHUMBERLAND, 1554.

Edmund Bonner, Bishop of London, a disgraceful enemy of the Reformers. On the accession of ELIZABETH he was committed to Marshalsea prison, in which he died. (1490—1569).

Stephen Gardiner, a notorious persecutor of the Protestants. His determined opposition to the Reformed religion caused EDWARD VI. to commit him to the Tower; but when MARY ascended the throne, he obtained his liberty and was appointed *Chancellor of England.* (1483—1555).

Thomas Cranmer, born at Aslacton in Nottinghamshire, 1489. Having suggested that HENRY VIII. should consult the Universities rather than the Pope, in reference to his contemplated divorce from CATHERINE, he came under the notice of that monarch, who created him Archbishop of Canterbury. He pronounced the divorce between the King and CATHERINE, was a zealous promoter of the Reformation, took a leading part in framing the Book of Common Prayer, the Homilies, and Articles of Religion, and caused an English translation of the Bible to be published and read in the churches. Being charged with heresy in the reign of MARY, he was committed to the Tower, and thence with RIDLEY and LATIMER, he was removed to Oxford for the purpose of holding a Public Disputation relating to Romish Ceremonies 1554. As the Archbishop and two Bishops could not be silenced by arguments, they were put down by clamour and pronounced heretics. The Archbishop was tried by the Pope's Commissioners, and convicted, but was afterwards induced, on the promise of life, to sign his abjuration of the Protestant Faith. Of this act he bitterly repented, and on being brought into St. Mary's Church, Oxford, to make a public recantation, instead of doing so, he asked God's forgiveness for his apostacy, and warned the audience against the errors of Rome. This so enraged his enemies that they dragged him to the stake, near Baliol College, where he endured his sufferings with great fortitude. While the fire was consuming the martyr's body, he often cried, "This unworthy right hand." 1556.

Peter Martyr, a noted Protestant divine, born at Florence in 1500. He was formerly an Augustine monk, but after reading the works of LUTHER, he embraced the Reformed religion. On the invitation of EDWARD VI. he came to England, and was appointed Professor of Divinity at Oxford, and Canon of Christ Church. In the reign of MARY, he retired to the continent, and ultimately died at Zurich in 1562. His writings consist of commentaries upon the Scriptures, and pieces against the errors of the Church of Rome.

John Hooper, Bishop of Gloucester, was burnt as a heretic. (1495—1555).

Hugh Latimer, Bishop of Worcester, born in 1472. He was very ardent in the cause of the Reformation, and received from HENRY VIII. the bishopric of Worcester, which he resigned on the passing of the Bloody Statute, and was imprisoned during the remainder of HENRY's reign. On the accession of MARY, he was condemned as a heretic and burnt with his friend RIDLEY at Oxford, 1555. When at the stake, LATIMER thus addressed RIDLEY, "We shall this day, my lord, light such a candle in England, as shall never be extinguished."

Nicholas Ridley, Bishop of London, was born in 1500, and received his education at Pembroke College, Cambridge, of which he was elected fellow in 1524. His abilities and learning brought him under the notice of CRANMER, whom he assisted in framing the Liturgy, Articles, and Homilies. He was a warm supporter of the Protestant cause, wrote against transubstantiation, and prevailed upon EDWARD VI. to endow St. Bartholomew's, St. Thomas's, and Christ's Hospitals. He joined the friends of Lady JANE GREY, and was burnt as a heretic at Oxford, 1555.

Reginald Pole, Cardinal and Statesman, succeeded CRANMER as Archbishop of Canterbury. He was the younger son of Sir RICHARD POLE, by MARGARET, daughter of GEORGE, Duke of CLARENCE, younger brother of EDWARD IV. He strongly opposed the divorce of HENRY VIII. from CATHERINE of Arragon, and wrote a Treatise against the Reformation, entitled "*Pro Unitate Ecclesiastica.*" He was born in 1500, and died a few hours after the Queen, Nov. 17, 1558.

Elizabeth was the daughter of Henry VIII. and Anne Boleyn. A.D. 1558—1603.

A   WARS.

1. As the Duke of GUISE began to persecute the Huguenots, as the French Protestants were called, Prince CONDE placed himself at their head, and obtained from ELIZABETH an army under the command of AMBROSE DUDLEY, Earl of Warwick. Havre was taken by the combined forces, but at the Battle of Dreux, the Catholics, under the Constable MONTMORENCY, defeated the Huguenots under CONDE, who was made prisoner, 1562, and in the following year the Duke of GUISE was assassinated while engaged in the Siege of Orleans.

2. Battle of St. Denis, in which the Huguenots under CONDE and COLIGNY were defeated by the Catholics under MONTMORENCY, who was slain, 1567.

3. Battle of Langside, near Glasgow, between the forces of the Earl of MURRAY, Regent of Scotland, and the army of MARY, Queen of Scots, in which the latter was completely defeated, May 13, 1568. After this battle MARY fled to England, and was soon afterwards imprisoned by ELIZABETH.

4. **Battle of Jarnac**, in which the Duke of ANJOU (afterwards HENRY III. of France) defeated the Huguenots, headed by CONDE, who is said to have been killed in cold blood by MONTESQUIEU, March 13, 1569.

5. **Battle of Moncontour**, in which the Huguenots under COLIGNY were again defeated by the Catholics, 1569.

6. **Battle of Zutphen**, in which the English, under the Earl of LEICESTER, were unsuccessful, and Sir PHILIP SIDNEY mortally wounded, Sep. 22, 1586.

7. The **Invincible Armada.**—PHILIP II. of Spain being piqued at ELIZABETH's refusal to marry him, and wishful to establish Popery in England, sent a tremendous fleet, under the **Duke of Medina Sidonia,** against the English. It was called "The Invincible Armada," and consisted of 130 ships and 30,000 men. This fleet was defeated by a very inferior force, under the following renowned seamen: Admiral Lord HOWARD of Effingham, assisted by DRAKE, HAWKINS, and FROBISHER. The loss of the Spaniards was eighty-one vessels and 13,000 men; that of the English, only one ship, 1588.

8. **Battle of Ivry**, in which the Huguenots, under HENRY IV. of France, defeated the Leaguers under MAYENNE, 1590.

9. **Battle of Cadiz**, in which the English, under the Earl of ESSEX and Admiral Lord HOWARD of Effingham, overcame the Spaniards, commanded by the Duke of MEDINA SIDONIA, 1596.

10. There was a **Rebellion** in Ireland, headed by HUGH O'NEAL, Earl of Tyrone, who defeated the English and slew their leader, Sir HENRY BAGNAL, the Lord-Deputy, at **Blackwater**, in Tyrone, Aug. 14, 1598. The Irish, however, were defeated by the Lord-Deputy MOUNTJOY (1601), and the rebellion suppressed by the defeat of their Spanish allies under D'AGUILAR, at **Kinsale**, 1602. TYRONE surrendered to MOUNTJOY, but was deprived of some of his lands, 1603.

CHIEF EVENTS.

ELIZABETH released all persons who had been imprisoned for their religious opinions, virtually rejected an offer of marriage made to her by PHILIP of Spain, and chose for her chief adviser Sir WILLIAM CECIL, afterwards Lord BURLEIGH, 1558.

ELIZABETH was crowned at Westminster by OGLETHORPE, Bishop of Carlisle, the other Bishops refusing to assist at the coronation, because she favoured the new religion, Jan. 15, 1559.

The Protestant Religion was re-established by Parliament, and the Acts of Uniformity and Supremacy passed in 1559.

All the Bishops, except KITCHEN of Llandaff, refused to take the oath of supremacy, and were removed from their sees. Nearly all the parish clergy obeyed the new laws.

Peace with France and Scotland was concluded at **Cateau Cambresis**, April 2, 1559; by which it was agreed, that Calais should be restored to England within eight years, and in case of failure France stipulated to pay 500,000 crowns, and still be obliged to give up the town.

Dr. MATTHEW PARKER, who had been Chaplain to ANNE BOLEYN, was made Archbishop of Canterbury, 1559.

As a measure of self-defence the Queen concluded a **Treaty at Berwick** with the leading Scotch Reformers, who were called **Lords of the Congregation**, and agreed to assist them against the Catholics, Jan. 1560.¶

The Treaty of Edinburgh, between England, France, and Scotland, was concluded July 6, 1560; the terms of which were:—

1. That FRANCIS should withdraw his troops from Scotland.

2. That the King and Queen of France and Scotland should cease to bear the arms of England, or to assume the title of that kingdom.

MARY, Queen of Scots, after the death of her husband, FRANCIS II. of France, Dec. 1560, returned to Scotland, and landed at Leith, Aug. 19, 1561.

In 1563 **The Articles of Religion**, originally **42** in number, were reduced to **39** by convocation; the three following being omitted:—

1. That the soul does not perish with the body.
2. That all men will not be saved.
3. That the resurrection of the dead is not passed already.

The two factions of Huguenots and Catholics concluded a **Truce at Amboise**, and besieged Havre, which the English under the Earl of WARWICK were, in consequence of the plague having crept in among the soldiers, obliged to quit, 1563. They brought the **plague** with them to England, where it destroyed multitudes.

The Bishops under PARKER finished a new Translation of the Bible, which was called the **Bishops' Bible, 1568.**

The Earls of NORTHUMBERLAND and WESTMORELAND raised an Insurrection in the north for placing MARY on the throne, but they were put down in Yorkshire by the Earl of SUFFOLK, and the two leaders fled into Scotland, 1569.

ELIZABETH was excommunicated by the Pope, 1570.

A terrible massacre of Protestants in France took place on St. Bartholomew's day, when 30,000 were cruelly slaughtered by the command of **Catherine de Medicis** and her son **Charles IX.** of France, who wished to exterminate the Reformed religion, Aug. 24, 1572.

Elizabeth concluded a **Treaty** with the Hollanders against Philip II. of Spain, from whom they had revolted, and stipulated to furnish them with 6,000 men, and £100,000, for the repayment of which she received ample security, 1578.

By the **Union of Utrecht** the seven revolted provinces threw off the Spanish yoke, united themselves for mutual defence, and thereby laid the foundation of the **Netherland** or **Dutch Republic,** so renowned by the name of the *Seven United Provinces*, 1579.

Francis Drake, who had made a voyage round the world, returned in 1580.

For the regulation of all Church matters, the **High Commission Court** was established, 1583.

A severe law was passed, ordering all Jesuits and Popish Priests to leave the Kingdom within 40 days, 1584.

Babington's Conspiracy—This plot was formed by some Roman Catholics, at the head of whom was Babington, a native of Derbyshire. The design of the conspirators was to assassinate Elizabeth, and to deliver Mary, Queen of Scots, 1586. Babington and 13 other conspirators were executed. By order of Elizabeth, Mary, Queen of Scots, was beheaded at **Fotheringay Castle** (Northamptonshire) for being concerned in the Babington conspiracy, Feb. 8, 1587.

Henry IV. of France, being favourable to the Protestants, was in consequence opposed by the Catholic Confederacy, known as **The League,** and also by Philip II. of Spain, and the Pope. He therefore requested aid from Elizabeth, who sent him £22,000, and 4000 men under Lord Willoughby, 1590. The Queen also despatched troops for Henry's assistance, under the Earl of Essex, 1591.

Among the Acts of Parliament passed in 1593, we may notice the following, which pressed heavily upon Roman Catholics and Dissenters :—

1. That any person above 16 years of age neglecting for the space of one month to attend divine service, established by law, should be committed to prison.

2. That **Popish Recusants** should be confined within five miles of their respective dwellings, on forfeiture of their goods and chattels, together with lands, during life.

An Act was passed for building Hospitals, Houses of Correction, and Workhouses for the Poor, 1597.

HENRY IV. of France, by the **Edict of Nantes**, granted the Protestants his protection, 1598.

The **East India Company** was established in 1600.

The famous **Poor Law Act** was passed, and great complaints made against monopolies, 1601.

The **Slave Trade** was introduced by JOHN HAWKINS of Plymouth, who employed three vessels for seizing African negroes, whom he sold to the Spanish Americans, 1562. This inhuman traffic continued till the reign of GEORGE III., when it was abolished by law, 1807.

Dissenters formed themselves into a distinct body, and were called **Puritans**, on account of their affecting to purify themselves from every mark of the Romish Church. The Puritans, who were specially supported by CECIL and LEICESTER, objected to—

1. **Bowing** at the name of JESUS, and the **ring** in marriage.

2. The sign of the **Cross** in Baptism, and ecclesiastical vestments.

3. **Kneeling** at the Communion, and ultimately to the Episcopacy.

The **Inventions and Discoveries** of this reign were :—

The **Stocking-Frame** was invented by the Rev. WILLIAM LEE of Nottingham, who, in consequence of this invention, was driven from the town, and fled to France, where he died in extreme poverty ; **Needles**, by ELIAS GROWSE, a German ; **Newspapers**, to acquaint the nation of the overthrow of the Spanish Armada ; **Fire Ships**, which were first used by Lord HOWARD, who filled some vessels with combustibles, and sent them into the midst of the Spanish Armada near Calais ; **Paper Mills**, the first being established at Dartford in Kent by a German in 1588 ; and in the same year **Bomb-shells** were invented at Venloo in the Netherlands. Cape Breton was discovered, 1584 ; Greenland, 1585 ; the Falkland Isles, 1592 ; and the Caribbee Isles, 1595. Sir THOMAS CHALONER discovered that **Alum** existed in abundance on his estate at Whitby. During this reign Knives were first made in England ; Starching was taught by a Flemish Lady named DINGHEN ; **Decimals** were invented by SIMON STEVIN, a Belgian ; Book-keeping by Double Entry taught by Sir James PEELE ; Tobacco was brought by Sir WALTER RALEIGH from Tobago (W. Indies) ; Potatoes from Santa Fé (S. America) by Sir FRANCIS DRAKE, who planted them in Lancashire ; Pocket watches and Gunpowder were introduced from Germany ; Carriages from France ; *false hair, fans, and muffs* from Italy. The **Colon** and **Semi-colon** *were first used* in printing.

The Bodleian Library was founded at Oxford by Sir THOMAS BODLEY; Westminster School was founded by the Queen, and Rugby School by L. SHERIFFE. The Custom House, the Stock Exchange, Dublin University, and Jesus, Sidney, and Emmanuel Colleges, Cambridge, were erected. Commerce flourished in this reign, and Art was much encouraged by the nobility. The great Naval power of England commenced in the present reign.

ELIZABETH died at Richmond, March 24, 1603, in the seventieth year of her age, and was buried at Westminster.

C   CELEBRATED PERSONS.

Roger Ascham, a distinguished scholar, assisted the Princess ELIZABETH in her classical studies, and on her accession to the throne, she appointed him her Latin Secretary. His most esteemed work is entitled " The Schoolmaster." (1515—1568).

John Fox, noted for his work entitled " The Acts and Monuments of the Church," or the " Book of Martyrs." (1517—1587).

Louis Camoens, a Portuguese poet, was born at Lisbon, 1517. His fame rests upon his epic poem, " The Lusiad." Died 1579.

Sir Thomas Gresham, a noted merchant, founded the Royal Exchange and Gresham College. (1519—1579).

Sir John Hawkins, a noted admiral, born at Plymouth in 1520. Having sailed to the coast of Africa, he procured 300 negroes, whom he conveyed to Hispaniola, and there sold them. He has the credit of being the *first* European that introduced the slave trade into the West Indies. He served as Rear-Admiral against the Spanish Armada, and for his bravery on that occasion received the honour of knighthood. Died in the West Indies, 1595.

William Cecil (Lord Burghley or Burleigh), the Queen's leading minister, and the greatest statesman of his age. The glory of ELIZABETH'S reign may in a great measure be ascribed to his policy. (1520—1598).

John Jewel, Bishop of Salisbury, a very learned prelate, born in 1522. He was one of the 16 divines selected to dispute with the same number of Romanists in the presence of the Queen. His chief work is entitled " An Apology for the Church of England." Died 1571.

Robert Dudley, Earl of LEICESTER, fifth son of JOHN, Duke of Northumberland, was born in 1532. He was suspected of murdering his own wife in anticipation of marrying ELIZABETH, with whom he had become a great favourite, and by whom he was appointed Lieutenant-General of the army at Tilbury Fort. Died, 1588.

David Rizzio, an Italian musician, and secretary to the Queen of Scots, was murdered by DARNLEY, who became jealous of him, 1566.

Charles Howard (Lord HOWARD of Effingham), Lord High Admiral of England, commanded the fleet by which the Spanish Armada was destroyed, 1588. He destroyed a Spanish Fleet in the harbour of Cadiz in 1596, for which he was created Earl of NOTTINGHAM. He suppressed the rebellion of ESSEX in 1601, and held important posts under King James I. (1536—1624).

Sir Francis Walsingham, born at Chiselhurst, in Kent, 1536. He was a profound politician, and in 1573 became Secretary of State. Died 1590.

Mary Stuart, Queen of Scots, was the daughter of JAMES V. of Scotland and MARY of Lorraine, daughter of the Duke of GUISE. She was educated at the French Court, and when 16 years of age married the Dauphin of France, who succeeded his father HENRY II. under the title of FRANCIS II. Instigated by HENRY II., MARY and Francis assumed the arms and title of the King and Queen of England, on the ground of ELIZABETH's illegitimacy. This step ultimately proved fatal to MARY. Soon after the death of her husband she returned to Scotland, which she found in a state of confusion, owing to the opposition between the Roman Catholics and Reformers. MARY being a Papist, ordered mass to be said in her chapel, which injunction gave great offence to the Protestants. Her second husband was HENRY STUART, Lord Darnley, to whom she was united in 1565. DARNLEY was murdered by BOTHWELL, who married MARY three months afterwards. These proceedings and an attempt on the part of BOTHWELL to secure the young Prince, caused great alarm among the principal nobility, who took up arms to defend the young Prince, and to punish the King's murderers. They were met by the forces of BOTHWELL and the Queen at **Carberry Hill,** near Edinburgh. MARY, finding that her own troops showed little inclination to defend her cause, was induced to throw herself upon the generosity of the Protestants, and was conducted to Edinburgh, and thence to the castle of **Lochleven** (near Dumbarton). After a year's confinement in this castle, MARY effected her escape, and raised a large army, but was defeated by the Regent MURRAY. After this defeat, MARY fled to England, and sought protection at the hands of ELIZABETH, who detained her as a prisoner for nearly 19 years; at the expiration of which *time she was* beheaded for aiding the Babington conspiracy, 1587.

John Knox, the great Scotch Reformer, was educated at St. Andrew's University, and became a priest before the age of 25. Having studied the works of St. AUGUSTINE and St. JEROME, he renounced Popery, and openly preached the new faith. Engaged with other Reformers in defending St. Andrew's, he was taken prisoner by the French (1547), who sent him to **Rouen,** where he was condemned to the galleys. After his detention there for 19 months, he came to England, and was appointed chaplain to EDWARD VI., from whom he refused to accept a bishopric, because he objected to the Common Prayer and Episcopacy. In the reign of MARY, KNOX retired to Frankfort, and thence to Geneva, where he became acquainted with CALVIN, whose writings he greatly admired. Having returned to his native country (1559) he began by preaching against the clergy, and the conduct of the Queen of Scots whom he called JEZEBEL. His sermons were attended with such an effect, that many of the Romish Cathedrals and Parish Churches were demolished. Knox died at Edinburgh, 1572.

Henry Stuart, Lord Darnley, the second husband of MARY, Queen of Scots, was murdered in a lonely house called "**The Kirk of Field,**" situated where the University of Edinburgh now stands, 1567. The house was blown up by gunpowder, and the bodies of DARNLEY and his valet were found lying in the garden.

James Hepburn, Earl of Bothwell, third husband of MARY, Queen of Scots, and the supposed murderer of DARNLEY. After MARY had fallen into the hands of the insurgents at Carberry Hill, he fled into Norway, where he was made prisoner by the Danish government, and thrown into the Castle of Malmoe, in which he went mad, and died a miserable death, 1576.

William Gilbert, an able physician, born at Colchester, 1540. He discovered several of the properties of the loadstone, and was appointed physician to the Queen. Died 1603.

Sir Francis Drake, a famous navigator, born at Tavistock, 1545. The globe was circumnavigated by DRAKE, who discovered New Albion, and aided in destroying the Invincible Armada. Died 1595.

Sir Martin Frobisher, a famous navigator, attempted the discovery of a North West passage to India. The Strait which bears his name was discovered by FROBISHER, who contributed by his bravery towards defeating the Spanish Armada, for which he was knighted, 1588. Being sent to aid HENRY IV. of France, he was wounded near Brest, and died on his homeward voyage, 1594.

Tycho Brahe, a noted Danish astronomer, was born 1546. His best works are the "Rudolphine Tables," and the "Historia Caelestis." Died 1601.

Cervantes, a celebrated Spanish novelist, author of Don Quixote. (1547—1616).

Christopher Marlowe, a dramatic writer, author of several plays, of which we may mention "Dr. Faustus," and "The Jew of Malta." He also translated Ovid's "Art of Love." Died 1593.

Edmund Spenser, an illustrious poet, was born in 1553. He wrote *The Faerie Queen*, which he presented to ELIZABETH, who granted him a pension of £50 per annum. Died 1599.

Sir Philip Sidney, a great statesman, soldier, and scholar, was born in 1554. He wrote sonnets, a prose romance called "Arcadia," and other works. He was mortally wounded at Zutphen, 1586.

William Camden, a learned antiquary, author of "The Britannia," "Annals of Queen ELIZABETH," and other works. (1551 —1623).

Richard Hooker, a most learned divine, author of an excellent work in defence of the established church, called "Hooker's Ecclesiastical Polity." Died 1600.

James Arminius, a Dutch Divine, founded the sect of Arminians. Being requested to refute a piece on Predestination, which had been written against BEZA, he became a convert to the doctrine he had to confute. His motto was, "A good conscience is a paradise." (1560—1609).

Galileo, a famous Italian astronomer, was persecuted by the Inquisition for teaching the true astronomical system. He discovered the inequalities on the surface of the moon, the satellites of Jupiter, and the nature of the Milky Way, &c. (1564—1642).

William Shakespeare, the most illustrious of our dramatic poets, born at Stratford-upon-Avon in 1564, was the son of JOHN SHAKESPEARE, a butcher. Having become proprietor of the Globe theatre, he realised a handsome fortune and purchased an estate in his native town, where he spent the close of his life. He wrote 35 plays, of which we may mention "Hamlet," "Merry Wives of Windsor," "Macbeth," "Othello," and "Merchant of Venice." Died 1616.

Charles Blount (Lord MOUNTJOY), became Lord Lieutenant of Ireland after ESSEX, and quelled TYRONE's rebellion. JAMES I. made him master of the Ordnance, but he fell into disgrace by marrying the divorced Lady RICH, daughter of the Earl of ESSEX. (1563—1606).

Robert Devereux, Earl of ESSEX, a favourite of ELIZABETH, was born in 1567. Having displeased the Queen through not suppressing the Irish Rebellion in 1599, and having afterwards attempted to raise an **Insurrection** among the citizens of London in his own favour, he was executed for treason, 1601.

John Kepler, a celebrated German astronomer, whose fame rests mainly upon his discovery that the orbits of the planets are elliptical. (1571—1630).

Benjamin Jonson, a poet and dramatist, born at Westminster, 1574. In the following reign he was appointed Poet-Laureate, with a yearly stipend of £100 and an annual butt of Canary wine. Among his dramas are, "Every Man in his Humour," "The Fox," "The Silent Woman," and "Cynthia's Revels." Died 1637. On his tomb in Westminster Abbey is inscribed, "O Rare Ben Jonson."

John Penry, was executed for a seditious book, called **"Martin-Mar-Prelate,"** 1594.

Francis Beaumont (1585-1616) and **John Fletcher** (1576-1625), two dramatic writers of great merit, who produced by their united efforts 52 plays.

Raphael Holinshed, a famous old English Chronicler. Died about 1580.

John Stow, an eminent antiquary and historian, noted for his *Chronicle of England* and *Survey of London.* (1525—1605).

Nicholas Hilliard, goldsmith and painter to the Queen. The portrait of ELIZABETH is one of his best works. (1547—1619).

Isaac Oliver, an artist, chiefly noted for his miniature paintings. (1556—1617).

John Whitgift, an eminent divine, was educated at Queen's College, and subsequently at Pembroke Hall, Cambridge. During the reign of MARY he strenuously exerted himself in advancing the principles of the Reformation. In 1563 he was appointed Lady MARGARET'S professor of divinity, and during the time he held that post he greatly distinguished himself by his learning and eloquence. He became chaplain to Queen ELIZABETH, who was a great admirer of his eloquence, and used to call him her little black husband. She appointed him, in 1567, master of Trinity College and regius professor. In 1573 Whitgift became dean of Lincoln; in 1576 bishop of Worcester; and in 1583 he was made Archbishop of Canterbury. He founded an hospital at Croydon, determinately resisted the encroachments of the Puritans, patronised learning, and was highly esteemed by the most pious clergy of his time. He was born at Great Grimsby, Lincolnshire, in 1530; and died in London, 1604.

REMARKS.

The prominent features of the TUDOR period were :—

1. *Establishment of the* Reformation, *and discovery of America.*

2. The basis of our present European System, which dates from the invasion of Italy by CHARLES VII. of France.

3. The foundation of English influence on the Continent.

4. A spirit of enterprise and the extension of commerce.

5. The production of some of the most famous characters, such as HOOKER, SHAKESPEARE, and SPENSER.

HENRY VII. was so fond of money, that nearly all the punishments inflicted by him consisted of fines. He was a hot Lancastrian, and did his utmost to put down the House of York. Even in the coronation of his Queen, he took no part in the ceremony. Finding his end approaching, he liberated all prisoners in London, desiring his successor to make restitution to such as he had wronged, and ordered 2,000 masses to be said for his soul, on condition that they should not cost more than sixpence each.

The annual value of the religious houses suppressed in the reign of HENRY VIII. was £160,000, and the immediate result of such spoliation was, that many persons were deprived of the means of subsistence, and in consequence became vagrants. Insurrections followed, and severe laws were enacted against vagrancy; while the money thus realised by the destruction of Church property, was disposed of in various ways. One portion was used in pensioning the monks; a second, for founding six bishoprics (already mentioned), fifteen new chapters, grammar schools, hospitals, Trinity College, Cambridge, and Christ Church, Oxford; another portion of the money was spent in the erection of castles at Southsea, Deal, Walmer, and Sandown, and also for improving Dover harbour; but the greater part fell into the hands of the King and his favourites.

On account of the encouragement given by ELIZABETH to nautical affairs, she was styled "The Restorer of the English Navy," and "The Queen of the Northern Seas."

Owing to the abundance of wheat and malt in 1553, a barrel of beer was sold for sixpence, and four large loaves for a penny.

Greek, Latin, and Hebrew were much cultivated, especially in the reign of ELIZABETH, who was well skilled in each of those languages.

In the time of the Tudors, children were treated with very great severity, being subjected to corporal punishment, and on no occasion allowed to sit in the presence of their parents, or to speak without permission.

The corrupt state of the Romish Church appears to have reached its climax at the beginning of the sixteenth century, for a Benedictine monk, who wrote a few years before, states, "That the law had departed from the priests, judgment from the rulers, and counsel from the elders, good faith from the people, reverence of superiors from the children, loyal affection from subjects, religion from the prelates, devotion from the monks, modesty from the nuns, discipline from the young, and learning from the clergy." The sale of indulgences became most flagrant at this time, because money was required for completing the

Church of St. Peter at Rome. TETZEL and his companions sold these indulgences to the highest bidders, that were foolish enough to believe that they could purchase salvation either for themselves or their deceased friends. TETZEL's form of Absolution ran thus :—

"May our Lord Jesus Christ have mercy on thee, and absolve thee by the merits of his most holy passion. And I, by his authority, that of his blessed apostles Peter and Paul, and of the most holy Pope, granted and committed to me in these parts, do absolve thee, first from all ecclesiastical censures in whatever manner they have been incurred, and then from all thy sins, transgressions, and' excesses, how enormous soever they may be, even from such as are reserved for the cognisance of the holy see ; and as far as the keys of the holy church extend, I remit to you all punishment which you deserve in purgatory on their account : and I restore you to the holy sacraments of the church, to the unity of the faithful, and to that innocence and purity which you possessed at baptism ; so that when you die, the gates of punishment shall be shut, and the gates of the paradise of delight shall be opened ; and if you shall not die at present, this grace shall remain in full force when you are at the point of death. In the name of the Father, and of the Son, and of the Holy Ghost."

In consequence of so many of the nobility being slain during the wars of the *Roses*, the TUDOR sovereigns were enabled to carry the royal prerogative much higher than their predecessors.

The **Tudor Dynasty** extended over a period of 118 years, beginning with the accession of HENRY VII., and ending with the death of ELIZABETH.

THE LEADING EVENTS AND PRINCIPAL DATES OF THE TUDOR PERIOD.

The Sweating Sickness prevailed in England ... ... A.D. 1485
Henry VII. united the Houses of York and Lancaster by marrying Elizabeth of York, and instituted a bodyguard of 50 men, called "Yeomanry of the Guard" 1486
Bartholomew Diaz discovered the Cape of Good Hope ... 1486
Battle of Stoke 1487
Edward Earl of Warwick, personated by Lambert Simnel, who aspired to the throne 1487
The brother of Columbus brought maps and sea-charts to England 1489
America discovered by Columbus 1492
Perkin Warbeck appeared in Ireland under the title of Richard Duke of York, the younger brother of Edward IV. 1492
Newfoundland discovered by Sebastian Cabot... 1495

Perkin, aided by James IV. of Scotland, invaded England A.D.

Perkin made a descent upon Cornwall, but was captured

Vasco de Gama made the voyage to India by the Capo of
Good Hope ...

The Earl of Warwick and Perkin executed ...

Prince Arthur married to Catherine of Arragon, but died
the following year, when she was contracted to
Prince Henry ...

The right of Sanctuary was limited, by which persons
could not be benefited a second time ...

Death of Henry VII. and accession of his son Henry VIII.

Murderers and Felons deprived of the benefit of clergy ...

For the furtherance of Navigation, the Trinity House was
founded ...

Battle of Spurs ...

Battle of Flodden Field ...

The first Thesis of Martin Luther affixed to the church-
door at Wittenberg ...

Luther published his 95 Propositions ...

Dr. Linacre founded the College of Physicians... ...

Six men and women were burnt at Coventry for having
instructed their children in the Apostles' Creed, the
Ten Commandments, and the Lord's Prayer ...

Luther excommunicated by the Pope ...

Henry and Francis held their interview at the "Field of
the Cloth of Gold" ...

The Pope's bull burnt by Luther ...

Henry VIII. received the title "The Defender of the Faith"

Bows and arrows fell into disuse among the English ...

The Spaniards invented muskets ...

A Portuguese ship under Ferdinando Magellan made the
first voyage round the world ...

Tonstal, Bishop of Durham, wrote a treatise on Arithme-
tic, which was the first printed in England ...

Hops were introduced into England from the Netherlands

William Tyndale translated into English the New Testament, the whole edition of which was bought by
the Bishop of London and burnt at St. Paul's Cross

Protest of 14 imperial cities of Germany against the
Second Decree of the Diet of Spires, from which
originated the term "Protestant" ...

Death of Cardinal Wolsey ...

Birth of Queen Elizabeth ...

Papal supremacy annulled in England ... ... A.D. 1534
Tyndale and Coverdale translated the whole Bible into
    English 1535
Sir Thomas Moore and Bishop Fisher executed for denying
    the King's supremacy 1535
Destruction of the English Monasteries began 1535
Wales incorporated with England and represented in the
    English Parliament 1536
Thomas Cromwell established the parochial registers of
    births, marriages, and deaths 1536
Edward VI. born 1537
"The Bloody Statute," or "Law of Six Articles" 1539
Cranmer's Bible ordered to be kept in the Churches ... 1539
Catherine Howard executed 1542
Copernicus the Astronomer died 1543
Henry VIII. married Catherine Parr 1543
Mortars and Cannon were cast in iron 1543
Boulogne captured 1544
The Treaty of Crepy 1544
The Litany published in English 1544
Interest on loans of money paid at ten per cent. 1545
Council of Trent commenced 1545
Ann Askew executed under the "Act of the Six Articles" 1546
Battle of Pinkie 1547
Death of Henry VIII. 1547
The whole Bible in English and the Paraphrase of Eras-
    mus ordered to be set up in every parish church ... 1547
The University of Jena founded 1548
The Liturgy revised 1549
Lord Seymour beheaded on a charge of high treason; his
    death-warrant being signed by Cranmer 1549
Ket's Rebellion 1549
Bucer, Professor of Divinity at Cambridge 1549
An Act passed authorising the marriage of the clergy, and
    one for the eating of fish on fast days, for the sup-
    port of the fisheries 1549
Shrewsbury School founded 1551
Somerset beheaded 1552
Death of Edward VI. 1553
Roman Catholic religion re-established 1553
Wyatt's rebellion, and execution of Lady Jane Grey ... 1554
Philip of Spain married Mary I. 1554
Marian persecution 1555

	A.D. 1
Cranmer burnt	1
First commercial treaty with Russia	1
Battle of St. Quentin	1
Death of Queen Mary, and loss of Calais	1
Protestant religion re-established	1
Reformation established in Scotland	1
Westminster College founded...	1
The Queen of Scots returned to Scotland	1
Reformation completed	1
English non-conformists acquire the name of "Puritans"	1
Separation of the Puritans from the Established Church...	1
Darnley murdered, and Mary married to Bothwell ...	1
Rise of the Independents	1
An insurrection in Ireland for the purpose of re-establishing Popery in that country	
University of Edinburgh founded	
An Act passed against Jesuits	
Babington's conspiracy against Queen Elizabeth	
Battle of Zutphen...	
Execution of Mary Stuart	
Defeat of the Spanish Armada	
The first English newspaper published	
The stocking-frame invented by the Rev. W. Lee, of Nottingham	
Trinity College, Dublin, founded	
Expedition to Cadiz	
The East India Company incorporated	
Conspiracy of Essex, and his execution	
Death of Elizabeth	

THE HOUSE OF STUART.

James I. of England and VI. of Scotland, was the son of Mary, Queen of Scots, and Lord Darnley. Queen of Scots, was the grand-daughter of Margaret was the daughter of Henry VII. Through his g father, James V., he was able to trace his descent Margaret, the sister of Edgar Atheling. A.D. 1603—

WARS.

1. The Bohemians refused to recognise the new Emperor, ...DINAND II., and chose for their King, FREDERIC, the Elector ...tine, son-in-law of JAMES. This step on the part of the Bo-...ians caused the **Thirty Years' War** (which began in 1618 and ...d by the **Peace of Westphalia** in 1648), and was followed by ...Battle of Prague, in which FREDERIC was defeated by the ...erialists, and forced to flee with his Queen and children to ...land, Nov. 7, 1620.

2. After FREDERIC had been thus driven from his dominions, ...the Protestant cause among the people of Bohemia in a fair ...· to be ruined, the force of public indignation moved the King ...and 12,000 men under Count MANSFELDT to aid in recovering ...Palatinate, but the expedition came to nought, two-thirds of ...men dying on the way, 1624.

CHIEF EVENTS.

By the accession of JAMES I., whose coronation took place at ...stminster, July 17, 1603, the **Crowns of England and** ...tland **were united;** on account of which he was called ...ing of Great Britain."

Before ascending the English throne, two conspiracies were ...ned against JAMES; one in 1582, called the **Raid of Ruthven,** ...n he was made prisoner by ALEXANDER RUTHVEN, Earl of ...vrie, but he managed to escape. The other conspiracy, desig- ...d the **Gowrie Plot,** was formed in 1600, on which occasion ...King's life was attempted by Lord GOWRIE, who had invited ...into his castle, but his attendants saved him.

After JAMES had come to the English throne, the following ...piracies were entered into for his overthrow :—

1. **The Main Plot** (so called to distinguish it from another ...d the "Bye Plot") was formed by Lord COBHAM and (as ...think) Sir WALTER RALEIGH. Its object was, by the aid of ...Spanish Government, to place on the throne ARABELLA ...RT, JAMES's cousin, 1603.

2. **The Bye Plot** (also called the **"Surprising Treason"**) ...leaded by BROKE, brother of Lord COBHAM, and Sir GRIFFIN ...KHAM, and aimed at imprisoning the King and improving the ...rnment, 1603. In this conspiracy both Puritans and Roman ...olics were engaged. The plotters were detected; BROKE and ...priests, named WATSON and CLARKE, were executed. Sir ...TER RALEIGH being suspected of participation in these plots, ...onfined 13 years in prison, and ultimately beheaded.

3. Gunpowder Plot.—This terrible scheme was formed by the Roman Catholics for blowing up the Houses of Parliament by means of 36 barrels of gunpowder, and thereby destroying the King, Lords, and Commons at one blow, Nov. 5, 1605. An anonymous letter addressed to MONTEAGLE, warning him not to attend the Parliament, which was to assemble Nov. 5, 1605, led to the discovery of the plot. The principal conspirators were ROBERT CATESBY, Sir HENRY PERCY, and GUY FAWKES, the last of whom was detected (Nov. 4) while arranging the powder in the vaults under the House of Lords. On being seized, CATESBY and PERCY were killed; GUY FAWKES, Sir EVERARD DIGBY, WINTER, and others, were executed.

To prevent the Courts of Common Law from interfering with the Ecclesiastical Courts, a series of petitions, entitled Articuli Cleri, were presented to the Star Chamber by Archbishop BAN-CROFT, but the application was unsuccessful, 1605.

Hampton Court Conference, was opened by JAMES (Jan. 4, 1604) for the purpose of settling the differences between the clergy of the Established Church and the Puritans, the latter of whom had presented to the King a petition, called the " **Millenary Petition**" (because it was signed by nearly a thousand persons) in which were contained the following demands :—

1. Alterations in the Book of Common Prayer.

2. Good and learned pastors, and reform in Church government.

The Conference did not terminate to the satisfaction of the Puritans, between whom and the clergy the following points were agreed upon :—

1. That there should be a new translation of the Bible.

2. That a few changes should be made in the Book of Common Prayer.

3. That a lawful minister only was to administer the rite of Baptism.

4. That the sacramental part of the Catechism should be added.

5. That no part of the Apocrypha opposed to Scripture should be read.

6. That the number of judges in the High Commission Court should be limited.

Peace was concluded with Spain, Aug. 18, 1604. James Town in Virginia was founded, which is said to have been the first permanent settlement of the English in North America, 1607.

ithorised **Version** of the Bible was published, 1611.
n was executed by 47 divines, who were employed
)m 1607 to 1611.

i English colony was planted in **Ulster**, and on pre-
ʒ money for its defence, JAMES created the title of
:h was sold to any one for £1,000.

iewed the Charter to the East India Company in
permission of the Great Mogul the first English
ablished at **Surat,** 1612.

V. of France was murdered by the fanatical
610, an event which caused the laws against the
ics in England to be executed with greater rigour.

death of Lord CECIL (1612) great differences con-
:d between the King and his Parliament, and in 1614
withheld supplies on the ground that their grievances
:dressed.

religious persecutions in their own country, about
om Holland, called the **"Pilgrim Fathers,"** emig-
England, and are said to have been the **Originators**
l **States of America.** They reached **Cape Cod**
hich they called **New Plymouth.**

nons quarrelled with the King for imprisoning one
rs, Sir E. SANDYS, but he informed them that their
derived from his ancestors and himself : upon which
the **Protestation,** in which they asserted that
privileges, and jurisdictions of Parliament are the
loubted birthright and inheritance of the subjects of

s son, Prince CHARLES, being engaged to the Infanta
:d to see her, and therefore he and BUCKINGHAM
ʒuise to Madrid, 1623. The engagement was after-
ff.

gn came into notice the three religious sects called
Baptists, and **Independents,** the originator of the
ion being ROBERT BROWN, whose followers were
wnists.

ance of Sir HUGH MIDDLETON, the **London New**
ny was founded, and that city supplied with water,
ight from Ware (Herts.) to Islington, a distance of
arithms were invented by Baron Napier, of Scot-
:e and farthings were coined, and broad-silk manu-
:ed. Hudson's Bay was discovered. The thermo-
er scientific instruments were invented. Charter-
as refounded. Licences were first granted to public

houses. A newspaper called "**The Weekly News**" was published. The circulation of the blood was discovered by Dr. HARVEY.

JAMES was educated by the famous BUCHANAN. The King published a work called "**Basilicon Doron**," or the "Royal Gift," which he intended for his son. He also wrote other books, and made such a show of his learning, that he was called by his flatterers, "The British Solomon," and by the Duke of SULLY, "The wisest fool in Christendom." He ordered a royal declaration to be drawn up, called the "**Book of Sports**," authorising the people after divine services on Sundays, to indulge in all sorts of amusements: such as dancing and archery. JAMES was passionately fond of hunting, and established horse-racing at Newmarket. Before he reigned three months, no fewer than 700 persons were knighted by him. On leaving Scotland for England, he said he was going to the "**Land of Promise**." The King lost the affections of his English subjects through his extreme partiality to the Scotch, and pompous display of the royal prerogative.

JAMES died of a tertia ague at Theobalds (Herts.), March 27, 1625, and was buried at Westminster.

C CELEBRATED PERSONS.

William Bird, a famous musician, composer of the fine canon, *Non Nobis, Domine*. (1543—1623).

Sir Thomas Bodley, a diplomatist in the reign of ELIZABETH, rebuilt the University Library of Oxford, ever since called the Bodleian Library. (1544—1612).

Prince Henry, the King's eldest son, died 1612.

Robert Cecil, Earl of Salisbury and JAMES's principal minister. Died 1612.

Arabella Stuart, cousin of the King, was imprisoned in the Tower for having married WILLIAM SEYMOUR, grandson of the Earl of HERTFORD. In consequence of her sufferings she lost her reason, and died 1615.

Sir Walter Raleigh, a distinguished navigator and historian was a native of Devonshire. Being a man of an enterprising spirit he attempted, in the preceding reign, to found a colony in North America, under the name of **Virginia**, in honour of Queen ELIZABETH, but it proved a failure. On his return to England he brought the **Tobacco Plant**. Being suspected of participation in the Main Plot, he was committed to prison, where he remained thirteen years, during which he wrote (among other works) his "**History of the World**." Having promised to point out in Guiana some

ines which he pretended he had discovered, RALEIGH (being
d from the Tower) sailed to that country. Instead of
g his followers the rich mines, he burnt the town of St.
s. The Spaniards, through their ambassador, GONDOMAR,
ined of this conduct to JAMES, who ordered RALEIGH to be
ed on his former charge, which rested upon the evidence of
COBHAM. He was therefore beheaded, 1618. Just before
his head upon the block to receive the executioner's blow,
GH felt the edge of the axe, and remarked that "It was a
but a sure remedy for all evils."

rancis **Bacon** (Lord Verulam), called the **Father of In-
ve Philosophy,** was born in London, 1561. Having become
ellor of England, he abused his high office by bribery and
tion, for which he was sentenced to pay a fine of £40,000,
be imprisoned during the King's pleasure. The fine was
ards remitted, and BACON released and pensioned on £1800
. Among the works of this philosopher may be named, the
i *Organum,* the *Advancement of Learning,* and the *Essays.*
.626.

eorge **Abbot,** became Archbishop of Canterbury, and was
: the forty-seven divines employed in translating the au-
ed version of the Bible. (1562—1633).

ames **I.,** author of the *Basilicon Doron,* or "Royal Gift,"
nterblast to Tobacco, and other works. Died 1625.

eorge **Chapman,** an English poet, who first translated
r. Died 1634.

ir **Everard Digby,** a participator in the Gunpowder Plot,
ich he was executed, 1606.

obert **Catesby,** was the leading conspirator in the Gun-
r Plot, 1605.

obert **Burton,** author of "The Anatomy of Melancholy."
—1640).

erardus Johannes **Vossius,** a German critic, historian,
ronologist, was created Doctor of Laws by the University
ord. Among his works may be named a *History of Pelag-
,* which offended the Calvinists. (1577—1649).

rilliam **Harvey,** an eminent physician, was born at Folk-
n Kent, 1578. Having received his education at Cambridge,
ceeded to Padua, where he took his degree of Doctor in
ne. In 1619 he discovered the circulation of the blood, and
3 published a treatise on the subject entitled *Exercitatio
nica de Motu Cordis et Sanguinis.* In 1651 he published
tationes de generatione Animalium. In 1645, HARVEY was
warden of Merton College, Oxford; and in 1654, elected

president of the College of Physicians, though the latter distinction, his infirm state of health compelled him to decline. He endowed the College of Physicians with his paternal estate, on condition that an annual oration should be delivered in the College, and provision made for the Keeper of the Library and Museum. Died 1657.

Edward Herbert, Lord Cherbury, noted as an ambassador, soldier, and writer, was born 1581. Among his works may be named, a "Life of HENRY VIII.," and *De Veritate.* Died 1648.

Edmund Gunter, an English mathematician, discovered the variations of the magnetic needle, invented a portable quadrant, which goes by his name, and a scale used by navigators. (1581—1626).

Philip Massinger, a distinguished dramatic poet, whose best play is entitled, *A New Way to Pay Old Debts.* (1584—1640).

William Drummond, a Scotch poet, was the son of Sir JOHN DRUMMOND, of Hawthornden, and friend of BEN JONSON. His poems consist of Epigrams, Madrigals, Sonnets, and other pieces, and are characterised by harmony of versification. (1585—1649).

Robert Carr, Duke of Somerset, and favourite of the King, poisoned Sir THOMAS OVERBURY, because the latter objected to his marrying the Countess of ESSEX. Having lost the King's favour, he and his wife retired into the country on a pension of £4,000 per annum. Died 1645.

Sir Thomas Overbury, became intimately acquainted with the King's favourite—ROBERT CARR or KER—by whose contrivance he was poisoned in the Tower, 1613. Sir THOMAS OVERBURY was the author of a poem called "The Wife," and a piece entitled "Characters," &c.

Thomas Carew, an English poet, author of a masque, called "Coelum Britannicum." (1589—1639).

Inigo Jones, a celebrated architect, who introduced into England the Palladian Style. He wrote a work on "Stonehenge," and in 1620 was appointed one of the commissioners for repairing St. Paul's Cathedral. Died 1652.

Charles I. was the second son of James I. A.D. 1625—1649.

A   **WARS.**

1. CHARLES, without any substantial reasons, declared war against Spain. An expedition under Viscount WIMBLEDON was despatched to Cadiz in 1625; but it proved unsuccessful. A peace was concluded between the two countries, Nov. 1630.

2. Instigated by BUCKINGHAM, CHARLES declared war against France, and made three attempts to relieve Rochelle, the stronghold of the Huguenots, at that time besieged by Cardinal RICHELIEU, the French minister, who wished to extirpate Protestantism.

1. The first expedition was undertaken by the Duke of BUCKINGHAM, whom the inhabitants of Rochelle refused to admit, as they had not been prepared for his arrival. He next directed his course to the Isle of Rhé, where, without gaining any advantage, he lost more than half his men, 1627.

2. Lord DENBIGH (BUCKINGHAM's brother-in-law) headed the second expedition for aiding the Rochellers, but it was without success, 1628.

3. The Duke of BUCKINGHAM resolved on heading the third expedition in person, but in the midst of his preparations was killed at Portsmouth by JOHN FELTON. The latter, an Irish lieutenant, was exasperated with the Duke for not conferring upon him a captaincy in the army. The expedition was now placed in the hands of the Earl of LINDSAY, but the attempt was again ineffectual (1628), and Rochelle, after losing numbers of its inhabitants, surrendered to the King of France, Oct. 18, 1628.

This war terminated by a **Peace** between the two countries, 1630.

3. CHARLES having attempted to enforce the Prayer Book and Episcopacy upon the Scots, they took up arms in defence of their national religion. The two armies met at Berwick, where the King concluded a **Treaty** called the "**Pacification of Berwick**," by which it was stipulated :—

1. That the armies on both sides should be disbanded.

2. That the King's authority should be acknowledged.

3. That a Parliament and General Assembly of the Kirk should be summoned to settle all differences, June 18, 1639.

4. As the Scots did not carry out the conditions of the Pacification of Berwick, war was renewed, and then followed the

Battle of Newburn-upon-Tyne, in which the Scotch under General LESLIE defeated the English under CONWAY, 1640. This encounter was immediately followed by the **Treaty of Ripon**, by which the parties agreed:—

1. That the Scotch were to be paid £5600 a week till matters should be arranged.

2. That in the meantime they should abstain from any hostilities.

THE CIVIL WAR, OR GREAT REBELLION.

This rebellion was chiefly caused—

1. By the King's unconstitutional measure in raising money.

2. CHARLES's great imprudence in going personally to the House of Commons for the purpose of seizing five of its leading members by whom he was opposed. This last proceeding induced the House to believe that he entertained some secret design against its members, and, therefore, amongst other demands, they asked permission to have control of the army for a short time. The King gave to this request a decisive refusal, after which both parties prepared for war.

The King's adherents were called **Cavaliers, Royalists, and Malignants**; and his opponents **Parliamentarians** and **Roundheads**; the latter name being given on account of their short hair.

CHARLES raised his standard at Nottingham, which was virtually a declaration of hostilities, Aug. 22, 1642.

The following were the principal battles:—

1. **Battle of Edgehill**, or **The Edgehill Fight** (Warwickshire). This was the first important engagement in the civil war. The forces of CHARLES (who was personally present in the battle) were commanded by the Earl of LINDSAY; Prince RUPERT commanded the horse, Sir JACOB ASTLEY, the foot; Sir ARTHUR ASHTON, the dragoons; and Sir JOHN HEYDON, the artillery: while the Parliamentarians were under the Earl of ESSEX. Though numbers fell on both sides, amounting to 12,000 men, neither party could justly claim the victory. LINDSAY was mortally wounded and taken prisoner, Oct. 23, 1642.

2. **Battle of Brentford** (Middlesex), in which the King's cavalry under RUPERT defeated the Parliamentarians, and took 500 prisoners, Nov. 12, 1642.

3. **Battle of Stratton** (Wilts). In this engagement the Parliamentarians were defeated, May 16, 1643.

4. **Battle of Chalgrove Field** (near Oxford), in which the Royalists were victorious. In this battle JOHN HAMPDEN, one of

the most celebrated Parliamentarian leaders, was mortally wounded, June, 19, 1643.

5. **Battle of Atherton Moor** (Yorkshire), in which the Roundheads under Lord FAIRFAX, were defeated by the Cavaliers under the Earl of NEWCASTLE, June 30, 1643.

6. **Battle of Lansdown** (near Bath). In this encounter great losses were sustained on both sides, the advantage being with the Royalists, July 5, 1643.

7. **Battle of Roundway Down** (near Devizes), in which the Parliamentarians, under Sir WILLIAM WALLER, were completely vanquished, July 13, 1643.

8. **Battle of Newbury** (Berkshire) was fought with desperate valour on both sides, and continued till midnight; but victory was undecided. Among the slain was LUCIUS CARY, Lord Falkland, a nobleman of great worth, who aided the cause of CHARLES, Sept. 20, 1643.

9. **Battle of Nantwich**, where the Royal forces, consisting of Irish troops, were vanquished by FAIRFAX, Jan. 25, 1644.

10. **Battle of Cropredy Bridge** (near Daventry) where the Parliamentarians, under WALLER, were routed by the Royalists commanded by RUTHVEN, Earl of Brentford, June 29, 1644.

11. **Battle of Marston Moor** (Yorkshire). In this engagement, CHARLES's army, under Prince RUPERT and NEWCASTLE, was completely defeated by the united forces of the Scots and Parliamentarians under FAIRFAX, OLIVER CROMWELL, and the Earl of LEVEN, who made a large number of the Royalists prisoners; capturing their guns, ammunition, and baggage. This was the first battle in which OLIVER CROMWELL came into notice. He was mainly instrumental in obtaining the victory, July 2, 1644.

12. **Second Battle of Newbury**, in which the Earl of MANCHESTER gained a partial victory over the King, Oct. 27, 1644.

13. **Battle of Naseby** (Northamptonshire), by which the affairs of CHARLES became altogether hopeless. The Royalists were commanded by Lord ASTLEY, Prince RUPERT, and Sir MARMADUKE LANGDALE; the King headed the body of reserve. The Parliamentary army was under FAIRFAX and CROMWELL, the latter of whom again distinguished himself. The Royalists were completely routed, and 500 taken prisoners. CHARLES abandoned the field and lost all his cannon and baggage, June 14, 1645. The King's enemies got possession of his cabinet, which contained his correspondence with the Queen, a correspondence which was afterwards published by order of the Parliament, and which showed that he could not be trusted.

14. Battle of Philiphaugh.—During the time that hostilities were raging in England, MONTROSE was fighting for CHARLES in Scotland, where he gained a series of victories—Tippermuir (Sept. 1, 1644); **Aberdeen** (Sept. 12); **Inverlochy** (Feb. 2, 1645); **Auldearn** (May 9); **Alford** (July 2); and **Kilsyth** (Aug. 15); but he was vanquished by LESLIE, at Philiphaugh, Sept. 13, 1645.

B   **CHIEF EVENTS.**

The First Parliament.—That CHARLES might be enabled to pay his father's debts, and prosecute his continental wars, he called his First Parliament and demanded £700,000; of which sum he obtained only £140,000, with tonnage and poundage for one year. The Commons refused to grant a larger sum, because the King would not redress certain grievances of which they complained. Indignant at this conduct on the part of his subjects, CHARLES dissolved the Parliament, which had been removed from Westminster to Oxford, on account of the plague then prevailing in London, 1625.

The Second Parliament was as difficult to manage as the first. Heavy charges were brought against the Duke of BUCK-INGHAM, the following being the principal :—

1. Negligence in guarding the seas.

2. Furnishing the French King with ships to be used against the **Huguenots.**

3. Administering medicine to the late King without the knowledge of his physicians.

To save the Duke from the consequence of these charges, the King dissolved the Second Parliament, 1626.

The Third Parliament.—Failing to raise a sufficient sum of money by forced loans and arbitrary taxes, CHARLES convoked his Third Parliament (1628), and obtained five subsidies, but only in consideration of his assent to the bill called the "**Petition of Right,**" by which some of the most important clauses of **Magna Charta** were confirmed. **The Petition of Right,** called the "**Second Great Charter of English Liberties,**" declared the illegality of the following grievances :—

1. Benevolences, forced loans, and arbitrary imprisonments.

2. The levying of taxes without the consent of Parliament.

3. The billeting of soldiers in private houses, and martial law.

In the second session of this Parliament (1629) the Commons drew up a **Protestation,** in which they complained :—

1. Against all innovations in religion.

2 Against the levying of tonnage and poundage without their consent; which provision declared that those who should favour either, were to be considered public enemies. For these proceedings nine of the members, viz., SELDEN, HOLLIS, ELIOT, HOBART, HAYMAN, CRITON, LONG, STROUD, and VALENTINE were stigmatized as "Vipers," and committed to prison by the King, who dissolved the Parliament, March 10, 1629.

From 1629 to 1640, there was no Parliament.

The Fourth or Short Parliament.—Want of money induced CHARLES to call his Fourth Parliament (in April 1640) which he dissolved in May, because he could not obtain unconditional supplies.

The Fifth or the celebrated **Long Parliament**, was opened by the King in person, Nov. 3, 1640, sat till CROMWELL turned it out (April 10, 1653,) and was ultimately dissolved in 1660. The chief proceedings of this Parliament were :—

1. The abolition of the Star Chamber, the High Commission Court, and the impressment of soldiers.

2. The impeachment of the Earl of STRAFFORD and Archbishop LAUD. The former was beheaded May 12, 1641; the latter suffered the same punishment, Jan. 10, 1645.

3. The passing of a statute by which it was enacted that Parliament should not be dissolved without its own consent.

4. The liberation and compensation of those who had been victimised by the Star Chamber.

5. Orders were issued for the removal of all images from the churches.

6. The passing of the **Triennial Act,** to prevent the King from governing without a Parliament, as CHARLES had done for eleven years, and to secure the calling of one at least every third year.

7. The first great dissension between the House of Lords and Commons was occasioned by the latter having passed a bill excluding bishops from Parliament, and clergymen from holding civil offices. This bill was rejected by the Lords.

8. Instead of giving the King supplies, the Commons voted £300,000 for the benefit of the Scots.

The opposition party in the House of Commons drew up a **Remonstrance,** which, after a long debate, was passed by a majority of eleven. The complaints were chiefly such as these :—

1. The bad administration of the King from the beginning of his reign.

2. The unsuccessful expeditions to France and Spain.

3. Aiding the French King by ships against the Huguenots.

4. Forced loans, and the violent dissolution of four Parliaments.

5. The fining and imprisonment of members for their conduct in the House.

6. Superstitious innovations in religion without legal authority, 1640—1642.

These proceedings were followed by some unreasonable demands on the part of the Commons, which were:—

1. That Parliament should have the disposal of the forts and castles.

2. That the same power should be exercised with regard to the militia.

Ship-money.—Among the many illegal exactions of CHARLES that of ship-money caused the greatest dissatisfaction. This tax was first levied in 1007, for providing a fleet against the Danes. At the suggestion of NOY, the Attorney-General, it was revived in 1634. The impost was not only laid on the seaport towns as formerly, but even upon the **inland counties.** JOHN HAMPDEN being rated at twenty shillings for his estate in Buckinghamshire refused to pay the tax on the ground of its illegality. The case was therefore tried before the twelve judges, who, with the exception of two, decided against HAMPDEN, June 12, 1637.

The Covenant.—The attempt of CHARLES to put down Presbyterianism by imposing the Prayer-Book and Episcopacy upon the Scots, caused that people to form at Edinburgh four committees, called the **Four Tables,** which consisted of the nobles, ministers, gentry, and burgesses. These four tables drew up what is called the **Covenant,** by which they renounced Popery, and engaged to resist all innovations upon their national religion, March 1, 1638. A few months afterwards a General Assembly met at Glasgow, and abolished the Court of High Commission, the Canons, Liturgy, and Episcopacy.

The Irish Rebellion.—Wishing to take advantage of the unsettled state of England, the Irish broke out into open rebellion in 1641, when 40,000 Protestants were massacred by the Roman Catholics. The leaders of this brutal proceeding were ROGER MORE, Sir PHELIM O'NEALE, and Lord MAGUIRE, whose object was the expulsion of the English.

The Solemn League and Covenant was a compact made between the Parliamentarians and the Scots, by the terms of which both parties bound themselves—

1. To defend each other against all opponents.

2. To put down Popery, Prelacy, Heresy, and Schism.

3. To maintain the rights and privileges of Parliaments.

4. To bring to justice all malignants and incendiaries.

5. The Scots to furnish 21,000 men to aid in the war, at the expense of the English, 1643.

The Assembly of Divines met at Westminster, for the purpose of effecting a uniformity of worship between England and Scotland, 1643.

A conspiracy to restore peace, and in favour of the King, was formed by EDMUND WALLER, TOMKINS, and CHALONER, 1643. The plot was discovered, and TOMKINS and CHALONER executed, while WALLER, a poet and Member of the House of Commons, was fined £10,000.

The Self-denying Ordinance was passed, by which Members of Parliament were excluded from holding any civil or military office, April 3, 1645.

The New Model.—Some alterations effected in the army by FAIRFAX and CROMWELL, were called the New Model, 1645.

Pride's Purge.—Instructed by Lord GREY, of Groby, Colonel PRIDE excluded from the House of Commons the leading Members of the Presbyterian party. This proceeding was called Colonel PRIDE's Purge. Those who remained were called the **Rump Parliament,** 1648.

By the **Peace of Westphalia,** between France, the Emperor, and Sweden, which was signed at Munster, 1648, the principle of a balance of power in Europe was for the first time recognised; Alsace was given to France; Sweden obtained part of Pomerania and some other districts; the Lower-Palatinate was restored to the Elector-Palatine; the independence of the Swiss Confederation recognised by Germany; and the civil and political rights of the German States were established.

In this reign Hackney-coaches were first used, letters sent by post, Barometers invented, the manufacture of Irish linen was established, and Epsom Salts discovered. Covent-garden market was built by the Earl of BEDFORD.

Trial and Execution of the King.—After the battle of Naseby, CHARLES delivered himself into the hands of the Scots (believing that they would protect him) but they sold him to the English Parliament for £400,000. After being imprisoned in various places, the unhappy King was brought to trial on a charge of high treason against the people. He was tried at Westminster Hall by a court, the authority of which he denied, condemned, and executed, Jan. 30, 1649. He was buried at Windsor.

C   **CELEBRATED PERSONS.**

Sir Edward Coke, an eminent lawyer, became Chief Justice of the King's Bench. The famous Petition of Right was drawn up by Coke, who wrote many works on legal subjects, the most esteemed being "Coke on Lyttleton." He was born at Mileham, Norfolk, in 1550, and died 1634.

John Donne, a divine and poet. Though brought up a Roman Catholic, yet he embraced the Protestant religion when only 19 years of age. He became chaplain to JAMES I. and was so distinguished as a preacher that, before he had been one year in the ministry, 14 different livings were offered to him. DONNE is called by DRYDEN "the greatest wit of our nation." (1573—1631).

William Laud, Archbishop of Canterbury, was born at Reading, in 1573, where his father was a clothier. He made enemies by influencing the King to attempt many arbitrary measures in Church matters, and was executed for high treason, Jan. 1645.

Joseph Hall, called **The English Seneca,** was born in 1574. He became Bishop of Norwich in 1641, and wrote many works, including the "Enochimus, or Treatise on the Mode of Walking with God," and "Satires." Died 1656.

Guido, an illustrious Italian painter, whose greatest work is the "Penitence of St. Peter after denying Christ." (1575—1642).

Peter Paul Rubens, the greatest painter of the Flemish School, sketched the design for the ceiling of the banqueting house at Whitehall. (1577—1640).

John Taylor, called "The Water-Poet," was bound an apprentice to a waterman, and during this employment produced some poetical pieces, on account of which he was styled "The King's Water-Poet." He was strongly attached to the Royal cause, which he aided by his songs and satires. His writings show a vigorous mind but deficient education. Born at Gloucester, 1580; and died in London, 1654.

Domenichino, a celebrated Italian painter, improved so slowly at the first that his companions called him "*the ox*," but he soon proved that he possessed talents of the highest order. (1581—1641).

William Juxon, Archbishop of Canterbury, was born at Chichester in 1582. During the progress of the civil war he continued faithful to CHARLES, whom he attended at his execution. *Just* before laying his head upon the block, CHARLES said to

Juxon, "Remember;" by which word the King intended to remind him of a wish already expressed that the authors of his death might be forgiven by his successor. Died 1663.

Hugo Grotius, a learned Dutchman, author of a masterly work entitled *De Jure Belli et Pacis*, a treatise on the *Truth of the Christian Religion*, and other works. (1583—1645).

John Pym, a celebrated statesman, and great opponent to the measures of CHARLES I., was one of the number of those who conducted the impeachment of the Duke of BUCKINGHAM. (1584—1643).

John Selden, a celebrated lawyer and antiquary, was a leading man in drawing up the "Petition of Right." He took the Covenant in 1643, and was afterwards appointed by the Parliament, Keeper of the Records in the Tower. His chief works are " The Law of Nature and Nations," "The History of Tithes," "Mare Clausum," and "The Table Talk." He was born in Sussex, 1584, and died in London, 1654.

Cornelius Jansen, an eminent Roman Catholic Prelate, became Bishop of Ypres, in West Flanders, and founded the sect of Jansenists. (1585—1638).

Richelieu, a distinguished French Cardinal and Minister of LOUIS XIII., besieged Rochelle, which he compelled to surrender, in 1628. He was a liberal patron of literary men, founded the French Academy, and wrote, his own " Memoirs." (1585—1642).

John Bradshaw, a noted lawyer, and President of the High Court of Justice by which CHARLES was condemned. For his services on that occasion the Parliament presented him with Summer Hill, a seat of the Earl of ST. ALBANS. (1586—1659).

Lucius Cary (Lord Falkland), an excellent man, was killed at Newbury, 1643.

John Hampden, a distinguished patriot, and celebrated for his opposition to ship-money, was slain at Chalgrove Field, 1643.

George Villiers, Duke of Buckingham, a special favourite of JAMES I. and also of CHARLES, was stabbed by FELTON, at Portsmouth, while making preparations for an expedition to Rochelle. The only words he uttered, after receiving the fatal blow, were: " The villain has killed me." (1592—1628).

Francis Quarles, an English poet, received the appointment of Secretary to Archbishop USHER, and also became Chronologer to the City of London. QUARLES wrote several books, and was the author of " Emblems, Meditations, and Hieroglyphics," a work chiefly remarkable for its quaint illustrations. He was born near Rumford (Essex) 1592, and died 1641.

Sir Thomas Wentworth (Earl of Strafford), an eminent statesman, born in London in 1593, was the eldest son of Sir WILLIAM WENTWORTH WOODHOUSE, of Yorkshire. For some years he advocated the popular cause, but subsequently joined the King's party, and in 1632, was appointed Lord Deputy of Ireland. He aimed at rendering the King an absolute monarch, and the scheme for accomplishing that object he designated, in his correspondence with LAUD as the "Thorough." His government of Ireland was severe, but in some respects beneficial to that country, for he encouraged agriculture, promoted the Protestant interest, and introduced flax-seed, from which originated the linen manufacture. He was impeached of high treason, and lodged in the Tower. The principal charges against him were :—

1. That he had by his own authority imposed a tax upon the inhabitants of Yorkshire.

2. That he had exacted arbitrary taxes by quartering soldiers in Ireland against the laws of the kingdom.

3. That he had raised an army in Ireland for subverting the laws of England, Scotland, and Ireland, and to introduce arbitrary and tyrannical government.

STAFFORD'S able defence make such an impression upon the spectators that many were moved to tears, while his enemies apprehensive that he might be acquitted, resorted to a bill of attainder, when he was condemned and executed, May 12, 1641.

James Graham, Marquis of Montrose, a firm adherent of CHARLES, for whom he achieved some brilliant victories in Scotland, but was defeated by General LESLIE at Philiphaugh, near Selkirk, Sept. 13, 1645. On the King's surrendering to the Scots, MONTROSE capitulated, and in 1646, retired to Norway. At the request of Prince CHARLES he again invaded his native country, but his forces were routed by STRACHAN, the Scottish general, and himself taken prisoner. He was conveyed to Edinburgh, and there hanged and quartered, May 21, 1650.

Sir Anthony Vandyck, a famous Dutch painter, studied under RUBENS. The portrait of the Earl of STRAFFORD is considered one of his masterpieces. He was much patronised by CHARLES, who conferred upon him the honour of Knighthood (1599—1641).

Henrietta Maria, daughter of HENRY IV. of France, was married to CHARLES in 1625. Died 1669.

William Prynne, an eminent lawyer, wrote a libel against the QUEEN, for which he had to pay a fine of £3000, to stand the pillory, and to lose both his ears. He was the author several works on politics and religion. Born at Swainswick (near Bath) 1600; and died in London, 1669.

illiam **Chillingworth,** an eminent theologian, author of a
ntitled "The Religion of Protestants, a Safe Way to Salva-
(1602—1644).

bert **Devereux,** Earl of Essex, son of the Earl of ESSEX who
ecuted in the reign of ELIZABETH. After serving under Sir
IO VERE, in the Palatinate, and under Prince MAURICE, in
1, he returned to England and became a leader of the Par-
:arians, but was deprived of his command by the **Self-denying**
ance in 1645. Died 1646.

rd **Thomas Fairfax,** a Parliamentarian leader, so distin-
l himself at the Battle of Marston Moor in 1644, that he
General of the Army in the place of the Earl of ESSEX,
R CROMWELL being appointed his Lieutenant-General. He
to act as one of the King's judges, resigned his commission
), and made peace with CHARLES II. Died 1671.

ulius **Mazarin,** a Roman Cardinal, and Minister of State
IIS XIV. of France. (1602—1661).

hn **Gauden,** Bishop of Worcester, is supposed by many
e been the author of the " Icon Basilike, or the Portraiture
Sacred Majesty in his Solitude and Sufferings." (1605—

rince **Rupert** and **Maurice,** sons of FREDERICK V., Elector
ie, and ELIZABETH, daughter of James, came to England and
he cause of their uncle, CHARLES I. The former was deprived
command for surrendering Bristol to the Parliamentarians.
eet was commanded by him in the reign of CHARLES II.,
which he gained considerable credit in several actions
t the Dutch. The remaining part of his life was spent in
ng the various branches of philosophy. (1619—1682).

THE COMMONWEALTH.

A.D. 1649—1660.

WARS.

As Ireland had declared in favour of CHARLES II., CROM-
landed in that country, and reduced many of the people to
sion. He struck great terror into the natives by slaughter-

ing the garrisons of **Drogheda** and **Wexford.** He now returned to England, leaving IRETON, his son-in-law, to complete the conquest of IRELAND, 1649—1650.

2. Though the Scots proclaimed CHARLES II. King, yet they refused to permit his coronation, unless he would first promise to observe the Covenant, and the Solemn League and Covenant. These terms being repugnant to CHARLES, he resolved on attempting an unconditional restoration, and for that purpose despatched from Holland some forces under the Marquis of MONTROSE, who was defeated by STRACHAN (the Scottish general) at Invercarron, and afterwards hanged at Edinburgh on a gallows thirty feet high, 1650.

3. **Battle of Dunbar,** was fought between the English under CROMWELL, and the Scots under General LESLIE. The Scots were completely vanquished, 4000 of whom were slain, and 10,000 taken prisoners, Sept. 3, 1650.

4. **Battle of Worcester.**—CHARLES II. having raised an army in Scotland, invaded England, but met with a severe defeat at **Worcester.** CROMWELL spoke of this battle as his "crowning mercy." Of the Royalists 2,000 were slain, and 8,000 taken prisoners, the greater part of whom were sold as slaves to the American colonies, Sept. 3, 1651.

THE DUTCH WAR.

The causes of this war were :—

1. Neglect on the part of the Dutch to punish the murderers of DR. DORISLAUS, who had been sent by the English Parliament as an envoy to Holland.

2. The refusal of the states to form an alliance with the Commonwealth, because they did not sanction the execution of the late King.

That the Dutch might be provoked to begin hostilities, the English Parliament inflicted a severe blow upon their commerce by passing a **Navigation Act,** forbidding the importation of foreign goods except in English vessels, or in the vessels of the country where the goods were produced.

1. BLAKE defeated the Dutch, under TROMP, off **Dover,** and captured two ships, May 19, 1652.

2. The Dutch under DE RUYTER, and the English under AYSCUE, fought an indecisive battle off **Plymouth,** Aug. 16, 1652.

3. The Dutch, commanded by DE WITT and DE RUYTER, were defeated by the English under BLAKE, BOURNE, and PENN, near the coast of **Kent,** Sept. 28, 1652.

4. TROMP, the Dutch Admiral, having a fleet of 90 sail vanquished BLAKE, who had only 37 sail, near the Goodwin Sands, Nov. 28, 1652. After this success, TROMP sailed in triumph through the English Channel, with a broom at his mast head, intimating that he had swept the English from the sea.

5. BLAKE defeated TROMP off Portsmouth, the latter losing 11 men-of-war and 30 merchantmen, Feb. 10, 1653.

6. The Dutch were again defeated with a loss of 40 vessels, near Portland, Feb. 18, 1653. This fight lasted three days.

7. Off the North Foreland, the English under BLAKE, DEAN, and MONK, defeated the Dutch under TROMP, who lost 21 sail and 1300 prisoners, June 2, 1653.

8. On the coast of Holland there was another battle, in which the Dutch lost 30 men-of-war, and their Admiral TROMP was killed, July 31, 1653. This war resulted in a league between the two countries, called the **Treaty of Westminster** (April 5, 1654), by which the Dutch were bound:—

1. To render due deference to the English flag.

2. In no way to aid the cause of CHARLES II.

3. To pay £85,000 for previous expenses.

4. To satisfy certain demands of the English East India Company.

THE SPANISH WAR.

As Spain had given little or no provocation to England, the cause of this war must be ascribed to some secret motives of CROMWELL. He was probably induced to adopt this policy from the following reasons:—

1. To render his Protectorate memorable by extending the British dominions.

2. To make himself less dependent upon Parliamentary supplies by realizing money from newly acquired possessions.

3. The then declining condition of Spain, and her weakness in the West Indies, led the Protector to believe the work could be easily accomplished.

4. It is likely that MAZARIN, the French minister, and successor of RICHELIEU, also influenced CROMWELL, as France was as that time waging war against Spain.

1. PENN and VENABLES with very little trouble took from the Spaniards Jamaica, which has ever since remained in the hands of the English, 1655. On returning to England, these two admirals were sent to the Tower for not having done more.

2. BLAKE sailed to **Leghorn, Algiers,** and **Tunis,** in each of which places he compelled the authorities to give satisfaction for injuries done to English commerce, 1655.

3. The English under Captain STAYNER, captured at Cadiz two galleons with two million pieces of eight, Sept. 1656.

4. BLAKE gained a signal victory over the Spanish at Santa **Cruz** (in the Canaries), April 20, 1657.

5. The Spaniards were defeated at **Dunes** by the united forces of the French and English, 1658. As a reward for aiding them in obtaining this victory, the French gave England **Dunkirk,** which was afterwards sold to France by CHARLES II.

B   **CHIEF EVENTS.**

After the death of CHARLES I., the Rump Parliament abolished Monarchy and the House of Lords, and denounced every one as a traitor who should proclaim a new King without the authority of Parliament. The country was governed by a Council of Regency, consisting of 38 persons, of which BRADSHAW was the President, and MILTON the Latin Secretary. A new **Great Seal** was also introduced, 1649. The Duke of HAMILTON, Lord CAPEL, and the Earl of HOLLAND, were executed for participation in the royal conspiracy during the past year. Through the vigorous policy of CROMWELL, the Channel Islands and the American Colonies were obliged to acknowledge the Commonwealth. As the Parliament became jealous of CROMWELL's power, and were trying to curtail it, he went to the House, accompanied by 300 soldiers, and after reprimanding the members in very strong language, turned them out and locked the door, April 10, 1653.

Barebone's Parliament.—In forming his first Parliament CROMWELL desired the ministers of religion to send in the names of the most pious men in their congregations, and from these he selected 6 Irishmen, 6 Welshmen, 4 Scotsmen, and 139 Englishmen. Of these names 120 assembled (July 4, 1653), and into their hands CROMWELL committed the supreme authority, which they were to exercise till Nov. 3, 1654. This assembly was called the **"Little Parliament,"** and also "Barebone's Parliament," the latter name being given in derision from one of its members, whose name was **"Praise God Barebone,"** a leather seller in Fleet Street. Of their proceedings we may notice the following :—

1. They aimed at abolishing the Universities and some of the Law Courts, especially the Court of Chancery.

2. They established a system of great economy in the government, and opposed the monthly property-tax (£120,000) by which *the* army and navy were supported.

3. To render the laws of England easily attainable, a proposition was made that they should be so reduced as to be comprised in one small volume.

4. They advocated the prosecution of the Dutch war for the purpose of amalgamating the United Provinces with the Commonwealth of England.

5. They provided for the registration of births, marriages, and deaths.

After sitting five months, BAREBONE's Parliament, at the suggestion of Colonel SYDENHAM, surrendered the supreme power into the hands of CROMWELL, and a document was now drawn up by the military council of officers, and called the **Instrument of Government,** in which were embodied the following particulars :—

1. CROMWELL received the title of **"His Highness the Lord Protector."**

2. A Parliament was to be called every three years, and not to be dissolved under five months.

3. The Protector's council not to exceed 21, nor be fewer than 13.

4. England to return 400 members, Scotland and Ireland 30 each.

5. Bills passed by Parliament and presented for the Protector's assent, if not confirmed within 21 days, to become law without him.

6. Parliament to enact laws and regulate taxes; the making of peace and war to be in the hands of the Protector.

7. The standing army of Great Britain to be 30,000 men.

8. The Protector to enjoy his office for life, and the council immediately after his death to choose another Protector.

CROMWELL, after reading this new constitution, took an oath to observe its conditions, and was immediately conducted to Whitehall with great ceremony (Dec. 16, 1653).

THE PROTECTORATE.

CROMWELL summoned a **Second Parliament** (Sept. 3, 1654), which he dissolved (Jan. 31, 1655) because some of the members began to question his authority. Two Royalist insurrections were crushed, one in the West, headed by Sir JOSEPH WAGSTAFF; the other in the North, by the Earl of ROCHESTER, 1655.

Decimation.—A few insurrections raised by the Royalists furnished CROMWELL with a pretext for imposing a special tax upon them. This impost was called decimation, because the

Royalists were compelled to pay the **tenth penny** of their possessions. He also divided England into eleven **military districts**, placed each under a Major-general, who was invested with authority :—

1. To levy the taxes imposed by the Protector and his council.

2. To imprison any suspicious persons (1655).

CROMWELL's Third Parliament met (Sept. 17, 1656), but he took care to exclude 100 members on account of their known opposition to him. The chief proceedings of this Parliament were :—

1. An act was passed securing CROMWELL's personal safety, and declaring it high treason to conspire his death.

2. A bill, called the **Humble Petition and Advice**, was voted by a majority of 123 to 62, according to which the title of **King** was offered to the Protector (March 25, 1657), but through the influence of others, especially the members of his family, he declined the dignity (May 8, 1657).

3. Another **Humble Petition** and advice was presented to CROMWELL, by which he had authority—

1. To nominate his successor.

2. To create a House of Lords.

CROMWELL was now inaugurated with all the splendours of royalty in Westminster Hall. The Parliament re-assembled (Jan. 20, 1658), but it was dissolved by the Protector (Feb. 4) because the Commons refused to acknowledge the House of Lords which he had a short time before created.

On finding that LAMBERT and other officers were conspiring against him, CROMWELL removed them from the army. Colonel HUTCHINSON discovered this **Conspiracy**, the object of which was to make LAMBERT Protector.

Another **Plot** was formed, chiefly by the London apprentices, against CROMWELL, but the Lieutenant of the Tower suppressed it. Sir HENRY SLINGSBY, DR. HEWIT, and three other conspirators, were executed, 1657.

During the Commonwealth, the **Air-pump** was invented by a German named OTTO DE GUERICK; and **Air-Guns** by GUTER also a German. The religious sect called **Quakers**, or the Society of Friends, was founded by GEORGE FOX, a Leicestershire shoemaker. The **Banking System** commenced, goldsmiths being employed as the Merchants' bankers. Clergymen were deprived of their livings, and episcopacy was abolished.

Commerce flourished greatly, the friendship of the Protector *being* ardently sought by foreign powers.

Owing to the numerous plots against his life, and the effect of a pamphlet styled "**Killing no Murder**," which was written by Colonel TITUS, to inflame the people against him, the Protector's health began to decline. These anxieties were increased by the death of his favourite daughter, Mrs. CLAYPOLE, for whom he entertained such affection that he withdrew from public business for fourteen days, during which time he continued at her bedside. CROMWELL died of a tertian ague, Sept. 3, 1658, and was buried in Westminster Abbey.

The Protectorate of Richard Cromwell.

A.D. 1658—1659.

CROMWELL was succeeded by his eldest son, RICHARD, Sept. 3, 1658. A Parliament assembled (Jan. 29, 1659), but the Council of Officers, among whom were his uncle, DESBOROUGH, and his brother-in-law, FLEETWOOD, forced the Protector to dissolve it (April 22, 1659).

The Council of Officers having the chief power, restored the **Rump** or remnant of the Long Parliament, May 7, 1659.

Finding the army unmanageable, RICHARD CROMWELL formally resigned the Protectorate (May 25, 1659), withdrew to the Continent, and afterwards returned to his estate, at Cheshunt (Herts.), where he died, 1712.

HENRY CROMWELL, also resigned his command in Ireland, (June 15, 1659) and spent the remainder of his days in Cambridgeshire. His death occurred 1674.

Disagreement between the army and Parliament induced the **Royalists** to attempt an **Insurrection**, headed by Sir GEORGE BOOTH. The insurgents surprised Chester, but were routed by LAMBERT, at Nantwich, Aug. 19, 1659.

The Committee of Safety.—As this parliament refused to sanction all the measures of the Council of Officers, it was expelled by LAMBERT, Oct. 13, 1659, and the supreme authority placed in the hands of twenty-three persons, who were styled "The Committee of Safety."

General MONK, commander of the army in Scotland, declared in favour of the Parliament, which re-assembled, Dec. 26, 1659. Returning with his troops to England, MONK was joined by Lord,

Fairfax at York, and entered London without opposition, Feb. 3, 1660; and those Members of Parliament who had been expelled by Colonel Pride, were restored to their seats, Feb. 21. This Long Parliament, which was opened by Charles 1., Nov. 3, 1640, after determining that a new Parliament should be called, dissolved itself, March 16, 1660.

The Convention Parliament, so named because it was not summoned in a regular mannner, met (April 25) when Sir Harbottle Grimstone was appointed Speaker.

The Declaration of Breda.—Shortly after the Meeting of Parliament, Sir John Granville presented from Charles a letter, accompanied by a document called "The Declaration of Breda" (Netherlands), in which were offered the following conciliatory terms:—

1. A general pardon to all persons (except those rejected by Parliament) who returned to their allegiance within forty days.

2. Liberty of conscience to all who should not otherwise disturb the peace of the kingdom.

3. The regulation of disputed estates to be settled by Parliament.

4. The arrears of the soldiers to be paid, and the men themselves to be taken into the Royal service. These conditions being approved by Parliament, His Majesty was invited to return. Charles embarked at Scheveling, landed at Dover (May 25, 1660), and entered London, May 29, the latter date being noted as the time of his Restoration.

C   **CELEBRATED PERSONS.**

James Usher, Archbishop of Armagh, was born in Dublin, 1580. Chief work, "Annals of the Old and New Testament." Died 1656.

William Lenthal, a lawyer, was Speaker of the Long Parliament, Commissioner of the Great Seal, Master of the Rolls, and also Chancellor of the Duchy of Lancaster. At the Restoration Lenthal was condemned, but afterwards obtained a pardon from the King. (1591—1662).

Robert Herrick, a famous poet, Vicar of Dean Prior (Devon), from which he was ejected by Cromwell, but restored by Charles II. His poems published (1648) were called *Hesperides*. (1591—1674).

Martin Happertzoon Tromp, a distinguished Dutch admiral, was born in 1597. By his own merit he rose from the *lowest* station to the supreme command, gained some advantage over the English fleet under BLAKE in 1652, but was defeated and killed in an engagement with the English under MONK, in 1653.

Robert Blake, a renowned admiral, was born at Bridgewater in 1599, and educated at Oxford. He greatly distinguished himself by his victories over the Dutch, for which he received the thanks of Parliament, and was presented with a diamond ring worth £500. Declining health induced BLAKE to return from Cadiz to his native country, which he longed to see once more; but he expired just as his ship was entering Plymouth Harbour, Aug. 29, 1658.

George Monk, Duke of Albemarle, distinguished himself in the civil war. At first he favoured the cause of the Royalists, but afterwards sided with the Parliamentarians. He was entrusted by CROMWELL with the command of the army in Scotland. After the death of the Protector, MONK showed in what direction his views ran by marching to London, and convoking a Parliament, which appointed him general of the forces. MONK now proposed and accomplished the restoration of CHARLES II. (1603—1670).

Bulstrode Whitelocke, an eminent statesman, was born in London, 1605. In 1640 he represented Great Marlow, Buckinghamshire, in the Long Parliament, and in 1656 he was chosen Speaker of the House of Commons. He was afterwards made a lord of the upper House, appointed President of the Council of State, and Keeper of the Great Seal. He was the author of "Monarchy asserted to be the best, most Ancient, and Legal Form of Government," and other works. Died 1676.

Sir William Dugdale, a learned antiquary, was born in Warwickshire, 1605. He obtained the situation of Poursuivant in the Herald's office, was with CHARLES I. in several engagements, wrote the "Baronage of England," the "History of St. Paul's Cathedral," the "History of Warwickshire," and other works. Died 1686.

Edmund Waller, an eminent poet, was committed to the Tower for conspiring to deliver the city to the King. He was condemned to be hanged, but saved himself by paying £10,000 and making an abject submission. Being elected to Parliament a second time, he is said to have become, by his wit and eloquence, "The delight of the House." He joined in the persecution of CLARENDON, because the latter had refused him the Provostship of Eton. (1605—1687).

Nathaniel Fiennes, a distinguished leader of the Independents, and a great favourite of CROMWELL, who made him one of his lords. On one occasion he was condemned to death for surrendering Bristol to Prince RUPERT, but his father's influence saved his life. (1608—1669).

John Milton, born in Bread Street, London, received his education at Christ College, Cambridge, and became Latin Secretary to CROMWELL. Through natural weakness and intense application to his studies, he became blind in 1654. MILTON was an illustrious poet, and much celebrated for his principal works: "Paradise Lost," and "Paradise Regained." (1608—1674).

Henry Ireton, a republican general, was born at Attenton, in Nottinghamshire, 1610. He married a daughter of OLIVER CROMWELL, sat as one of the judges of CHARLES I., and was appointed Commander-in-Chief in Ireland, where he died of the plague, 1651. His body was conveyed to England, and buried in Westminster Abbey; but at the Restoration it was taken up and hung at Tyburn, the head being cut off and exposed on Westminster Hall.

Sir Henry Vane, became a Member of the Long Parliament, and at the commencement of the civil war took an active part against the King. He afterwards opposed the usurpation of CROMWELL, who caused him to be imprisoned. Being among the number of those excluded from the general pardon after the Restoration, he was executed for high treason, 1662.

Charles Fleetwood, a violent republican, married one of OLIVER CROMWELL'S daughters, and became Lord-Deputy of Ireland. He induced RICHARD CROMWELL to resign the office of Protector, and thereby opened a way for the Restoration. His death took place soon after that event.

Abraham Cowley, a distinguished poet, author of "Poetical Blossoms." (1618—1667).

John Lambert, was educated for the Bar, but on the breaking out of the civil war, joined the Parliamentarians, and became major-general. As the Rump Parliament would not concede to all his demands, LAMBERT expelled it and formed the *Committee of Safety.* He opposed General MONK, who aimed at the restoration of Charles II., and being defeated, he was banished for life to the Island of Guernsey, where he lived for more than thirty years, occupying himself with horticulture and flower painting. Born 1620, and died about 1691.

Sir William Penn, a noted admiral, born at Bristol in 1621. He commanded the fleet, and **Venables** the land forces, at the taking of **Jamaica** from the Spaniards in 1655. He was engaged under the Duke of YORK in the naval action against the Dutch, who were defeated in 1665. Died at Wanstead in Essex, 1670.

George Fox, a shoemaker, founder of the **Society of Friends** or **Quakers,** was born at Drayton in Leicestershire. (1624—1690).

The House of Stuart restored. Charles II. was the eldest son of Charles I. A.D. 1660—1685.

A WARS.

Owing to some disputes about the **African Trade**, CHARLES was induced to declare war against Holland, Feb. 22, 1665.

1. **Naval engagement off Lowestoft**, Suffolk, in which the Duke of York, Prince RUPERT, and the Earl of SANDWICH, defeated the Dutch under Admiral OPDAM, who lost 19 ships; the victors losing only one, June 3, 1665. The mode of fighting in Line was during this war introduced into naval tactics by the Duke of YORK.

2. Two India ships and twelve men-of-war were captured by the Earl of SANDWICH, Sept 4, 1665. LOUIS XIV. of France now joined the Dutch; and Denmark also declared war against England.

3. **Battle off the North Foreland**, Kent, in which the English under the Duke of ALBEMARLE, were defeated by the Dutch under DE RUYTER and the youngest VAN TROMP. This encounter continued four days, during which the English lost 9 ships, and the enemy 15, June 1—4, 1666.

4. DE RUYTER was severely beaten at the Mouth of the Thames by Prince RUPERT and ALBEMARLE, July 25, 1666. The loss of the Dutch on this occasion was 24 men-of-war, 4000 officers and seamen, and 4 admirals. On finding that he was vanquished, DE RUYTER was so exasperated that he frequently exclaimed, "My God, what a wretch am I! Among so many thousand bullets is there not one to put an end to my miserable existence?"

5. The French fleet of 30 sail was defeated by the English of 16 sail, near **Martinico**, 1667.

6. The Dutch under DE RUYTER, having succeeded in taking Sheerness, and in destroying some ships at Chatham, sailed up the Thames as far as **Tilbury**, where they were repulsed by Sir EDWARD SPRAGUE, June 29, 1667.

These hostilities were followed by the **Treaty of Breda**, between the English, French, and Dutch, according to the terms of which the Dutch settlement (New Amsterdam), on the coast of America, now the city of **New York**, was ceded to England, July 21, 1667.

7. CHARLES joined France in a declaration of war against the Dutch, who, under De RUYTER, were defeated in **Southwold Bay** by the English under the Duke of YORK, May 28, 1672.

This was a bloody action, during which the ship of the Earl of SANDWICH was blown up, and some thousands of men perished. The Dutch were pursued to their own coasts by the Duke of YORK.

8. DE RUYTER and D'ETREES were several times defeated by Prince RUPERT off the **Coast of Holland, 1673.**

9. During 1673 other warlike actions took place, to the disadvantage of the Dutch; and in 1674 **Peace** was concluded with Holland.

10. **A Battle off Tangiers** was fought between the English and the Moors, which engagement continued 11 **days,** 1679.

11. The Covenanters of Scotland rose in arms, and put to death Archbishop SHARP; but they were defeated by the Duke of MONMOUTH at **Bothwell Bridge** (near Glasgow), June 22, 1679.

B   **CHIEF EVENTS.**

The Convention Parliament continuing to sit after the **Restoration,** settled on the King an income of £1,200,000, abolished the remains of the **Feudal System,** with the revenues thence arising: and instead thereof, imposed an excise duty on beer and other liquors. They also voted tonnage and poundage for the King's life. **An Act of Indemnity** was passed, by which pardon was extended to all that had been engaged in the late wars, except such as were directly concerned in the King's death. Ten regicides were executed, while the bodies of CROMWELL, IRETON, and BRADSHAW, were taken from their graves, and hanged upon a gibbet at Tyburn; after which their heads were cut off, and exposed to public gaze on Westminster Hall. The Convention Parliament was dissolved by the King, Dec. 29, 1660. The army was also disbanded, except 1000 horse and 4000 foot.

The Pension Parliament, so called because some of its members received bribes from the Kings of France and England, assembled 1661 and lasted till 1679.

The Corporation Act was passed 1661, by which every member of a corporation was required to comply with the following regulations:—

1. To take an oath of **non-resistance** against the King's authority.

2. To abjure the Solemn League and Covenant.

3. To take the oaths of allegiance and supremacy.

4. To receive the Sacrament of the Lord's Supper in the Church of England at least once every year.

The Savoy Conference.—This was a conference held at the Savoy Palace, between 12 bishops and the same number of Presbyterian ministers, for the purpose of adjusting their differences; but it ended with still greater dissatisfaction, 1661.

CHARLES sold **Dunkirk** to the French for £400,000, and married the Infanta CATHERINE OF PORTUGAL, who received for her dowry £350,000, Tangiers in Africa, and Bombay in the East Indies, 1662.

The Act of Uniformity was passed (1662) by which every clergyman was bound:—

1. To receive **episcopal** ordination.

2. To take the oath of canonical obedience.

3. To abjure the Solemn League and Covenant.

4. To renounce the lawfulness of taking up arms against the King.

5. To declare his assent to everything contained in the Book of Common Prayer.

The act was to be put into force about three months afterwards, the time appointed being St. Bartholomew's Day (Aug. 24), and all that refused to comply with these conditions were to be deprived of their benefices. The result was that 2000 incumbents resigned their livings on the day in question.

The Conventicle Act.—As the non-conforming ministers sought other places than the Church in which to preach, a bill called the Conventicle Act was passed, which prohibited all meetings of more than five persons, (except in the case of families) for religious purposes, not in accordance with the Prayer Book. The punishment for the first offence was a fine of £5, or three months' imprisonment; for the second, £10, or six months' imprisonment; and for the third, £100, or transportation for seven years, 1664.

The Five Mile Act was passed (1665), and prohibited clergymen, who had refused to take the oath of non-resistance, from coming within five miles of any corporate town, unless when travelling. They were also by this act prevented from keeping schools. The four acts already mentioned are called the "Clarendon Code."

The Great Plague, which broke out in the suburb of St. Giles, ravaged London; during which more than 100,000 persons perished, 1665. In consequence of this plague, 40,000 servants are said to have been dismissed from their situations, and left to perish in the streets, as none were willing to give them a home.

In 1666 the **Great Fire of London** broke out, in a baker's shop near London Bridge, and destroyed property to the amount of £7,000,000. Eighty-nine churches, including St. Paul's, 13,200 houses, Guildhall, the Custom-house, and 4 stone bridges were reduced to a mass of ruins.

The Cabal.—After the dismissal of Lord CLARENDON, the King's chief minister, a new administration, called the Cabal, was formed, 1667. The word "Cabal" is by some historians supposed to be derived from the initial letters of its five leading members, Sir THOMAS CLIFFORD, Lord ASHLEY, the Duke of BUCKINGHAM, Lord ARLINGTON, and the Earl of LAUDERDALE ; others inform us that the word signified, at the time in question, a "secret committee," and therefore had nearly the same meaning as our word **Cabinet** at the present day.

The Triple Alliance.—As LOUIS XIV. had married MARIA THERESA (the daughter of PHILIP IV. of Spain), on the death of her father he claimed, in right of his wife, the Spanish Netherlands ; and with a powerful army invaded the country in 1667. In order to check the ambitious designs of the French King, a league, called " The Triple Alliance," was formed between England, Holland, and Sweden, Jan. 13, 1668. In consequence of this league LOUIS was under the necessity of signing the **Treaty of Aix-la-Chapelle,** the conditions of which were :—

1. That Spain should give up to LOUIS all the towns conquered by him.

2. That LOUIS should renounce all claims on the rest of Flanders (April 25, 1668).

The Treaty of Dover.—This was a secret agreement between CHARLES and LOUIS, the conditions of which were the following :—

1. That CHARLES should openly profess the Roman Catholic religion.

2. That he should aid LOUIS in his war against Spain and Holland.

3. That LOUIS should give CHARLES a pension of £120,000 a year during the continuance of the war.

4. That LOUIS should furnish CHARLES with 6000 men, if the latter required them, to put down any insurrection that might occur in consequence of the Treaty of Dover (May 22, 1670).

By the **Second Conventicle Act,** passed in 1670, preachers, and those who allowed them the use of their houses for preaching purposes, were fined, but the penalty on the hearers was mitigated.

The Crown jewels were stolen from the Tower by Colonel BLOOD, a disbanded officer, who was pardoned by the King, and also received from His Majesty an estate in Ireland worth £500 a year, May 9, 1671.

In 1672 CHARLES issued "The Declaration of Indulgence," which he pretended should be of special service to the Nonconformists, in giving them liberty to adopt and practise their own methods of Worship; but Parliament suspecting that its real object was to benefit the Roman Catholics, whose growing power they wished to check, passed a bill (1673) called the **Test Act**, by which none could hold any office, either civil or military, who refused compliance with the following conditions:—

1. To abjure the doctrine of transubstantiation.

2. To take the oaths of allegiance and supremacy.

3. To receive the sacrament according to the rites of the Church of England.

In consequence of this act, the Duke of YORK (the King's brother), who was a Roman Catholic, resigned his office of Lord High Admiral.

In order to prepare for a Dutch war, CHARLES seized £1,300,000, contained in the exchequer, which he closed (Jan. 2, 1672.) This shameful conduct was followed by great stagnation in trade, and the ruin of many families.

CHARLES finding that he could not obtain money from the Commons to carry on war against Holland, concluded a separate peace with that country, called the **Treaty of Westminster** (Feb. 9, 1674), by which it was agreed:—

1. That the English flag should be honoured by the Dutch.

2. That the states should pay CHARLES £300,000.

3. That all possessions obtained before the war should be restored.

The war, however, was continued by LOUIS, who concluded a peace with Holland at **Nimeguen**, Aug. 10, 1678.

The statute which authorised the burning of heretics was repealed, 1677, and in the same year WILLIAM, Prince of Orange, married MARY, daughter of JAMES, Duke of York.

The Popish Titus Oates Plot.—This Plot was framed by TITUS OATES, who asserted that the Roman Catholics had formed a conspiracy for taking the King's life, and securing the Duke of YORK's accession to the throne, 1678. Many Papists were in consequence executed, the most distinguished of whom was Lord STAFFORD. TITUS OATES received for this pretended discovery a pension of £1200 a year.

The Papists' Disabling Bill, or the Parliamentary Test. Owing to the discovery of a supposed Popish plot by which the country became alarmed, a bill was passed (1678) by Parliament, and called by the above name, because it disabled Papists from holding office either in the House of Lords or the House of Commons.

The Habeas Corpus Act was passed in 1679, and contained the following important provisions :—

1. That no person shall be tried **twice** for the **same** offence.

2. That the body of every prisoner must be produced on his trial.

3. That no person shall be sent to prison beyond the seas.

4. That the prisoner undergo his trial **the first term** after he is taken into custody.

The Exclusion Bill was passed by the Commons, but rejected by the Lords, 1679. Its object was to exclude from the throne the Duke of YORK, because he had embraced the Roman Catholic religion.

The Meal-Tub Plot was concocted by one DANGERFIELD, for the discovery of which he hoped to obtain money, 1679. Both Papists and Presbyterians were accused by this new fabrication, which was called by the preceding name, because the papers containing the scheme was found concealed in a meal-tub in the house of a disreputable woman.

The Rye-House Plot was formed for the purpose of assassinating the King on his return from Newmarket, 1683. The plot failed, because the house in which CHARLES lodged caught fire, and therefore compelled him to leave eight days sooner than was expected. It was so named because the conspirators assembled at a place called the "Rye-house Farm" (Herts). Among the conspirators were Lord RUSSELL and ALGERNON SIDNEY, who (without sufficient evidence) were executed.

The Third Parliament assembled (March 6) and was dissolved (July 10, 1679). It passed two acts, one for disbanding the army, the other was the Habeas Corpus Act. After the dissolution of this Parliament, TEMPLE and RUSSELL withdrew from the ministry, and the King had for his chief advisers, ESSEX, HALIFAX, and SUNDERLAND; who were called the Triumvirate.

The Fourth Parliament, though called in 1679, did not assemble till Oct. 1680, and was dissolved (Jan. 10, 1681). The Exclusion Bill already explained, again passed the House of Commons, but was rejected by the House of Lords. Owing to the long interval of time between the calling and meeting of this Parliament, many addresses were presented by the country party, praying for a speedy assembling of Parliament; these were opposed by the addresses from the Court party, who declared their abhorrence of what they called an interference with the prerogative of the Crown. Hence the country party were called **Addressers;** and the Court party, **Abhorrors.** The former were shortly afterwards called **Whigs,** and the latter **Tories.**

The Fifth Parliament, the last in the reign of CHARLES, met at Oxford (March 21) and was dissolved (March 28, 1681) because the Commons would insist upon an Exclusion Bill.

To secure uncontrolled power in the Metropolis and throughout the country, CHARLES, on the most trivial pretext, by a writ of **Quo Warranto** deprived the city of London of its **Charter,** and returned it only on condition that the appointment to any municipal office should be subject to his approbation, 1683. Many other Corporations also surrendered their charters on similar terms.

For calling the Duke of YORK a traitor, TITUS OATES was fined £100,000, and imprisoned because he was unable to pay the money, 1684.

In this reign the **Royal Society** for the advancement of science was instituted; **Toll-gates** were erected; a periodical paper called **The Public Intelligencer,** was published by Sir ROGER L'ESTRANGE; **Guineas** were first coined, and so named because they were made of gold brought from Guinea, on the Western Coast of Africa; the **Triennial Act** was repealed; **Magic Lanterns,** invented by ROGER BACON (1260), were manufactured by a German named KIRCHER; **Tea** began to be used in England, and the **First Fire Insurance Office** established; **Looms** were introduced into Derby from Holland by Sir THOMAS LOOM; **Plate Glass** from Venice, by the Duke of BUCKINGHAM; the art of **Dyeing** from Holland, by ANTHONY BREWER; **Pendulums** by CHRISTIAN HUYGENS, a Dutchman; **Flags** for sea-signals were first used by the Duke of YORK; **Glass Coaches** were invented at Brussels; Bombay was granted to the East India Company; the salt mines of Staffordshire were discovered; the exemption of juries from fines on account of their verdicts was established; judges and barristers began to wear wigs in the Courts of Justice; the **Royal Observatory** was founded at Greenwich; a **Penny-Post** for conveying letters about London and its vicinity was established; a new kind of tapestry was invented by GILES GOBELIN, a French dyer; St. Paul's Cathedral, and other magnificent structures were commenced by CHRISTOPHER WREN; Chelsea Hospital for aged soldiers was founded by the King, who became almost despotic towards the end of his reign.

CHARLES died somewhat suddenly, Feb. 6, 1685, and was buried at Westminster.

Isaac Walton, a distinguished biographer, and author of the "Complete Angler, or the Contemplative Man's Recreation." (1593—1683).

Sir Thomas Browne, an eminent physician, who took the degree of M.D. at the University of Leyden, and was the author of "Religio Medici," and "Vulgar Errors." (1605—1682).

Michael Adrian Ruyter, a brave Dutch Admiral, was born at Flessingen in 1607. He served under TROMP against the English in 1653, and aided the King of Denmark against the Swedes in 1659. He was killed on the Coast of Sicily in an engagement with the French, 1676.

John de Witt, a famous Dutch statesman and Admiral, by whom the naval war against England was conducted. He was killed at the Hague in 1672.

Edward Hyde (Earl of CLARENDON), became Prime Minister and Lord Chancellor. Having incurred the displeasure of the King, and that of the people, he retired to France, where he wrote "A History of the Rebellion." The Duke of YORK married CLARENDON's daughter. (1608—1674).

Sir Matthew Hale, Lord Chief Baron, noted for his learning and piety. (1609—1676).

Samuel Butler, a distinguished poet, author of "Hudibras." (1612—1680).

John Pearson, Bishop of Chester, author of a masterly exposition on the Creed. (1612—1686).

Jeremy Taylor (called "The English Cicero") the son of a barber, was educated at Caius College, Cambridge. TAYLOR became such an eminent preacher, that through the influence of Archbishop LAUD, he obtained a fellowship at All-Souls' College, Oxford. He was afterwards made Bishop of Down and Connor. Among his works we may mention "Holy Living and Holy Dying." (1613—1667).

Richard Baxter, a most distinguished Presbyterian minister, was the author of 126 volumes, among which were "The Saint's Rest," and "A Call to the Unconverted." (1615—1691).

Ralph Cudworth, a learned divine, and author of "The Intellectual System," a work which was levelled against the atheism of the time. (1617—1688).

Sir Peter Lely, a Westphalian painter, whom CHARLES II. patronised. (1617—1680).

Andrew Marvell, a poet and politician. (1620—1678).

Sir B. Gomme, engineer.   (1620—1685).

Anthony Ashley Cooper (Earl of Shaftesbury), at first aided the Royal cause, then joined the Parliamentarians, and afterwards assisted MONK in bringing about the Restoration.   On the accession of CHARLES II., he was made Governor of the Isle of Wight, and Chancellor of the Exchequer.   He belonged to the Cabal Ministry, and in 1679 drew up and carried the **Habeas Corpus Act,** which at that time was called **"Lord Shaftesbury's Act."** Though the cause of national liberty was furthered by him, SHAFTESBURY was an intriguing statesman.   (1621—1683).

Heneage Finch, the son of Sir HENEAGE FINCH, Recorder of London, was born in 1621.   He received his education at Westminster School, Christ Church College, Oxford, and the Inner Temple, and became the first Earl of Nottingham, and Lord Chancellor.   FINCH is the *Amri* of Dryden's Poem "Absalom and Ahitophel."   Died 1682.

Thomas Sydenham, one of the most eminent physicians of his day, is noted as the first prescriber of the cool regimen in the treatment of small-pox.   His works on consumption and nervous disorders are considered very valuable.   (1624—1689).

Edward Montague (Earl of Sandwich), a brave admiral, served under CROMWELL and CHARLES II.   In the battle of Southwold Bay, he displayed the utmost valour, and saved the fleet from destruction.   His own ship having caught fire, he jumped into the water and was drowned.   (1625—1672).

Samuel Morland, Master of Mechanics to CHARLES II., and inventor of the **Speaking Trumpet.**   (1625—1695).

Robert Boyle, a noted philosopher, and improver of the air-pump.   (1626—1691).

John Bunyan, a Bedford tinker, whose education had during the early part of his life been neglected, applied himself to the study of the Scriptures, and became a Baptist preacher at Bedford. At the Restoration he was committed to prison for preaching, and confined in Bedford jail for more than 12 years, during which time he wrote his **"Pilgrim's Progress."**   (1628—1688).

Sir William Temple, an eminent statesman and diplomatist, was mainly instrumental in effecting the **"Triple Alliance."** (1628—1699).

Isaac Barrow, D.D., an illustrious mathematician and divine, was born in London.   He had a great love for the works of BACON, DESCARTES, and GALILEO, chiefly on account of their profundity.   In 1672 he became Master of Trinity College, Cambridge, and was pronounced by the King the most learned man in

England.   Sir Isaac Newton was a pupil of Barrow, who wrote many works, among which we may mention his "Lectiones Mathematicæ."   (1630—1677).

Edward Cocker, arithmetician, and author of several works. (1632—1675).

John Wilmot (Earl of Rochester), a poet and celebrated wit, was very intemperate in his habits, and paid the penalty by an early death.   He wrote the following mock-epitaph upon the bedroom door of Charles II. :—

> "Here lies our sovereign lord the king,
>   Whose word no man relies on ;
>   Who never says a foolish thing,
>   Nor ever does a wise one."

His poems were characterised by general obscenity.   Towards the close of his life he became truly penitent, and expressed a wish that all his licentious writings should be burnt.   (1647—1680).

Thomas Otway, a dramatic writer and author of numerous works, was a native of Sussex, and is said to have died of want. (1651—1685).

Henry Jenkins, a Yorkshire peasant, was born in the reign of Henry VII., and died a beggar in the present reign, at the age of 169.

James II. was the second son of Charles I. and brother of Charles II.   A.D. 1685—1688.

A   WARS.

1. The Earl of Argyle, an exile in Holland, for the security of the Protestant religion attempted an invasion by landing in Cantire (Scotland).   He raised 2,500 men, but they were soon dispersed ; while he was captured, conveyed to Edinburgh, and executed, June 30, 1685.

2. Battle of Sedgemoor (Somersetshire).—James, Duke of Monmouth, also an exile in Holland, landed at Lyme Regis (Dorset.) and asserted his claim to the crown on the ground that his mother Lucy Walters, and Charles II. had been married in private.   Monmouth was defeated by the Earl of Feversham (July 5, 1685), and executed ten days afterwards on Tower Hill.   The last battle fought on English ground was that of Sedgemoor.

JAMES II. began his reign by making the following promise to the **Privy Council**; and by repeating it in Parliament:—

"I shall endeavour to preserve this government both in **Church** and **State,** as it is now by law established. I know the principles of the **Church of England** are for **monarchy,** and the members of it have shewed themselves good and loyal subjects; therefore I shall always take care to defend and support it."

This open declaration appeared so straightforward and satisfactory to the people, that some went so far as to style the new monarch "James the Just." His words were contradicted by his actions. The following proceedings of the King will speak for themselves:—

1. He went openly to mass, endeavoured to bring England under the dominion of the Romish Church, and ordered the release of all persons confined for refusing to take the oaths of allegiance and supremacy.

2. He published two papers to show that the late King died a Papist, and without Parliamentary sanction ordered the customs duties to be collected.

3. In order to carry out his arbitrary measures, JAMES put Romish officers in places of trust, aimed at the establishment of a standing army, violated the Test Act, and instituted a **High Commission** Court of the same character as that which had been abolished in the reign of CHARLES I. The notorious Judge JEFFREYS was the president of this court.

4. The Jesuits received royal encouragement to erect colleges in various parts of England, and four Roman Catholic Bishops, consecrated in the King's Chapel, and called **Apostolic Vicars,** had authority to exercise their episcopal functions thoughout the kingdom.

5. JAMES still continued his career by invading the rights of the Universities of Oxford and Cambridge. The latter seat of learning was ordered to confer the degree of M.A. upon one Father FRANCIS (a Benedictine monk) without the usual oaths. Doctor PEACHELL, the Vice-Chancellor, disobeyed the injunction, on account of which he was deprived of his office by the High Commission Court, 1687.

When the President of Magdalen College, Oxford, died, JAMES sent a mandatory letter, electing to that office ANTHONY FARMER, a Roman Catholic convert, who was a man of indifferent character. For refusing compliance the fellows were ejected, 1687.

The Bloody Assize, or **Jeffreys' Bloody Campaign.**—After the defeat of MONMOUTH at Sedgemoor, Judge JEFFREYS, assisted by Colonel KIRK, was sent to try the prisoners, who were treated with the utmost cruelty. By the command of their brutal judges, 300 persons were hanged, and nearly 1000 sold as slaves to the **West Indian Plantation,** 1685.

A Declaration of Indulgence was issued by the King, authorising Catholics and Dissenters to free and open exercise of their religion, 1687.

The Second Declaration of Indulgence was issued (April 25, 1688) with an injunction that it should be twice publicly read in all their churches. Seven bishops refused to obey this proclamation, and were sent to the Tower, brought to trial, ably defended by Somers, and acquitted, June 30, 1688.

These indulgences were really intended for the furtherance of Popery.

The Revocation of the Edict of Nantes by Louis XIV. caused some thousands of Protestants to seek refuge in England, and settle at Spitalfields (London), where they commenced the silk trade. The Edict of Nantes, for granting religious tolerance to Protestants, was passed by Henry IV. of France, 1598.

The arbitrary proceedings of JAMES (especially against the bishops) and the birth of his son (1688), who they concluded would be educated in the Romish faith, induced some of the English noblemen and others to invite WILLIAM, Prince of Orange, (Stadtholder of Holland) to take the crown and protect **The Protestant Religion** and the **Liberties of the People.** WILLIAM landed with a Dutch army at **Torbay** (Devonshire), Nov. 5, 1688, and JAMES fled to France, where he met with a kind reception from LOUIS XIV., from whom he obtained a pension, and the palace of St. Germains for himself and family.

THE INTERREGNUM.

Dec. 11, 1688—Feb. 13, 1689.

After the flight of JAMES and the arrival of WILLIAM, a Convention Parliament was called (Jan. 22, 1689), which passed the following vote:— "That King James the Second having endeavoured to subvert the Constitution of the Kingdom, by breaking the Original Contract between King and people, and by the advice of Jesuits and other wicked persons, having violated the fundamental laws, and withdrawn himself out of the kingdom, hath abdicated the government, and that the throne has thereby become vacant."

The next day the Commons further voted—"That it hath been found by experience to be inconsistent with this Protestant Kingdom, to be governed by a Popish prince."

An **Act of Settlement,** by which it was resolved that the crown should be settled on the PRINCE of ORANGE jointly with MARY (son-in-law and eldest daughter of JAMES), and in failure of issue on JAMES'S youngest daughter, the Princess ANNE of Denmark, and the heirs of her body; and that any sovereign embracing Romanism, or marrying one of that creed should be deprived of the crown and succeeded by the next Protestant heir.

The Declaration of Rights was drawn up and declared:—

1. The arbitrary proceedings of the late King.

2. The illegality of raising money without the consent of Parliament, creating the late Commission Court for ecclesiastical purposes, and all other Commissions or Courts of like nature.

3. The raising or keeping a standing army in times of peace, unless sanctioned by Parliament.

It is also declared:—

1. That Protestant subjects may have arms for their defence such as are by law established.

2. That the election of Members of Parliament ought to be free.

3. That excessive fines ought not to be imposed, nor cruel nor unusual punishments inflicted.

It also contained new oaths of allegiance and supremacy.

This declaration was read in the presence of WILLIAM and MARY, who assented to it, and accepted the crown. The following answer was returned by the Prince:—

"My Lords and Gentlemen,—This is certainly the greatest proof of the trust you have in us, that can be given, which is the thing that makes us value it the more, and we thankfully accept what you have offered. And as I had no other intention in coming hither, than to preserve your religion, laws, and liberties, so you may be sure that I shall endeavour to support them, and shall be willing to concur in anything that shall be for the good of the kingdom, and to do all that is in my power to advance the welfare and glory of the nation."

On the same day the Prince and Princess were proclaimed by the names of WILLIAM and MARY, King and Queen of England, France, and Ireland, Feb. 13, 1689.

The foregoing events which ended in the crown passing from JAMES to WILLIAM, are called **The Revolution** or **The Glorious Revolution** of 1688, and terminated Feb. 13, 1689. JAMES died about twelve years afterwards at St. Germains (France) Sept. 6, 1701.

C   CELEBRATED PERSONS.

Sir J. Child, a noted merchant. (1630—1699).

Edward Stillingfleet, Bishop of Worcester, was a man of profound learning, and a great opponent of Romanism and Nonconformity. Chief work, " Origines Sacrae, or a Rational Account of the Grounds of Natural and Revealed Religion." (1635—1699).

James, Duke of Monmouth, a natural son of CHARLES II., was born at Rotterdam, 1649. His father banished him for aspiring to the throne, to the exclusion of the Duke of YORK. On the accession of JAMES II., he landed at Tyne with some followers, whose numbers increased so rapidly that he asserted the legitimacy of his birth, and assumed the title of King. His forces were defeated ; while he, being found shortly after at the bottom of a ditch overcome by hunger and fatigue, was taken and executed, 1685. He refused to betray his companions, and was so great a favourite that he was called "The Darling of the English people."

Samuel Parker, a divine, who for the zeal with which he carried out the measures of JAMES, was appointed Bishop of Oxford. The character of this prelate seems to have been marked by hypocrisy, and it is said that he concerted with King JAMES the overthrow of the English Church, and its ultimate subjection to the Pope. PARKER was the author of "A History of his own Time." (1640—1687).

George Jeffreys, commonly called **Judge Jeffreys,** born at Acton in Denbighshire about 1640, was educated at Shrewsbury School and Westminster, whence he removed to the Inner Temple, where he prosecuted his legal studies. He became Recorder of London, a Welsh Judge, Chief Justice of Chester, and Chief Justice of the King's Bench. He earned for himself an infamous character by his cruelties and gross violation of justice, especially in his brutal treatment of the adherents of the Duke of MONMOUTH. As a reward for his sanguinary proceedings on that occasion he was made Lord Chancellor. When JAMES abdicated *the throne,* JEFFREYS attempted to leave the kingdom in the disguise of a sailor, but was detected in a low pothouse in Wapping by a lawyer whom he had formerly insulted. This information coming to the ears of the people, they rushed in and carried him before the Lord Mayor, and thence to the Lords of Council, who committed him to the Tower, where he died in 1689.

Archibald Campbell (Earl of ARGYLE) rebelled, but was captured, and executed at Edinburgh, 1685.

Richard Talbot (Earl of TYRCONNEL), a bigoted Roman Catholic, was appointed by JAMES II. Lord-Lieutenant of Ireland. After the Revolution of 1688 had terminated, TYRCONNEL tried to achieve the independence of his native country, but was unsuccessful. Died 1691.

The following were the seven bishops who refused to read JAMES's Declaration of Indulgence in their cathedrals; in consequence of which they were brought to trial, but acquitted:—

1. Archbishop Sancroft, held a fellowship in the University of Cambridge, but was deprived of it, because he refused to take the Solemn League and Covenant. He wrote a Latin Dialogue against Calvinism, called "The Predestinated Thief." (1616—1693).

2. Ken. Chaplain to CHARLES II., by whom he was nominated to the bishopric of Bath and Wells. Ken attended the dying-bed of that monarch, but his services were interfered with by Romish priests.

3. Lloyde, Bishop of St. Asaph.

4. Turner, Bishop of Ely.

5. Lake, Bishop of Chichester.

6. White, Bishop of Peterborough.

7. Trelawney, Bishop of Bristol.

THE REVOLUTION DYNASTY.

William III. and **Mary II.**—William was the son of William II. (Stadtholder of Holland) and **Mary,** daughter of Charles I. Mary II. was the eldest daughter of James II. A.D. 1689—1702.

William and **Mary** reigned together, A.D. 1689—1694. **William** reigned alone, 1694—1702.

WARS.

1. Battle of Killiecrankie (Perthshire), in which William's forces under General Mackay, were defeated by 2000 Highlanders, headed by Graham of Claverhouse (Viscount DUNDEE), who favoured the cause of JAMES. As DUNDEE fell in the battle, the enemy ceased to offer further resistance, July 27, 1689.

2. Siege of Londonderry.—Aided by LOUIS XIV. of France, JAMES II. landed in Ireland for the recovery of his crown. He was joined by TYRCONNEL at Cork with Irish troops. James now commenced the siege of Londonderry, which was blockaded for 105 days by Marshal ROSEN ; during which the inhabitants were reduced to the necessity of eating dogs and horses. The garrison and people were inspired to make a vigorous resistance, by a clergyman named WALKER, and Major BAKER. The siege was at last raised by General KIRK, with a loss of 9000 men to the assailants, July 30, 1689.

3. Battle of Newton-Butler (Ireland), in which the Protestants of Enniskillen routed some of JAMES's Irish forces under Lord MOUNTCASHEL, July 30, 1689.

4. Battle of the Boyne (Ireland), in which WILLIAM defeated JAMES, who fled to France, July 1, 1690.

5. Battle of Aughrim (Ireland). This was the last battle in favour of JAMES, whose forces under St. RUTH, a French General, were defeated by those of WILLIAM under GINKELL. In this engagement St. RUTH was killed, July 12, 1691.

6. Siege of Limerick, which capitulated in six weeks (Oct. 1, 1691), on the following conditions, called **The Treaty** or **Pacification of Limerick:**—

1. The Irish Catholics to have the free exercise of their religion.

2. The Irish who submitted to WILLIAM to be put in possession of those estates and rights which were held by them in the reign of Charles II.

3. All that chose could leave their own country and go to any other, except England and Scotland.

This treaty induced **Patrick Sarsfield** (an Irish leader) and 12,000 others who had fought on behalf of JAMES, to enter the service of LOUIS XIV. These men were called "**The Irish Brigade,**" and the Parliament which subsequently met, did not altogether adhere to this treaty.

The aid given by LOUIS XIV. to JAMES caused England to declare war against France, 1689.

1. The English and Dutch fleets under the Earl of TORRINGTON, were defeated off **Beachy Head** (Sussex), by the French Admiral TOURVILLE (June 30, 1690).

2. Battle of Cape La Hogue, between the combined English and Dutch fleets under Admirals RUSSELL and ROOKE, and the French fleet commanded by Admiral TOURVILLE. The French were attacked by the English near La Hogue, and defeated with a loss of 21 ships, May 19, 1692.

3. Battle of Steinkirk (Belgium), in which WILLIAM was defeated with heavy loss by the French, while trying to raise the siege of Namur, July 24, 1692.

4. At the Bay of Lagos, TOURVILLE captured three Dutch men-of-war and 80 ships of the Smyrna fleet (which consisted of 400 English, Dutch, and Hamburgh merchantmen) under Sir G. ROOKE, 1693.

5. Battle of Landen (Belgium), between the Allies and French. Owing to the cowardice of the Dutch horse, WILLIAM was defeated by the French, who were commanded by Marshal LUXEMBOURG, July 16, 1693. The Duke of BERWICK (an illegitimate son of JAMES II.) was taken prisoner by CHURCHILL, afterwards Duke of MARLBOROUGH.

6. Dieppe and **Havre** were nearly destroyed by the English, 1694. The attempt upon **Brest** failed through MARLBOROUGH'S treachery.

7. Namur was besieged and captured by WILLIAM, Aug. 26, 1695.

This war was brought to a close by the **Peace** or **Treaty of Ryswick,** concluded between England, France, Spain, Holland, and the Emperor of Germany, Sept. 20, 1697. Its conditions were :—

1. That WILLIAM should be acknowledged King of England.

2. That no rebellions or intrigues should be favoured by LOUIS and WILLIAM against each other.

3. That there should be a restoration of unrestricted commerce.

B   **CHIEF EVENTS.**

A bill was carried for changing the Convention into a Parliament, in which were passed (1689);—The **Mutiny Act,** by which the army was put under martial law, owing to an outbreak in a Scotch regiment.

A Toleration Act, by which freedom of worship was granted to such dissenters as should make a declaration against transubstantiation, and take the oaths of allegiance and supremacy; but its benefits were not extended to Unitarians and Papists.

The Bill of Rights, which was a confirmation of the Declaration of Rights, and called the **Third Great Charter of English Liberty,** declared the illegality of the following proceedings without the consent of Parliament :—

1. The suspending of, or dispensing with laws; the erecting of Commission Courts; levying of money for the use of the Crown, on pretence of prerogative; the raising or keeping of a standing army in time of peace.

It also declared :—

1. That subjects have a right to petition the King, and if Protestants, to carry arms for defence.

2. That Members of Parliament ought to be freely elected, and that their proceedings ought not to be impeached or questioned in any place out of Parliament.

3. That neither ought excessive bail to be required, excessive fines imposed, nor unusual punishment inflicted.

4. That juries ought to be chosen without partiality.

5. That all grants and promises of fines and forfeitures before conviction, are illegal.

6. That for redress of grievances and preserving of the laws, Parliament ought to be held frequently.

It also contained an enactment for the settlement of the crown, as already mentioned.

A New Parliament assembled (March 20, 1690) sat till May, and voted WILLIAM :—

1. £1,200,000 for carrying on the war in Ireland.

2. An act of pardon and indemnity was passed.

3. Marshal SCHOMBERG was presented with £100,000.

4. An annual pension of £20,000 was settled upon the Princess ANNE.

The Non-jurors.—Archbishop SANCROFT, seven bishops, and 400 of the clergy, were deprived of their livings, and called non-jurors, because they refused to take the oath of allegiance to WILLIAM, 1691.

The Massacre of Glencoe.—As there were in Scotland a few of the Highland chiefs not disposed to acknowledge WILLIAM, an Act of Indemnity was passed for the benefit of such as would *take* the oath of allegiance before Dec. 31, 1691. The MAC-DONALDS of Glencoe (a vale in Argyleshire) being a few days late in coming to take the prescribed oath, were, through the treachery of the Earl of BREADALBANE and Sir JOHN DALRYMPLE (Secretary of State), slaughtered by the military, Feb. 14, 1692.

The Freedom of the Press was established by the expiration of **the Licensing Act,** which prohibited unlicensed printing, 1693.

By the **Triennial Bill,** it was enacted that a new Parliament should be summoned every three years, 1694.

Queen MARY died of small-pox, much lamented, 1694.

A Parliament met (Nov. 1695) and passed an act for regulating trials for treason. By this statute it was enacted :—

1. That the prisoner should have the aid of counsel, a copy of the indictment, and of the panel of the jury.

2. That every overt act should be proved by two witnesses, and that the prisoner could compel his witnesses to appear.

Anticipating the death of CHARLES II., King of Spain, and wishful to maintain the balance of power, WILLIAM and LOUIS entered into the **First Partition Treaty,** so called because it was formed for the purpose of dividing the Spanish dominions among the Electoral Prince of Bavaria, the Dauphin of France, and the Archduke of Austria, 1698.

As the Electoral Prince died (1699), a **Second Partition Treaty** was formed, 1700; but the Spanish dominions were left by CHARLES II. to PHILIP OF ANJOU, the grandson of LOUIS, who, in violation of his treaty with WILLIAM, resolved on enforcing the claims of PHILIP.

These proceedings of LOUIS caused :—

1. The war concerning the Spanish succession, in the reign of ANNE.

2. A **Grand Alliance** against France to advance the claims of the Archduke CHARLES to the throne of Spain, 1702.

The Second Act of Settlement (1701) for regulating the succession to the throne, was occasioned by the death of the Duke of GLOUCESTER (the Princess ANNE's only surviving son, who was heir to the crown) and provided :—

1. That every succeeding sovereign shall join the communion of the Church of England, as by law established.

2. That in event of a foreigner coming into possession of the crown, the nation shall not be obliged to engage in war for the defence of any dominions not belonging to England, without the consent of Parliament.

3. That no sovereign shall go out of great Britain or Ireland *without the consent of* Parliament.

4. That all matters relating to the well-governing of the kingdom, which are properly cognizable in the Privy Council, shall be transacted there, and all resolutions passed shall be signed by such of the Privy Council as shall advise and consent to the same.

5. That none, except born of English parents, shall be capable of holding any office under the crown, or receiving a grant from it, or becoming a member of Parliament.

6. That no person in the service of the crown, or receiving a pension, shall be capable of sitting in the House of Commons.

7. That judges shall hold their offices *quamdiu se bene gesserint* (during good behaviour) but they might be removed on an address of both houses.

8. That no pardon under the great seal shall be pleadable to an impeachment by the Commons.

As WILLIAM and ANNE died without issue, the succession devolved upon **Sophia of Hanover,** and her descendants, **being Protestants.** SOPHIA was the grand-daughter of JAMES I.

Plots for taking the life of WILLIAM were formed, but they proved unsuccessful. One by the partizans of JAMES, who were called **Jacobites,** ended in the execution of the conspirators.

The Darien Scheme was undertaken in Scotland to found a colony on the Isthmus of Darien for the purpose of establishing a trade with America and India. It is said that 1200 men, besides their wives and children, embarked for the spot (1688) but owing to the opposition they had to encounter, the plan failed, and most of the emigrants perished.

The Banks of England and Scotland were founded, the former by PATERSON, a Scotchman, and the latter by an Englishman, named HOLLAND.

A tax was imposed upon malt, the land-tax increased to four shillings per acre, and hawkers subject to an annual payment for their licence.

In this reign commenced the **National Debt,** or according to others, it began in that of HENRY VI. **Bayonets** were invented at Bayonne in France; the first **Public Lottery** was drawn in England; **Fire Engines** were invented; the first **real Cabinet Council** was formed; Ministers became responsible for the acts of the Sovereign; the King and Queen generously gave up Greenwich Palace to be converted into an hospital for disabled sailors.

WILLIAM fell from his horse, and in a few days afterwards died at Kensington, March 8, 1702, and was buried at Westminster.

Elias Ashmole, a celebrated antiquary, who is said by some historians to have founded the Ashmolean Museum at Oxford, which contains the museum of Tradescant. (1617—1692).

Duke of Schomberg, a Dutch general, commanded some of WILLIAM'S forces at the Battle of the Boyne. The French refugees of his own regiment shot him by mistake, while he was crossing that river. The success of the battle was considered a poor compensation for the loss WILLIAM had sustained in the death of the Duke. (1619—1690).

John Evelyn, the author of several works, became one of the first members of the Royal Society. His book called **Sculptura,** or the **History and Art of Chalcography, and engraving in copper,** is a valuable work. Exotics were introduced into England by EVELYN. (1620—1706).

Francis Henry de Montmorency (Duke of Luxembourg), a distinguished French general. (1628—1695).

George Saville (Marquis of Halifax), Speaker in the House of Lords in the Convention Parliament, tendered the crown to the Prince of Orange. (1630—1695).

John Dryden, a famous poet and satirist, was the author of numerous works, and one of the best prose writers in the English language. He translated Virgil. (1631—1700).

Samuel Pepys, author of an excellent book entitled "Memoirs relating to the Navy," and other works, including his famous "Diary." In 1684 he was made President of the Royal Society. (1632—1703).

John Locke, a philosopher, and author of a work on **"The Human Understanding."** (1632—1704).

Tourville, a distinguished French admiral. (1642—1731).

William Bentinck, page to WILLIAM, Prince of Orange, became the first Earl of Portland, and was promoted to high civil and military offices. He earned the affection of WILLIAM by his devotion and fidelity. (1648—1709).

John Benbow, a distinguished admiral. He was severely wounded during a naval engagement with the French in the West Indies, and died soon afterwards. (1650—1702).

George Walker, an Irish Divine, who offered a vigorous resistance to the forces of JAMES II. in the siege of Londonderry. He was killed at the Battle of the Boyne in 1690.

Godart de Ginkill, first Earl of Athlone, was born in Holland. In 1688 he accompanied WILLIAM to England, and at the Battle of the Boyne, fought 1690, commanded the Dutch horse. Being left by WILLIAM to conduct the war in Ireland, he brought it to a termination by the capture of Limerick. In 1692 he was created a Peer of Ireland, and afterwards served under MARLBOROUGH in the reign of Queen ANNE. Died 1703.

Anne was the second daughter of James II., by his first wife Anne Hyde. A.D. 1702—1714.

A   **WARS.**

The War of the Spanish Succession.—Induced by French influence, CHARLES II. of Spain (who had no immediate heirs) left the whole of his dominions to the Duke of ANJOU, the grandson of LOUIS XIV. of France, and lineal descendant of PHILIP III. of Spain, whose grand-daughter was married to LOUIS. The French monarch therefore determined to secure all the Spanish dominions for his grandson, and was aided by Spain, Bavaria, Cologne, and Mantua.

The Grand Alliance, comprising England, Holland, Austria, Germany, Portugal, and Savoy, wishful to maintain the balance of power, resolved on supporting the claims of the Archduke CHARLES, who was also a lineal descendant of PHILIP III. of Spain.

1. **Battle of Blenheim** (Bavaria), between the English and their allies, under the Duke of MARLBOROUGH and Prince EUGENE, and the French and Bavarians, under Marshal TALLARD and the Elector of Bavaria. The former gained a splendid victory ; 27,000 of the enemy being killed, and 13,000 (including TALLARD) made prisoners, Aug. 13, 1704. As a reward for this great success, the Queen gave MARLBOROUGH Woodstock Park, on which she built for him the spacious palace called Blenheim House.

2. **Battle of Ramillies** (Belgium), in which MARLBOROUGH defeated the French, commanded by Marshal VILLARS and the Elector of Bavaria. This encounter was fought on Whitsunday, May 23, 1706. As a reward for these services, Parliament settled the honours which had been conferred upon MARLBOROUGH, on the male and female issue of his daughter.

3. **Battle of Turin** (Italy), in which Prince EUGENE defeated the French, who had besieged the city, Sept. 7, 1706.

4. **Battle of Almanza** (Spain), in which JAMES FITZJAMES, Duke of Berwick, (the illegitimate son of JAMES II.) at the head *of the French* and Spanish, defeated the confederates under the

Earl of GALWAY, April 14, 1707. Many of the English were killed or taken prisoners, because they were deserted at the very onset by the Portuguese.

5. **Battle of Oudenarde (East Flanders),** in which MARL-BOROUGH and EUGENE defeated the French (under Marshal VENDOME) who were besieging Oudenarde, July 11, 1708.

6. **Battle of Malplaquet (France),** in which the Duke of MARLBOROUGH and Prince EUGENE gained a great victory over the French under Marshal VILLARS. There were about 120,000 men on each side. The conflict was a most sanguinary one, both for the victors and the vanquished; the former losing 18,000, and the latter 10,000 men, Sept. 11, 1709.

7. **Battle of Almenara (Spain),** in which PHILIP V. of Spain was defeated by the allies under General STANHOPE and Count STAREMBERG, July 27, 1710.

8. **Battle of Saragossa (Spain),** in which the allies under STANHOPE were victorious over PHILIP, Aug. 20, 1710.

9. **At Brihuega,** (Spain) 5,000 men under General STANHOPE were surprised by the Duke of VENDOME, and obliged to capitulate, Dec. 9, 1710.

10. **Battle of Villa Viciosa,** between the Duke of VENDOME and a portion of the allied army under Count STAREMBERG, who suffered heavy loss, and was compelled to retreat, Dec. 10, 1710.

11. **Battle of Denain (France.)**—MARLBOROUGH being superseded in the command of the allied forces by the Duke of ORMOND, who was ordered to give no further aid in the war, France gained some advantages over the allies, and defeated EUGENE at Denain, July 24, 1712.

During this war were the following successes :—

1. **Venloo, Ruremonde,** and **Liege** were taken by MARL-BOROUGH, 1702.

2. Some of the Spanish Plate fleet were captured and destroyed in the **Bay of Vigo** by Sir GEORGE ROOKE, Oct. 1702.

3. **Bonn, Huy, Limburg,** and **Gueldres** were captured in 1703; and in the following year the allies took **Donawerth, Traerbach,** and **Landau.**

4. **Gibraltar,** called by ancient writers "The Pillars of Hercules," was attacked by the English under Sir GEORGE ROOKE, Sir JOHN LEAKE, Admiral BYNG, and the Prince of HESSE-DARMSTADT. After a cannonading of three days, it was surrendered by the Marquis de SALINES (the governor), and it has remained ever since in the hands of the British, July 24, 1704. *After the taking of Gibraltar by the English, it was besieged by*

the Spanish and French, who were not only defeated but lost 10,000 men, the victors only 400, Oct. 11, 1704.

Catalonia and **Valentia** were reduced and **Barcelona** captured by Sir CLOUDESLEY SHOVEL, and CHARLES MORDAUNT, Earl of Peterborough, 1705.

Sardinia was taken from the Spaniards by Sir JOHN LEAKE, and **Minorca** captured by General STANHOPE, 1708.

Quebec was besieged by the English under HILL, but the attempt failed, 1711.

Bouchain, a fortified town of France, was captured by MARLBOROUGH, 1711, but retaken by the French, 1712.

B   **CHIEF EVENTS.**

The first Parliament met (1702) when a bill was passed by the Commons against **Occasional Conformity,** but it was rejected by the Peers.

There occurred the **Great Storm,** which caused the destruction of Eddystone Lighthouse and 13 ships of war ; damage in London amounting to £1,000,000, and killed 1,500 persons, including Bishop KIDDER and his wife, 1703.

By the Act of Union, England and Scotland were united into one kingdom, May 4, 1707. The provisions of this act were :—

1. That the succession should be in SOPHIA and her Protestant heirs.

2. That Scotland should be represented in the House of Lords by 16 elective Peers, and by 45 members in the House of Commons.

3. That both nations should have the same rights and privileges in respect of trade.

4. That Scotland should retain her national religion and courts of law, unaltered.

This union of the two countries produced much dissatisfaction among the Scotch ; but the advantage has been great to the commerce and civilisation both of England and Scotland.

The First British or United Parliament of Great Britain assembled, Oct. 23, 1707.

The Pretender attempted an invasion of Scotland, but he was prevented by Sir GEORGE BYNG, 1708.

In a sermon preached before the Lord Mayor and Corporation of London, Dr. SACHEVERELL, rector of St. Saviour's (Southwark), *spoke strongly against Dissenters, condemned the Revolution, and* declared the Church of England to be in danger. For this offence he was suspended for three years, and his sermons were ordered to be burnt, Feb. 27, 1710.

The New Parliament met (1710) in which the Tories were the stronger party. It passed:—

1. An Act against **Occasional Conformity**.

2. **The Schism Act,** by which dissenters were prohibited from becoming schoolmasters. The Queen's death prevented the enforcement of this law.

3. MARLBOROUGH was charged with peculation, and dismissed.

The Treaty of Utrecht ended the war of the Spanish succession, and was signed by France, Great Britain, and her allies, with the exception of Germany, April 11, 1713. Its leading conditions were :—

1. That the protestant succession should be recognised by France.

2. That there should never be a union between the two crowns of France and Spain.

3. That England should have Gibraltar, Minorca, Hudson's Bay, Nova Scotia, and Newfoundland.

4. That the fortifications of Dunkirk should be destroyed.

5. That PHILIP (the grandson of LOUIS) should hold Spain.

6. That the Duke of SAVOY should have Sicily; and the Emperor, Sardinia, Milan, Naples, and the Netherlands.

By this war, whose termination was not very beneficial to England, our **National Debt** was increased by £21,932,622.

During this reign there was no rebellion, and only one person (GREGG) was executed for high treason. A **General Post Office** for all the British dominions was established in 1710; St. Paul's Cathedral, after 37 years' labour, was finished by WREN, and cost £1,000,000; the Queen gave up the *first fruits* and *tenths* for the benefit of poor livings, which gift is well known as **Queen Anne's Bounty.** Newspaper stamps and promissory notes are said to have originated. THOMAS NEWCOMAN, a locksmith of Devonshire, invented the **Steam-engine.** Owing to the eminent literary characters who flourished at this time, the reign of ANNE has been styled the **Augustan Age of English Literature.**

ANNE died at Kensington, Aug. 1, 1714, and was interred at Westminster.

Robert South, an eminent divine, and author of sermons, which are characterised by wit and eloquence. (1633—1716).

Sir Isaac Newton, one of the greatest philosophers ever known, was born at Woolsthorpe, Lincolnshire, 1642. He invented the reflecting telescope, discovered the law of gravitation, and is the author of the *Principia* (Mathematical Principles of Natural Philosophy). He also wrote on theological subjects. Died 1727.

Gilbert Burnet, a native of Edinburgh, and Bishop of Salisbury, wrote a "History of the Reformation," and of "His Own Times." (1643—1715).

Leibnitz, an eminent German philosopher and metaphysical writer. (1646—1714).

Matthew Prior, poet, chief author of "The Country Mouse and City Mouse." He also wrote a "History of His Own Times." (1664—1721).

Lord Somers, Chancellor, wrote "A History of the Succession of the Crown of England." (1650—1716).

Sir Cloudesley Shovel, a famous admiral, and the son of a peasant. His activity against the French at the battle of Bantry Bay caused him to be knighted by WILLIAM III. and made Rear-Admiral. (1650—1707).

Sir George Rooke, a renowned admiral, who distinguished himself in several engagements with the French, and was mainly instrumental in the capture of Gibraltar. The influence of the Whigs compelled Rooke to resign his command, after which he withdrew to his estate in Kent. (1650—1709).

John Churchill, Duke of Marlborough, a celebrated general, was born at Ashe in Devonshire, June 24, 1650. Having given early proofs of great military talents, he was appointed by the Queen to command the allied forces in the war of the Spanish Succession; during which he gained a series of the most brilliant victories, especially those of **Blenheim, Ramillies, Malplaquet,** and **Oudenarde,** which considerably raised the military reputation of England. It is said "that he never besieged a town which he did not take, or fought a battle which he did not win." He afterwards lost the favour of the Queen, and was deprived of his military command. Died June 10, 1722.

Fenelon, a celebrated French archbishop, and author of several theological works. (1651—1715).

Marshal Tallard, a celebrated French officer, whom MARL-BOROUGH defeated and made prisoner at the battle of Blenheim. (1652—1728).

Marshal Villars, a distinguished French general, was op-posed to MARLBOROUGH at the battles of Ramillies and Mal-plaquet. In the latter engagement he was severely wounded. (1653—1734).

Charles Mordaunt (Earl of Peterborough), a noted general, who distinguished himself against the Moors at the siege of Tangiers. As commander of the English troops in Spain, he displayed the utmost valour, and captured Barcelona. (1658—1735).

Robert Harley (Earl of Oxford), a statesman, who was im-peached by the Whigs, and imprisoned for two years on a charge of treason. He had a large collection of manuscripts, which were sold to the British Museum for £10,000. (1661—1724).

Matthew Henry, a learned Nonconformist divine, and emi-nent Biblical Commentator. (1662—1714).

Sir John Vanbrugh, architect and dramatist. Blenheim House (the seat of the Duke of MARLBOROUGH) was built by him. (1666—1726).

Dean Swift, born in Dublin, 1667, author of "Gulliver's Travels," the "Tale of a Tub," and "Drapier's Letters." Died insane, 1745.

Sir Richard Steele, a distinguished essayist, was an Irishman by birth, and the originator of the *Tatler* and *Spectator*. (1671—1729).

Colley Cibber, a poet and play-writer, whose first play was "Love's Last Shift." The "Careless Husband" is considered his best work. (1671—1757).

Joseph Addison, a poet and elegant prose writer, was one of the contributors to the *Spectator*, *Tatler*, and *Guardian*. He also became Secretary of State. (1672—1719).

William Congreve, a dramatic poet, author of "The Old Bachelor," "The Double Dealer," "The Mourning Bride," and other works. (1672—1729).

Nicholas Rowe, a dramatic poet, became Poet-Laureate in the reign of George I. Among his plays may be named *Jane Shore*, and *The Fair Penitent*. He also translated Lucan's *Pharsalia* and Quillet's *Callipædia* into verse. (1673—1718). .

George Farquhar, a comic writer, whose best work is con-sidered "The Beau's Stratagem." (1678—1707).

Thomas Parnell, a poet, contemporary with POPE, author of "The Hermit." (1679—1718).

Alexander Pope, a celebrated poet, translator of HOMER, author of an "Essay on Man," an "Essay on Criticism," and other works. (1688—1744).

John Gay, a poet, and author of " Rural Sports," "The Beggar's Opera," and other works. (1688—1732).

George Frederick Handel, born at Halle, Saxony, in 1685, was an eminent musical composer.　In 1741 he produced the " Messiah," which is considered one of his masterpieces.　The " Creation " is also one of his grand conceptions.　Died 1759.

REMARKS.

The prominent features of the STUART period were :—

1. Frequent contentions between the Sovereigns and their Parliaments ; the former endeavouring to make the royal prerogative almost absolute, the latter struggling for constitutional freedom.

2. The civil war, which resulted in the execution of CHARLES I.

3. The establishment of the Commonwealth and the Protectorate of OLIVER CROMWELL.

4. The great military and naval reputation of England under CROMWELL and QUEEN ANNE.

5. A manifestation of strong party-feeling both in religion and politics.

6. The Restoration of the STUART Dynasty.

7. The Revolution.

8. The present authorised translation of the Scriptures.

9. The Augustan Age of English literature.

After the death of CHARLES I., the Queen of SWEDEN bought his jewels ; and the Duke of AUSTRIA, most of his splendid collection of pictures.　His wife fled to France, accompanied by two of her children; CHARLES (afterwards CHARLES II.) escaped to the Netherlands.　After CHARLES's defeat at Worcester, he was loyally sheltered by farmer PENDERELL and his four brothers at a house called Boscobel, in Shropshire.　Finding the enemy were in search of those who had escaped, CHARLES concealed himself in an oak-tree, and thus baffled the vigilance of his pursuers.　He was at last enabled to land in safety at Fecamp in Normandy.　Owing to the great fire, and other events of the year 1666, it was called by DRYDEN *Annus Mirabilis,* or the wonderful year.　In the statutes enacted in 1624, we have the first mention of *interest* instead of *usury.*

In London, 51 churches are said to have been built by CHRISTOPHER WREN, the noted architect.

During a part of this period, it is only right to say that agriculture did not improve. Education was neglected, social evils were unrestrained, and no attempt was made to ameliorate the sanitary conditions of the poor, whose destitute children in the large towns were compelled to sleep in the open streets. Many of the wretched and unhealthy dwellings in the metropolis were destroyed by the great fire, through which means a check was put upon the ravages of the plague. The French Protestants were called **Huguenots**, which is said to be a corruption of the German *Eidgenossen*, meaning *bound together by oath*.

The partizans of JAMES were called **Jacobites**, from *Jacobus*, the Latin for JAMES.

The **Stuart Dynasty**, including the Commonwealth and the joint reigns of WILLIAM and MARY, extended over a period of 111 years, commencing with JAMES I. in 1603, and ending with the death of ANNE in 1714.

THE LEADING EVENTS AND PRINCIPAL DATES
OF THE STUART PERIOD.

	A.D.
Accession of James I.; Union of England and Scotland	1603
Hampton Court Conference...	1604
The Gunpowder Plot	1605
James-Town in Virginia founded...	1607
The present authorised translation of the Bible finished ..	1611
Sir W. Raleigh executed; commencement of the Thirty Years' War...	1618
The circulation of the Blood discovered by Dr. Harvey ...	1619
Death of James I.; and accession of Charles I.	1625
First English Settlement in the West Indies	1625
Petition of Right, and the assassination of the Duke of Buckingham	1628
Hampden tried for resisting the payment of ship-money..	1637
The Covenant made in Scotland	1638
England invaded by the Scots, and battle of Newburn-upon-Tyne; the Long Parliament began	1640
Abolition of the Star Chamber and High Commission Court; Irish Rebellion	1641
Battle of Edgehill	1642
Death of Hampden at Chalgrove Field	1643
Battle of Marston Moor	1644
Execution of Archbishop Laud	1645
Battle of Naseby	1645
Colonel Pride's Purge...	1648
Execution of Charles I.	1649
Battle of Dunbar	1650

	A.D.
Battle of Worcester	1651
War against Holland	1652
Cromwell made Protector	1653
Peace concluded with Holland; and Jamaica captured	1655
Refusal of the Crown by Cromwell	1657
Capture of Dunkirk and death of Cromwell	1658
Watch-making commenced in England	1658
Richard Cromwell resigned the Protectorate	1659
The Committee of Safety formed	1659
Charles II. restored to the throne	1660
Incorporation by Charter of the Royal Society	1662
The Act of Uniformity passed, and 2000 Ministers in consequence resigned their livings	1662
Guineas coined for the first time in England	1663
The erection of Toll-gates	1663
The Conventicle Act passed	1664
The Great Plague of London	1665
The Five-mile Act passed	1665
The Fire of London	1666
Treaty of Breda concluded	1667
The ministry called the Cabal formed	1667
Triple alliance; grant of Bombay to the East India Company	1668
The use of Tea became general	1669
Secret Treaty of Dover, between Charles II. and Louis XIV. of France	1670
War declared against Holland	1672
The Test Act	1673
Peace with Holland	1674
The Royal Observatory founded at Greenwich	1676
Peace of Nimeguen	1678
The Habeas Corpus Act passed	1679
The Exclusion Bill passed	1679
Meal-tub Plot	1679
Chelsea Hospital founded	1682
Rye-house Plot	1683
Battle of Sedgemoor	1685
Death of Charles II. and accession of James II.	1685
Edict of Nantes revoked by Louis XIV.	1685
Trial of the seven Bishops	1688
Landing of the Prince of Orange	1688
Accession of William and Mary	1689
Bill of Rights	1688
Battle of the Boyne	1690

<table>
<tr><td>The Massacre at Glencoe ... ...</td><td>A.D. 1692</td></tr>
<tr><td>The Battle of La Hogue ... ...</td><td>1692</td></tr>
<tr><td>Foundation of the National Debt... ... ...</td><td>1692</td></tr>
<tr><td>Bill passed for Triennial Parliaments ... ...</td><td>1694</td></tr>
<tr><td>Death of the Queen ... ...</td><td>1694</td></tr>
<tr><td>The Bank of England Incorporated ... ...</td><td>1694</td></tr>
<tr><td>Treaty of Ryswick ... ...</td><td>1697</td></tr>
<tr><td>The Act of Settlement passed ... ...</td><td>1701</td></tr>
<tr><td>The grand Alliance ... ...</td><td>1702</td></tr>
<tr><td>Death of William III.... ... ...</td><td>1702</td></tr>
<tr><td>Accession of Queen Anne ... ...</td><td>1702</td></tr>
<tr><td>War of the Spanish Succession ... ...</td><td>1702</td></tr>
<tr><td>Battle of Blenheim ... ...</td><td>1704</td></tr>
<tr><td>Gibraltar Captured ... ...</td><td>1704</td></tr>
<tr><td>Battle of Ramillies ... ...</td><td>1706</td></tr>
<tr><td>The Union of Scotland ... ...</td><td>1707</td></tr>
<tr><td>Battle of Oudenarde ... ...</td><td>1708</td></tr>
<tr><td>Battle of Malplaquet ... ...</td><td>1709</td></tr>
<tr><td>A General Post Office for all the British dominions established... ... ...</td><td>1710</td></tr>
<tr><td>Marlborough stripped of his offices ... ...</td><td>1711</td></tr>
<tr><td>The Treaty of Utrecht ... ...</td><td>1713</td></tr>
<tr><td>Death of Queen Anne... ... ...</td><td>1714</td></tr>
</table>

THE HOUSE OF HANOVER OR BRUNSWICK.

George I. was the son of Sophia (daughter of Elizabeth), and Ernest Augustus, Elector of Hanover. Elizabeth was the daughter of James I. A.D. 1714—1727.

A   WARS.

1. Battle of Sheriffmuir (Perthshire). This was a rebellion in favour of the Old Pretender, the son of James II.; the insurgents under the Earl of MAR were partially beaten by the Royalists, commanded by the Duke of ARGYLE, Nov. 13, 1715.

2. There was an Insurrection for advancing the interests of the Pretender, headed by Lord DERWENTWATER and others, but the insurgents being met at Preston in Lancashire by the Royal-

ists, under Generals CARPENTER and WILLES, were obliged to surrender, Nov, 13, 1715. Some of the offenders were executed, and others banished.

3. The Pretender himself embarked at Dunkirk, and shortly after landed at **Peterhead** (Dec. 25, 1715), but finding no possibility of enforcing his claims, he re-embarked at Montrose, landed at **Gravelines,** and ultimately died at **Rome,** 1766.

4. There was another **Jacobite Conspiracy** for placing the Pretender on the throne, but it ended in the execution of LAYER and the banishment of ATTERBURY, Bishop of Rochester, 1722.

5. The Spanish Fleet of 27 sail was completely defeated off **Cape Passaro** (Sicily), by Sir GEORGE BYNG, Aug. 11, 1718. Two years after, **Peace** was concluded with Spain.

6. **Gibraltar** was unsuccessfully besieged by the Spaniards for four months, 1727.

B   **CHIEF EVENTS.**

The **Crowns of England and Hanover were united in the person of George I.,** who came to the throne without opposition, although there were many of the Jacobite party, under the Earls of OXFORD and BOLINGBROKE and the Duke of ORMOND, who had been scheming for the restoration of the STUARTS, by advancing the claims of the "Old Pretender," the son of JAMES II.

The unexpected death of the Queen, and the vigilance of the Whigs, who had the lead in this reign, caused the scheme to fail, and in the Parliament (which met March 17, 1715) the Duke of ORMOND, BOLINGBROKE, and HARLEY, Earl of OXFORD, were impeached for their conduct in the Treaty of Utrecht. The first two fled to France; the last was confined two years in prison, and then released.

The Riot Act.—As party spirit ran high, causing several riots to break out in different parts of the kingdom, it was found necessary to pass a bill, called the Riot Act, for the prevention of such assemblies as tended to disturb the peace, July 1715. Persons joining such meetings rendered themselves punishable by this law, if they did not disperse within one hour after receiving warning by the proclamation of any one justice.

The Septennial Act.—The enactment of this law, by which Parliaments were to last seven years, was caused by the " rebellion" in favour of the "Old Pretender," whose claims might have been advanced by an accession of Tories had Parliament been dissolved every three years according to the Triennial Act, 1716.

The **Triple Alliance**, comprised England, Holland, and France, and was signed by the three powers for protection against Spain under Cardinal ALBERONI, Jan. 4, 1717.

The **Quadruple Alliance**, between Great Britain, France, the Emperor, and Holland, was signed in London, for securing the rightful succession of sovereigns in Great Britain and France, and the partition of Spain, Aug. 2, 1718.

The **Mississippi or Law's Bubble**, was a fatal speculation in France, devised by a Scotchman named JOHN LAW; the scheme of this individual was the liquidation of the French national debt by the profits arising from the establishment of a bank, an East India and a Mississippi Company. The plan had been accepted by the French government in 1710, and in 1720 came the failure of the scheme, and thereby the ruin of some thousands of families.

By the **Peace of Stockholm**, between England and Sweden, the former acquired the duchies of Bremen and Verden, Nov. 20, 1719.

The **South-Sea Scheme or Bubble.**—A ruinous speculation in England, was started at the suggestion of Sir JOHN BLUNT; the plan proposed and accepted was the following:—

1. That the South-Sea Company should take the responsibility of the National Debt.

2. That in consideration thereof, the Company should be invested with the exclusive privilege of carrying on the South-Sea trade.

Deluded by the false representations of the Company's directors, thousands of persons became speculators in the dishonorable scheme, by the failure of which they were reduced to the condition of beggars (1720). The shares at first were sold for £100, but the directors had by their deception succeeded in raising them to £1000. The financial salvation of England at this particular juncture is attributed to ROBERT WALPOLE, and in 1721 the estates of the directors, valued at £2,014,000, were confiscated for the benefit of those who suffered by the South-Sea Bubble.

Lord TOWNSHEND was made Secretary of State, and WALPOLE, succeeded AISLABIE as Chancellor of the Exchequer, 1721.

Wood's Coinage.—Copper money being wanted in Ireland, WILLIAM WOOD was authorised by the English government to coin a number of halfpence and farthings, amounting in value to £108,000. This coinage caused a great tumult in Ireland, which DEAN SWIFT encouraged by his Drapier's Letters, 1724. The vigorous resistance of the Irish against the new coinage ended in WOOD losing his patent, and receiving instead a pension of £3000.

For selling offices in his gift, and for robbing widows and orphans of their money, Lord Chancellor MACCLESFIELD was fined £30,000. (1725).

By the **Treaty of Vienna** between the Emperor of Germany and the King of Spain, they confirmed to each other their respective parts of the Spanish dominions; Spain guaranteed the Pragmatic Sanction; and the Emperor engaged to employ a force to procure the restoration of Gibraltar to Spain, and to use means for placing the Pretender on the English throne, 1725.

The **Treaty of Hanover** was entered into by England, France, Holland, Denmark, Prussia, and Sweden, against the Treaty of Vienna, 1725.

Owing chiefly to the **Bangorian Controversy**, which originated from a sermon by DOCTOR HOADLEY, Bishop of Bangor, the **Convocation** was prorogued by government (1717), and it did not sit again for the transaction of business till the reign of VICTORIA; in 1718, the **Schism Act**, passed in the reign of ANNE, was **repealed**; THOMAS GUY, a bookseller, founded Guy's Hospital, 1721; Inoculation for the **small-pox** was introduced into England from Turkey by Lady Mary WORTLEY MONTAGUE, (1721) and tried for the first time upon some criminals with satisfactory results; the King **re-established** the order of **Knight** of the **Bath**, 1725, no one having received that honour since the time of CHARLES II.; a Charter of Incorporation for the three towns of Calcutta, Bombay, and Madras, was granted to the East India Company, 1726.

The King died from an apoplectic fit at Osnaburgh, June 11, 1727, and was buried at Hanover.

C   CELEBRATED PERSONS.

Humphrey Prideaux, Dean of Norwich, author of "The connection of the Old and New Testaments;" "The Original Right of Tithes," and other works. (1648—1724).

Dr. Samuel Clarke, a divine and philosopher, was appointed Chaplain to Queen ANNE. Of the works published by CLARKE, we may mention his twelve books of HOMER's "Iliad," with Annotations, a paraphrase of the Gospels, and his Latin translation of NEWTON's "Optics," for which Sir ISAAC NEWTON presented him with five hundred pounds. (1675—1729).

William Lowth, a learned divine, who, among other works, wrote "Directions for the Profitable Reading of the Holy Scriptures," and "Commentaries on the Four Greater Prophets." (1661—1732).

Dr. Daniel Waterland, Archdeacon of Middlesex, wrote a "History of the Athanasian Creed," and a "Vindication of the Doctrine of the Trinity." (1683—1740).

Dr. Isaac Watts, a famous Nonconformist divine, author of Hymns, a "Treatise on Logic," an "Essay on the Improvement of the Mind," besides other works. (1674—1749).

Dr. N. Lardner, a noted Dissenting minister, author of the "Credibility of the Gospel History." (1684—1768).

George Berkeley, Bishop of Cloyne, who, according to POPE, possessed every virtue under Heaven. He published his "Theory of Vision," "Principles of Human Knowledge," "Dialogues between Hylas and Philonus," a work against infidelity, called the "Minute Philosopher," &c., &c. (1684—1753).

John Potter, Archbishop of Canterbury, author of "Antiquities of Greece," and some theological works. (1674—1747).

Joseph Butler, Bishop of Durham, celebrated for his work called *The Analogy of Religion*. (1692—1752).

Sir Robert Walpole, Earl of Orford, an eminent statesman, was a leading man among the Whigs in the House of Commons, He became First Lord of the Treasury and Chancellor of the Exchequer. By his pacific policy the National Debt was greatly reduced. WALPOLE continued in office for twenty years, at the end of which time he was obliged to resign, but received a pension of £4000 a year, and was created Earl of Orford. (1676—1745.)

Sir James Thornhill, chief painter to Queen ANNE and GEORGE I., became a member of the House of Commons. The dome of St. Paul's was painted by THORNHILL. (1676—1734).

Richard Bentley, celebrated as a divine and critic. His editions of HORACE and TERENCE are well known to the classical scholar. (1661—1742).

Henry St. John, (Lord Bolingbroke) was one of the principal leaders of the Tory party, and a great political writer. (1678—1751).

James Stuart, commonly called the *Old Pretender*, was the son of JAMES II., and born in 1688. After an unsuccessful attempt to regain the English crown in 1715, he returned to the continent. Being expelled from Paris by the Treaty of Utrecht, he went to Italy, and there remained till his death, which took place at Rome in 1766. By his wife, MARIA CLEMENTINA, grand-daughter of JOHN SOBIESKI, King of POLAND, he had CHARLES EDWARD, and HENRY.

Lord Nithisdale, an adherent of the Old Pretender, was committed to the Tower, but through the heroic conduct of his

Thomas Sherlock, Bishop of London, a ve
author of "Sermons on the Use and Intent o
" Defence of the Miracle of Christ's Resurrection,"
in justification of the Test Act.   (1678—1761).

Benjamin Hoadley, Bishop of Bangor, but
moted to the See of Winchester.   His sermon o
Kingdom of Christ gave rise to the **Bangorian**
(1676—1761).

Lady Mary Wortley Montague, eldest c
Duke of KINGSTON, noted for her " Letters," whicl
models of the epistolary style.   (1690—1762).

Anthony Ashley Cooper, third Earl of Salis]
as a metaphysician.   Chief work, " Characteristics
ners, Opinions, and Times."   (1671—1713).

Daniel Defoe, novelist and Miscellaneous w
"Robinson Crusoe," a "History of the Union o
Scotland," &c.   (1661—1731).

2. Anson headed an expedition against Spanish America, during which he circumnavigated the globe, took the town of Paita, and captured a Spanish galleon (the Manilla) in which was found treasure to the amount of £300,000. This undertaking commenced in 1740, and ended by the return of Anson in 1744.

II. War of the Austrian Succession.

In 1713, Charles VI., Emperor of Germany, published a decree, called The Pragmatic Sanction, securing his hereditary Austrian dominions to his daughters in preference to the sons of his brother Joseph I. In accordance therewith, Charles, at his death in 1740, left these said territories to his daughter, Maria Theresa, by whom he was succeeded in the same year, but her rights were opposed by the Elector of Bavaria, and Frederic of Prussia, who claimed certain portions of the dominions. As the Queen would not yield to these demands, war was the result, Maria Theresa being aided by England; France uniting with the other two powers against her.

1. **Battle of Molwitz** (Silesia), in which the Austrians were severely beaten by the Prussians under Frederic, to whom Silesia yielded, April 10, 1741.

2. **Battle of Dettingen** (Bavaria).—This was an engagement between the British, Hessian, and Hanoverian army of 52,000 men, commanded by the King in person, and the Earl of Stair, against the French forces of 60,000 men, headed by Marshal Noailles and the Duc de Grammont. The French were defeated with a loss of 5000 men, June 27, 1743. This battle is noted as being the last in which an English monarch was personally engaged.

3. **Battle of Fontenoy** (Belgium).—This great battle was fought between the French, consisting of 76,000 strong, under Marshal Saxe, and the allied army (50,000) of the English, Dutch, Hanoverians, and Austrians, commanded by the Duke of Cumberland. Through the disgraceful flight of the Dutch, France was victorious. The allies lost 12,000 men, and the enemy nearly the same number, May 11, 1745.

4. **Louisbourg**, the capital of Cape Breton, was besieged and captured from the French, June 15, 1745.

.5. Admirals Anson and Warren defeated the French in a battle off Cape Finisterre, and took or destroyed the greater part of their fleet, May 3, 1747.

6. Seven men-of-war, belonging to the French, were captured by *Admiral Hawke*, off Belle-Isle, Oct. 14, 1747.

3. That the King of Prussia, the only one who
the treaty, should retain Silesia.

4. That the **Pragmatic Sanction** should be ol

5. That the fortifications of **Dunkirk** next tl
be destroyed.

6. That the duchies of **Placentia, Parma,** an
should be surrendered to the infant Don Philip, heii
the Spanish throne.

III. Rebellion in Scotland for the Restoration of

1. **Battle of Prestonpans** (near Edinburg]
Charles Edward Stuart, the **Young Pretend**
of James II., at the head of his Scotch followers,
King's forces under Sir John Cope, Sept. 21, 1745.

2. **Battle of Falkirk** (Scotland), in which tl
under General Hawley, were defeated by the You
Jan. 17, 1746.

3, **Battle of Culloden** (Scotland). betweer
forces commanded by the Duke of Cumberland, an
rebels, under the Young Pretender. The latter wer
with a loss of 2500 men, April 16, 1746. After this d
Charles wandered for six months in the wilds of S
though the sum of £30,000 was offered for his captur
to France. His death took place at Rome, 1788

2. Calcutta, a principal British fort, was besieged and captured by Surajah Dowlah, the Viceroy of Bengal. It was on this occasion that 146 Englishmen were cast into a dungeon somewhat less than 18 feet square, called the **Black Hole of Calcutta**. Owing to the heat and close confinement in so small a place, 123 were found dead the next morning, June 21, 1756.

3. Calcutta was retaken in two hours by the English under Admiral Watson and Lord Clive, who had resolved on punishing the offenders for the Black Hole cruelty, Jan. 2, 1757.

4. **Battle of Plassey** (Bengal), in which 70,000 native Hindoos and some French forces, under Surajah Dowlah, were complety vanquished by 3000 British under Lord Clive, June 23, 1757.

The result of this victory was:—

1. **The foundation of the British Indian Empire.**

2. The English received as a compensation from Meer Jaffier, the successor of Surajah Dowlah, who was put to death, a sum of money amounting to nearly three millions sterling.

5. **The Closter-seven Convention.**—The French army under Duc De Richelieu, having surrounded 38,000 Hanoverians under the Duke of Cumberland, the latter agreed to disband his soldiers, Sept. 10, 1757.

6. **Fort Louis** and the **Isle of Goree** in Africa, were taken from the French by Commodore Keppel; Louisburg, the capital of Cape Breton, was captured by Boscawen and Amherst, who also took Prince Edward's Island, 1758. Fort Duquesne was captured by Forbes, who gave it the name of **Pittsburgh**, 1758.

7. **Battle of Minden** (Prussia), in which 80,000 French were vanquished by a force of 9000, consisting of English, Hessians, and Hanoverians, under Prince Ferdinand and Lord George Sackville, Aug. 1, 1759.

8. The French under De la Crue were defeated off **Cape Lagos** (Portugal), by Admiral Boscawen, Aug. 18, 1759. The Admiral De la Crue lost both his legs in the engagement, and expired the following day.

9. In **Quiberon Bay**, the French, commanded by Conflans, were defeated by Admiral Hawke, whose success on this occasion is said to have prevented a French invasion of England, Nov. 20, 1759.

10. **Quebec** was taken from the French by General WOLFE, Sept. 13, 1759; but the gallant officer had the misfortune to be killed in the action. MONTCALM, the French commander, and Governor of Canada, shared the same fate as WOLFE. By this victory England gained Canada, which has ever since remained in her possession.

B   **CHIEF EVENTS.**

The new Parliament met, Jan. 23, 1728, and in 1729, some London, Liverpool, and Bristol merchants presented petitions, in which they complained of losses in their trade caused by Spanish depredations in the West Indies. The **Treaty of Seville**, including England, France, and Spain, was concluded, 1729.

The **East India Company** obtained a new Charter, by agreeing to pay £200,000, and reducing by one per cent. the interest on money lent by them to the public, 1739.

Georgia was founded by General OGLETHORPE in 1732.

Sir ROBERT WALPOLE, the King's chief minister, introduced his **Excise Bill**, but he was obliged to abandon it on account of violent opposition, 1733.

The **Porteous Riot**, at Edinburgh, arose from Captain PORTEOUS having ordered his men to fire on the mob for throwing stones at the guard when a smuggler named WILSON was executed. For this order he was condemned to die, but was afterwards reprieved by the Queen. The people, however, were so exasperated with PORTEOUS, that they broke into the Tolbooth prison, dragged him to the Grassmarket, and hanged him on the sign-post of a dyer, Sept. 7, 1736.

The King and the Prince of Wales quarrelled, in consequence of which the latter with his Princess removed from Hampton Court to St. James's, 1737.

Queen CAROLINE died this year, lamented by all.

The religious sect called **Wesleyan Methodists** was founded by JOHN WESLEY in 1739.

ANSON commenced his voyage round the world, 1740.

As WALPOLE resigned, Lord CARTERET and the Earl of BATH were appointed the King's chief ministers, 1742.

Halifax in Nova Scotia, so called after the Earl of HALIFAX, was founded, 1750.

The **Prince of Wales** was killed by a blow from a cricket ball, 1751.

The **Calendar** was altered, and the **New** or **Gregorian Style** of Computation adopted, by which eleven days were taken from September, the *third* of that month being called the *fourteenth*, and the year made to begin on the *first* of January, and not on the *twenty-fifth* of March, as was formerly done by the old or Julian style of computation, 1752.

The Law of Marriage.—As people were in the habit of entering into matrimony without licence, banns, or parental sanction, a bill was passed (1753), and provided:—

1. That marriages should be effected either by licences obtained from the bishops, or by publishing the banns three successive Sundays in the parish church.

2. That the authority to grant **Special Licences** for solemnizing a marriage *at any time or place*, should be vested in the Archbishop.

3. That all marriages not in accordance with this law should be *null and void*, and the clergyman by whom such were solemnized, transported for seven years.

The British Museum was founded at Montague House by **Act** of Parliament, 1753.

Lisbon was destroyed by an earthquake, Nov. 1, 1755. For the relief of the survivors, England sent £100,000.

During this reign FAHRENHEIT invented his **Thermometer**, 1730; HADLEY's **Quadrant** was invented 1731; **Stereotyping,** by WILLIAM GED of Edinburgh, 1734; **Ventilators,** by Dr. HALES, 1741; HARRISON constructed his first **Time-piece**, 1735; FRANKLIN invented the **Lightning Conductor**, 1752; BRINDLEY commenced the Bridgewater Canal, 1758; and the first improvement in the stocking loom known as the "**Derby ribs,**" was effected by GEDEDIAH STRUTT, 1759.

The first Eddystone Light-house was built, the Mansion House, the Foundling Hospital for deserted children, and Black-Friars Bridge were erected; the Military Academy at Woolwich, and the College of Surgeons were founded, and the Manufacture of carpets was introduced into London by two Frenchmen.

The Gentlemen's Magazine, first published in 1731, is said to have laid the chief foundation of our periodic literature. Newspapers too became of more weight in public estimation, because politics were discussed in them.

The wars in this reign increased the **National Debt** by £30,000,000.

GEORGE II. died suddenly from disease of the heart, Oct. 25 1760, and was buried at Westminster.

C **CELEBRATED PERSONS.**

Charles Edward Stuart, designated the *Young Pretender,* and the *Chevalier de St. George,* was the son of the Old Pretender, and born in 1721. He made an effort in 1745 to regain the English crown, and at first obtained some advantages, but was defeated at the Battle of Culloden in Inverness-shire, 1746. After many dangers and difficulties, he escaped to France, and subsequently fell into habits of drunkenness. In 1772, he married the Princess LOUISA of Stolberg, and they afterwards lived at Florence under the title of the Count and Countess of ALBANY. In 1780, she, eloped with ALFIERI, the dramatic poet. CHARLES died at Rome, Jan. 30, 1788.

Henry Benedict Stuart, the last descendant of the royal line of the STUARTS, was the younger brother of CHARLES, called the Pretender. On the failure of the final attempt to restore his family in 1745, he entered into holy orders, and in 1747, Pope BENEDICT XIV. created him a cardinal. He ultimately received a pension from the English government. (1725—1807).

DIVINES.

John Lawrence Von Mosheim, a German divine and historian, born at Lübeck in 1694. GEORGE II. of England appointed him in 1747 Professor of Theology at Gottingen, and Chancellor of the University. He is well known for his "Ecclesiastical History." Died 1755.

Philip Doddridge, a distinguished Nonconformist, noted for his "Family Expositor of the New Testament," and the "Rise and Progress of Religion in the Soul." He was born in London, 1702, and died at Lisbon, 1751.

James Hervey, author of "Meditations among the Tombs," and many popular theological works. (1714—1758).

STATESMEN.

William Pulteney (Earl of Bath), a noted political opponent of WALPOLE. (1682—1764).

William Pitt, created Earl of Chatham by GEORGE III., was illustrious as a statesman and orator. He gave extraordinary tone to the administration, by the vigour of which the British arms flourished in every direction. (1708—1778).

Mr. **Pelham,** who died March 3, 1754.

Sir **Robert Walpole,** mentioned in the preceding reign.

GENERALS.

Duke of Cumberland, second son of GEORGE II., defeated CHARLES STUART, at the Battle of Culloden. (1721—1765).

Lord Clive, gained the Battle of Plassey, and thereby laid the foundation of our Empire in India. (1725—1774).

James Wolfe, who was killed at Quebec in Canada. (1726—1759).

ADMIRALS.

Edward Vernon, who captured Porto Bello. (1684—1757)

George Anson, sailed round the world, and returned with much treasure, which he had taken from the Spaniards. Lord ANSON commenced his memorable voyage in 1740, and completed it in four years. (1697—1762).

Edward Boscawen, who captured Madras, Cape Breton, and Louisburg. (1711—1761).

Edward Hawke, by whom CONFLANS was defeated. (1715—1781).

George Brydges (Lord Rodney), by whom Martinique, St. Lucia, and Granada were taken. (1718—1792).

John Byron, grandfather to the famous poet of that name, was appointed governor of Newfoundland, and Commander of the fleet in the West Indies. (1723—1786).

HISTORIANS.

Thomas Carte, wrote a history of England, and the life of JAMES, Duke of Ormond. (1686—1754).

Tobias Smollet, published a History of England, and was also a distinguished novelist. (1721—1771).

POETS.

Edward Young, author of "Night Thoughts." (1684—1765).

Allen Ramsay, wrote a pastoral called "The Gentle Shepherd. (1685—1758).

James Thomson, author of "The Seasons," and "Castle of Indolence." (1700—1748).

William Shenstone, author of "The Schoolmistress." (1714—1763).

Thomas Gray, who wrote a fine poem, entitled the "Elegy in a Country Churchyard." (1716—1771).

William Collins, author of an "Ode on the Passions," and "Oriental Eclogues." (1720—1756).

Mark Akenside, wrote "The Pleasures of Imagination." (1721—1770).

LITERARY MEN.

William Whiston, wrote a new theory of the earth, and translated "Josephus." (1667—1752).

Le Sage, a French novelist, author of "Gil Blas." (1668—1747).

Conyers Middleton, wrote the life of Cicero. (1683—1750).

Samuel Richardson, novelist; "Clarissa Harlowe" being esteemed his best production. (1689—1761).

Richard Savage, author of plays and some poetical pieces. (1698—1743).

Henry Fielding, a celebrated author, the novel of "Tom Jones" being considered one of his best productions. (1707.—1754).

Gilbert White, wrote a "Natural History of Selborne." (1720—1793).

Ephraim Chambers, compiled a Cyclopædia. Died 1740.

ANTIQUARIES.

Sir Hans Sloane, whose museum was made the basis of the British Museum. (1660—1753).

Dr. Thomas Tanner, author of a "History of the Spanish Monasteries." (1674—1735).

ASTRONOMER.

Dr. Halley, Astronomer Royal. (1656—1742).

ARTIST.

William Hogarth, well known for his "Rake's Progress," and other pictures. (1697—1764).

George III. was the eldest son of Frederick, Prince of Wales, and grandson of George II. A.D. 1760—1820.

A   •   WARS.

I. Continuation of the Seven Years' War.

1. **Battle of Wandewash (East Indies)**, in which the English, under Sir EYRE COOTE, defeated the French, under LALLY TOLLENDAL, and thereby secured for the former the **Carnatic**, a country of Southern Hindostan, Jan. 22, 1760.

2. **Pondicherry**, formerly the capital of French India, **Dominica**, in the West Indies, and **Belle-Isle** on the coast of Britany, were taken by the English in 1761.

3. After the capture of **Martinique** by Admiral RODNEY and General MONKTON, **Grenada, St. Lucia, St. Vincent**, the **Grenadines**, and **Tobago** surrendered to the English, 1762.

4. As Spain had formed with France (1761) a secret treaty, called the "**Family Compact**," England declared war against that country, and in addition to much treasure, captured **Havannah**, the capital of Cuba, and the **Phillipine Islands**, 1762.

5. The Spanish invaded Portugal, because the latter country would not join in hostilities against England, but they were vanquished by the British troops, who quickly drove them into their own country, 1762.

The Seven Years' War ended with the **Treaty of Paris**, Feb. 10, 1763, by which it was stipulated :—

1. That England should give up some of her conquests, Martinique and Guadaloupe being among the number.

2. That she should have **Minorca** for Belle-Isle, and **Florida** for Havannah, and also retain Canada, Senegal, Dominica, Louisiana, Cape Breton, Grenada, St. Vincent, and Tobago.

This war added £60,000,000 to the **National Debt**, which now amounted to £138,000,000.

II. The War with America,

Whose chief allies were France, Spain, and Holland. This contest originated from England imposing some taxes upon the Americans, and laying restrictions upon their commerce for the benefit of the mother country.

1. **Battle of Lexington** (near Boston), was the *first* fought in the War of Independence between England and America. The advantage was with the British, who destroyed the stores of the enemy, but lost in killed and wounded 273 men, April 19, 1775.

4. **Battle of Brooklyn** (Long Island), in
WILLIAM HOWE gained a victory over the America
2000 men in killed and wounded, and 1000 prisone
1776.

5. **Battle of White Plains,** in which the Ame
vanquished with heavy losses by HOWE, Nov. 30, 177(

6. **Battle of Brandywine.**—The British in
ment were again victorious over the Americans, w
great loss; the victors taking possession of **Philade**
11, 1777.

7. **Battle of Saratoga,** ended in the surrender
lish forces (5791 men) under BURGOYNE, to the Ame
General GATES, Oct. 17, 1777. This was the *turn*
favour of the Americans.

8. **Battle of Briar's Creek,** in which 2000
under General ASHE, were routed by the English, u
PREVOST, March 16, 1779. Altogether the British
victories at this place.

9. **Battle of Camden,** in which the Amer
GATES, were defeated by the English, under Lord C
Aug. 16, 1780.

10. **Second Battle of Camden,** between the
commanded by General GREENE, and the British
RAWDON. The latter were again victorious, April
CAMDEN was burnt by the English, May 13, 1781.

11. Siege of York Town, when Lord Corn

14. CLINTON marched to South Carolina, and reduced Charleston, May 12, 1780. DE GRASSE, placed at the head of the French Navy by LOUIS XVI., was signally defeated in a naval engagement off St. Lucia by RODNEY and HOOD, April 12, 1782.

15. The Dutch fleet under Admiral ZOUTMAN was defeated off the Doggerbank, by Admiral HYDE PARKER, 1781.

16. The Island of St. Eustatia was taken from the Dutch by RODNEY, Feb. 15, 1781.

17. Minorca, after a siege of six months, was taken from the English by DE CRILLON, Feb. 5, 1782.

18. In 1782, the French and Spanish bombarded Gibraltar, but it was bravely defended by General ELLIOT, the governor, who for his gallant services was created Lord HEATHFIELD. The siege of this place began in July 1779, and did not end till Feb. 1783.

19. Lord Rodney gained a great victory over the French fleet off Guadaloupe, in the West Indies, April 12, 1782.

In Nov. 1782, the **Independence** of the United States was acknowleged, and the **Treaty of Versailles** concluded between England, France, Spain, Holland, and America, Sept. 3, 1783.

By this treaty, England—

1. Recognised the **Independence** of the United States.

2. Recovered from France, Dominica, St. Vincent, Grenada, St. Christopher's, Nevis, and Montserrat.

3. Gave up her claim for demolishing the fortifications of Dunkirk.

4. Restored to France, Tobago, St. Lucia, Chandernagore, and Pondicherry, besides other possessions.

5. Ceded to Spain the two Floridas and Minorca, and in return obtained right to cut logwood in Honduras.

6. Kept from Holland only **Negapatam**.

The expense of this war added £100,000,000, to the **National Debt**, which now amounted to £240,000,000.

III. War with France.

The **French Revolution** began in 1789, but did not involve England till 1793. The causes which induced England to enter into war with France were:—

1. The declaration of the French National Convention, containing a *promise of aid* to all people wishful to recover their

liberty, and the suppression of the nobility and all the taxes in those countries in which the Republic should be victorious.

2. The execution of LOUIS XVI. and MARIE ANTOINETTE, his Queen, with other excesses, which showed the necessity of stopping the revolutionary career.

1. **Valenciennes** was taken by the English under the Duke of YORK, July 25, 1793.

2. The French fleet of 26 ships under JEAN BON St. ANDRE, was defeated off **Ushant** by Lord HOWE, who captured six ships of war and sank several, June 1, 1794.

3. As the **Dutch** had entered into a treaty with France, war was declared against Holland, and the **Cape of Good Hope** captured by Admiral ELPHINSTONE and General CLARKE, Sept. 16, 1795.

4. Spain, in 1796, united with France, and declared war against England, but Admirals JERVIS, NELSON, and COLLINGWOOD vanquished the Spanish fleet off **Cape St. Vincent**, Feb. 14, 1797.

5. The Dutch fleet under Admiral DE WINTER was almost destroyed off **Camperdown** by Admiral DUNCAN, Oct. 11, 1797.

6. **Battle of the Nile**, also called the **Battle of Aboukir**, in which the French were signally defeated by NELSON. Nine of the French line-of-battle ships fell into the hands of the conquerors, two were burnt and two escaped, Aug. 1, 1798.

7. BONAPARTE besieged **Acre**, but he was repulsed by Sir SIDNEY SMITH, 1799.

8. The Madras and Bombay armies, under Generals HARRIS and BAIRD, captured **Seringapatam** from TIPPOO SAHIB, who was killed, May 4, 1799.

9. Major-General PIGOT took **Malta** from the French, Sept. 5, 1800.

10. **Battle of Alexandria**, was fought between the French under MENOU, and the English under Sir RALPH ABERCROMBIE. The French were beaten, but ABERCROMBIE was mortally wounded, March 21, 1801.

11. **Battle of Copenhagen**, when the Danish fleet was almost destroyed by the English under Lord NELSON and Admiral PARKER. Of twenty-three ships of the line, eighteen were taken or destroyed, April, 1801.

12. **Battle of Assaye** (India), in which the British, under General ARTHUR WELLESLEY (afterwards Duke of WELLINGTON), gained a decisive victory over SCINDIAH and the RAJAH OF BERAR,

get. 23, 1803. This was WELLESLEY's first great battle, in which his army amounted only to about **one-tenth** of that of the enemy.

13. **Battle of Trafalgar**, in which the combined fleets of France and Spain under Admiral VILLENEUVE, were defeated by the British under the illustrious NELSON, who was killed in the engagement. The enemy lost nineteen ships, and about 20,000 prisoners. On commencing the fight, NELSON gave as his last signal, "**England expects every man will do his duty**," Oct. 21, 1805. This glorious victory was so destructive to the naval power of France, that NAPOLEON was in consequence compelled to abandon his projected invasion of England.

14. **Battle of Austerlitz**, in which the French, commanded by the Emperor NAPOLEON, gained a decisive victory over the Austrians and Russians, under the Emperors ALEXANDER of Russia and FRANCIS of Austria. The killed and wounded of the allies are said to have exceeded 40,000 men, Dec. 2, 1805.

15. **Battle of Maida** (Italy), between the French under General REGNIER, and the British commanded by Sir JOHN STUART. Though the French were double the number of the English, yet the latter gained a great victory. STUART is known as the **Hero of the Plains of Maida**, July 4, 1806.

16. As NAPOLEON had issued his **Berlin Decree** (Oct, 14, 1806), forbidding all commercial transactions with Great Britain, it was deemed advisable to secure the Danish fleet, lest it should be used by NAPOLEON against England. **Copenhagen** was therefore bombarded, and the Danish fleet taken by Admiral GAMBIER, Sept. 7, 1807.

V. The Peninsular War, in which Spain was aided by England.

1. **Battle of Vimeira** (Portugal), in which the English, under Sir ARTHUR WELLESLEY, defeated the French under Marshal JUNOT, Aug. 21, 1808. This victory was followed by the Convention of Cintra, by which the French army, which might have been taken, was allowed by Sir HARRY BURRARD and Sir H. DALRYMPLE, who had superseded WELLESLEY, to evacuate Portugal, Aug. 30, 1808.

2. **Battle of Corunna** (Spain).—In this engagement the French forces, 20,000 strong, were defeated by 15,000 of the English, under Sir JOHN MOORE, who was killed in the moment of victory, Jan. 16, 1809.

3. **Battle of Talavera (Spain)**, in which Sir ARTHUR WELLESLEY, at the head of 19,000 British and 30,000 Spaniards, gained a great victory over the French, amounting to 47,000, commanded by Marshals VICTOR and SEBASTIANI, July 27-28, 1809. For this victory WELLESLEY was created **Viscount Wellington of Talavera.**

4. **Battle of Busaco.**—In this engagement Lord WELLINGTON defeated the French army under MASSENA, Sept. 27, 1810. Owing to the great numbers of the enemy, WELLINGTON afterwards retreated into the lines of **Torres Vedras,** which were impregnable.

5. **Battle of Barrosa or Barosso** (near Cadiz), in which the French under Marshal VICTOR were beaten by the British, whose commander was Major-General GRAHAM, afterwards Lord LYNDOCH, March 5, 1811.

6. **Battle of Albuera or Albuhera** (near Badajos), where the French under Marshal SOULT were vanquished by the united army of the English and Anglo-Spanish, commanded by Marshal BERESFORD, May 16, 1811.

7. **Badajos** was stormed and taken by WELLINGTON, April 6, 1812. This success compelled the French to make a speedy retreat from Portugal.

8. **Battle of Salamanca (Spain).**—In this memorable battle, the French, commanded by Marshal MARMONT, were defeated by the English and allies under Lord WELLINGTON, July 22, 1812. Of the enemy 8,000 were killed and wounded, and 7,141 taken prisoners. **Madrid** was captured after this battle, and 2,500 more prisoners taken.

9. **Battle of Vittoria (Spain).**—In this terrible battle, the allied English, Spanish, and Portuguese, under the famous WELLINGTON, gained a brilliant victory over the French, under JOSEPH BONAPARTE, King of Spain, and Marshal JOURDAN, June 21, 1813.

10. **Battle of the Pyrenees,** in which the English under Lord WELLINGTON, vanquished the French, who were commanded by Marshal SOULT, July 28, 1813.

11. **Battle of Orthes.**—In this engagement the combined English and Spanish forces commanded by WELLINGTON, obtained a glorious victory over the French, headed by SOULT, Feb. 27, 1814.

12. **Battle of Toulouse,** was one of the most sanguinary conflicts in the Peninsular War. The French under SOULT were defeated after twelve hours' fighting, with a loss of 10,000 men; the *English* and allies under WELLINGTON, losing half that number, *April* 10, 1814.

13. **Battle of Quatre Bras,** when the French under Marshal NEY were repulsed by the English and allies, under the Duke of BRUNSWICK, the Prince of ORANGE, and Sir THOMAS PICTON. The British fought under great disadvantage, as their numbers were very inferior to those of the enemy. The Duke of BRUNSWICK was killed in this engagement, June 16, 1815.

14. **Battle of Waterloo.**—This memorable and decisive battle was fought on Sunday, June 18, 1815, when the French under NAPOLEON were totally routed by the British and their allies under the Duke of WELLINGTON. BLUCHER, who had done his utmost to reach the field of battle, just arrived in time to take up the pursuit of the enemy.

V. War with America.

The United States of America declared war against England, because the latter power would insist upon her right to search for English sailors in American vessels, June 18, 1812.

1. In the contest between the American frigate **Chesapeake** and the **Shannon,** the latter being commanded by Captain BROOKE, the former was taken in fifteen minutes, June 1, 1813.

2. **Washington,** the capital of the United States, was captured by the British under General Ross, and all its national structures burnt, Aug. 14, 1814.

3. An attack was made upon **Baltimore,** a maritime city in Maryland, by the British under Ross, but that general was killed, Sept. 12, 1814. Colonel BROOKE, who then took command of the army, routed the Americans, killing 600, and making 300 prisoners.

4. **New Orleans** was attacked by the British in Dec. 1814, but they were repelled with considerable loss by the Americans under General JACKSON, Jan., 1815. This war ended with the **Peace of Ghent.**

VI. The Irish Rebellion.

Though great dissatisfaction had prevailed in Ireland, it seems to have been ripened into a rebellion through the French Revolution. In the year 1791, a society, called the United Irishmen, was formed by THEOBALD WOLFE TONE, the object of which was to procure a reform of the Legislature. The time fixed for a general rising was May 23, 1798, but the discovery of this plot led government to arrest EMMETT, BOND, FITZGERALD, and other leaders. General LAKE finally defeated the insurgents at Vinegar Hill, near Wexford, June 21, 1798.

VII.

The British under Lord Exmouth, bombarded Algiers, destroyed the fleet in the harbour, and compelled the Dey to give up 1068 Christians, whom he had reduced to the condition of slaves, Aug. 27, 1816.

B   CHIEF EVENTS.

On the accession of George III., who was in his 22nd year, Pitt, Earl of Chatham, was Prime Minister, but he resigned because government refused to declare war against Spain, 1761, and was succeeded by John, Earl of Bute.

George married Charlotte of Mecklenburg Strelitz, Sept. 8, 1761, and in the same year, Sept. 22, the coronation took place.

In 1763, John Wilkes, a member of Parliament, and editor of a newspaper, called the *North Briton*, was prosecuted for publishing articles in his paper against the government. Being arrested on the strength of a general warrant, he was committed to the Tower, but when brought to Westminster Hall, he obtained his release on the ground that he was a member of Parliament. Wilkes now preferred an action against the Secretary of State for illegally arresting him, and got damages to the amount of £1000. Chief Justice Pratt at the same time declared general warrants to be illegal. Wilkes was, however, in 1764 expelled from the House of Commons, and his papers ordered to be burnt by the common hangman. After spending some time abroad, he returned to England, and being elected a member for Middlesex in 1768, the House declared that he was disqualified for holding a seat in Parliament. In 1769 he prosecuted Lord Halifax for illegally seizing his papers, and obtained £4000 damages. He was ultimately re-admitted a member of Parliament.

The American Stamp Act, which led to the American war, was passed, March 22, 1765. As the Americans were under British protection, Grenville considered it right that they should pay a part of the British taxes, and therefore he ordered certain documents to be stamped as in England. The Americans, on the other hand, insisted that it was unreasonable for them to pay taxes to the mother country, as they were not represented in the British Parliament.

In 1765, the Marquis of Rockingham became Prime Minister, and by the advice of Pitt, the American Stamp Act was repealed in 1766.

During Pitt's absence from ill health, Townshend, the Chancellor of the Exchequer, succeeded in passing a bill for imposing taxes on *glass, paper, tea,* and *painters' colours,* in the American colonies, 1767.

The **Royal Academy** was founded in 1768.

An unknown writer, who signed himself **Junius,** but who is supposed by many to have been Sir PHILIP FRANCIS, began a series of able letters in the *Public Advertiser,* in which he attacked both the King and his ministers, 1769.   On the resignation of the Duke of GRAFTON, Lord NORTH became Prime Minister (1770), and in the same year opposition from the American colonists led the British government to repeal all the taxes except that on tea, three ship-loads of which, belonging to English merchants, a mob cast into the sea at Boston in 1773.

The **Declaration of Independence** of the United States of North America was signed by the Members of Congress, July 4, 1776.

The death of the Earl of CHATHAM took place, 1778.

MARGARET NICHOLSON attempted the life of the King in 1780.

The **Gordon Riots.**—These were terrible riots in London, headed by Lord GEORGE GORDON, 1780.   The object of the rioters was to procure the repeal of an act which had been passed by Parliament in 1778 for the benefit of Roman Catholics.   Many of the rioters were executed, but GORDON, who was said to be insane, died in Newgate Prison, where he had been confined for a libel on MARIE ANTOINETTE, 1793.

The **Independence of the United States of America** was recognised by England, Nov. 30, 1782.

WILLIAM PITT, second son of the Earl of CHATHAM, became Premier, 1783.   WARREN HASTINGS, who had been appointed Governor-General of India, 1772, was tried on a charge of having used corrupt means for enriching the East India Company.   His trial began in 1789, and did not end till 1795, when he was pronounced innocent.   BURKE, SHERIDAN, and FOX were among his accusers.

The first settlement of the English made in Australia, at Botany Bay, 1788.

ROBERT RAIKES, a printer, established **Sunday Schools,** the first of which was opened in 1788.

The trial of HARDY, HORNE, TOOKE, and others for high treason, caused a great sensation in England in 1794, but they were all acquitted.

An attack was made upon the King while going to Parliament in 1795.

The marriage of the Prince of WALES took place in 1795.

In 1797, a Mutiny broke out in the fleet at Spithead, and no sooner was it suppressed, chiefly by the influence of Lord HOWE, than a second commenced at the Nore under RICHARD PARKER, who, with other ringleaders, was executed; while the rest obtained pardon. The sailors complained of low wages, severity of discipline, want of attention when sick, and of their provisions, which they said were deficient in weight and measure.

The Bank of England suspended Cash payments in 1797, which were not resumed till 1817.

On the return of BONAPARTE to France in 1799, he was declared First Consul, and in the same year he put a stop to the French Revolution.

The Rev. J. SMITH, of Wendover, founded Savings' Banks, 1799.

In the Union Bill by which Great Britain and Ireland were to be united, Jan. 1, 1801, the following terms were agreed upon:—

1. That Great Britain and Ireland should be called the United Kingdom of Great Britain and Ireland.

2. That in the United Parliament, Ireland should be represented by 100 Commoners, 4 Spiritual and 28 Temporal Peers.

3. That the churches of England and Ireland should be united into one Protestant Episcopal Church, and designated *the United Church of England and Ireland.*

4. That the commercial privileges should be the same in both countries.

5. That the laws of each country should remain the same as before, or be altered as the United Parliament might determine.

Treaty of Amiens, between England, France, Spain, and Holland, was effected, March 18, 1802, but lasted only till May, 1803.

By this treaty England agreed:—

1. To restore Malta to the Knights of St. John.

2. To retain out of her conquests only Trinidad and Ceylon.

3. France retained Belgium, Savoy, Geneva, Nice, &c.

BONAPARTE was created Emperor of France, 1804.

Both PITT and Fox died in 1806.

The Slave Trade was abolished by Parliament, March 25, *1807.*

Of the Societies founded in this reign, we mention the following:—

1.   Linnæan Society, 1778.

2.   The Tract Society, whose main work is the distribution of religious books, 1799.

3.   The Church Missionary Society, for the maintenance of Missionaries in foreign parts, 1800.

4.   Royal Institution, 1800.

5.   The Bible Society, for promoting the circulation of the Scriptures both at home and abroad, in 1804.

6.   Horticultural Society, 1804.

7.   Medico Chirurgical Society, 1805.

8.   London Institution, 1805.

9.   Geological Society, 1807.

10.   Russell Institution, 1808.

11.   The Jews Society, for the conversion of Jews, 1808.

12.   Institution of Civil Engineers, 1818.

13.   The Hibernian Society, the object of which is to furnish the Irish with Bibles and schools.

Besides the above mentioned societies, there were many others founded, such as the Humane, Philanthropic, National, Medical, Philosophical, and Agricultural Societies.

The "Orders in Council" were decrees issued by the British Privy Council, by which all commerce was forbidden to be carried on with French ports, 1807.

The Peace of Tilsit, was concluded between Russia, France, and Prussia (July 7, 1807), the terms of which were:—

1. That the Emperor of Russia should recognise the Confederation of the Rhine.

2. That Napoleon should restore to the Prussian monarch one-half of his dominions.

3. That Russia should recognise Napoleon's three brothers, Joseph, Louis, and Jerome, as Kings of Naples, Holland, and Westphalia.

Through the insanity of the King, the Prince of Wales was appointed Regent in 1811.

Spencer Perceval, the Premier, was shot in the House of Commons by Bellingham, May 11, 1812.

In 1814 Bonaparte had retired to Elba, but in the following year (1815) he invaded France, and met with a final defeat by Wellington at Waterloo, after which he delivered himself up to an English vessel called Bellerophon, of which MAITLAND was captain. He was banished to the Island of St. Helena, and there died, May 5, 1821.

The Peace of Ghent, between Great Britain and the United States of America, was effected, Dec. 24, 1814.

The Treaty of Paris, by which England obtained some islands in the West Indies, Malta, Ceylon, Mauritius, and the Cape of Good Hope, was concluded, May 30, 1814.

Princess CHARLOTTE, daughter of the Prince Regent, died, 1817.

An attack on the Prince Regent led to a suspension of the Habeas Corpus Act in 1817.

The Peterloo Massacre was occasioned by a Reform Meeting in Manchester in Aug. 1819, when some persons lost their lives.

An act for the regulation of the currency was passed by Secretary PEEL, 1819.

The passing of the **Six Acts** for preventing the use of arms, and seditious meetings, was accomplished by Lord SIDMOUTH, 1819.

The Duke of KENT, father of our present Queen, died, Jan. 23, 1820.

The chief leaders of the **French Revolution,** which commenced in 1789, were DANTON, ROBESPIERRE, MARAT, and CARRIER, all of whom met with untimely deaths. During two months of this shocking period, justly called the "**Reign of Terror,**" 50 persons were guillotined every day.

After the Union, in 1801, the National Banner was altered, and called "**The Union Jack.**" This flag bears three crosses; England being represented by St. George, her Patron Saint; Ireland by St. Patrick; and Scotland by St. Andrew.

GEORGE III. gave up the title of "King of France," which had been adopted by English monarchs since the reign of EDWARD III.

Three millions of subjects were lost to the Crown on the occasion of the American war, and the **National Debt** was increased by a hundred millions.

Among the additional **Taxes** imposed during the present reign may be mentioned those upon windows, quack medicines, and horses, as well as the game licence.

The Inventions, Discoveries, &c., of this reign :—

WATT made his first improvement in the **steam-engine,** *1765;* the **Spinning-Jenny** was invented by an humble weaver, named HARGREAVES, and the **Spinning Frame**, by ARKWRIGHT, 1767; **Botany Bay** discovered by Captain COOK, 1770; the **Mule-Jenny** invented by CROMPTON, 1775; COOK discovered the **Sandwich Islands**, 1778, but was killed at Owyhee in the following year; Sir W. HERSCHEL discovered a new planet, called, in honour of the King, **Georgium Sidus**, 1781; **Air Balloons** were invented by a Frenchman named MONTGOLFIER, in 1783, but they were introduced into England by VINCENT LUNARDI, an Italian; **Mail Coaches** began to run, 1784, and came into general use in 1785; the **power-loom** was invented by CART-WRIGHT; the steam first applied to cotton spinning, 1785. **The Times**, then called the *London Daily Universal Register*, was first issued, Jan. 13, 1785; **Coal gas** first applied for lighting purposes, 1792; **Vaccination** introduced by Dr. JENNER, 1796; penny pieces were issued 1797, London was first lighted by gas, 1807; steam applied for printing the "Times," 1814; the first steam-boat appeared on the Thames, 1815, and the Atlantic Ocean was first crossed by a **Steamer** in 1816: **India-rubber** was introduced through the influence of Dr. PRIESTLEY; and umbrellas by JONAS HANNAY, the introduction of the latter causing a riot among the cabmen of London, who were apprehensive that their business would suffer; the London Docks, Southwark Bridge, and the New Mint were erected.

GEORGE III., called the "**Christian King**," expired Jan. 29, 1820, after a reign of nearly sixty years, the longest in our history, and was buried in St. George's Chapel, Windsor.

C   CELEBRATED PERSONS.

DIVINES.

William Warburton, Bishop of Gloucester, author of several works, the chief being his "Divine Legation of Moses." (1698—1779).

John Wesley, the noted founder of the religious denomination of Christians called Arminian Methodists. WESLEY became Fellow of Lincoln College, Oxford, and was distinguished for his zeal, piety, and learning. (1703—1791).

Thomas Newton, Bishop of Bristol, author of "Dissertations on the Prophecies." (1704—1782).

Charles Wesley, who aided his brother JOHN WESLEY, was the author of "Hymns," &c. (1708—1788).

George Whitefield, celebrated as a preacher, and as the founder of the Calvinistic Methodists. He published some sermons and controversial tracts, and was patronised by the Countess of HUNTINGDON. (1714—1770).

Dr. Hugh Blair, a Scotchman, wrote "Sermons" and "Lectures on Belles Lettres." (1718—1800).

Richard Hurd, Bishop of Worcester, whose writings are numerous, among which, his "Twelve Discourses on the Prophecies," and his "Commentary on HORACE's Art of Poetry," may be mentioned. (1720—1808).

John Parkhurst, a learned divine, author of a Hebrew and English, and a Greek and English, Lexicon. (1728—1797).

George Horne, Bishop of Norwich, wrote a commentary on the Book of Psalms. (1730—1792).

Samuel Horsley, who became Bishop of Rochester and St. Asaph, opposed the unitarianism and materialism of Dr. PRIESTLEY. He published many theological works, chiefly of a controversial character. (1733—1806).

John Horne Tooke, wrote the "Diversions of Purley." He was born in London in 1736, and died at Wimbledon in 1812.

Dr. William Paley, Archdeacon of Carlisle, author of "The Evidences of Christianity," and "Natural Theology." (1743—1805).

Gilbert Wakefield, who left the Established Church and joined the Socinians. Among his chief works were a "Translation of the New Testament," and "The Evidences of Christianity." (1756—1801).

Dr. Adam Clarke, a great Oriental scholar, and author of a "Bibliographical Dictionary," a "Commentary on the Bible," &c., &c. (1762—1832).

Robert Hall, an eminent Baptist preacher, and author of "Modern Infidelity Considered." (1764—1831).

Reginald Heber, Bishop of Calcutta, author of the prize poem "Palestine," &c. (1783—1826).

STATESMEN.

Edmund Burke (1728—1797).

George Washington, the first President of the United States. (1732—1799).

Charles James Fox, son of the first Lord HOLLAND. (1749—1806).

R. B. Sheridan (1751—1816).

William Pitt, son of the great Earl of CHATHAM. (1750—1806).

Lord Castlereagh, was, on the death of Mr. Perceval, the ministerial leader of the House of Commons. (1769—1822).

George Canning, who became Governor of India, and afterwards Premier. (1770—1827).

William Huskisson, most efficient in Finance and Political Economy, was killed at the opening of the railway between Liverpool and Manchester. (1770—1830).

Sir Francis Burdett, a distinguished Political Reformer. (1770—1844).

Sir Thomas Stamford Raffles, distinguished not only as a statesman, but also as a naturalist, and as the founder of the Zoological Society, of which he was the first President. (1781—1826).

MILITARY COMMANDERS.

Sir Ralph Abercrombie, defeated the French at Alexandria, but was mortally wounded. (1738—1801).

Blücher, who came with the Prussian army to assist Wellington at the Battle of Waterloo. (1742—1819).

Sir John Moore, distinguished himself in the West Indies, Ireland, Holland, and in the Peninsular War. He gained the Battle of **Corunna,** but fell in the moment of victory. (1761—1809).

Napoleon Bonaparte, was born in Corsica, and became in 1804 Emperor of the French. He overran Europe with his victories, but was thoroughly defeated by the Duke of Wellington at Waterloo, June 18, 1815. After his defeat he was banished to St. Helena, where he died in 1821.

Nicholas Soult, Marshal of France, and Duke of Dalmatia, was much esteemed by Napoleon, who considered him the ablest tactitian in Europe. He had the chief command of the French army in the Peninsular War, and was defeated by Wellington in many engagements. In 1838, Soult represented France at the coronation of Queen Victoria, and met on that occasion with his old opponent, the Duke of Wellington, and also received an enthusiastic welcome from the English people, with which he was much gratified. Died 1851.

Junot, Marshal of France, was defeated by Wellington at the Battle of Vimiera. (1771—1813).

Jourdan, Marshal of France, whom Wellington defeated at Vittoria. (1762—1833).

Arthur Wellesley, (Duke of Wellington) an illustrious military commander and eminent statesman, was the third son of the

Earl of MORNINGTON, by ANNE, daughter of ARTHUR VISCOUNT DUNGANNON. He was educated at Eton College, then under a private tutor at Brighton, and finally at the Military Academy of Angers in France. He entered the army in 1787, and first distinguished himself in India, particularly at the Battle of Assaye. On his return to England he was elected a member of Parliament for Rye. In 1808, Sir ARTHUR WELLESLEY was sent to the Peninsula to aid the Spanish and Portuguese against the French, whom he defeated in many engagements, and ultimately drove them from the Peninsula. For these signal services he received £400,000, and was created Duke of Wellington and Field-Marshal of Great Britain. He next marched against NAPOLEON, who had escaped from Elba, and defeated him at the Battle of Waterloo. He was born in Dublin, 1769, and died at Walmer Castle in 1852.

NAVAL COMMANDERS.

Richard Howe, relieved Gibraltar and gained a decisive victory over the French fleet. (1725—1799).

Captain James Cook, aided in the re-taking of Newfoundland, and is noted for having thrice navigated the globe. He was killed in a quarrel with the natives 'of Owyhee, one of the Sandwich Islands. (1728—1779).

Adam Duncan, who defeated the Dutch, under DE WINTER, off Camperdown, for which achievement he received an annual pension of £2,000. (1731—1804).

John Jervis, (St. Vincent) was of great service to KEPPEL, aided Lord HOWE in the relief of Gibraltar, and commanded the expedition through which were captured Guadaloupe, Martinique, and St. Lucia. (1734—1823).

Horatio, Lord Viscount Nelson, Duke of Bronte, &c., one of the most renowned and successful admirals that England ever produced. He was killed at the Battle of Trafalgar. (1758—1805).

Sir Sidney Smith, who obliged NAPOLEON to raise the siege of St. Jean d' Acre. (1764—1840).

Lord Gambia, a distinguished admiral, was entrusted with the squadron which compelled the surrender of the Danish fleet in 1707. For his services on this occasion he received a peerage with a pension of £2,000. Died 1833.

HISTORIANS.

David Hume, author of a "History of England," "Essays," and a "Treatise on Human Nature." (1711—1776).

Robert Henry, wrote a History of Great Britain to the reign of HENRY VII.   (1718—1790).

William Robertson, a learned Scotch divine, who published a History of Scotland and a History of America.   (1721—1793).

Edward Gibbon, wrote the "Decline and Fall of the Roman Empire."   (1737—1794).

William Mitford, wrote a History of Greece.   (1744—1827).

POETS.

William Cowper, author of "The Task," "The Sofa," "John Gilpin," and a "Translation of Homer."   (1731—1800).

Dr. James Beattie, author of a volume of poems, and other works, but his fame rests chiefly on his *Minstrel.*   (1735—1803).

James Macpherson, chiefly known by a translation of poems, of which OSSIAN is said to have been the author.   (1738—1796).

Thomas Chatterton, the boy-poet, extended his fame through pretending to have discovered some poems, whose author was asserted to be THOMAS ROWLEY, a Bristol priest, who lived in the fifteenth century.   CHATTERTON published "Miscellanies in Prose and Verse."   He was born at Bristol in 1752, and owing to poverty he committed suicide in London, 1770.

Robert Burns, the National Poet of Scotland, was a man of humble origin, fine genius, but intemperate habits.   (1759—1796).

Robert Bloomfield, author of "The Farmer's Boy."   (1766—1823).

William Falconer, author of "The Shipwreck," was born in 1730, and is said to have been shipwrecked in the Mozambique Channel, about 1770.

Henry Kirke White, a youthful poet, who taught himself several languages, but was cut off by death at an early age.   He was born at Nottingham, 1785, and died at Cambridge, 1806.

Percy Bysse Shelley, wrote "Queen Mab," and "Revolt of Islam." (1792—1822).

Rev. George Crabbe, whose chief poems were "The Library," "The Village," &c.   (1754—1832).

Sir Walter Scott, novelist, author of many works, "Marmion" and "The Lady of the Lake" being his productions. (1771—1832).

Lord Byron, author of "Childe Harold's Pilgrimage."   He died at Missolonghi in Greece.   (1788—1824).

LITERARY MEN.

Lord Chesterfield, a man of great wit, author of Letters to his Son.   (1694—1773).

Lord Kaimes, a Scotch judge, author of the "Elements of Criticism," &c.   (1696—1782).

Dr. John Jortin, among whose works we find Latin poems entitled "Lusus Poetici," "Miscellaneous Observations upon Authors Ancient and Modern," and his "Life of Erasmus." (1698 —1770).

Soame Jenyns, author of a "Free Inquiry into the Origin of Evil."   (1704—1787).

Dr. Samuel Johnson, whose chief work is his Dictionary of the English Language.   (1709—1784).

Laurence Sterne, author of "The Sentimental Journey." (1713—1768).

Horace Walpole, Earl of Orford, author of "Historic Doubts concerning RICHARD III.," was considered by Sir WALTER SCOTT the best letter-writer in the English language.   (1717—1797).

Joseph Warton, son of THOMAS WARTON, wrote poems, and translated Virgil.   (1722—1800).

Adam Smith, Professor of Logic and Moral Philosophy in the University of Glasgow, and author of a work entitled "The Wealth of Nations."   (1723—1790).

William Gilpin, published an Exposition of the New Testament, and wrote the lives of LATIMER, HUSS, WICKLIFFE, and CRANMER.   (1724—1804).

Oliver Goldsmith, wrote "The Vicar of Wakefield," "The Deserted Village," &c.   (1728—1774).

Thomas Warton, another son of THOMAS WARTON, became Poet-Laureate, and Camden Professor of Modern History at Oxford. (1728—1790).

James Boswell, wrote "Memoirs of Dr. JOHNSON."   (1740 —1795).

John Louis de Lolme, a native of Switzerland, was a political writer, his chief work being a "History of the Constitution of England."   (1740—1806).

Sir William Jones, an accomplished Oriental scholar, is said to have been well versed in twenty-seven languages.   His works were published in six volumes.   (1746—1794).

Dr. Richard Porson, whose most important works were his criticisms on Greek writers, and his edition of a Lexicon of Photius. *(1759—1808).*

Mungo Park, author of a History of his own Travels. (1771—1805).

Alexander Cruden, who compiled "The Concordance." Died in 1774.

Dr. Abraham Rees, who compiled a Cyclopædia. (1743—1825).

William Roscoe, lawyer and banker, and also an eminent biographer and miscellaneous writer, whose best works were, "The life and Pontificate of LEO X.," and "The life of LORENZO DE MEDICI." He was the son of a market-gardener, near Liverpool. (1753—1831).

Dr. Gall, a German, who originated the science of Phrenology. (1758—1828).

William Hazlitt, a critic, author of "Table Talk," "Characters of Shakespeare's Plays," &c. (1778—1830).

PHILOSOPHERS.

Dr. Joseph Priestley, author of various works. (1733—1804).

Dugald Stewart, whose chief works were "Elements of the Philosophy of the Human Mind," "Outlines of Moral Philosophy," and "Philosophical Essays." (1753—1828).

Sir Humphrey Davy, inventor of the safety lamp, became Professor of Chemistry in the Royal Institution of London. He was the author of "Chemical and Philosophical Researches." (1778—1829).

ASTRONOMERS.

James Ferguson, author of "Astronomy explained upon Sir ISAAC NEWTON's principles, and made easy to those who have not studied Mathematics," &c. (1710—1776).

Sir William Herschel, private astronomer to GEORGE III., discovered Uranus and its satellites, &c., &c. (1738—1822).

LAWYERS.

Charles Pratt, (Earl Camden) a noted lawyer and statesman, was born in 1713. In 1762 he was appointed Chief Justice of the Common Pleas, created a Peer in 1765, and in 1766 became Lord Chancellor. It is said that only one of his decisions was reversed. Died 1794.

William Murray, (Lord Mansfield) an illustrious lawyer and upright man, became Chief Justice of the King's Bench, and was so eloquent that his friend POPE styled him the "silver-tongued

Murray." His conduct on the bench during the trials of the publisher of *Junius's* letters, and of Wilkes, rendered him unpopular, and in the riots of 1780 his house in Bloomsbury Square was burnt down by the mob. (1704—1793).

Sir William Blackstone, was one of the Judges of the Common Pleas, a member of Parliament, and author of "Commentaries on the Laws of England." (1723—1780).

MEDICAL MEN.

John Hunter, author of "Observations on the Animal Economy." (1728—1793).

William Buchan, a Scotch physician, author of a work called "Domestic Medicine." (1729—1805).

Dr. Edward Jenner, discovered vaccination. (1749—1823).

John Abernethy, was very eminent in his profession, and the first to teach that local diseases are not independent maladies, but the result of a disordered constitution. (1764—1831).

MUSICIANS.

Dr. Samuel Arnold, composed an oratorio called "The Prodigal Son," &c. (1740—1802).

Mozart, among whose works it will be sufficient to mention his magnificent "Requiem," which he composed on his death-bed. (1756—1792).

Joseph Haydn, a celebrated and extensive composer of music, was the son of a poor wheel-wright, and born at the village of Rohran in Austria. On his second visit to London in 1794, he met with a grand reception, and the degree of doctor of music was conferred on him by the University of Oxford. In 1798, appeared his *chef d'œuvre*, the splended oratorio of "The Creation." His numerous works included "The Seasons," a "Te Deum,' a "Stabat Mater," 116 symphonies, 14 operas, 83 violin quartetts, 60 pianoforte sonatas, 4 oratorios, 15 masses, 42 duets and canzonets, 200 concertes, &c. Died at Vienna in 1809.

Beethoven, an eminent German composer, was born at Bonn in 1770. He was a pupil of Haydn, and produced many symphonies, of which the Battle of Symphony is considered one of the finest. Of his operas, *Fedelio* is the most admired. Died 1827.

Dr. Callcott, author of a "Musical Grammar," and several compositions. (1766—1821).

Carl Maria Von Weber, a German, who composed "Der Freischutz." (1786—1826).

PHILANTHROPIST.

John Howard, noted for his zeal in endeavouring to ameliorate the condition of prisoners, both at home and abroad. He died while engaged in this occupation. (1726—1790).

INVENTORS.

John Harrison, invented the Marine Chronometer. (1693—1776).

Josiah Wedgewood, invented the "Queen's Ware," which is composed of ground flint and Dorsetshire white clay. (1730—1795).

Sir Richard Arkwright, a hairdresser by trade, invented the spinning-frame, on account of which he is considered the founder of our cotton manufacture. (1732—1792).

James Watt, by whose inventions the steam-engine was greatly improved. (1736—1819).

Edmund Cartwright, inventor of the powerloom. (1743—1823).

Samuel Crompton, who invented the spinning-frame called the "Mule." (1753—1827).

Sir William Congreve, inventor of rockets and lucifer matches. (1772—1828).

William Hyde Woollaston, discovered the metals palladium and rhodium, and invented the Camera-lucida. (1776—1828).

ENGINEERS.

James Brindley, was employed by the Duke of BRIDGE-WATER in the construction of the canal from Worsley to Manchester. (1716—1772).

John Smeaton, the successful constructor of the third Eddystone Lighthouse. (1724—1792).

John Rennie, constructed the Aberdeen canal, designed the East and West India docks, London, and built the Waterloo Bridge over the Thames. (1761—1821).

Thomas Telford, a Scotchman, constructed the Menai Bridge, the Caledonian Canal, &c. (1757—1834).

MATHEMATICIAN.

Dr. Charles Hutton, author of a course of Mathematics. (1737—1823).

ARTISTS.

Sir Joshua Reynolds, President of the Royal Academy. (1723—1792).

Thomas Gainsborough, a famous landscape painter. 1727 —1788).

Benjamin West, an American, became President of the Royal Academy, London. His chief paintings were "Cromwell Dismissing the Long Parliament" and "St. Paul on the Island of Melita." (1738—1820).

Thomas Bewick, who gave a stimulus to wood engraving by the illustration of his "History of Quadrupeds." (1753—1828).

Sir Thomas Lawrence, called the **English Titian,** whose best works are considered "John Kemble," "Mrs. Siddons," and "Benjamin West." He also became President of the Royal Academy. (1769—1830).

SCULPTORS.

John Flaxman, whose last statues were a group from Ovid's Metamorphoses, entitled "The Fury of Athamas." (1755—1826).

Sir Francis Chantrey, was born at Norton, near Sheffield, in 1781. His group of the Sleeping Children, which appeared in 1817, was universally admired. Died 1841.

ACTORS.

James Quin, the first actor of his time till GARRICK appeared. FREDERICK, Prince of Wales, engaged QUIN to instruct the royal children in elocution, and on learning that GEORGE III. delivered his first speech from the throne in a graceful manner, QUIN said—"Ay, it was I who taught the boy to speak." (1693—1766).

David Garrick, whose histrionic representations were of the highest order. (1716—1779).

John Philip Kemble, more particularly distinguished as a tragedian. (1757—1823).

Mrs. Siddons, sister of JOHN and CHARLES KEMBLE, became the leading actress of her time. (1755—1831).

**George IV. was the eldest son of George III.   A.D. 1820—
1830.**

A   **WARS.**

I.   War with Burmah.

War arose between the East India Company and the Burmese,
in consequence of the latter encroaching on the frontiers of Bengal,
1824.   After the enemy had been beaten in several engagements, a
Treaty was concluded, (1826) by which the Burmese monarch
agreed :—

1.   To pay the Company a large sum of money for the
expenses of the war.

2.   To cede to Great Britain the provinces of **Aracan,
Assam,** and **Tenasserim.**

II.   War with the Ashantees.

These disturbances began in 1824, and are said to have been
caused by the British interfering in the quarrels of the native
Ashantees, who live on the Coast of Africa.

1.   The British under Sir CHARLES MACCARTHY, governor of
Sierra Leone, were terribly slaughtered by an army under the
Ashantee monarch.   Sir CHARLES was also slain, 1824.

2.   After the Ashantee King had been several times defeated
by the British under Colonel SUNDERLAND, a **Treaty** was concluded between England and the Ashantees, 1826.

III.   War with the Turks.

Battle of Navarino (Greece).—The revolt of Greece against
Turkey led to war between those two countries. England favoured
the former, and Lord BYRON went to render them personal aid,
but he caught a fever and died at Missolonghi.   As the contest had
continued some time, England, France, and Russia requested the
Turks to cease hostilities, but this advice was not heeded.   The
combined fleets, therefore, of these three powers, under Admiral
CODRINGTON, almost destroyed the Turkish and Egyptian fleet
under IBRAHIM PASHA, Oct. 20, 1827. Greece was made an
independent kingdom, and OTHO, of Bavaria, became its sover-
ign.   The Duke of WELLINGTON called the destruction of the
Turkish fleet an **Untoward Event.**

The Cato Street Conspiracy.—This plot was devised by ARTHUR THISTLEWOOD and others, for murdering the King's ministers, but it was detected and the leaders executed, May 1, 1820.

A Bill of Pains and Penalties was introduced by Lord LIVERPOOL, Prime Minister, against CAROLINE, the King's consort, for the purpose of depriving her of such rights as she was entitled to as Queen. She had for some time been separated from her husband, and in 1816 retired to the continent. Learning that her husband had become King, she returned to England in order to assert her rights. She was charged with immoral conduct, and her name was erased from the Liturgy. Owing to the able defence made in her favour by BROUGHAM, WILLIAMS, DENMAN, and LUSHINGTON, the bill was abandoned, 1820. On the day of His Majesty's coronation, the Queen attempted to enter Westminster Abbey in order to see the ceremony, but she was refused admittance. This so distressed her that she died soon after, Aug. 7, 1821. She had given orders that her body might be buried in her own country with this inscription engraved on her tomb—"Here lies Caroline of Brunswick, the injured Queen of England."

The Royal Society of Literature was founded by the King, 1821, and **Mechanics' Institutes** in the same year by Dr. GEORGE BIRKBECK.

The Caledonian Canal, after a labour of 20 years and an expenditure of £900,000, was opened, 1822.

GEORGE IV. visited Ireland, where he met with a hearty welcome. He is said to have been the first English King that paid a peaceful visit to that island, 1821. He also went to Scotland, and was warmly received there, 1822. During the King's stay in Scotland, Lord LONDONDERRY committed suicide, and was succeeded by GEORGE CANNING as Foreign Secretary.

The Spanish colonies in South America revolted, and their independence was recognised by England, 1823.

Mr. HUSKISSON, President of the Board of Trade, introduced **Free Trade,** 1823.

The National Gallery was founded, 1824.

Owing to the numerous foolish speculations in 1825, many banks stopped payment, and bankruptcy became very general.

The weights and measures of the United Kingdom were investigated and equalised by law, 1825.

Lotteries were prohibited, 1826.

The leading events of the year 1827 were :—

1. Death of the Duke of York, by which the Duke of Clarence, afterwards William IV., became heir to the throne.

2. Death of Lord Liverpool.

3. Death of Canning, who became Premier after Lord Liverpool.

4. The suspension bridge over the **Menai Strait** was opened in January.

5. On the death of Canning, Lord Goderich became Premier, but he soon resigned.

The Duke of Wellington became Prime Minister after Goderich in 1828, and in the same year was founded King's College, London.

The Test and Corporation Acts, which prevented Dissenters and Roman Catholics from holding office in the State, were **repealed,** 1828.

The Catholic Emancipation Bill, by which Roman Catholics were placed nearly on a level with Protestants as regards privileges, was introduced by Mr. Peel, and passed in 1829.

The London **Police Force** was founded by Mr. Peel in 1829.

The Treaty of Adrianople, by which the **Independence of Greece** was recognised by Turkey, was concluded, 1829.

A part of **York Minster** was burnt by a man named Martin, who was insane, 1830.

To this reign are to be ascribed the planting of **Regent's Park,** the opening of the **Zoological Gardens,** and the Colosseum.

Omnibuses were introduced from France by a coachman named Shillibeer, 1830.

The King died at Windsor, June 26, 1830, and was buried at the same place.

C   CELEBRATED PERSONS.

William Wordsworth, was born in Cumberland, 1770. Among his poetical effusions may be named "The White Doe of Rylston," "Sonnets on the River Duddon," and a philosophical poem in blank verse, called "The Excursion." Died 1850.

Thomas Moore, author of the "Irish Melodies," "Lalla Rookh," &c. (1779—1852).

Samuel Taylor Coleridge, author of numerous poems, the most popular being "Christabel," and "The Ancient Mariner." (1772—1834).

Thomas Campbell, was born in Glasgow in 1777. Of hi poetical productions we may mention the " Pleasures of Hope and " Ye Mariners of England." Died 1844.

Robert Southey, Poet-Laureate, wrote " Joan of Arc," an other works. (1774—1843).

George Canning, became Governor of India, and afterwar Premier. (1770—1827).

Sir Astley Cooper, an eminent surgeon and anatomist, be came President of the College of Surgeons. (1763—1841).

Edmund Kean, a celebrated tragedian. (1787—1833).

Henry Fox, (Lord Holland) a great advocate for Parliamer tary Reform, aided in the abolition of the Corporation and Te Acts. (1773—1840).

John Shore, (Lord Teignmouth) statesman and author " Considerations on communicating to the inhabitants of India tl knowledge of Christianity." (1751—1834).

Earl Spencer, statesman. (1759—1834).

John Scott, (Earl of Eldon) was born at Newcastle-upo: Tyne in 1751, and received his education at the University Oxford. He was called to the bar in 1776, and joined the Nort ern Circuit, but made little progress till his success at the Clither Election, by which he obtained some celebrity. In 1793 he becar Attorney-General; in 1799 Chief Justice of the Common Ple and in 1801 he succeeded Lord LOUGHBOROUGH as Lord Chancell which office he finally relinquished in 1827, and spent the remai der of his life in retirement. Died 1838.

Charles Abbott, (Lord Tenterden) a celebrated judge, a author of a treatise upon the law relative to " Merchant Ships a Seamen." (1762—1832),

Edward Pellew, (Lord Exmouth) naval commander. (17 —1833).

William Wilberforce, a celebrated philanthropist, was be at Hull in 1759, and is ever to be remembered with gratitude his unwearied exertions during a period of twenty years for 1 abolition of Negro Slavery. In 1807 the Abolition Bill passed 1 House of Lords. After Sir SAMUEL ROMILLY had spoken in fav of the bill, he concluded by " contrasting the feelings of NAPOLE in all his greatness with those of that honoured individual w would this day lay his head upon his pillow, and remember tl the Slave-trade was no more." WILBERFORCE wrote a work titled, " Practical View of the prevailing Religious System of P. fessed Christians in the Higher and Middle Classes of this Coun contrasted with Real Christianity." He expended more than or *fourth* of his income in private charities, and a short time bef is death he said, " Thank God ! that I should have lived to witness day in which England is willing to give twenty millions sterling r the Abolition of slavery." He died in London in 1833, and his mains were honoured with a public funeral, and interred in Westminster Abbey.

Joseph Lancaster, who founded the Lancasterian Schools. 778—1838).

Hannah More, authoress of " Christian Morals," and an essay on the Character and Writings of St. Paul, &c. (1745—. 333).

Jeremy Bentham, noted for endeavouring to improve egislation and Jurisprudence. Of his numerous works, we need nly mention his "Introduction to the Principles of Morals and egislation," and " Panopticon," a work on prison discipline. 747—1832).

Dr. John Gillies, historiographer for Scotland, wrote a istory of Greece, translated the Ethics, and Politics of Aristotle, c. (1747—1836).

William Cobbett, a political writer, and author of an English rammar. (1762—1835).

George Colman, a dramatic writer. (1762—1836).

Sir James Mackintosh, a distinguished lawyer and author a History of England. (1765—1832).

Baron Cuvier, a French naturalist, author of a Theory of the arth. (1769—1832).

Sir John Malcolm, Persian Ambassador, published a History Persia, and a Political History of India. (1769—1833).

James Hogg, a Scotch poet, called the *Ettrick Shepherd,* rote " Madoc the Moor," " The Pilgrim of the Sun," and was a ntributor to " Blackwood's Magazine." (1772—1835).

Charles Lamb, a great wit and essayist. (1775—1834).

Felicia Hemans, whose chief works were " Songs of the ffections," and " Records of Woman." (1794—1835).

Henry Bell, is said to have been the first that made a uccessful application of steam to purposes of navigation. (1767— 830).

William IV., Duke of Clarence, was the third son of George III. A.D. 1830—1837.

A   WARS.

I. The Second French Revolution.—Interference with the freedom of the Press led to another revolution in France, and ended in the abdication of CHARLES X., who fled to England. The Duke of ORLEANS, under the title of LOUIS PHILIPPE I., then became "King of the French," 1830.

II. Revolution in Belgium.—Belgium participated in the revolutionary feelings manifested in France, and separated from Holland, 1830. In securing her independence, Belgium was aided by England, and in 1831, LEOPOLD of Saxe Coburg, widower of Princess CHARLOTTE of England, was elected King of the Belgians.

III. Revolution in Poland.—A revolution broke out at Warsaw, Nov. 29, 1830, when the Poles tried to free themselves from the bondage of Russia; but they were finally subdued by the large armies of the Emperor NICHOLAS in 1831. Many of the Poles fled to England, where they met with kind treatment.

IV. Portugal was the scene of **Civil War** between DONNA MARIA (daughter of DON PEDRO) and her uncle, DON MIGUEL, who had usurped the throne. DONNA MARIA'S fleet was commanded by Admiral NAPIER, who vanquished that of DON MIGUEL, July, 1833. The contest ended in DONNA MARIA becoming Queen, and in the expulsion of MIGUEL from Portugal.

V. A contest for the crown of **Spain** arose between ISABELLA (daughter of FERDINAND VII.) and DON CARLOS. As Englishmen were allowed by government to engage in the dispute, a force called the **British Legion** was despatched under Colonel DE LACY EVANS, who fought for ISABELLA. The British were chiefly instrumental in gaining the battles of **Bilboa** (1836), and of **Irun** (1837). DON CARLOS was ultimately defeated.

B   CHIEF EVENTS.

Earl GREY succeeded the Duke of WELLINGTON as Prime Minister, and formed an Administration, in which Lord ALTHORPE became Chancellor of the Exchequer; Mr. BROUGHAM, Lord Chancellor; Lord PALMERSTON, Foreign Secretary; Lord LANDS-DOWNE, President of the Council; Lord GODERICH, Colonial ecretary; Lord MELBOURNE, Home Secretary; while Lord JOHN RUSSELL was Paymaster of the Forces, and Lord STANLEY (the present Earl of DERBY), Secretary for Ireland, (1830).

The Railway between Liverpool and Manchester was opened, Sept. 15, 1830, on which occasion Mr. HUSKISSON was accidentally killed by one of the trains.

Lords-Lieutenant of counties in Ireland were appointed, 1831.

The first meeting of the **British Association for the Advancement of Science** was held in York, 1831.

The **New London Bridge** was opened by the King, Aug. 1, 1831.

That formidable disease, called the **Asiatic Cholera**, which appeared in 1817 on the banks of the Ganges, visited England for the first time, breaking out at Sunderland, Oct. 1831. After ravaging the country for 12 months, and destroying 60,000 persons, disappeared towards the end of the year 1832.

The Reform Bill.—The events in France considerably influenced the English mind, and caused it to be extremely urgent for reforms in Parliament. A bill, therefore, for that purpose was introduced by Lord JOHN RUSSELL, March 1, 1831, but it was rejected. This caused much discontent among the people, and serious riots followed in Derby, Bristol, and Nottingham, the castle of the last mentioned town being burnt as a retaliation on the Duke of NEWCASTLE for his aversion to Reform. The bill, notwithstanding the most determined opposition on the part of the Tories, who were now called **Conservatives**, passed, and received the Royal Assent, June 7, 1832.

The leading changes effected by the Reform Bill were:—

1. Some insignificant boroughs (56 in number) were **disfranchised.**

2. Some important towns which had not been represented Parliament, now obtained the right of sending members there.

3. An extension of the **Franchise**, by which the political power of the middle classes was much increased. Those who owned houses from which they realised ten pounds per annum, or who paid a rental to that amount, were entitled to vote for town members. All who owned land worth ten pounds a year, or who paid a rent not under £50, had a right to vote for *county* members.

The Scotch and Irish Reform Bills, similar to the above, also received the Royal Assent in 1832.

The **Reformed Parliament** was opened by the King in person, Feb. 5, 1833, and during its first session the following measures were passed:—

The Irish Coercion Bill.—It was found necessary to pass this Bill in order to suppress the numerous outrages committed in Ireland. O'Connell, who wanted a repeal of the Legislative Union, and the abolition of the Protestant Church, kept the people of that country in a state of incessant agitation, which resulted in many deeds of violence.

The Irish Church Bill.—This Bill was passed for the purpose of regulating the revenues of the Irish Church, and for abolishing ten bishoprics.

The Charter of the Bank of England was renewed, the government of British territories in Hindostan vested as before in the East India Company, but the trade to India and China was no longer monopolised by that Company, but thrown open to any who liked to engage in it.

Annual Parliamentary Grants, for the furtherance of education, began in this session, when £20,000 were voted and given for that purpose.

The Emancipation Bill, for abolishing Slavery in the **West Indies,** was passed, and in 1834 the law came into operation, when some thousands of Colonial slaves were emancipated, and their owners received £20,000,000 by way of compensation. The celebrated Mr. Wilberforce was the first in 1787 to move for the Emancipation of Slaves, and he pursued that humane course till his wishes were accomplished.

The Factory Bill was also passed, by which children working in factories had their hours of labour shortened, and provision made for their education.

The University of Durham was founded, and Quakers were admitted into Parliament, Mr. Pease, member for South Durham being the first, 1833.

The events of the year 1834 were:—

1. Through disputes about the Irish Coercion Bill, Earl Grey resigned, and was succeeded by Lord Melbourne as Prime Minister, with whom was Lord Palmerston and Lord John Russell.

2. Continued crime in Ireland, arising in a great measure from O'Connell's inciting the people of that country to demand a Repeal of the Union, made it necessary to renew the Irish Coercion Bill, which now became more stringent.

3. The New Poor Law Act was passed, authorising local *boards* to be placed under government inspection, and prohibiting

ut-door relief to able-bodied paupers, except they would enter
ie workhouses and earn it there. This Bill was calculated to
rike at the root of idleness, to diminish pauperism, lessen the
>or-rates and elevate the lower classes. At this time £7,000,000
ere spent annually for the support of the poor.

4. Both Houses of Parliament were destroyed by fire.

5. On the resignation of the ministry, Sir Robert Peel was
lled to the head of the Government in December, but in a few
onths Lord Melbourne again became Premier.

The English began to **colonise South Australia** in 1834.

The **Overland Route to India** was adopted in 1834.

The Municipal Act, for reforming the town councils, passed
1835, when boroughs obtained the right to appoint their own
>uncillors and magistrates.

Fieschi attempted to assassinate the King of the French,
835.

The Statutes enacted in the year 1836 were:—

1. **The Tithe Commutation Act**, which authorised clergy-
en to receive money instead of tithes from the landlord.

2. **The New Marriage Act**, giving dissenters permission to
s married in their own chapels, and by their own ministers.

An act was also passed for establishing a general system for
ie **Registration of Births, Marriages, and Deaths**; another
>r reducing stamped duty on newspapers; while a third was enacted
ranting to criminals the assistance of counsel in cases of felony.
he law for executing murderers on the third day after conviction
as repealed.

Louis Napoleon attempted to raise an **Insurrection** at
trasburg, 1836.

That debilitating disease called **Influenza** appeared in 1836.

The two new **Bishoprics** of **Ripon** and **Manchester** were
reated, 1836.

England was visited by a terrible storm, which did much
amage, 1836.

The King died at Windsor, June 20, 1837. Provision was
lade for Adelaide, the Queen-dowager, by a grant of £100,000
er annum, and also the residence of Marlborough House and
lushey Park.

C   **CELEBRATED PERSONS.**

William Lamb, (Lord Melbourne) became, on the resignation of Earl GREY in 1834, Prime Minister.   (1778—1848).

Dr. Thomas Chalmers, a most eloquent and powerful Scotch preacher, founded the **Free Church** of Scotland.   Among his writings, he produced a treatise "On the Adaptation of External Nature to the Moral and Intellectual Constitution of Man." (1780—1847).

Dr. Thomas Arnold, head master of Rugby School, wrote a History of Rome, translated "Thucydides," and published several volumes of Sermons.   (1795—1842).

Daniel O'Connell, called *the great agitator*, whose main object was the repeal of the union of England and Ireland. (1775—1847).

Sir John Franklin, who perished while engaged in a voyage to discover the North West Passage.   Many expeditions were fitted and sent out in search of FRANKLIN, the last being undertaken by Captain McCLINTOCK, who ascertained that the gallant commander and the greater part of his crew were lost.   (1786—1847).

Sharon Turner, author of a valuable History of the Anglo-Saxons from the earliest period to the reign of Queen ELIZABETH. (1768—1847).

Thomas Clarkson, united with WILBERFORCE in strongly advocating the abolition of slavery.   (1760—1846).

Elizabeth Fry, one of the Society of Friends, devoted much time to the improvement of prisons and the reformation of convicts. (1780—1845).

Rev. John Foster, author of "Essays on Decision of Character," "On the Evils of Popular Ignorance," &c.   (1770—1843.)

Sir Charles Bell, one of the most celebrated anatomists of modern times, discovered the arrangement and operation of the Nervous System.   (1774—1842).

Sir Francis Chantrey, a famous monumental sculptor.   The statue of PITT, in Hanover Square, London, is one of his works. (1782—1841).

Benjamin Robert Haydon, painted "The Judgment of Solomon," "Christ's Entry into Jerusalem," &c.   (1786—1846).

Sir David Brewster, author of a "Treatise on Optics," and of "Letters on Natural Magic."   Died 1840.

Sir Alexander Barnes, author of "Travels into Bokhara *and Cabool.*"   Died 1841.

Allan Cunningham, a celebrated poet, author of "Paul Jones," and the Lives of "Burns" and "Sir David Wilkie." (1785—1842).

Thomas Dibdin, a famous dramatic song writer, to whose pen we are indebted for "The English Fleet," and "The High Mettled Racer." Died 1841.

George Dyer, a miscellaneous writer, whose greatest labour was in contributing to the production of VALPY's Edition of the Classics, in 141 volumes. He also wrote a "History of the University of Cambridge." Died 1841.

Rowland Hill, (Viscount) distinguished himself as a general, and in 1828 became Commander-in-Chief. Died 1842.

Queen Victoria, daughter of Edward, Duke of Kent (fourth son of George III.) and niece of the late King, began to reign, A.D. 1837.

A   **WARS.**

I. The Canadian Rebellion.

Headed by PAPINEAU and MACKENZIE, broke out Dec. 1837, but was suppressed by Sir JOHN COLBORNE, Nov. 1838. In order to maintain peace for the future, the union of the two Canadas was effected by law, and the seat of government transferred from Quebec to Montreal, Feb. 10, 1841.

II. War in Syria.

As MEHEMET ALI, vassal of the SULTAN OF TURKEY, and PASHA OF EGYPT, had rebelled against his master, and had over-run Syria, a **Quadruple Treaty** between England, Austria, Prussia, and Russia, for aiding the Sultan, was formed. The English fleet under Sir CHARLES NAPIER and Sir ROBERT STOPFORD, with the assistance of Austria, bombarded **Sidon, Beyrout,** and **Acre,** and the forces of MEHEMET ALI, under his son IBRAHIM PASHA, were compelled to evacuate Syria. MEHEMET ALI, however, obtained for himself Egypt, and a promise that the title of Pasha should be hereditary in his family, 1840.

III. War with China.

British merchants having imported into **China** large quantities of opium, which had been prohibited by the Emperor, the **Chinese** authorities seized the smuggled article, and destroyed it, and at the same time committed Captain ELLIOTT and other British subjects to prison.   For these proceedings war was declared against China, 1840.   After the capture of several towns by the British under Generals GOUGH and POTTINGER, hostilities ended with the **Peace of Nankin** in 1842, by which the Chinese agreed :—

1. To cede to the English the **Island of Hong Kong.**

2. To pay above four millions for the expenses of the war.

3. To open to British merchants the ports of **Canton**, Amoy, **Ningpo, Foo-choo**, and **Shanghae.**

4. To release all British prisoners.

IV. The Affghan War.

As the throne of AFFGHANISTAN had been usurped by DOST MOHAMMED, who was inimical to the British, the latter, under Sir JOHN KEANE, aided SHAH SUJAH in deposing the usurper and securing the throne, 1839.   The Affghans, however, did not like their new monarch, and, therefore, in 1841 they broke out in open rebellion.   The British, to the number of 20,000, commenced their retreat from Cabul, and on their march through the mountain-passes, were attacked by the Affghans under AKHBAR KHAN, (the son of DOST MOHAMMED) and some thousands of them slaughtered; the remainder either perished through cold and hunger or were made prisoners.   The only one that escaped was Dr. BRYDON, 1842. Generals POLLOCK and NOTT afterwards entered Cabul, chastised the Affghans for their treachery, and released the ladies and children who had been made captives.   Having restored the honour of the British flag, our troops were ordered by Lord ELLENBOROUGH, the Governor-General, to evacuate Affghanistan, Oct. 12, 1842.

V. War with the Ameers, or Chiefs of Scinde.

1.   **Battle of Meanee**, in which 30,000 of the Ameers' forces were signally defeated by 2,500 British under Sir CHARLES NAPIER, who was styled "The bearded vision that swept o'er Scinde," Feb. 17, 1843.

Battle of Dubba, (near Hyderabad) in which the Ameers were again worsted, March 24, 1843.   Shortly after these victories, *Scinde* was joined to the British Indian possessions.

VI. War in Gwalior, a Mahratta State.

1. **Battle of Maharajpoor,** in which the English unde Gough were victorious, Dec. 29, 1843.

2. **Battle of Punniar,** in which the British, headed by Grey, vanquished their opponents, Dec. 22, 1843. **Peace** followed these victories; and in 1844 Sir Henry Hardinge was appointed Governor-General in place of Lord Ellenborough.

VII. War with the Sikhs.

1. **Battle of Moodkee,** in which the Sikhs were repulsed by Sir Hugh Gough and Sir Henry Hardinge, Dec. 18, 1845. The losses of the Sikhs were considerable; Sir Robert Sale received a mortal wound here.

2. **Battle of Feroze-shah.**—In this battle, which lasted two days, the Sikhs were defeated with heavy loss by the British under Gough and Hardinge, Dec. 21-22, 1845.

3. **Battle of Aliwal,** in which the Sikh army, 24,000 strong, (and armed with 68 pieces of cannon) under Sirdar Runjoor Singh Majerthea, were completely vanquished by the British under Sir Henry Smith, who had 12,000 men and 32 guns. The Sikhs lost 6000, some of whom were drowned in attempting to re-cross the river Sutlej, Jan. 28, 1846.

4. **Battle of Sobraon.**—In this engagement, which closed the campaign, the British under Sir Hugh Gough routed the Sikhs, who lost 10,000 men, Feb. 10, 1846.

VIII. Renewal of War with the Sikhs.

1. **Battle of Kineyree,** in which the Sikhs were overcome by Lieutenant Edwards, June 18, 1848.

2. **Battle of Ramnuggar.**—This was an indecisive engagement between the Sikhs and the British under Lord Gough, Nov. 22, 1848.

3. **Battle of Chillianwallah.**—This was a most sanguinary battle between the Sikhs and the English under Lord Gough. The former were routed, but the loss of the English was very severe, Jan. 13, 1849.

4. **Battle of Goojerat,** in which a decisive victory was gained over 60,000 Sikhs by 25,000 British under Lord Gough, Feb. 21, 1849.

The Punjaub, or territory of the Sikhs, was annexed to the British empire by Lord Dalhousie, (the Governor-General) March 29, 1849.

IX.   The Second War with the Burmese.

This war was of short duration, and ended in the annexation of **Pegu** and **Rangoon** to the **British dominions**, Dec. 20, 1852.

X.   War with the Kaffirs.

Battle of Berea, in which 2000 British troops, under the late Governor-General CATHCART, routed 6000 Kaffirs, Dec. 28, 1852; and in March 9, 1853, **Peace** was concluded between the two countries.

XI.   The Crimean War.

This war arose from an attempt on the part of NICHOLAS, the Emperor of Russia, to annex Turkey to his dominions. His encroachments were resisted by England and France, who resolved on aiding Turkey; and therefore declared war against Russia, 1854.

Sardinia joins the Allies, Jan. 26, 1855.

1. Odessa was bombarded and most of its batteries destroyed by the English, April 21, 1854.

2. Silistria was besieged by the Russians under Prince GORTSCHAKOFF and General SCHILDERS, but they were repulsed with great loss by the Turks under the command of BUTLER and NASMYTH, two British officers, who compelled them to raise the siege, June, 1854.

3. Battle of the Alma, in which 46,000 Russians under Prince MENSCHAKOFF were routed by the allies (consisting of 48,000 men) commanded by Lord RAGLAN and Marshal St. ARNAUD, Sept. 20, 1854.

4. Battle of Balaclava, in which 30,000 Russians under General LIPRANDI were defeated by the allies. It was in this battle that through some misunderstanding **The English Light Cavalry** under Lord CARDIGAN made an extraordinary charge upon the Russians, celebrated in history as "The charge of the Light Brigade," Oct. 25, 1854.

5. Battle of Inkermann.—In this remarkable battle, 8,000 British soldiers are said to have held their ground for several hours against an attack of 60,000 Russians. The English were afterwards joined by 6000 French, led by General BOSQUET, when the Russians were routed with a loss which exceeded in number the whole allied army, Nov. 5, 1854.

6. Battle of the Tchernaya, in which 50,000 Russians, under Prince GORTSCHAKOFF, were repulsed with heavy loss by the allies.

In this battle MONTEVECCHIO, the Sardinian General, and READ, the Russian Commander, were both slain, Aug. 16, 1855.

7. **Bomarsund,** a Russian fortress in the Baltic, was destroyed by Admiral NAPIER, Aug. 1854; but great dissatisfaction manifested itself in England, where it was thought **Cronstadt** ought to have shared the same fate.

8. **Kerch** and **Yenikale,** in the Sea of Azoff, were captured by Sir EDWARD LYONS, May, 1855.

9. **Kars,** in Asiatic Turkey, was bravely defended by the Turks, under our countryman, General WILLIAMS, who was pensioned on £1000 a year for his "eminent and distinguished services." He was at last obliged to capitulate, but on being dismissed by the Conqueror MOURAVIEFF, the latter complimented WILLIAMS for his extraordinary bravery, Nov. 1855.

10. The memorable **Siege of Sebastopol** began October, 17, 1854, and lasted till September 8, 1855, when the Southern part of the town was evacuated by the Russians, and entered by the Allies. The losses of the English, French, and Russians, during this period, are said to have been nearly 100,000 men.

11. **Sweaborg** was bombarded by the English fleet under Admiral DUNDAS (who had succeeded NAPIER) and heavy losses were inflicted on the Russians, 1855.

The Treaty of Paris.—The fall of Sebastopol and other successes of the Allies induced Russia to sue for peace, which England would scarcely have granted on such terms as she did, had not France exhibited a strong desire to discontinue the war.

The conditions of this Treaty were :—

1. That the fortifications of Sebastopol should be demolished.

2. That both Turkish and Russian ships of war should be discontinued in the Black Sea.

3. That the **Danubian Principalities** should cease to be under the power of Russia.

That the Christians of Turkey, without any preference to Russia, should have the protection of all the Powers concerned in the Treaty, March 30, 1856.

The cost of this war to the British was £32,793,303.

XII. The Persian War.

Instigated by the Russians, the Shah of Persia violated his treaty with Great Britain by besieging **Herat**; and war was in consequence declared in November, 1856.

1. **Bushire** was bombarded, and surrendered to the English under Admiral **Leeke**, December 10, 1856.

Battle of Mohammerah, in which the Persians were defeated by the British, March 26, 1857.

Peace, however, had been concluded between the two countries at **Paris**, March 3, 1857.

XIII. War with China.

These hostilities were caused by the Chinese insulting the British flag, (in 1856) when an apology was demanded by the English Ambassador, but was refused by the Commissioner **Yeh**, in consequence of which war followed; but after the capture of **Canton**, the combined fleets of England and France, with Lord **Elgin** (Her Majesty's Ambassador) reached **Tien-Tsin**, where a treaty of peace was concluded, June 26, 1858, the terms of which were:—

1. Additional ports were to be opened for commerce.

2. The toleration of Christianity throughout the empire.

3. That there should be a Chinese minister in London, and a British one at Pekin.

XIV. The Indian Mutiny.

This was a formidable rebellion of the **Sepoys**, or native soldiers, for overthrowing the British power in India. The causes which led to it are said to have been the following:—

1. A report that the religion of the natives was about to be abolished by the English.

2. A Hindoo prophecy that the dominion of the East India Company after an existence of 100 years, which were now expiring, should be destroyed.

3. The introduction of greased cartridges for the Enfield rifles. To rouse the people, it was rumoured that the grease consisted of cow and swine fat, which greatly shocked the religious notions both of the Hindoo and Mohammedan.

This mutiny broke out at **Meerut**, May 11, 1857, and was suppressed, 1858. The Queen's forces were efficiently aided by the Sikhs, and the Ghoorkas (who inhabited Nepaul). In many places, among which are **Delhi, Meerut, Bareilly, Lucknow,** and **Cawnpore,** the British were massacred with the utmost barbarity. Through the treachery of that monster, **Nana Sahib,** the *women* and children were butchered at Cawnpore. For checking this rebellion we are indebted to our brave soldiers under the valiant HAVELOCK, Sir JOHN LAWRENCE, (the Saviour of India,) Generals OUTRAM, WILSON, BARNARD, REED, NEILL, and NICHOLSON; and for its final suppression, to Sir COLIN CAMPBELL, (afterwards Lord CLYDE) who was sent out as the Commander-in-Chief. After the termination of the rebellion, the following changes were effected :—

1. The government of India was now taken from the East India Company, and vested in the Queen of England.

2. A Secretary of State was appointed for India.

3. The appointment of a council of 15 persons, by whom the affairs of that country are virtually managed.

XV. War renewed with China.

This war was undertaken for the purpose of compelling the Chinese to observe the Treaty of Tien-Tsin, which they had violated by refusing to admit Mr. BRUCE, the English Ambassador, at Pekin.   The united forces of England and France having captured the **Taku Forts**, took possession of **Tien-Tsin**, and thence proceeded to **Pekin**, where the treaty of Tien-Tsin was ratified, and the **Convention of Pekin** signed, (October 24, 1860) by which it was stipulated :—

1. That **Cowloon** should be ceded to the British.

2. That the Emperor should pay nearly three millions, instead of the indemnity formerly agreed upon.

3. That a British minister should reside at Pekin.

4. That British subjects should be allowed to trade at the port of Tien-Tsin.

B   **CHIEF EVENTS.**

On the accession of Queen VICTORIA, who came to the throne in her eighteenth year, **Hanover**, by virtue of the **Salic Law**, was separated from England, and ERNEST (fifth son of GEORGE III.) being the next male heir, was proclaimed its King, 1837.

The Queen was crowned in Westminster Abbey, June 28, 1838.

In 1838, a numerous body of people called **Chartists**, arose, and caused great disturbances in various parts of the country, because they failed to obtain Government sanction to the following six points, which they embodied in a petition, designated The **People's Charter**:—

1. Universal suffrage.

2. Annual Parliaments.

3. Vote by ballot.

4. Abolition of the property-qualification for holding a seat in the House of Commons.

5. Division of the country into Electoral Districts.

6. Payment of Members of Parliament.

There were **Riots** in several towns, and one at Newport (Monmouthshire) ended with the loss of 20 lives, and the transportation of the principal leaders, FROST, JONES, and WILLIAMS, 1839.

The English took possession of **Aden**, in Arabia, 1840.

Her Majesty was married to her cousin, Prince ALBERT of Saxe Coburg Gotha, Feb. 10, 1840.

The **Uniform Penny Post** came into operation, Dec. 10, 1840.

The **Thames Tunnel** was completed, and a great portion of the Tower of London destroyed by fire, 1841.

A disruption occurred among the Scotch Presbyterians, which resulted in the establishment of the **Free Church**, 1843.

Rebekah Riots.—These disturbances occurred in Wales for the purpose of destroying the toll-gates. The rioters were clad in women's bed-gowns and night-caps, and called themselves "Rebekah's Daughters," from the passage in Genesis (xxiv. 60) where we find a prayer to the effect that the seed of REBEKAH might possess the gates of their foes, 1843.

In consequence of using seditious language at the **Repeal Meetings** in Ireland, DANIEL O'CONNELL was arrested in 1843, and in 1844 sentenced to pay £2000, and to undergo 12 months' imprisonment. The House of Lords soon after reversed the sentence.

The **New Royal Exchange** was opened by the Queen in 1844.

The Association called the **Anti-Corn Law League**, which had been formed by Mr. RICHARD COBDEN in 1834, for repealing the Corn Laws, succeeded in carrying their measure by the powerfull advocacy of Sir R. Peel, in 1846.

A blight in the potato crop of 1845 caused a terrible **Famine and Pestilence** in Ireland (1846-7). Though that starving country received considerable aid from England and America, yet disease and emigration reduced the population by two millions.

In England there was a great **Commercial Panic,** 1847, a year noted for the discovery of the gold region in California.

Through another **Revolution in France,** LOUIS PHILIPPE abdicated the throne, which was immediately followed by a proclamation in favour of a republic, of which LOUIS NAPOLEON was elected **President,** 1848. " By the *coup-d'état* of December 2, 1852, he dissolved the existing constitution, and made himself the supreme ruler of France under the name of **Consul,** which he changed into the title of **Emperor,** in 1853." LOUIS PHILIPPE fled to England, and died in 1850.

SMITH O'BRIEN did his utmost to raise an **Insurrection in** Ireland, but his attempts ended in the transportation of the leaders, who were afterwards pardoned. O'BRIEN himself was taken at Thurles, 1848.

The **Bishopric of Manchester** (created in 1836) was erected into a see in 1847, and its first bishop (the Rev. Dr. Lee) consecrated, 1848.

The events of the year 1849 were :—

1. England was ravaged by **Cholera,** which carried off vast numbers in London and other places.

2. Repeal of the Navigation Laws.

3. Visit of Her Majesty to Ireland, where her reception was of the most gratifying character.

4. Death of ADELAIDE, the Queen Dowager.

The Ecclesiastical Titles Bill.—An attempt by the Pope to establish a Roman Catholic hierarchy in England, by creating Dr. WISEMAN Archbishop of Westminster, was vehemently opposed, and led to the passing of the above bill, by which the assumption of Ecclesiastical titles over places in the United Kingdom is punishable by law, 1850.

Sir ROBERT PEEL (who had fallen from his horse) died in 1850, and in the same year the **Submarine Telegraph** between **Dover** and **Calais** was laid.

The year 1851 is memorable for the opening in Hyde Park of the **Great Exhibition of the Industry of all Nations.** It was open nearly six months, during which time the number of visitors is said to have been about 7,000,000. The Exhibition was suggested by Prince ALBERT, and the building designed by Sir JOSEPH PAXTON. This noble example was followed by Dublin in 1853, and by Paris in 1855. In this year gold was discovered in Australia by Mr. HARGREAVES, but a proclamation claiming the gold field for the Crown was issued by the Governor.

The year 1852 is noted for the death of the Duke of WELLINGTON; and the first telegraphic communication between England and Ireland.

The Crystal Palace at Sydenham was opened by the Queen, 1854.

NICHOLAS, Emperor of Russia, whose ambition led to the Crimean War, died very suddenly, March 2, 1855.

The Queen visited France, Aug. 18, 1855.

Oude, in the East Indies, was annexed to the British Empire 1856.

England was materially affected by numerous failures in America, where speculations had been carried on to a great extent, 1857.

LOUIS NAPOLEON visited England in 1857.

A Bill for admitting Jews into Parliament was passed, and Baron ROTHSCHILD became M.P. for London, 1858.

An important Commercial Treaty between Great Britain and Japan was effected at Jeddo by Lord EGLIN, our Chinese Ambassador, 1858.

The French and English Consuls were massacred at Jiddah, (Arabia) which was afterwards bombarded by the English, 1858.

Marriage of the Princess Royal with Prince FREDERICK WILLIAM of Prussia, 1858.

Orsini and others attempted to assassinate the Emperor of the French, Jan. 14, 1858.

The East India Company was abolished, 1858.

The Leviathan or Great Eastern Steamship, was launched on the Thames, 1858.

Sardinia and France commenced war against Austria, and after the latter had been defeated at the Battles of Montebello, Magenta, Malegnano, and Solferino, hostilities were brought to a close with the Treaty of Villafranca, by which Lombardy was ceded to Sardinia; Savoy and Nice to France; while Austria retained her rule of Venetia, 1859.

The warlike proceedings of NAPOLEON caused some uneasiness in England, and led to the Volunteer Movement in 1859; and in 1860 the number of Volunteers in the United Kingdom amounted to more than 120,000.

GARIBALDI expelled from the Two Sicilies the Spanish Bourbon dynasty in 1860, and VICTOR EMMANUEL was elected King of Italy in 1861.

A **Commercial Treaty** between England and France (for reducing the duties on articles exported from one country to the other) was effected chiefly by Mr. COBDEN, Jan. 23, 1860.

The Duchess of Kent, mother of the Queen, died 1861. Her Majesty suffered another sad bereavement in the death of the Prince CONSORT, by which the whole nation was involved in the utmost grief, Dec. 14, 1861.

The Secession of the Southern States of America took place in 1861, and was followed by a sanguinary war; which continued with varying success till April, 1865, when the **Confederates** were overpowered by the **Federals,** and obliged to surrender. While the Northerners were rejoicing at the successful issue of the war, they sustained a terrible shock by the **assassination of President Lincoln** on Good Friday, April 14, 1865.

The seizure of Messrs. SLIDELL and MASON, two Confederate Commissioners, from a British mail-packet, by Captain WILKES, commander of an American war-steamer, caused great indignation throughout England. Our Government on this occasion adopted the most decisive measures, by demanding the release of the commissioners, who were at once given up, 1861.

The abolition of the Paper Duty was effected in 1861.

The Second International Exhibition was opened May 1, 1862, a year also memorable for great distress in the cotton districts, which did not receive their usual supply of that material on account of the **American Civil War.** The sufferings of the operatives were, however, greatly alleviated by the practical sympathy of all classes.

The Educational Code, which had been issued in 1861, underwent some alterations in 1862.

The **Princess Alice was married** to Prince LOUIS of Hesse-Darmstadt, 1862.

The marriage of the Prince of Wales with Princess Alexandra of Denmark, took place, March 10, 1863.

Lords LYNDHURST and ELGIN died, the latter of whom was succeeded by Sir JOHN LAWRENCE as Governor-General of India, 1863.

England ceded the Ionian Islands to Greece, 1863.

In the beginning of the year 1864, war broke out between Denmark and Prussia, the latter being aided by Austria, in reference to Schleswig and Holstein, which resulted in the **Annexation** of those duchies to Prussia by the Gastein Convention of 1865.

The **Dublin Exhibition** was opened by the Prince of WALES in May, 1865.

A terrible plague, called the **Rinderpest**, broke out among the cattle, and destroyed many thousands, thus inflicting upon farmers and others most serious losses, 1865.

A **Fenian Conspiracy** was discovered in Ireland, its object being the formation of a republic in that country, 1865.

After great perseverance and several failures the **Atlantic Cable** was laid between Ireland and America, 1866.

Princess HELENA, daughter of her Majesty, married to Prince CHRISTIAN, 1866.

Prussia and Italy declared war against Austria, June 18, 1866, and after some engagements in favour of the allies, peace was in a short time concluded between the belligerents.

Great Commercial Depression commenced in 1866, which was followed by the stoppage of several Metropolitan and Provincial Banks.

Schleswig and **Holstein** were formally incorporated with Prussia in 1867.

The **New Reform Bill**, which extended the Franchise to small householders and lodgers, was passed in 1867.

The **Abyssinian Expedition** was undertaken for the liberation of certain English and German Prisoners, and ended in the death of King Theodore and with the Capture of Magdala by Sir ROBERT NAPIER, who was afterwards created **Lord Napier of Magdala,** 1868.

The **General Election** took place in 1868, which resulted in a great majority of liberal members, and in the Right Hon. W. E. GLADSTONE becoming **Premier.**

A **Bill for Disestablishing and Disendowing the Irish Church** was introduced into the House of Commons by Mr. GLADSTONE, which, after protracted debates and some modification was accepted by the House of Lords, and received the Royal assent, 1869.

During this reign the new **Divorce Court** has been opened; **Wellington College** in honour of the *Iron Duke* founded; the *Armoury* of the London Tower, **Covent Garden Theatre,** and *Cotton's* **Wharf,** near London Bridge, have been burnt; **Drinking Fountains** erected; the **Palace of Westminster** opened;

Gutta Percha brought from Malay by Dr. WILLIAM MONT-GOMERIE; the Museum of Science and Art in South Kensington established; the **Electric Telegraph, Submarine Telegraph,** and **Photography** have been invented; ARMSTRONG and WHITWORTH have improved **cannon**; in cases of arson, burglary, forgery, and highway robbery, **Transportation** has been substituted for the punishment of **Death**; a **Book-post** established, by which 4 ounces of matter can be sent for one penny; **Bronze pence,** halfpence, and farthings have been coined.

During the reign of VICTORIA, the Prime Ministers have been :—

1. **Lord Melbourne,** a Whig, who continued in office till 1841.

2. **Sir Robert Peel,** a Conservative (1841—1846).

3. **Lord John Russell,** a Whig, (1846—1852).

4. **Lord Derby,** a Conservative, 1852.

5. **Lord Aberdeen,** at the head of a Coalition Ministry (1852—1855).

6. **Lord Palmerston** (1855—1858).

7. **Lord Derby** (1858—1859).

8. **Lord Palmerston** (1859—1865).

9. **Earl Russell** (1865—1866).

10. **Lord Derby** (1866—1868).

11. **The Right Honourable Benjamin Disraeli,** 1868.

12. **The Right Honourable William Ewart Gladstone** 1868.

C   **CELEBRATED PERSONS.**

DIVINES.

Thomas Hartwell Horne, a celebrated Biblical writer, whose "Introduction to the Study of the Scriptures" was held in such high estimation by the Bishop of London, that he ordained him without his having taken a degree at any University. (1780—1862).

John Bird Sumner, became Bishop of Chester in 1828, and in 1848 Archbishop of Canterbury, was distinguished for his learning. (1780—1862).

Dr. John Kitto, editor of "Knight's Pictorial Bible." (1803—1854).

John Oxlee, born at Guisborough in the North Riding of Yorkshire, Sept. 25, 1779, was an eminent divine of the Church of England, a deep and original thinker, a man of high literary attainments, and justly allowed by many competent judges to have been one of the most accomplished and profound Hebrew scholars ever produced in this or any other country. If great abilities, piety, and sound scholarship were the leading qualifications for preferment, Mr. OXLEE must in his generation have ranked amongst the first of mitred heads, and it is a matter of deep regret, and a reproach to the Church, that such sterling worth and rare merit as Mr. OXLEE undoubtedly possessed, should have been so little recognised and appreciated. Among the many learned works of this great scholar and divine may be named a masterly production in three volumes, " On the Christian Doctrines of the Trinity, the Incarnation, and Atonement, considered and maintained on the Principles of Judaism." " Three Sermons on the Power, Origin and Succession of the Christian Hierarchy ;" and " Six Letters to the Late Archbishop of Canterbury," concerning the way and manner generally adopted for the conversion of the Jews to the Christian faith.   Mr. OXLEE died at Molesworth, Huntingdonshire, of which place he was rector, Jan. 30, 1854.

Dr. Raffles, an eminent nonconformist divine and author, was for many years minister of Great George Street Chapel, Liverpool.   Dr. RAFFLES was born in Spitalfields, London, May 17, 1788, and died much lamented at Liverpool, Aug. 18, 1863.

Dr. Whately, Archbishop of Dublin, author of " The Elements of Logic," " The Elements of Rhetoric," " Introductory Lectures on St. Paul's Epistles," &c., (1787—1863).

Nicholas Wiseman, a learned priest and Cardinal of the Church of Rome, author of sermons, " Lectures on the Connection between Science and Revealed Religion," &c. His nomination by the Pope (1850) to be Archbishop of Westminster, led to the enactment of a law which forbids the assumption by Romanists of ecclesiastical titles.   He was born at Seville in 1802, and died in London, 1865.

Rev. Canon Howell, M.A., 1865.

STATESMEN.

George Hamilton Gordon (Earl of Aberdeen) who secured the alliance of Austria against France in 1813, and in 1852 became Premier after Lord DERBY.   He wrote an Inquiry into the Principles of the Beauty of Grecian Architecture. (1784—1860).

Sir Robert Peel, who effected the abolition of the Corn Laws. (1788—1850).

Richard Cobden, the distinguished advocate of **Free Trade,** took an active part in the abolition of the Corn Laws, and effected a very important and beneficial treaty between England and France. (1804—1865).

Sir George Cornewall Lewis, statesman and historian, became Chancellor of the Exchequer, but resigned that office in 1858. He translated MULLER's "History and Antiquities of the Doric Race." (1806—1863).

Count Cavour, an eminent Italian statesman, whose efforts for the regeneration of his country gained him a high reputation. His death was an irreparable loss to Italy. (1110—1861).

Richard Lalor Shiel, an Irish politician and diplomatist, became in 1846 Master of the Mint, and in 1850 was appointed British Minister at the Court of Tuscany. (1793—1851).

Joseph Hume, distinguished himself as a financial reformer. (1777—1855).

Sir William Molesworth, became Secretary for the Colonies. (1810—1855).

Sir James Graham, who filled many official positions, and took an active part with Sir ROBERT PEEL in effecting the repeal of the Corn Laws. (1792—1861).

James Wilson, economist, became in 1852 Financial Secretary to the Treasury. (1805—1831).

Henry Pelham Clinton (Duke of Newcastle), was a Member of Parliament for South Nottinghamshire, became Secretary for the Colonies, under PALMERSTON, and accompanied the Prince of WALES on his visit to America. (1811—1864).

Henry John Temple (Viscount Palmerston), a great diplomatist, born in 1784, was educated at Harrow School, then at the University of Edinburgh, and finally at St. John's College, Cambridge. He was first returned to Parliament for the borough of Bletchingley, and subsequently represented the University of Cambridge and Tiverton. At the commencement of his Parliamentary career, Lord PALMERSTON exhibited great business talents, and in 1809 was appointed Secretary of War, upon the resignation of Lord CASTLEREAGH. After filling other important posts, he became in 1855 First Lord of the Treasury, but was compelled in 1858 to resign through public indignation aroused against his Cabinet in reference to the **Conspiracy Bill,** which was introduced soon after an attempt on the life of the Emperor of the French by ORSINI and others. He again became Premier in 1859, and continued to hold that office till his death in 1865. Lord PAL-MERSTON was honoured with a public funeral, and buried in Westminster Abbey.

MILITARY COMMANDERS.

William Carr (Viscount Beresford), who organised the Portuguese army in the Peninsular campaign. (1768—1854).

Henry William Paget (Marquis of Anglesea), who rendered signal service at the battle of Waterloo. He headed the last charge, by which the French Guards were completely routed. (1768—1854).

Sir Charles James Napier, who served in the Peninsular, Affghan, and Sikh Wars. (1782—1853).

Viscount Hardinge, won for himself a high military reputation. He also became Governor-General of India. (1785—1856).

Lord Raglan, was engaged in the Peninsular War, Battle of Waterloo, and the Crimean War, in the last of which he was Commander of the British Forces. He was born in 1788, and died before Sebastopol, 1855.

General Sir George Brown, whose services were very efficient in the bombardment of Copenhagen, and in the Peninsular, American, and Crimean Wars, during the last of which he was wounded. (1790—1865).

Radetzky (Field-Marshal), an eminent Austrian commander, distinguished himself at the Battle of Leipsic, and quelled the Italian Insurrection of 1848. Died 1858. His funeral was honoured by the presence of the Emperor, Empress, and Officers of State.

Sir Colin Campbell (Lord Clyde), distinguished himself in the Peninsular and Crimean Wars, &c. During the Indian Mutiny he was Commander-in-Chief of the British Forces. (1792—1863).

Sir Henry Havelock, was born near Sunderland, and is to be remembered with gratitude for his great services in the Indian Mutiny of 1857. The victory of Mohumna is in a great measure ascribed to the plans of HAVELOCK. (1795—1857).

Joseph Garibaldi, an Italian patriot and General, was born at Nice in 1807. He is noted for having in 1860 expelled from the Two Sicilies the Spanish Bourbon Dynasty, which was followed *in 1861* by the proclamation of VICTOR EMMANUEL as King of Italy. *In 1864,* GARIBALDI visited England, where he met with a most cordial reception.

NAVAL COMMANDERS.

Thomas Cochrane (Lord Dundonald), a brave admiral, commanded a fleet of fire-ships with which he destroyed the French fleet in the Basque Roads, and for this service he was rewarded with the knighthood of the Bath. It having been alleged that he had spread a report concerning the abdication of the Emperor NAPOLEON I., he was sentenced to pay £1000, to stand in the pillory, and to be imprisoned for one year. This sentence roused public indignation, and the punishment of the pillory was remitted, and the fine paid by public subscription. He subsequently aided the Chilians and the Greeks in their struggles for Independence. In 1854 he became Admiral of the United Kingdom, and in 1858 offered to blow up the walls of Sebastopol, but his plan was rejected. (1775—1860).

Sir Charles John Napier, a gallant admiral, served in the Portuguese war and signalized himself in the wars of Syria. (1786—1860).

Lord Lyons, who, in addition to his other achievements, rendered the most signal aid in the Crimean War. (1790—1858).

HISTORIANS.

John Lingard, a Roman Catholic priest, wrote a History of England from CÆSAR's Invasion to the year 1688. For his literary labours the Queen granted Dr. LINGARD a pension of £300 a year. (1771—1851).

John Mitchell Kemble, an eminent Anglo-Saxon scholar. Chief work, "The Saxons in England: a History of the English Commonwealth till the period of the Norman Conquest." (1807—1857).

Henry Hallam, wrote "The Constitutional History of England," from the accession of HENRY III. to the death of GEORGE II., and other excellent works. (1778—1859).

Lord Macaulay, author of a History of England and "The Lays of Ancient Rome," &c. (1800—1859).

Sir Francis Palgrave, wrote many works on British history and antiquities, and was for a long time the Deputy-keeper of the Public Records. (1788—1861).

POETS.

Thomas Haynes Baylay, author of "I'd be a butterfly," and many other graceful Lyrics. (1799—1839).

Mrs. Browning, a most distinguished poetess, whose productions occupy a high place in our poetical literature. (1809—1861).

Thomas Moore, wrote the "Irish Melodies," "Lallah Rookh," &c. (1779—1852).

Thomas Hood, wrote "Eugene Aram's Dream," "The Song of the Shirt," and " Bridge of Sighs," &c. (1798—1845).

James Montgomery, author of " Original Hymns for Public, Private, and Social Devotion," and other works. (1771—1854).

Sheridan Knowles, an eminent dramatic author, whose best productions are "William Tell," "The Love-Chase," and "The Hunch-Back." (1784—1862).

LITERARY CHARACTERS.

William Hazlitt, a distinguished critic, author of "The Literature of the Elizabethan Age," "Table Talk," "The Spirit of the Age," and other works. (1778—1830).

Maria Edgeworth, authoress of novels, and tales of fashionable life. (1767—1849).

Miss Mitford, novelist, died 1855.

Douglas Jerrold, novelist, essayist, and dramatist. (1803—1857).

Andrew Ure, author of a "Dictionary of Chemistry," "The Philosophy of Manufactures," &c. (1778—1857).

William Yarrell, wrote popular histories on Fishes and Birds. (1784—1856).

John Wilson, poet, novelist, and miscellaneous writer, became Professor of Moral Philosophy in the University of Edinburgh. (1785—1854).

Charles James Blomfield, Bishop of London, published an edition of the tragedies of AESCHYLUS. 1786—1857).

Dr. Dionysius Lardner, author of the "Museum of Science and Art," &c. (1793—1859).

William M. Thackeray, a clever novelist, who wrote "Vanity Fair," "Pendennis," "Lectures on the Four Georges," &c. He was born in Calcutta in 1811, and died in London, 1863.

Dr. William Whewell, the son of a carpenter, was educated at the Free Grammar School, Lancaster, and thence, by the aid of the Head Master, proceeded to the University of Cambridge. He ultimately became Vice-Chancellor and Master of Trinity. He wrote a *History of the Inductive Sciences*, and other works. (1795—1866).

Mrs. Gore, novelist. (1800—1861).

Charles Dickens, a celebrated novelist, author of "David Copperfield," "The Pickwick Papers," and other works. (1812——).

Samuel Lover, novelist and song writer. (1797—1868).

PHILANTHROPIST.

Miss Florence Nightingale, an accomplished lady, who, with a number of nurses, proceeded to the hospitals of Scutari, for the purpose of attending on our sick and wounded soldiers, 1854.

LAWYERS.

John Campbell (Lord), an eminent judge, was born at Cupar in 1781. He was called to the bar in 1806, entered Parliament in 1830 as member for Stafford, became Attorney-General in 1834, was made Lord Chief Justice in 1850, and in 1859 Lord Chancellor. Died June 23, 1861.

Lord Lyndhurst, born at Boston in the United States, 1772. He was Solicitor-General during the trial of Queen CAROLINE, and in 1827 became Lord Chancellor. As a Chancery judge, his reputation was great. Died Oct. 12, 1863.

Lord Denman, who, in 1820, was appointed Solicitor-General to Queen CAROLINE, and afterwards became Chief Justice of the King's Bench. (1779—1854).

Lord Brougham, distinguished as a lawyer, statesman, orator, scholar, and writer. (1779—1868).

James Parke, Lord Wensleydale. (1782—1868).

MEDICAL MEN.

Dr. John Ayrton Paris, a distinguished physician, wrote, among other works, "Philosophy in Sport made Science in Earnest," and "The Life of Sir Humphrey Davy." (1785—1856).

Jonathan Pereira, an eminent physician, rose by his talents and perseverance to be one of the greatest ornaments of his profession. His works are numerous and valuable, but his reputation is chiefly based upon a work entitled *Elements of Materia Medica and Therapeutics.* He was appointed physician to the London Hospital, and became Professor of Materia Medica to the Pharmaceutical Society of Great Britain. Died 1853.

Dr. Robert Bentley, a noted physician, author of "The Physiological Anatomy and Physiology of Man," and other works. (1809—1860).

Sir Benjamin Brodie, author of "Experiments and Observations on the Influence of the Nerves of the Eighth Pair on the Secretions of the Stomach," and various other works. (1783—1863).

MUSICAL COMPOSER.

Sir Henry Rowley Bishop, one of the first musical composers, became Professor of Music at the University of Oxford. Among his best works may be named *The Slave, Guy Mannering,* and *The Virgin of the Sun.* (1780—1855).

ACTOR.

Charles Kean, tragedian, son of Edmund Kean. (1811—1868).

CHEMISTS.

Baron Liebig, a most celebrated chemist, was for some time Professor of Chemistry in the University of Giessen, an **Alma Mater** in which the best chemists, both in England and Germany, have been educated. Baron LIEBIG's writings are numerous, among which we may mention "Chemistry in its application to Agriculture and Physiology," and "Familiar Letters on Chemistry." (1803—).

Michael Faraday, an eminent chemist and natural philosopher, author of "Researches on Electricity," and "Popular Lectures on the Chemistry of a Candle." (1794—1867).

William Herapath, chemist and toxicologist. (1868).

ENGINEERS.

George Stephenson, son of a fireman at a colliery, greatly improved the locomotive engine, and made a railway over Chat Moss. (1781—1848).

Robert Stephenson, son of GEORGE STEPHENSON, constructed the Tubular Bridge over the Menai Strait, and the Victoria Bridge over the River St. Lawrence. He also wrote two valuable works entitled, "The Locomotive Steam-Engine," and "The Atmospheric Railway System." (1803—1859).

Sir Mark Isambard Brunel, constructed the Thames Tunnel. (1769—1849).

Isambard Kingdom Brunel, son of Sir MARK ISAMBARD BRUNEL, whom he assisted in constructing the Thames Tunnel. Among his own great works may be named, the Great Western Railway ; the *Great Western, Great Britain,* and the *Great Eastern Steam Ships.* His death, which took place in 1859, was hastened by the anxiety he felt for the successful completion of the last mentioned vessel.

GEOLOGISTS.

Dean Buckland, by whose exertions the science of Geology has considerably advanced. (1784—1856).

Hugh Miller, a native of Scotland, and a mason by trade. He wrote the "Testimony of the Rocks," "Footprints of the Creator," and other works. He was born in 1802, and while suffering from disease of the brain committed suicide in 1855.

ARTISTS.

Joseph William Turner, a landscape painter, of great eminence. (1775—1851).

Sir Charles Lock Eastlake, became President of the Royal Academy. One of his greatest works is "Christ weeping over Jerusalem." (1793—1865).

George Cattermole (1800—1868).

Benjamin Robert Haydon (1786—1846).

BOTANISTS.

Sir Joseph Paxton, wrote many works on horticultural subjects, the chief being "Paxton's Flower Garden," and "The Pocket Botanical Dictionary." He designed the building for the Great Exhibition of 1851, and the terraces, fountains, and gardens of the Crystal Palace of Sydenham. (1803—1865).

Dr. John Lindley, author of "The Ladies' Botany," "School Botany," and other works. (1799—1865).

ARCHITECTS.

Sir Charles Barry, designed the new Houses of Parliament. (1795—1860).

John Britton, author of many works on architecture and the fine arts. (1771—1857).

SCULPTORS.

Sir Richard Westmacott, whose fame mainly rests on his monumental statues of Fox, Pitt, Sir Ralph Abercrombie, &c. (1775—1856).

John Gibson, whose first work was a group of " Mars and Cupid." (1791—1866).

Baron Charles Marochetti, born at Turin (1805—1867).

PHILOSOPHER.

Sir David Brewster, one of the most eminent philosophers of his day. (1781—1868).

REMARKS.

The prominent features of the Hanoverian Period are :—

1. Independence of the American Colonies.

2. Civil War in the United States.

3. Numerous inventions—Railroads, Gas-Lighting, Steam-Printing, Photography, and Electric Telegraph.

4. Three French Revolutions.

5. Two International Exhibitions.

6. Great acquisition of new territories to the British dominions, upon which it is justly said the sun never sets.

7. Freedom of the Press.

8. Great scientific improvements.

9. Foundation of Religious Societies, and diffusion of the Scriptures by translations into many different languages.

10. Establishment of the Penny Postage.

11. Mitigation of the severity of our Criminal Laws.

12. Augmentation of the National Debt, which, on the accession of George I., was £50,000,000, but now amounts to £790,000,000.

13. Immense increase in the population of England and Wales, which amounted in 1688 to five and a-half millions ; and in 1801, to 9,872,980 ; but the year 1861 shows a population of 20,205,504.

At no period of our history has the national progress been so great as in the reign of Queen Victoria.

The available military forces of each country in Europe at the present time (1866) are thus estimated :—

Prussia, 650,000; Austria, 651,000; Italy, 424,000; France, 900,000; Russia, 1,200,000; England, 265,000, besides 230,000 Volunteers; German Confederation, 405,000; Spain, 170,000; Portugal, 64,000 ; Holland 90,000 ; Belgium, 80,000 ; Sweden and Norway, 188,000 ; Denmark, 42,000 ; Switzerland, 192,000 ; Turkey, 340,000 ; the Danube Principalities, 50,000 ; Rome, 12,000 ; making altogether nearly six millions of soldiers.

Five attempts have been made upon the life of the Queen ; one in 1840, by a boy named EDWARD OXFORD, who was confined in a lunatic asylum ; another in 1842, by JOHN FRANCIS (a lad), who was transported for life ; and in the same year, a boy named BEAN, committed the like offence, for which he underwent eighteen months imprisonment ; and in 1850, an Irishman tried to shoot her, and ROBERT PATE attempted to strike her.

We must not omit to mention another important step, viz., the stimulus given to education through the examination of schools by the Universities of Oxford and Cambridge. These tests are held twice every year at specified local centres, where any scholastic establishment can send its pupils for examination, a faithful account of which comes in due course before the public. Such competition is calculated to raise the standard of education, to excite a laudable emulation among the candidates, and to lay the foundation of a sound and accurate scholarship, which, in after years, must prove of the utmost benefit to its possessor in what sphere of life soever he may be engaged.

THE BRITISH CONSTITUTION.

The Constitution of England is a **Limited Monarchy**, comprising **King, Lords**, and **Commons**, each having peculiar powers. The Sovereign is invested with exclusive authority :—

1. To Convoke, prorogue, or dissolve Parliament.

2. To wage war, make peace, or conclude treaties with Foreign States.

3. To create different ranks of nobility, to appoint officers in the army and navy, all Ministers of State and Bishops.

4. To pardon those who break the law ; but he is, notwithstanding these privileges, obliged to keep the law.

The House of Lords is composed of Lords Spiritual and Lords Temporal. The former comprise the Archbishops and Bishops ; the latter, Dukes, Marquises, Earls, Viscounts, and Barons. It is the highest Court of Law in the kingdom, and to it appeals from inferior courts can be made. A Peer who has committed any crime can be tried only by Peers.

The House of Commons consists of 658 Members, who are returned by Cities, Boroughs, Counties, and the three Universities of Oxford, Cambridge and Dublin. The Chairman of the House of Commons is called

The Speaker. A bill in which is proposed a new law, must go through seven stages before it can become the law of the land. It must pass the House of Commons three times, the House of Lords three times, and then must be signed by the Sovereign, who can prevent it becoming law by withholding his signature, which is seldom, if ever, done.

Money raised annually for the purpose of defraying the different public expenses, is called the **Revenue.**

The Annual Financial Statement given in the House of Commons by the Chancellor of the Exchequer concerning the National Debt, expenditure, income, and taxation, is called the **Budget.**

Taxes levied on articles imported or exported, are called **Customs**; while those imposed on articles made for home use, are known by the name of **Excise.**

The expenditure for the support of the Sovereign or Household, is designated the **Civil List.**

As a standing army is illegal, the **Mutiny Act** is passed every year, by which it becomes lawful to maintain that force.

The Sovereign is by law bound to be a **Protestant.**

For the administration of justice the kingdom is divided into **Circuits,** which are visited by judges at stated periods of the year.

As the control of the supplies is in the hands of the Commons, they can by that means check the power of the Sovereign, who by unconstitutional measures, such as raising taxes without the consent of Parliament, forfeits the allegiance of his subjects.

By the **Septennial Act,** the dissolution of Parliament must take place every seven years.

The accession of a Sovereign to the throne must be followed by a new Parliament before the expiration of six months.

THE LEADING EVENTS AND PRINCIPAL DATES

of the HANOVERIAN or BRUNSWICK PERIOD.

The Crowns of Hanover and England united by the Accession of George I.	A.D. 1714
Townshend made Prime Minister	1714
Death of Louis XIV. ; Mar's Rebellion	1715
James, the Old Pretender, in Scotland	1715
The Riot Act passed	1715
The Septennial Bill enacted	1716
Stanhope became Prime Minister	1717

CHARACTERS OF THE SOVEREIGNS SINCE THE CONQUEST.

William I.—A man of great mental calibre and physical strength, brave, ambitious, and tyrannical.

William II.—Intemperate, covetous, and cruel.

Henry I.—Learned, courageous, cruel, and avaricious.

Stephen.—Brave and energetic.

Henry II.—Possessed of great natural endowments, but haughty and revengeful.

Richard I.—A man of singular courage; he was magnanimous, proud, and vindictive.

John.—Almost destitute of every good quality.

Henry III.—Not absolutely vicious, but in many respects showed great weakness of character.

Edward I.—A monarch of great wisdom and valour, but not free from ambition and cruelty.

Edward II.—Wanting in resolution and energy, fickle and partial.

Edward III—Wise, brave, and magnanimous.

Richard II.—Brave, but ostentatious and frivolous.

Henry IV.—Enterprising, courageous, gloomy, and severe.

Henry V.—Profligate in his youth, but afterwards became temperate. He was brave and impartial.

Henry VI.—Amiable and gentle in his disposition, but weak-minded, and, therefore, unfit to govern.

Edward IV.—Possessed all the qualities of a soldier, but was extremely voluptuous and cruel.

Edward V.—An amiable and promising youth.

Richard III.—A man of great abilities, but unscrupulous, cruel, and deceitful.

Henry VII.—Efficient as a ruler, but crafty and avaricious.

Henry VIII.—Remarkable for his learning, vigour of mind, vanity, cruelty, and despotism.

Edward VI.—A youth of great promise, but cut off by an early death.

Mary.—Probably sincere in her religious convictions, yet she was morose, bigoted, and cruel.

Elizabeth.—She was a woman of great capacity and judgment, a most sagacious ruler, but somewhat despotic and open to flattery.

James I.—Distinguished for his learning, pedantry, sagacity, and folly.

Charles I.—Though he had many good qualities, he lacked discretion, and was haughty, arbitrary, and faithless.

Oliver Cromwell was born in the town of Huntingdon in 1599, and in 1653 became Lord Protector of England. Passing over his private character, which was irreproachable, we notice his public career. He was a renowned warrior and distinguished statesman, as evinced by the greatness to which he aised England during the Commonwealth. Many of the acts of cruelty with which he was charged seem to have been caused by the numerous plots against his life, and frequent rebellions in the kingdom. He was undoubtedly one of the greatest men of his age, but the part he took in the death of Charles I. cannot be justified. The extraordinary dissimulation spoken of by his enemies, was rather of a defensive character, and resulted from the dangers to which he was exposed.

Charles II.—A man of great wit and little virtue, insincere, and sensual.

James II.—Attentive to his royal duties, but cruel, arbitrary, and dishonest in religious matters.

William III.—Cold and reserved in his manners, sincere and brave, of great mental capacity and inflexible determination.

Anne.—A tender mother, an affectionate wife, charitable, but somewhat undignified in manners

George I.—A man of moderate capacity, great determination and industry. His want of feeling is shown by the fact that he detained his own wife a prisoner in Hanover for a period of 40 years.

George II.—Illiterate, parsimonious, obstinate and violent in his temper, but one who adhered to his word.

George III.—He was in every respect a man of excellent character, and a good king.

George IV.—Engaging in his appearance and manners, sensual in his youth, but towards the end of his life he became tyrannical.

William IV.—Simple in manners, frank, hearty, and a great lover of his people. He has been justly called **The father of his country.**

Contemporary European Sovereigns

ENGLAND.	SCOTLAND.	FRANCE.
William I.............1066	Malcolm III. 1057	Philip I. 1060
William II. 1087	Donald VII. 1093	
	Duncan II. 1094	
Henry I. 1100	Donald VII. restored	
	Edgar 1098	
	Alexander 1107	Louis VI. 1108
	David 1124	
Stephen.............1135		Louis VII. 1137
Henry II. 1154	Malcolm IV. 1153	
	William the Lion 1165	
		Philip II. 1180
Richard I.. 1189		
John 1199		
Henry III. 1216	Alexander II.......1214	Louis VIII. 1223
		Louis IX..............1226
	Alexander III. ...1249	
Edward I............1272		Philip III. 1270
	Margaret 1285	Philip IV. 1285
	John Baliol........ ...1292	
Edward II. 1307	Robert I. (Bruce) 1306	Louis X. 1314
		Philip V. 1316
Edward III. 1327	David II. (Bruce) 1329	Charles IV. 1322
	Edward Baliol ...1332	Philip VI............1328
	David II. restored 1342	John II. 1350
		Charles V.......... ..1364
	Robert II. (Stuart)1371	
Richard II. ... .1377		Charles VI. 1380
	Robert III. 1390	
Henry IV. 1399		
	James I. 1406	

and Popes since the Conquest.

GERMANY.	SPAIN.	POPES.
Henry IV. 1056		Alexander II. 1061
	CASTILE.	Gregory VII. 1073
		Victor III. 1086
	Sancho II. 1065	Urban II. 1088
	Alfonso VI.........1072	Pascal II. 1099
	Alfonso VII. 1109	Gelasius II. 1118
Henry V. 1106	Alfonso VIII.......1126	Calixtus II. 1119
Lothaire II. 1125	Sancho III. 1157	Honorius II. 1124
Conrad III. 1138	Alfonso IX. 1158	Innocent II. 1130
	Henry I. 1214	Celestine II..........1143
	Ferdinand III. ...1217	Lucius II............1144
	Alfonso X. 1252	Eugenius III. 1145
Fred. Barbarossa...1152	Sancho IV. 1284	Anastasius IV......1153
	Ferdinand IV.. ...1294	Adrian IV. 1154
	Alfonso XI. ...1312	Alexander III......1159
	Peter the Cruel ...1350	Lucius III. 1181
	Henry II. 1368	Urban III. 1185
	John I. 1379	Gregory VIII......1187
	Henry III. 1390	Clement III. 1187
Henry VI. 1190	John II. 1406	Celestine III. 1191
Philip 1198	Henry IV. 1454	Innocent III. 1198
Otho IV. 1208		Honorius III. 1216
Frederick II. 1212		Gregory IX.........1227
		Celestine IV. 1241
Conrad IV. 1250		Innocent IV. 1243
William.............1250		Alexander IV.......1254
Interregnum.........1256	ARRAGON.	Urban IV. 1261
		Clement IV.........1265
Rodolph 1273	Sancho Ramirez...1063	Gregory X. 1271
	Peter of Navarre...1094	Innocent V. 1276
	Alfonso I. ...1104	Adrian V...........1276
	Ramiro II. 1134	John XXI. 1277
	Petronilla and	Nicholas III. 1277
	Raymond........1137	Martin IV. 1281
	Alfonso II. 1162	Honorius IV. 1285
Interregnum.........1291	Peter II. 1196	Nicholas IV. 1288
Adolphus 1292	James I. 1213	Celestine V..........1294
	Peter III. 1276	Boniface VIII.......1294
Albert 1298	Alfonso III. 1285	Benedict XI. 1303
Henry VII. 1308	James II............1291	Clement V. 1305
Interregnum.........1313	Alfonso IV.........1327	John XXII. 1316
Louis IV. and	Peter IV...........1336	Benedict XII. 1334
Frederick 1314	John I.............1387	Clement VI.........1342
Louis IV............1330	Martin I...........1396	Innocent VI. 1352
Charles IV. 1347	Ferdin. of Sicily...1412	Urban V. 1362
Wenceslaus 1378	Alfonso V. 1416	Gregory XI.........1370
	John II. 1458	Urban VI. 1378
		Boniface IX. 1389
		Benedict XIII.......1394
Frederick 1400	CASTILE.	Innocent VII. 1404
Rupert 1400		Gregory XII. 1406
Jossus ... .1410	Ferdinand V.......1474	Alexander V. 1409

ENGLAND.	SCOTLAND.	FRANCE.
Henry V. 1413		
Henry VI.............1422		Charles VII. 1422
	James II.............1437	
Edward IV. 1461	James III. 1460	Louis XI.............1461
Edward V. 1483		Charles VIII. 1483
Richard III..........1483		
Henry VII. 1485	James IV. 1488	Louis XII, ...1498
Henry VIII.........1509		
	James V.............1513	Francis I.............1515
Edward VI..........1547	Mary 1542	Henry II.............1547
Mary 1553		Francis II. 1559
Elizabeth 1558	James VI. 1567	Charles IX. 1560
		Henry III. 1574
	(Unites the crowns on the death of Elizabeth, 1603.)	Henry IV. 1589
	RUSSIA.	
	Emperors from Peter the Great.	
James I................1603	Peter the Great ...1689	Louis XIII...........1610
	Catherine I..........1725	
	Peter II. 1727	
Charles I.............1625	Anne 1730	Louis XIV. 1643
Commonwealth ...1649	Ivan VI. 1740	
Charles II. 1649	Elizabeth 1741	Louis XV. 1715
(Restored 1660.)	Peter III............1762	
	Catherine II. 1762	Louis XVI. 1774
	Paul 1796	
James II. 1685	Alexander I. 1801	Louis XVII. 1793
William III..........1689	Nicholas 1825	(Died in prison, 1795,
Anne 1702	Alexander II. 1855	aged 10.)
George I. 1714		
George II...........1727	—	
	PRUSSIA.	**REPUBLIC.**
		Napoleon I., Emperor 1804
	From the Establishment of the Kingdom.	
George III. 1760		Louis XVIII. 1814
	Frederick I..........1701	
	Frederick Wm. I...1713	Charles X............1824
	Frederick II. (the	Louis Philippe ...1830
George IV. 1820	Great) 1740	
William IV.........1830	Fred. Wm. II.......1786	Republic 1848
	Fred. Wm. III......1797	Napoleon III. Emperor 1852
Victoria.............1837	Fred. Wm. IV. ...1840	
	William I.............1861	

GERMANY.	SPAIN.	POPES.
Sigismund 1410	(Marries Isabella of Castile, 1479, and unites Castile and Arragon.)	John XXIII. 1410
Albert II............1438		Martin V............1417
		Eugenius IV. 1431
Frederick III.......1440	Joan 1504	Nicholas V..........1447
		Calixtus III.........1455
		Pius II...............1458
		Paul II..............1464
		Sixtus IV...........1471
		Innocent VIII......1484
Maximilian I. 1493		Alexander VI.......1492
	SPAIN.	Pius III. 1503
		Julius II............1503
Charles V. 1519	Ferdinand V. 1512	Leo X. 1513
	Charles I.............1506	Adrian VI. 1522
		Clement VII. 1523
		Paul III. 1534
		Julius III. 1550
Ferdinand I. 1558	Philip II....... 1556	Marcellus II. 1555
Maximilian II......1564	Philip III. 1598	Paul IV. 1555
Rodolph II..........1576		Pius IV. 1559
		Pius V....... 1566
		Gregory XIII.......1572
		Sixtus V............1585
		Urban VII..........1590
		Gregory XIV.......1590
		Innocent IX. 1591
		Clement VIII......1592
Matthias 1612		Leo XI. 1605
Ferdinand II. 1619	Philip IV. 1621	Paul V............1605
Ferdinand III. ...1637	Charles II. 1665	Gregory XV. 1621
Leopold I. 1658		Urban VIII.........1623
Joseph I.............1705	Philip V. 1700	Innocent X.........1644
Charles VI. 1711		Alexander VII......1655
Maria Theresa......1740		Clement IX.........1667
Charles VII........1742	Ferdinand VI.......1745	Clement X. 1670
Francis I. 1745		Innocent XI. ...1676
Joseph II. 1765	Charles III..........1759	Alexander VIII....1689
Leopold II..........1790	Charles IV..........1788	Innocent XII. ..1691
Francis II. 1792		Clement XI.........1700
(With this prince the title of Emperor of Germany was dropped for that of Emperor of Austria).		Innocent XIII......1721
		Benedict XIII......1724
		Clement XII. 1730
		Benedict XIV......1740
		Clement XIII.......1758
		Clement XIV.......1769
—		Pius VI. 1775
		Pius VII............1800
AUSTRIA.		
Francis I. (the preceding............1804	Ferdinand VII. ...1808	Leo XII. 1823
	Jos. Bonaparte.	Pius VIII. 1829
Ferdinand 1835	Ferdin. restored ...1814	Gregory XVI......1831
Francis Joseph ...1848	Isabella II. 1833	Pius IX............1846

FOREIGN POSSESSIONS BELONGING TO GREAT BRITAIN.

Aden, a seaport town of Arabia, ceded to England in 1839, and taken possession of in 1840, is now used as a depôt and halting place for steamers employed in the passage between Bombay and Suez.

Anguilla, or Snake Island, so called from its winding form, one of the West India Islands, colonised by the British in 1650.

Antigua, one of the Leeward West India Islands, discovered by COLUMBUS in 1493; the first settlement being made by some British families in 1632. *Productions*—sugar, rice, tobacco, and arrowroot.

Ascension, an African Island in the Southern Atlantic Ocean, so named because it was discovered on Ascension Day, 1501. This Island, famous for its *turtle,* was taken by the English in 1815, and garrisoned to prevent the followers of NAPOLEON BONAPARTE from any attempt to rescue the deposed Emperor from St. Helena.

Australia, the largest Island in the world, was first discovered by the Dutch in the beginning of the seventeenth century, and called by them New Holland. It seems, however, to have been little known till Captain COOK discovered **Botany Bay,** so named from its beautiful flowers, in 1770. Owing to the favourable account given of it by COOK, British colonies were soon after formed. These settlements comprise ; **New South Wales,** chief town, Sydney, established as a penal colony in 1788 ; **Van Dieman's Land,** now **Tasmania,** established as a penal colony in 1803 ; **Western Australia,** capital, Perth, established in 1829 ; **South Australia,** capital, Adelaide, established in 1834 ; the *Port Philip district,* now called **Victoria,** whose chief town is Melbourne, established in 1837, was formerly a dependency of New South Wales ; **North Australia** was colonised in 1838 ; **New Zealand,** though colonised some time before, was not officially established till 1840 ; and **Queensland** in 1859. Gold was discovered in 1851. *Chief productions* —gold, wool, and copper.

Bahamas, or Lucayo Islands, in the Atlantic Ocean, opposite to the coast of Florida, one of which, **San Salvador,** was the first land discovered by COLUMBUS in his voyage of 1492. The Bahama Islands were first colonised by the English in 1629, possessed by Spain in 1781, and restored to Britain in 1783. *Chief products*—cotton, maize, salt, sugar, turtle, Guinea corn, vegetables, and pine apples.

Barbadoes, the most eastern of the West India Islands, was colonised by Britain in 1625. *Products*—sugar, cotton, arrowroot, aloes, and ginger.

Bermudas, or Somers Islands, a group of about 300 small Islands in the Atlantic, about 800 miles east from South Carolina, discovered in 1522 by a Spaniard named BERMUDEZ. Here, in 1609, Sir GEORGE SOMERS, while on his voyage to Virginia, was wrecked, and soon after they were colonised from England. *Products*—coffee, arrowroot, and cotton.

British Columbia, on the north-west coast of North America, formed part of the territory held by the Hudson Bay Company till 1858, when it was made into a colony, the name of British Columbia being given to it by Sir E. BULWER LYTTON, at that time Secretary for the Colonies. Its products are similar to those of England. Gold was discovered in 1857.

British Guiana, on the north-west coast of South America, produces sugar, coffee, cotton, wheat, maize, cocoa, tobacco, vanilla, and cinnamon. Here 49,000 emigrants arrived from Great Britain in 1853.

Burmese Colonies—Arracan, conquered by the British in 1826 ; Tenasserim, taken in 1826 ; and Pegu, in 1852.

Barbuda, one of the West India Isles, produces corn, cotton, tobacco, and pepper.

British Kaffraria, capital, King William Town, was taken from the Kaffirs in 1853.

Canada, was taken by the British in 1759, and in 1840 the two Canadas, called Upper and Lower, were united. *Chief Productions*—fish, furs, and timber.

Cape of Good Hope, or **Cape Colony**, but commonly known as **The Cape**, in Southern Africa, discovered by DIAZ, a Portuguese admiral, in 1486, and called by him the **Cape of Storms**; but JOHN II., of Portugal, altered the title to that of *Good Hope*, because he believed it would open the way to the Indies. The Dutch founded a colony at the Cape in 1652, which the British took in 1795. It was restored to Holland by the Treaty of Amiens, but recaptured by the English in 1806, and confirmed to Britain at the Congress of Vienna. *Chief Products*—aloes, wines, gold, and copper.

Cape Breton, an Island of Nova Scotia, was first colonised by the French in 1712, and taken by the British in 1758, to whom it was finally ceded by the Treaty of Paris in 1763.

Ceylon, a large Island in the Indian Ocean, separated from the southeast point of Hindostan by Palk Strait and the Gulf of Manaar. It is 270 miles long and 140 broad. Little was known of it till 1505, when the Portuguese began a regular intercourse with its inhabitants, and received from the King of **Candy**, to whom it belonged, a tribute in cinnamon, for defending the Island against the Arabian pirates. The Portuguese were afterwards expelled by the Dutch, from whom it was taken by the English about the year 1796, and ceded to the latter by the Treaty of Amiens in 1802. The kingdom of Candy, situated in the centre, was subdued in 1815, when the *whole* Island became subject to the British. *Productions* - cinnamon, coffee, sugar, rice, teak, cocoa-nuts, tin, lead, iron, and precious stones in great variety.

Channel Islands, annexed to Britain in 1066.

Chatham Island, situate 380 miles east of New Zealand, and has similar productions.

Dominica or Domenica, an Island in the West Indies, belonging to the Leeward group, was discovered by COLUMBUS in 1498, and ceded by France to Great Britain in 1763. It was afterwards taken by the French but restored to Britain by the Treaty of Versailles in 1783. Its *products* are—coffee, sugar, maize, cotton, tobacco, timber trees, and cabinet wood. Hogs, bees, and poultry are very plentiful.

Falkland Islands, situate in the Southern Atlantic Ocean, were discovered by DAVIS in 1592; colonised by the French 1763; taken by the Spaniards, 1767 ; and ceded in 1771 to the English, who have held peaceable possession of them only since 1833.

Gambia, in Western Africa, has a flourishing trade, and *exports* hides, wax, ivory, gold-dust, rice, horns, palm oil, and timber.

Gold Coast, a country of Guinea in Western Africa, was discovered by the Portuguese, who, in 1482, formed a settlement at Fort Elmina. The English first established themselves here in 1664, and the Danish settlements in it were given up to England in 1850.

Gibraltar, near the Southern extremity of Spain, was ceded to Spain by the Moors in 1462, and taken by the English, under Sir G. ROOKE, in 1704. Under General ELLIOT, it successfully withstood a memorable siege by the French and Spaniards, the operations continuing from 1779 to 1783.

Grenada, an Island in the West Indies belonging to the Windward group, was discovered by COLUMBUS in 1498, originally settled by the French, and in 1762 was taken by the British, and confirmed to them in 1763.

India, an extensive region in the south of Asia, first visited by VASCO DE GAMA in 1498. At a subsequent period settlements were formed on this peninsula by the Portuguese and the Dutch, the former never obtaining more than a small territory on the West Coast, the latter only a few commercial factories. The French power in India was once great, but it finally yielded to that of the British. The origin of our Indian Empire is said to have been connected with a Mr. BROUGHTON, an English surgeon, who, having been sent from Surat to Agra, in 1636, on a professional visit to a daughter of the Emperor **Shaw-Gehan**, succeeded in curing her of her malady. As a reward for his skilful services, the Emperor granted him the privilege of a free commerce throughout his dominions. Having returned to Bengal to purchase goods, for transmission by sea to Surat, he was requested to attend the favourite of the **Nabob**, or Governor of the province, who was dangerously ill. His efforts being again crowned with success, BROUGHTON was pensioned by the Nabob, who also confirmed the privilege of the Empire, at the same time promising that the right should be extended to all the English going to Bengal. These facts being communicated by BROUGHTON to the Governor of Surat, the latter induced the Company to send from England in 1640 two ships to Bengal. Such was the real commencement of a commerce which has become so great and has led to such extensive territorial possessions.

For political purposes British India is divided into the three Presidencies of **Bengal, Madras, and Bombay,** and its leading historical events are comprised in the following summary :—

1. First charter granted by Queen ELIZABETH to the East India Company, 1600.
2. Second charter granted to the same Company, 1609.
3. The English made a settlement at Madras, 1620.
4. CHARLES II. by his marriage with CATHERINE, Infanta of Portugal, obtained **Bombay**, it being given as part of her dowry, 1662.
5. Seat of the East India Company's Factory removed from Hoogly to Calcutta, 1698.
6. Fort William, Calcutta, so named after WILLIAM III., built, 1698.
7. Calcutta taken by SURAJAH DOWLAH, and the Black Hole cruelty, 1756.
8. CLIVE recaptured Calcutta in two hours, and was victorious at Plassey, 1757.
9. WARREN HASTINGS became Governor of Bengal, 1772.
10. The Carnatic overran, and the British defeated by HYDER ALI, 1780.
11. Death of HYDER, and accession of his son TIPPOO SAIB, 1782.
12. **Seringapatam** taken by the British, and TIPPOO SAIB killed, 1799.
13. Overthrow of the Mahrattas by Sir ARTHUR WELLESLEY at **Assaye,** 1803.
14. Treaty of Peace with SCINDIAH the Mahratta Chief, 1805.
15. The Affghan War began in 1839 and ended in 1842.

16. Annexation of **Scinde**, 1843.
17. The **Punjaub** conquered, 1849.
18. **Pegu** annexed, 1852.
19. **Oude** annexed in 1856.
20. Indian Mutiny, caused in a great measure by the annexation of **Oude**, 1857.
21 Government of India transferred from the East India Company to the Crown, 1858.

The preceeding outline of historical facts will afford some notion of the rise, progress, and territorial acquisitions of Great Britain in India, the possession of which not only extends her influence among other nations, but also gives her control of the trade of the Eastern seas. *Chief products*— barley, wheat, rice, indigo, tobacco, cotton, sugar-cane, opium, ginger, and other spices, tea in Assam, and very fine timber, &c. The minerals consist of copper, gold, iron, tin, coal, and diamonds.

Jamaica, one of the largest and most valuable of the West Indian Islands, was discovered by COLUMBUS in 1494, colonised by the Spaniards in 1510, and taken by the English in 1655. *Exports*—coffee, sugar, cocoa, rum, molasses, pimento, ginger, cotton, indigo, arrowroot, and logwood.

Kitt's. St., or **St. Christopher's**, one of the West Indian Islands in the Leeward group, discovered by COLUMBUS in 1493, then thickly populated by Caribs. The French and English colonies took possession of this Island about the same time in 1625, from which period it became the scene of much contention between the two nations till 1783, when it was finally ceded to the British by the Treaty of Versailles. *Chief product*—sugar.

Lucia, St., a West Indian Island in the Windward group, held by the French from 1763 till 1803. *Chief product*—sugar.

Malta. an Island of the Mediterranean, taken from the French by the English in 1800, and confirmed to the latter by the Treaty of Paris in 1814. *Chief products*—cotton, wheat, barley, oats, fine oranges, figs, and splendid honey.

Malacca or **Malaka**, on the west coast of the Malay Peninsula, obtained from the Dutch in 1825, in exchange for Bencoolen in Sumatra. *Chief products*—cocoa-nuts, nutmegs, cloves, pepper, gums, ivory, gold-dust, tin, rice, sago, and poultry.

Montserrat, a West Indian Island in the Leeward group, discovered by COLUMBUS in 1493, recovered from France by the Treaty of Versailles, in 1783. *Chief products*—coffee, sugar, and tamarinds.

Mauritius. or **Isle of France**, an Island of the Indian Ocean, discovered by the Portuguese in 1505, taken by the Dutch in 1598, and received the name of *Mauritius* in honour of Prince MAURICE. Came into possession of the British in 1810. *Chief products*—wheat, maize, sugar, and yams.

Man, (Isle of) Mona or Menavia, an Island in the Irish Sea, originally peopled by the **Manx** (Menaviae), a tribe of the **Celtic** race. It was alternately possessed by the Scotch and English, subsequently held as a feudal sovereignty by the Stanleys, and finally became the property of the Dukes of ATHOL, from whom it was purchased by the British Crown in 1806, and finally in 1826, some remaining privileges were ceded by the Duke, in consideration of which he received £416,000. Ruled by a Governor, a Council of Public Affairs, and the House of Keys, comprising 24 members. *Chief products*—corn, eggs, potatoes, lime, stone, fish, ore, linens, and sail-cloth.

New Brunswick, a province of North America, ceded to Britain by the Treaty of Paris in 1763. *Chief products*—wood, potatoes, maize, barley, oats, wheat, iron, coal, and manganese.

Newfoundland, an Island in North America, ceded to the English by the Treaty of Utrecht in 1713. Famous for its cod, seal, and salmon fisheries, and fine breed of dogs.

Norfolk Island, an Island in the South Pacific, discovered by Captain COOK in 1774, and colonised by Governor PHILLIP, was used for some years as a penal colony.

Nova Scotia, a peninsula of North America, discovered by CABOT in 1497, and under the name of Arcadia was afterwards settled by the French. It came into British possession at the peace of Utrecht in 1713. *Chief products*—potatoes, turnips, rye, oats, and wheat. Hogs in abundance.

Natal, situated on the eastern coast of South Africa, and so named by the Portuguese, because they discovered it on **Christmas-day** in 1498. It came into British possession at a recent date. *Products*—wheat, oats, sugar, coffee, cotton, tobacco, and indigo.

Nevis, a Leeward West Indian Island, exports molasses, sugar, and rum.

New Zealand, comprising a chain of three Islands, with smaller isles in the Pacific, discovered by TASMAN, a Dutch navigator, in 1642, and by COOK, on the *East Coast,* in 1769. Taken possession of as a British colony in 1840. Chief articles of commerce—wheat, flour, potatoes, wool, flax, and timber.

Penang, Pinang, or Prince of Wales' Island, in the Straits of Malacca, bought from the King of Quedah. *Chief products*—rice, cotton, tobacco, ginger, indigo, coffee, cocoa-nuts, and sugar.

Sierra Leone, a small peninsula of Western Africa, colonised in 1787. *Exports*—ginger, pepper, rice, palm-oil, hides, timber, and ivory.

Singapore, or **Sincapore,** an Island in the south-east of Asia, was purchased from the Sultan of Johore, and settled by the English in 1819. *Products*—nutmegs, pepper, coffee, catechu, and fine fruits.

Tasmania, or **Van Diemen's Land,** an Island in the Southern Ocean, discovered by TASMAN, a Dutchman, in 1633, visited by FURNEAUX in 1773, and by Captain COOK in 1777. Occupied by the British as a penal colony in 1803. *Products*—barley, wheat, oats, apples, gooseberries, and currants. Iron, coal, and copper, are the chief minerals.

Trinidad, the most southern of the West Indian Islands in the Windward group, discovered by COLUMBUS in 1498; taken from the Spaniards by Sir WALTER RALEIGH in 1595; taken from the English by the French in 1676; but capitulated to the British under Sir RALPH ABERCROMBIE in 1797. *Chief products*—asphalt, cacao, coffee, sugar, and cotton.

Tobago, a West Indian Island in the Windward group, settled by the Dutch in 1642; taken by the British in 1672; retaken in 1674; ceded to the English by the Treaty of Paris in 1763. Abounds in fruit &c.

Vincent, St., an Island in the West Indies, Windward group, ceded to Britain by the Treaty of 1783. *Products*—dyewoods, arrowroot, cocoa, sugar, and rum.

Virgin Islands, a group in the West Indies.

Vancouver's Island, an Island in North America, whose coast was *traced* by Captain GEORGE VANCOUVER in 1793. *Chief products*—grain, and coal.

WORKS

BY THE

Rev. GEORGE BARTLE, D.D.

Crown 8vo., Price Five Shillings.

THE SCRIPTURAL DOCTRINE OF HADES, comprising an Inquiry into the State of the Righteous and Wicked Dead between Death and the General Judgment, and demonstrating from the Bible that the Atonement was made neither on the Cross nor yet in this world.

OPINIONS OF THE PRESS.

Great obscurity hangs over the grave. Such, however, is not the opinion of our Author, who discusses all passages in the Old and New Testaments that appear to him appropriate, and he brings forth a tolerably clear picture of the future. The reader who goes along with Dr. BARTLE in his animated reasoning will feel at the end that his ideas are marvellously enlarged.—**Athenæum.**

The work is a masterpiece of research, of thought, and of the energetical handling of Scripture.—**Liverpool Leader.**

Though we cannot agree with many of the conclusions of the Author of this able work, we are constrained to admire his subtlety in argument, and the extent of his erudition.—**The Rock.**

We have never observed so large an accumulation of Scripture proofs and so appositely put to demonstrate an argument; and we think Dr. BARTLE's theory more than plausible, in fact, the true one.—**The Press and St. James's Chronicle.**

That Dr. BARTLE's Work on "Hades" will create a profound sensation in the religious world there is no doubt, and all credit will be given to the intelligent and learned Author for his masterly handling of his most difficult subject.—**Ipswich Free Lance.**

sion as would be produced on a candid and unprejudiced reader of the formularies of our Church. This ought to be esteemed great praise, for what can be more unbecoming in a minister of that church than to write a book which will startle the reader by suggesting difficulties, or the deficiencies of his own Catechism and Church Services? Dr. Pusey does this in his *Eirenicon*, and the Bishop of Salisbury in his essentially Roman charge. This *should* be the test of faithfulness to the Church in any theological work by its clergy, namely, that their statements harmonise generally with those of the formularies intended to instruct the body of the faithful and do not startle the reader by novelties and paradoxes. We can sincerely give Dr. BARTLE this praise.—Clerical Journal.

After careful examination, we are satisfied that it is the work of a *liberal* churchman, who has his own opinions, *and his reasons for them*, but who can conceive of others differing from him without a feeling of bitterness or intolerence arising in his heart. A cursory persual only of the portion of the book devoted to the Sacraments, and to the definition and office of the Church, will amply suffice to support this view. The arrangement of the book is excellent, and bears the mark of a practised hand; and not the least valuable portions of its contents are the directions as to the best mode of using it, the questions for examination, the biblical references, and the explanatory notes.—Liverpool Leader.

A full and complete exposition of the various portions of the Church Catechism is to be found in this work. With this Analysis in hand a candidate for examination on the subject need not fear plucking. The introduction of questions and advice to pupils cannot fail to be of great service.—Ipswich Express.

After a careful examination of Dr. BARTLE's "Analysis and Expotition of the Church Catechism," we now commend it with confidence to our readers. The Student will derive not only assistance from the Author's explanations, but a thorough appreciation of the essential doctrines of our Church. The Catechism is too frequently acquired by mere rote, and hence the inability of many professing church people to give an account of their faith. This book will be invaluable to the Student, and by no means wanting in didactic worth and suggestiveness to the teacher.—Church and School Gazette.

This excellent Analysis ought to be in the hands of every school boy and girl, especially those who are preparing for public examination, or intend to become candidates for Confirmation. The Biblical references are multitudinous, while the notes and remarks are highly valuable and interesting. In many cases they throw a great and new light upon the subject.—*Liverpool Mercury.*

Dr. BARTLE's Analysis and Exposition of the Catechism may be safely recommended.—**Oxford University Herald.**

This work, with Dr. Bartle's Synopsis of English History, ought to be in the possession of every teacher, and every intelligent head of a household.—**Cheltenham Chronicle.**

An elaborate Exposition of the Catechism.—**The Rock.**

Contains much information in a brief compass. The Analysis of the Apostles' Creed is particularly full and comprehensive.—**Our Own Fireside.**

Notwithstanding the many publications of this class issuing constantly from the press, the book before us will find a high place amongst families, students, and candidates for competitive examinations, for whom it is principally designed. The explanatory notes. copious references to Scripture texts—the clearness with which the Author states and conveys his well-digested and excellently arranged information for the catechist and catechumen—is worthy of all praise. In fact, nothing seems wanting to render the book a most complete manual of teaching in the Catechism of the Church of England.—**Liverpool Mail.**

Second Edition.—Price Sixpence.

A DISSERTATION ON THE SACRIFICE OF CHRIST,
designed for all Class of Readers.

This work displays both talent and scholarship. We commend it to the perusal of Theologians.—**Northern Herald.**

A learned and masterly Dissertation. Every Christian ought to procure it.—**Liverpool Albion.**

This is a subject of equal interest and importance at the present time, and Dr. BARTLE's Dissertation cannot, therefore, fail to be acceptable. His premises are well chosen, the argument is clear and logical, and the *Dissertation* throughout will more than repay the reader.—**Church and School Gazette.**